Speech Craft has **personality**

Speech Craft brings purpose and personality to the discussion of traditional public speaking topics. Josh Gunn's voice is conversational, vivid, humorous, and energetic.

Practical illustrations and activities help students with the **speechmaking process**.

Strong **scholarship** appears throughout the text; the author references the psychological theories of Freud, Maslow, and Erikson, as well as the rhetorical theories of Diane Davis and Barry Brummett.

The speech traditions of the Ancient Greeks are covered in a modern way.

Examples from current and classic **pop culture** are interspersed throughout the text. Examples include listening skills at a Beyoncé concert, the style philosophy of *Project Runway*, and the global popularity of Adele.

dpa picture alliance archive/Alamy Stock Photo

MPI/Getty Images

Examples from **history** give the text a balanced **perspective**.

a focus on **community**

Speech Craft has a focus on public speaking for the community and as a vocation. The text helps students connect public speaking to their own lives, making an ethical connection with the audience.

A minister speaks to his congregation.

A dear friend makes a toast to you at your birthday party.

A colleague explains a new technology.

and speaking for **change**

A unique chapter on Speaking for Social Change shows how speaking for social change connects speakers to their communities. The history of activism is presented through examples like Rosa Parks, the protests in Tahrir Square in Cairo, and the Women's March in Washington, DC, in 2017.

Bettman/Getty Images

Chuck Fishman/Getty Images

Modern and historic examples of **activism** and **advocacy** lay the groundwork for students' social justice involvement.

powerful digital tools

LaunchPad for _Speech Craft_ reflects the interactive, student-friendly, and fun spirit of the book. Digital Dives, a feature in most chapters, drives students to LaunchPad, which also includes:

- **LearningCurve adaptive quizzing**, which gives individualized question sets and feedback based on each student's correct and incorrect responses. All the questions are tied back to the e-Book to encourage students to read the book in preparation for class time and exams.
- **The video assignment tool**, which makes it easy to assign and assess video-based activities and projects, as well as provides a convenient way for students to submit video coursework.
- **Easy LMS integration** into your school's learning management system.
- **_Speech Craft_ Activities** created by the author for students to work on in groups or as homework assignments.
- **_Speech Craft_ e-Book**

Full set of instructor resources included!

from where you say it:
feeling **accents** and **dialects**

DIGITAL DIVE

The late Ann Richards, former governor of Texas, spoke with a discernible Texas accent, which she often referenced to impart her authority as a political leader for Texans. *Ken Geiger/KRT/Newscom*

Adopting appropriate vocalics varies by venue, community, and the background of the speaker. In general, the more formal the speaking situation, the more proper one's vocalics should be. The most obvious example of vocalic diversity is one's **accent**, which refers to the way a person's voice *sounds* and how they pronounce words. A **dialect**, on the other hand, can reference both an accent *and* certain turns of phrase, speaking styles, and grammatical conventions particular to a community, class allegiance, or geographical region. For example, many Americans born in the Deep South speak with a melodic "southern drawl" or accent, which not only has a particularly "twangy" sound, but also has grammatical inventions that specify a regionally specific dialect, such as the term "y'all." If you are speaking to an audience that may be unfamiliar with your accent or dialect, consider speaking more slowly and articulating words more clearly than you normally would. If you're listening to a speaker who has an accent or speaks in a particular dialect, be generous as a listener and try to accept his or her ways of pronouncing things as simply *different* rather than wrong, bad, or uneducated.

LaunchPad *macmillan learning*

For a striking example of how one's vocal tone, accent, and dialect influence the perceptions of listeners, visit LaunchPad at launchpadworks.com and listen to an audio clip featuring a speaker delivering a speech by Ann Richards. The speaker reads Richards's speech in what is termed a "north central" or "midwestern" dialect, which is routinely adopted by radio and television personalities. Next, link out to the video of Ann Richards delivering her speech.

After listening, consider the following questions:
- Trying to ignore the actual words spoken, which speaker is more appealing to you? Why?
- In what ways do the speakers' accents and dialects differ? Do these ways influence how you *hear* the speech? How?

Digital Dives: A special feature found in most chapters that drives students to LaunchPad to take a deep dive into a topic, either by listening to a podcast or watching a video, and then answering critical thinking questions.

Speech Craft video collection contains a curated collection of **speech clips** and **full-length speeches**, including professionally shot speeches such as "The Science of Dreams" and "Car Cookery: The Real Fast Food," which appear in this text. "Needs improvement" clips highlight typical speech delivery challenges. Model student speeches show techniques such as gestures and effectively citing sources.

about the **author**

Courtesy of Dan Gunn

Dr. Joshua Gresham Gunn (Ph.D., University of Minnesota, 2002) teaches and researches at the University of Texas at Austin, where he is an Associate Professor of Communication Studies and a Faculty Affiliate in the Department of Rhetoric and Writing. He also taught public speaking as an adjunct professor at Southwestern University in Georgetown, Texas.

Josh received the Outstanding Graduate Teaching award from the University of Texas at Austin in 2015.

Josh's research tends to focus on the concept of the "ineffable," and in particular, how people use and abuse signs and symbols to negotiate ineffability. In this context, his attention to music, religion, and human affective experiences (e.g., love) are part of a deeper interest in the limits of human representation, self-understanding, and self-fashioning. As teacher and student of popular culture, Josh is currently completing an academic book on ghosts and haunting in U.S. culture.

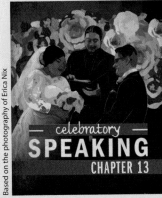

Based on the photography of Erica Nix

celebratory
SPEAKING
CHAPTER 13

SPEECH CRAFT

SPEECH CRAFT

Joshua Gunn
University of Texas at Austin

with illustrations by
Brian and Michelle Sharkey Vaught

bedford/st.martin's
Macmillan Learning
Boston | New York

For Bedford/St. Martin's

Vice President, Editorial, Macmillan Learning Humanities: Edwin Hill

Senior Program Director, Communication and College Success: Erika Gutierrez

Senior Development Manager: Susan McLaughlin

Senior Development Editor: Lorraina Morrison

Senior Content Project Manager: Jessica Gould

Editorial Assistant: Kimberly Roberts

Senior Media Editor: Tom Kane

Assistant Editor: Mary Jane Chen

Media Project Manager: Sarah O'Connor

Senior Workflow Project Supervisor: Joe Ford

Marketing Manager: Kayti Corfield

Senior Photo Editor: Martha Friedman

Photo Researcher: Julie Tesser

Permissions Editor: Angela Boehler

Senior Art Director: Anna Palchik

Text Design: Maureen McCutcheon

Cover Design: William Boardman

Cover Art: Brian and Michelle Sharkey Vaught

Composition: Lumina Datamatics Inc.

Printing and Binding: LSC Communications

Manufactured in the United States of America.

2   1   0   9   8
f   e   d   c   b

For information, write: Bedford/St. Martin's, 75 Arlington Street, Boston, MA 02116

ISBN 978-0-312-64488-8 (Paperback)
ISBN 978-1-319-06462-4 (Loose-leaf Edition)

Acknowledgments

Text acknowledgments and copyrights appear at the back of the book on page A-1, which constitutes an extension of the copyright page. Art acknowledgments and copyrights appear on the same page as the art selections they cover.

For Karlyn Kohrs Campbell,

Teacher, Mentor, & Friend

contents

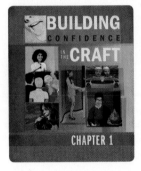
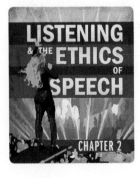

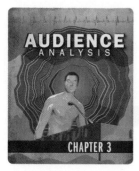

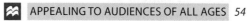

The Advertising Archives

Lambert/Getty Images

CHAPTER 5

RESEARCHING YOUR SPEECH TOPIC   *91*

Neal Hamberg

CHAPTER 6

SUPPORTING MATERIALS & CONTEXTUAL REASONING   *109*

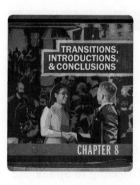

REUTERS/Fred Prouser

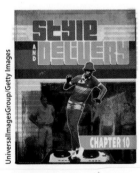

UniversalImagesGroup/Getty Images

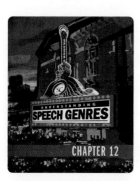
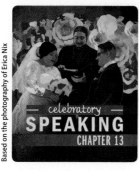

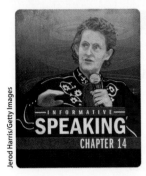

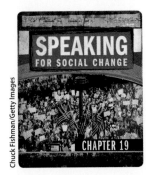

preface

What you hold in your hands or see on your screen is like all the other introductory textbooks on public speaking and presentations—**except that it's not.** *Speech Craft* is similar to its siblings because the way public speaking has been taught has changed very little for over a century,[1] despite the technological revolutions of telephony and television, despite the cultural reconfigurations wrought by radio and wireless. As with the first college courses in public speaking, most of us still teach three or four speeches, from celebrating to informing to persuading. As the postmodern prophet David Byrne of the aptly named musical group Talking Heads once intoned, "same as it ever was!"

I would argue that the craft of public speaking has not changed much for *thousands* of years. The renowned scholar of oratory Herbert A. Wichelns put it well in 1925: "Human nature being what it is, there is no likelihood that face-to-face persuasion will cease to be a principal mode of exerting influence." There is an enduring relation between the human and speech, and our need and desire to influence each other in flesh and voice has seldom wavered for any democracy.[2] Perhaps because we define our humanity in speech, in a broad sense, the principles of public speaking have remained relatively intact since the time of Aristotle. *Speech Craft* shares with its kind in this century—and with so very many in centuries past—the continuation and celebration of the principles and methods of a very old art. Like other books on public speaking, this guide strives to uphold the values of public belonging and betterment through the cultivation of earnest and humane calls and responses. As teachers and scholars of speech, our shared mission is to better behold how good it is to dwell together in speech, to paraphrase a famous Hebrew psalm.

Speech Craft's difference is one of emphasis: speechmaking is presented, first and foremost, as the indispensable art of community-building, as the primary means of constituting or reconstituting a common company through oratory. Whether a speaker calls for rallying

> Whether a speaker calls for rallying behind a cause or simply explains to others how to make a green smoothie, a community of listeners must be created prior to that, and to this end the bonds between people must be forged or renewed *first*.

behind a cause or simply explains to others how to make a green smoothie, a community of listeners must be created prior to that, and to this end the bonds between people must be forged or renewed *first*. Among the dominant genres of speaking today, such an emphasis is most discernable in celebratory or *epideictic* speaking: celebratory speeches often honor or praise a person or event, but really these are about reckoning with a community through commonly shared beliefs and values. Speaking to inform and persuade others does this too, of course, but the celebratory speech puts the community-building purpose front and center. Similarly, *Speech Craft* spotlights the fostering of community.

Over the last century, the introductory public speaking course—or the "basic course," as it is sometimes called—has shifted to accommodate the needs of students and society alike. As we know it today, the public speaking course was created to address the new kind of students seeking higher education after the Civil War, especially after U.S. President Abraham Lincoln signed the Morrill Land Grant Act of 1863 into law. Unlike the more privileged students attending American private schools at the time, the newer students enrolling in Land Grant colleges and universities needed additional instruction in writing, speaking, and basic English fluency. Aiding the development of "oral English" and composition classes was the rapid publication of textbooks penned with these new students in mind. The related fields of rhetoric, rhetoric and composition, speech, public speaking, and communication studies were as much a product of this new ecology of textbooks as they were emergent curricula.[3] Public speaking and presentation-skills classes are no longer the purview of public education, since these are needed by virtually any student today. What remains common to the basic course, wherever it is taught, are the ideals behind the creation of our great, public institutions of learning: vibrant, diverse communities; social

> What remains common to the basic course, wherever it is taught, are the ideals behind the creation of our great, public institutions of learning: vibrant, diverse communities; social mobility; and the access to civic participation that fluency and literacy better enable.

mobility; and the access to civic participation that fluency and literacy better enable. Listening and speaking well are no guarantee that these ideals will become a reality, but these skills will benefit students' lives because, ultimately, they are valuable in and of themselves.

A Focus on Community

For public speaking textbooks, the close association of speech with the functions of citizenship in the early to mid-twentieth century led to an emphasis on public deliberation and debate,[4] while a general trend toward the cultivation of workplace skills shifted textbooks toward a more professional or vocational direction in the later twentieth century. As educators in various locations continue to adapt the basic communication course for local needs, it seemed to me and my collaborators at Bedford/St. Martin's that a guide re-centered on time-tested methods and principles, yet adapted to newer generations of students and teachers, would be both welcome and helpful.

Rather than emphasizing this or that particular end, benefit, or consequence, what if we produced a guide to the craft of speech that returned to the heart of the art as an *ethical, cultivated practice*? Learning the skills of writing and delivering a speech will help students in their education, in their careers, in participating in public life, and most certainly in advocating for social change. But more fundamental to all of these ends is the means of building relationships with groups, which ultimately form the net of an audience in a moment and with a community over time.

Jake Lyell/Alamy Stock Photo

Public speaking is an art that aspires toward being with others, toward sharing, and, however paradoxically, toward listening better. I wager this labor of communing—this *networking*, especially among presumed strangers—is really what public speaking is about for us today.

> Public speaking is an art that aspires toward being with others, toward sharing, and, however paradoxically, toward listening better.

For years I taught the basic interpersonal communication course, which is a class that introduces students to the insights of social scientific research for the purpose of helping them to create and maintain meaningful and fulfilling relationships at a personal level.[5] *Speech Craft* has been written in parallel to such aims, but with a focus on relationships to a group or an audience, or more to the point, to a community or "public." To put the difference of the emphasis of *Speech Craft* bluntly: the craft of speaking is not about *you*, it's about *us*.

Notes

[1] For a robust account of the reasons why the public speaking course has changed little, see William Keith, "Understanding the Ecology of the Public Speaking Course," *Review of Communication* 16 (2016): 114–124.

[2] Herbert A. Wichelns, "The Literary Criticism of Oratory." In *Readings in Rhetorical Criticism*, ed. Carl R. Burgchardt (State College, PA: Strata Publishing, Inc., 2010), 4.

[3] See Herman Cohen, *The History of Speech Communication: The Emergence of a Discipline, 1914–1945* (Annandale, VA: Speech Communication Association, 1994), esp. 13–28. Also see Pat J. Gehrke, *The Ethics and Politics of Speech: Communication and Rhetoric in the Twentieth Century* (Carbondale: Southern Illinois University Press, 2009); and J. Michael Sproule, "Discovering Communication: Five Turns Toward Discipline and Association." In *A Century of Communication Studies: The Unfinished Conversation*, Eds. Pat J. Gehrke and William M. Keith (New York: Routledge, 2015), 26–45.

[4] See William M. Keith, *Democracy as Discussion: Civic Education and the American Forum Movement* (Lanham, MD: Lexington Books, 2007).

[5] For an introduction, see Steven McCornack, *Reflect & Relate: An Introduction to Interpersonal Communication*, 4th Ed. (New York: Bedford/St. Martin's, 2016).

Public Speaking with Passion and Purpose

> I committed to writing a public speaking and presentation textbook because the field that pioneered its teaching and study *committed to me.*

I committed to writing a public speaking and presentation textbook because the field that pioneered its teaching and study *committed to me.* You see, I am a first generation college student; I became a professor of communication, in large part, because the field and its teachers encouraged me in high school. At the time and place I grew up, many young people were not expected to attend college. Whereas my loquacious loafing in high school hallways frustrated more than a few teachers, a somewhat unconventional history teacher encouraged me to channel my chatter into competitive speech events and eventually mock trial and competitive debate. It was through my experiences with what is dubbed "policy debate" that I began to discover I had a passion for crafted speaking—not just speaking, but planning and researching it ahead of time.

I eventually got to college because of a debate scholarship. Regardless, communication or communication studies, the field formerly known as "Speech," introduced me to the life of the mind by helping me to better coordinate my ears and mouth. In fact, the sample speech in Chapter 14 is a revised version of the first speech I gave in my own college public speaking class during my first year of college. And you'll never guess what the first class I ever taught was (yes, it was public speaking in the fall semester of 1996).

Communication studies is an academic field, but it is also a community of like-minded professionals who study and teach others to make connections to create, maintain, and transform their communities. *Speech Craft* underscores this purpose and attempts to impart how finding one's own passion is key to communicating well. By stressing the significance of developing speeches on topics of personal import and interest throughout, *Speech Craft* encourages beginning speakers to temper their anxiety with excitement about their topics and goals, which in turn makes it easier to connect with audiences.

AP Photo/Paul Sakuma

Speech Craft was composed and developed interactively and in tandem with Bedford/St. Martin's online and digital content platform, LaunchPad. Not only is *Speech Craft* available in a digital format, but both print and digital versions of the book can be used interactively with online example speeches, speech texts, and helpful tools (e.g., the outlining tool for composing speeches).

Speech Craft can be read and studied without any online content, of course. Each chapter has a stand-alone, interactive section called a "Digital Dive" that encourages students to apply the concepts introduced in the book to online examples and scenarios. As I write this preface, I am currently developing two asynchronous online courses for my university, and the insights I learn from this process will contribute to future online content for *Speech Craft*.

> *Speech Craft* . . . attempts to impart how finding one's own passion is key to communicating well.

Digital Options

For more information on these resources, please visit the online catalog at **macmillanlearning.com/speechcraft/catalog**.

Digital tools for *Speech Craft* are available in LaunchPad, a dynamic new platform that combines a curated collection of video, homework assignments, e-Book content, and the LearningCurve adaptive quizzing program, organized for easy assignability, in a simple user interface.

- **Easy to start.** Ready-made interactive LaunchPad units give you building blocks to assign instantly as is or customize to fit your course.
- **Intuitive and useful analytics.** The gradebook allows you to quickly review progress at the class and individual level, providing information you can use to make the most of the teaching and learning experience.
- **Fully interactive e-Book.** Every LaunchPad e-Book comes with powerful study tools, multimedia content, and easy customization for instructors.

LaunchPad for *Speech Craft* helps students learn, study, and apply communication concepts:

- *Speech Craft's* **Digital Dives** are special features in the print book that explore a special topic in depth; in LaunchPad, students can watch and critique videos or compare audio files and answer critical thinking questions.
- **Speech Craft's video collection includes** professionally filmed versions of Victoria Filoso's speech on dreams and Joshua Gunn's speech on car cookery, as well as other model speeches, short speech clips, and "needs improvement" clips.
- **LearningCurve provides adaptive quizzing and a personalized learning program.** In every chapter, call-outs prompt students to tackle the game-like LearningCurve quizzes to test their knowledge and reinforce learning of the material. Based on research on how students learn, LearningCurve motivates students to engage with course materials, while the reporting tools let you see what students understand so you can adapt your teaching to their needs.
- **With video assignment tools.** The functionality of video tools enables instructors to create video assignments. Instructors and students can add video, use time-based comments to discuss video, and assess video using rubrics.

Speech Craft e-Book Options

E-Books meet students where they already live—online and digital—and *Speech Craft* is available in a variety of e-Book options. Visit **macmillanlearning.com** to learn more about these options.

Resources for Students and Instructors

For more information on these resources or to learn about package options, please visit the online catalog at **macmillanlearning.com/speechcraft/catalog**.

Resources for Instructors

For more information or to order or download the Instructor Resources, please visit the online catalog at **macmillanlearning.com/communication**. The Instructor's Resource Manual, Test Bank, and lecture slides are also available on LaunchPad: **launchpadworks.com/speechcraft**.

Online Instructor's Resource Manual for Speech Craft, by Laura Sells, Nicolet College. This extensive Instructor's Resource Manual is available on LaunchPad and from the Instructor Resources tab at **macmillanlearning .com/communication**. It includes teaching notes on managing a public speaking course, organization, and assessment; sample syllabi; and tips for using the pedagogical features of *Speech Craft*. Every chapter also includes chapter summaries, key terms, lecture outlines and class discussion starters, class and group exercises, assignment suggestions, video and music recommendations, and website suggestions.

Computerized Test Bank for Speech Craft. Available on LaunchPad and from the Instructor Resources tab at **macmillanlearning.com /communication**, the Test Bank includes eighty multiple-choice, true/false, short-answer, and essay questions for every chapter. This easy-to-use Test Bank also identifies the level of difficulty for each question, includes the book page the answer is found on, and connects every question to a learning objective.

Lecture slides for *Speech Craft* provide support for important concepts addressed in each chapter, including graphics of key figures and questions for class discussion. The slides are available for download on LaunchPad and from the Instructor Resources tab at **macmillanlearning .com/communication**.

Resources for Students

The Essential Guide Series: This series gives instructors flexibility and support in designing courses by providing brief booklets that begin with a useful overview and then address the essential concepts and skills students need. Topics covered that will interest public speaking students include presentation software, rhetoric, intercultural communication, small group communication, and interpersonal communication. For more information, go to **macmillanlearning.com**.

Media Career Guide: Preparing for Jobs in the 21st Century, **Eleventh Edition,** by Sherri Hope Culver (Temple University). Practical, student-friendly, and revised with recent statistics on the job market, this guide includes a comprehensive directory of media jobs, practical tips, and career guidance for students considering a major in the media industries.

Acknowledgments

As both a pedagogy and practice, thousands of teachers and scholars in the fields that pioneered public speaking as a college and university course—in departments of communication, English, and others—are the actual authors of this book, and I am grateful to them for teaching me and encouraging me by example how to continue transmitting the tradition. I've dedicated this text to my mentor and friend, Karlyn Kohrs Campbell, who is not only among the most brilliant theorists and critics of communication in our time, but an activist, a gifted speaker, and one of the most talented teachers I have ever learned from.

Much gratitude is similarly shared for my instructional material collaborator Laura Sells, my colleague for many years at the Louisiana State University, who mentored me as a teacher and scholar in my early professorship days, and whose pedagogical approach and encouraging attitude toward students has infused every page. Less directly but nonetheless influentially, I am especially grateful to David Zarefsky and Stephen Lucas, whose work *and example* taught me public speaking and whose scholarship I have taught in turn.

Many thanks are owed to the late, great Harold Lloyd "Bud" Goodall, former director of the Hugh Downs School of Human

Communication at Arizona State University, who recommended Bedford/St. Martin's work with me after he attended my lecture on Kenny and Dolly's hit duet, "Islands in the Stream" (thanks, too, to Daniel Brouwer for inviting me to speak that day). Senior Program Director Erika Gutierrez and Program Manager Simon Glick shepherded the project in the early years, and I am grateful for their ideas, their unflagging enthusiasm, and their foodie sensibilities. I am especially appreciative of Erika's *tireless* cheerleading for almost nine years on this project. This book would not have been published were it not for Erika's patience, careful guidance, and indefatigable good cheer.

Sincere and deep gratitude is owed to my editor Lorraina Morrison, whose goodwill, empathy, and brilliance guided every page—paper and digital—to completion. Lorraina is truly two parts Owl and one part Tigger to my Eeyore, and *Speech Craft* wouldn't exist without her. I would also like to thank Senior Development Manager Susan McLaughlin for her tireless support and cheerleading during the editing process, and am thankful for her sensitivity and keen anticipation of the expectations of a diverse readership. An enthusiastic thank-you also goes to Brian and Michelle Sharkey Vaught, artful mind readers! Their talent and sense of humor appears in every chapter, and it's impossible to imagine this book without their contribution.

As with Hollywood films, an extended editorial, production, and marketing team works on a textbook project of this scope; *Speech Craft* would not have been completed were it not for Kimberly Roberts, Editorial Assistant; Kayti Corfield, Marketing Manager; Lindsey Jaroszewicz, Director of Market Development; Lisa Kinne, Managing Editor; Tom Kane, Senior Media Editor; Mary Jane Chen, Assistant Editor; Sarah O'Connor, Media Producer; Jesse Hassenger, Senior Development Editor; Kate George, Development Editor; and William Hwang, Editorial Assistant. Very special thanks to Jessica Gould, Senior Content Project Manager, for her extraordinary efforts. Thanks to Edwin Hill for his support and leadership throughout the development of the book. Special thanks to our voice talent Daniel Johnson, Alison Lorber, and Nik Toner.

Finally, gratitude of a personal nature goes to my colleagues Diane Davis and Dana Cloud, whose professional advice and friendship have been invaluable during the writing of this text. I am also very appreciative of my colleagues at Southwestern University, Davi Thornton and Valerie Renegar, for their friendship and for graciously inviting me to teach public speaking—and agreeing to let me test out this book! I am thankful for my wonderful students at Southwestern University as well, who read and commented on the penultimate draft of *Speech Craft*. Also many thanks to my partner, Andrea Alden, and my mother, Jane Gunn, for patiently listening to me talk about this project for years (and years).

I began these acknowledgments by stressing the true authorship of this book is communal, and this certainly consists of the teachers and scholars of public speaking currently teaching the course! So many colleagues have contributed to *Speech Craft* through their feedback on earlier drafts, and no doubt they will recognize places where their recommendations and suggestions ended up in the book. A hearty thank-you is due, then, to:

Editorial Advisory Board

Andrea Davis, *Western New England University*
Erica Cooper, *Roanoke College*
Sandy Pensoneau-Conway, *Southern Illinois University Carbondale*
Tami Martinez, *Indiana University South Bend*

Reviewers and Focus Group Participants

Karen Alman, *Wenatchee Valley CC*
Kaylea Annen, *Ohio State University*
Bernard Armada, *University of St. Thomas*
Mary Beth Asbury, *Middle Tennessee State University*
Leonard Assante, *Volunteer State Community College*
Suzanne Atkin, *Portland State University*
Ray Bell, *Calhoun Community College – Decatur*
Jeff Bennett, *Vanderbilt University*
Mardia Bishop, *University of Illinois*

Keith Bistodeau, *Ohio University*

Jason Edward Black, *University of North Carolina at Charlotte*

Sandra Bowen, *Fayetteville Technical Community College*

James Bowman, *University of South Florida*

Ferald Bryan, *Northern Illinois University*

Joni Butcher, *Louisiana State University*

Rya Butterfield, *Nicholls State University*

Steven Cameron, *Caldwell University*

Charles Campbell, *Dixie State University*

Chantele Carr, *Estrella Mountain Community College*

Shera Carter, *San Jacinto College Central*

Rafael Cervantes, *St. Catherine University*

Shaun Clerkin, *Gannon University*

Rachel Cobb, *Greenville Technical College*

Diana Cooley, *Lone Star – North Harris*

Kevin Cummings, *Mercer University*

Amber Davies-Sloan, *Yavapai College*

Alyssa Davis, *Clemson University*

Michael Eaves, *Valdosta State University*

Amber Edwards, *Dean College*

Jason Edwards, *Bridgewater State University*

Vanessa Ferguson, *Mott Community College*

Diane Ferrero-Paluzzi, *Iona College*

Nancy Fisher, *Ohio State University*

Vanessa Forcari, *California State University – East Bay*

Tonya Forsythe, *Ohio State University*

Rebecca Franko, *California State Polytechnic University*

Bonnie Gabel, *McHenry County College*

Roger Gatchet, *West Chester University*

Sara Green-Hamann, *University of Maine*

Joseph Harasta, *Kutztown University*

Lynn Harper, *College of Lake County*

Laura Harrison, *Georgia Regents University*

Carrisa Hoelscher, *University of Oklahoma*

Mary Hogg, *Western Illinois University Quad Cities*

Tracey Holden, *University of Delaware*

Gary Hughes, *Western Kentucky University*

Arthur Hunt, *The University of Tennessee at Martin*

Daniel Hunt, *Worcester State University*

John Hyatt, *Trident Technical College*

Raphaella Ianniello, *Chabot College*

Elena Jarvis, *Daytona State College*

Christa Tess Kalk, *Minneapolis Community & Technical College*

Kyle Kelly, *Johnson & Wales University*

Cindy King, *University of North Texas Dallas*

Staci Kuntzman, *University of North Carolina, Charlotte*

Alex Liles, *University of Arkansas*

Nikoloas Linardopoulos, *Rutgers University*

Darren Linvill, *Clemson University*

Benjamin Lohman, *Orange Coast College*

Robert L. Mack, *Arizona State University*

Steven Madden, *Coastal Carolina University*

David Majewski, *Richard Bland College*

Jodie Mandel, *College of Southern Nevada*

Josh Matthews, *Pitt Community College*

Pauline Matthey, *Clemson University*

Samuel McCormick, *San Francisco State University*

Janet McCoy, *Morehead State*

Audra McCullen, *Towson University*

Laurie Metcalf, *Blinn College*

Josh Misner, *North Idaho College*

Daniel Mistich, *University of Georgia*

Charles E. Morris III, *Syracuse University*

Steve Ott, *Kalamazoo Valley Community College*

Lisa Packard, *Gateway Technical College*

John L. Pauley II, *Eastern University*

Kendall Phillips, *Syracuse University*

Elizabeth Popp, *University of Illinois*

Amy Powell, *Central Michigan University*

Helen Prien, *Lock Haven University*

Claire Procopo, *Southeastern Louisiana University*

Amy Ramsay, *Western Technical College*

Ulrich Regler, *University of Maine – Orono*

Gail Reid, *University of West Georgia*

R. Joseph Rodríguez, *The University of Texas at El Paso*

Chelsea Shore, *CSUF/ESGVROP*

Liz Sills, *Louisiana State University*

Kate Simcox, *Messiah College*

Brent Sleasman, *Gannon University*

John M. Sloop, *Vanderbilt University*

Pam Solberg, *Western Technical College*

Richard Soller, *College of Lake County*

Karen Solliday, *Gateway Technical College*

Glenn Standly, *Hill College*

Sarah Steimel, *Uber State University*

L'Oreal Stephens, *Middle Tennessee State University*

Brad Stevens, *Hill College*

James Monroe Stewart, *Tennessee Technological University*

Charlotte Toguchi, *Kapiolani Community College*

Shaun Treat, *Independent scholar*

Lori Trumbo, *Greenville Technical College*

Lisa Turowski, *Towson University*

Shawn Wahl, *Missouri State University*

Jill Weber, *Hollins University*

Christopher Westgate, *Johnson & Wales University*

Amy Wolgamott, *Holmes Community College*

Anna M. Young, *Pacific Lutheran University*

About the Illustrators

Brian and Michelle Sharkey Vaught have designed for print, web, television, and all imaginable forms of collateral. Both Brian and Michelle hold advanced degrees emphasizing media studies, and in 2016, Little, Brown & Co. published their adult coloring book, *American Road Trip: Color Your Way to Calm from Coast to Coast*. When not designing together, they love traveling with their four boys, enjoying the incredible richness of the Deep South, and working on their 1965, 41' Hatteras.

BUILDING
CONFIDENCE

IN THE CRAFT

CHAPTER 1

Have you ever listened to a speaker and lost track of time? Have you ever been persuaded to do something you've never considered before because of a speech? Have you ever been moved to tears by the heartfelt words of a friend at a wedding or a funeral?

However much we are separated from each other physically in our changing social landscape — especially by screens — we still have the ability to move each other with speech: we entrance, we inform, we console, and we love, both in person and from afar.

In a variety of contexts, the craft of public speaking is about the many and varied rhythms and movements of hearts and minds. Across centuries, teachers of public speaking have argued the reason to study the craft is its primary purpose: the creation of relationships with others and the strengthening of community bonds.

This textbook was written and designed as a conversational guide to help you conquer your jitters, with practical tips for speaking in different kinds of situations. This text was also undertaken to center public speaking as an art that concerns community building. Rather than focusing strictly on public speaking as a civic mission, or on vocational or business speaking, or on the complexities of platform speaking so popular in our time (public lectures, TED talks, preaching, and so on), the thesis of *Speech Craft* is to demonstrate how building relationships with other human beings is *the common core of every type of speaking in public.*

The Celebrated and Feared Power of Speech

> **You will learn to**
>
> **EXPLAIN** why the craft of public speaking is powerful, in both good and bad ways.

The power of speech has been studied, celebrated, and even feared since the beginning of its formal study about two thousand years ago. Because human speech *moves* people, because it can influence how people think, act, and feel about the world around them, it has incredible power. Throughout human history, public speaking has been regarded as a robust skill or tool—like a painter's brush or a chef's cooking techniques—that can both magically enchant or enflame anger.

Some of the first teachers of public speaking, such as the ancient Greek orator Gorgias, compared the exciting and fearful effects of a good speech to "witchcraft" or "spell binding," which references public speaking's exciting and fear-inspiring power. Gorgias's old analogy can be explained this way: in varied cultures around the world, shamans and spiritual guides have used "spells" or rituals to heal people of physical or psychological pain, while in other cultures, those who use incantations are feared as sinful or harmful. Similarly, the *craft* of speaking, or "speech craft," can be used as an artful tool to soothe or hurt, to help or harm (see "A First Teacher of Public Speaking" on page 5).

Bettmann Archive/Getty Images

Congresswoman Barbara Jordan (1936–1996)

We tend to celebrate public speaking as a right and honorable thing, which is the message behind this book. We can easily think of great civil rights leaders or politicians in American history, such as Congresswoman Barbara Jordan or President John F. Kennedy, whose moving speeches helped change the minds and hearts of citizens, as well as U.S. laws and policies. But the craft of speech can also be used for wrongdoing and deception. We can think of many historical instances when large numbers of people were moved by the speeches of misguided leaders to support discrimination, hatred, and even warmongering (Joseph McCarthy, Adolf Hitler, and Osama bin Laden to name a few). Whether speech inspires the "divinest works," like bringing communities together to do or think constructive things, or the most depraved deeds, like deceiving others or promoting destruction, usually depends on the motives of both the speaker *and* listeners.[1]

Moral character is something that Isocrates—another early teacher of oratory from ancient Greece—insisted that the craft of public speaking *cannot* teach. The study of public speaking can help you "more speedily towards honesty of character," he said, *but it cannot make you a good person.* You have to be a good person on your own. Make no mistake about it, argued Isocrates, "there does not exist an art" of any kind that can "implant sobriety and justice in depraved natures."[2] For this reason, public speaking is *almost always* taught with a study of ethics, even though learning about ethics or morality will not make you ethical or moral (again, you have to will that for yourself). Nevertheless, because an understanding of ethics and morality goes hand in hand with the *risks* of public speaking, it is an important issue for us to address, which we will do so together in the next chapter.

Freedom of Speech

> *You will learn to*
> **EXPLAIN** why public speaking is rarely studied outside of democracies.

In the centuries-long study of public speaking, its teaching has never flourished outside of democratic societies. In some cultures, particularly nondemocratic cultures, leaders and influential citizens sometimes feared the craft of public speaking: if people are moved by speech, then they can be persuaded to think, do, believe, or feel things that are contrary to the interests of those in power. Influential speaking can be perceived as threatening to those in power because a community could be persuaded to disobey laws or, for example, the will of a dictator. Throughout history, rulers and other leaders have sometimes feared or outright banned the study of public speaking simply because it is founded on the ideal of free speech—an ideal that makes

a first teacher
of public speaking: gorgias

Way back in time — over two thousand years ago — there was an itinerant, or "wandering," teacher named Gorgias. He taught various subjects, including philosophy and oratory ("public speaking" in today's lingo). As a kind of paid tutor termed a "sophist," Gorgias traveled around the Mediterranean world looking for work. He advertised his craft by delivering fancy, rhythmic speeches that reportedly entranced his audiences.

A particularly famous speech, which has been described for centuries as one of the most eloquent speeches of all time, is about Helen of Troy. In Greek myth, Helen is described as the most beautiful woman in the world, "the face that launched a thousand ships." In his speech about Helen, Gorgias creates an analogy to persuade his audience to study public speaking, one of the subjects he taught for payment. Gorgias considered public speaking the most important of all the arts.

The myth that Gorgias uses to describe the power of oratory has many versions: Helen either left with or was abducted by a hot dude named Paris, ending up at his home in Troy (presently in the area that is currently called Turkey), thereby causing the famous Trojan War. Contrary to popular Greek accounts that describe Helen's departure as a betrayal, Gorgias provocatively insinuates that the power of oratory was responsible for her leaving.

In his speech, Gorgias compares the powers of persuasion to seduction. "Speech is a powerful lord," argues Gorgias, because it can cause the "divinest works: it can stop fear and banish grief and nurture pity."[3] Gorgias argues that the power of the spoken word can be compared to an irresistible passion or even intoxication (e.g., that Helen was overcome by her passions for Paris just like audiences can be overcome by a passionate orator).

Finally, Gorgias compares the power of persuasive speaking to "spell binding" and "witchcraft." The title of this textbook is something of a playful joke on Gorgias's analogy: *Speech Craft* is meant as a reference to the ways in which a good speech is spellbinding as well as the ways in which speech making is a craft or an art.

LaunchPad
macmillan learning

Gorgias's speech, "Encomium of Helen," is regarded as one of the most eloquent of recorded history. Listen to a dramatic reading of the speech by visiting LaunchPad at **launchpadworks.com** and clicking on "Encomium of Helen."

Consider the following questions:

- Gorgias likens good oratory to drugs, witchcraft, and spell binding. What qualities of the speech delivered orally try to intoxicate the audience? Do these qualities influence you at all?

- Is Gorgias's speech persuasive to you? Why or why not?

> The fact that you are reading this book at all means that you are in a society and culture that protects the right to speak freely. Viva la public speaking!

it possible to criticize, critique, and disagree with others without fear of punishment. Not surprisingly, then, the formal study of public speaking has rarely flourished outside of a democracy because the precondition of being moved by speech is the freedom to be moved in the first place. In a society in which people are not free to listen to others and speak their minds, there is no need for public speaking and certainly few opportunities for public persuasion, because speaking freely in such a culture could result in punishment or even death. There are many historical examples of the suppression or banning of speech due to a fear of its power. The fact that you are reading this book at all means that you are in a society and culture that protects the right to speak freely. Viva la public speaking!

The lofty ideals of free speech and democracy, however, register the highest aims of public speaking and their associated fears in ways that may seem far removed from where you sit and read at this moment. So let's cut to the chase: another reason why public speaking is feared is that you might be asked—even required—to do it. Unlike many other subjects of formal study that you will take in college, public speaking is one that many of your classmates, maybe even you, do not want to be required to take.

Many public speaking teachers will tell you that public speaking is one of the hardest subjects to teach because so many students dread it. In this respect, the study and craft of public speaking is not simply about appreciating the talents of gifted speakers and trying to learn from them, but also working through the apprehension or fear many of us feel when anticipating the prospect of speaking in public ourselves. We begin our study of public speaking, then, with a joke about death, courtesy of stand-up comedian Jerry Seinfeld.

What is the relationship between public speaking and democracy? ❷

The First Amendment of the U.S. Constitution

"Congress shall make no law respecting an establishment of religion, or prohibiting the free exercise thereof; or abridging the freedom of speech, or of the press; or the right of the people peaceably to assemble, and to petition the Government for a redress of grievances."

High Anxiety: The Fear of Public Speaking

> **You will learn to**
>
> **DESCRIBE** "speech anxiety," and explain why people have it.
>
> **LIST** the things speakers can do to reduce speech anxiety.

> I read a thing that actually says that speaking in front of a crowd is considered the number one fear of the average person. I found that amazing—number two was death! Number two! That means to the average person, if you have to be at a funeral, you would rather be in the casket than doing the eulogy.
>
> —Jerry Seinfeld[4]

Like heights, bugs, drowning, and clowns, students report that speaking publicly in front of a group is among their biggest fears—and yes, even more than death itself.[5] Although Jerry Seinfeld's joke is based on a dated study from the early 1970s, more recent research has demonstrated that public speaking remains a persistent and common fear for most people. In part, we are apprehensive about public speaking because of what we imagine it to be: a solitary figure in formal attire approaches a podium, and before her is a sea of people—hundreds of people, no, *thousands of people*! She must move them all, and she hopes her antiperspirant is working. She opens her mouth and prepares to speak but nothing comes out. All she hears is the sound of the silent scream in her head.

This nightmare image makes for great film or television, but it is not very realistic. Most of the times you will be asked to speak publicly will not resemble the grand images of political leaders or movie stars addressing thousands. Rather, you will be speaking in a home or a place of worship, in your workplace, online, or, of course, in a classroom.

Looking to Your Audience for Support

The term "public" is something of a contradiction, because it connotes a large group of people; in reality, public speaking is often a performance before a small group of people in a private setting (like your classroom). Whether you are speaking to inform, entertain, or persuade, public speaking is about bringing a group together, or constituting a "public," at the moment of speaking.

We tend to remember those speakers who have an ability to encourage audience members to feel like a group or experience a sense of togetherness. If you think about public speaking as a group effort, which means it is as much about listeners as it is speakers, then the challenge of giving a speech may seem much less daunting. In most public speaking situations, an audience wants to hear the speaker and can empathize with the task of speaking.

When we are listening to a public speaker, many of us imagine ourselves—however briefly—standing in the speaker's shoes. This empathy is often shared by those who assemble to hear *you* speak. Most people are respectful when they congregate to hear a speech, even when they disagree with what the speaker says.

Navigating Speech Anxiety

Still, let's be honest: what we fear about public speaking is the judgment of others. We worry about what others think about our speech, of course, but also about our style, our appearance, and even how our voice sounds. We get nervous because we fear messing up or forgetting our words, or that we are speaking in front of a group wearing unfashionable clothes. All these worries are normal, are widely shared, and contribute to what scholars of public speaking term "speech anxiety" or "communication apprehension." **Communication apprehension** concerns fears that we all have about verbal communication with others. **Speech anxiety** is communication apprehension specific to making speeches (it is sometimes termed "stage

Simply defined, public speaking is the craft of speaking to a group of people.

fright" in popular culture). Most beginning public speakers tend to feel anxiety because of a lack of experience, which is precisely what a public speaking class is designed to help you with. Here's a little secret: even advanced public speakers *still* feel anxiety because they want to do a good job. In general, speech anxiety or nervousness when speaking is something all speakers, from the beginner to the expert, contend with as the "center of attention."[6] One trick is to tell yourself that your anxiety is actually just excitement. Research has shown that the mental reframing of stress can improve performance in sports and speaking alike.[7] Another trick is to channel your nervous energy into planning and preparation. Those who teach public speaking tend to focus on reducing speaking anxiety in two ways: (1) by teaching you how to prepare and plan your speech, and (2) by getting you to practice public speaking. These are the basic tenets of the craft of teaching public speaking, and they will be what this course will focus on for the rest of the quarter or semester.

Most of the time we experience speech anxiety as we anticipate making a speech, not when we are actually speaking. We tend to obsess on our own speaking abilities long before we stand up to speak.[8] Once we start speaking, many of us become *less* nervous the longer we speak. Our tendency to obsess on "what ifs" prior to speaking goes back to antiquity and the first formal studies of public speaking by Plato and Aristotle in ancient Greece. Perhaps the oldest image of the public speaker is that of a man imploring a public while wearing a toga. For centuries, the study of oratory characterized the public speaker as an expert authority speaking to the inexpert or ignorant, a burden—and certainly a cause for anxiety for any aspiring speaker. Although the solitary-speaker situation is still common today, speakers don't always have to be experts, and sometimes a person may be asked to speak as a member of a group or team.

communication apprehension refers to the anxiety or fear experienced by communicators.

speech anxiety is the communication apprehension specific to speech making.

> When we are listening to a public speaker, many of us imagine ourselves — however briefly — standing in the speaker's shoes. This empathy is often shared by those who assemble to hear *you* speak.

> **?** What are the reasons for communication apprehension or speech anxiety? How can speakers manage it?

Public Speaking as a Civic Conversation

> **You will learn to**
> **NAME AND DESCRIBE** two models of public speaking in our time.

Over the past century, the formal study of speaking has shifted away from the expert speaker addressing an inexpert audience toward two different but related models. The first is a conversational model, in which the speaker and audience are understood to be in dialogue with each

Vermont senator and former presidential candidate Bernie Sanders holds a town hall meeting. The town hall combines the conversational and civic models of public speaking.[9]

other. The second is a civic model, in which public speaking is understood as a component of a much larger democratic dialogue among communities, or "publics."[10] Today we tend to think about public speaking as the building, maintaining, or reinforcing of a sense of community—in addition to whatever it is a speaker has to say.

The more recent turn toward thinking about public speaking as a civic conversation more equally balances the roles of listeners and speakers. A kind of "we're-in-this-together" attitude has emerged in the last century, which characterizes public speaking as a transaction, or a kind of give and take, between a speaker and an audience: more convo, less toga. Today, the formal study of public speaking is less focused on unique gifts or skills and more about the study of expectations, or what audiences bring to a speaking situation and anticipate hearing in a speech. Consequently, our focus in this book will be to answer questions like:

Who is my audience?
What is the best way to address my audience?
What kind of message is expected by this particular audience?
How is a speech like the one I am going to give supposed to go?
What am I having for dinner after I give my speech?

While that last question is a joke, it's an instructive one for understanding public speaking. Humor, the ability to amuse another (or oneself), is a metaphor for the process of public speaking in general. To amuse someone, you have to have some knowledge of that person and what he or she may find amusing. This is to say that humor often brings people together over something they share in common, which is precisely what public speaking is supposed to do, from the funniest to the most serious topics.

Public speaking is not simply about addressing a group of people, but is also about determining what constitutes a group of people or holds them together. While speaking the same language (English, Spanish, French) is what we most fundamentally have in common with an audience, we also share the human condition in all its varieties: common experiences, common feelings, and like-minded thoughts. Perhaps one of the biggest challenges we face as speakers is reminding ourselves that when we address any public, we are actually speaking to human beings, and that we are more alike than we are different. This challenge can be met by first understanding how we are similar and then by planning ahead based on those similarities.

The Craft of Speech

> **You will learn to**
>
> **EXPLAIN** why public speaking is an art or craft and not a science.

The character and function of public speaking have changed as radically as our communication technologies have changed over thousands of years—from oral traditions to parchment paper, the printing press, radio, television, and the Internet. Despite these changes, three elements of the craft have remained the same. Teachers of public speaking in the time of Aristotle as well as today have stressed that a speaker understands and gets better at public speaking by doing three things:

- practicing and having good role models to emulate;
- studying and understanding the expectations of audiences;
- planning or preparing speeches in advance.

No textbook can teach you how to be a good speaker. The experience of public speaking—and learning from these experiences—is the best and most fundamental teacher of the craft. A textbook on public speaking can help you *prepare* for speaking by providing you with an understanding of what different kinds of audiences *expect* and by introducing you to planning strategies for meeting those expectations. How you practice the craft is up to you and your instructor.

Practice!

Although the formal study of public speaking can help you prepare to speak, it is no substitute for practice, which is why so many of us who write about public speaking struggle to teach it (or, to make the same point by altering a cliché, "public speaking is more easily written about than said and done"). Another fact compounds your teacher's challenge: there are no hard-and-fast rules for public speaking. There is no absolute right or wrong way to speak. Your instructor cannot teach you universal principles that apply to every context of speaking, because how you speak and what you say depends on the speaking situation and your audience.

Appropriate and accepted ways of addressing publics differ from community to community and from culture to culture. For example, how you learn and practice public speaking in North America will differ from the way you learn and practice it in other parts of the world. The Chicago-based marketing expert Magda Walczak describes her experience listening to speakers in China at a conference. The speakers and listeners were "much different than what I'm used to in the [W]estern world. For example, the audience doesn't necessarily look at the speaker when he or she is talking. In the [conference] sessions I went to, people were texting, browsing the Internet[,] and even talking on their mobiles during presentations."[11] In North America, such audience behavior would be considered rude, but in other parts of the world, it's not.

> We describe public speaking as an art or craft instead of a science.

How audiences react to speakers really does depend on where and in what culture you are speaking. This is why we describe public speaking as an art or a craft instead of a science. The sciences concern rules or laws that apply across most contexts most of the time. Unlike the sciences, crafts concern skills that must be adapted to ever-changing contexts, situations, and events.

Crafting Your Speech

The way public speaking is studied today — as an art — comes most directly from ancient Greek manuscripts from the fourth and fifth centuries BCE. This is the reason why so many ancient Greek thinkers appear in this book — we still depend on their teachings. The ancient Greeks described public speaking or oratory — which they eventually called "rhetoric" — as a **techne**. *Techne* is usually translated as "craftsmanship" or "art" for many reasons. A craft emphasizes *doing* something; it is concrete and hands-on, and it is situational (context dependent).

techne is a habit of mind and body that is cultivated to make something; a craft.

Orators and philosophers like Isocrates, Plato, and Aristotle often objected to the teachings of sophists like Gorgias, some of whom boasted that they could teach public speaking like a science, specifying principles and magical techniques that could help speakers manipulate audiences. Plato famously criticized the teaching of public speaking as a science in a number of his writings, and he found the view of public speaking as manipulation unethical. He said that teaching public speaking as if it were law-based ignored the crucial component of adapting to the "soul of the hearer," including the listener's welfare or well-being, which is always context dependent.[12] His student, Aristotle, was not as harsh and said that although public speaking is a highly context-dependent craft, there are a number of general guidelines and principles that could be helpful to beginners and seasoned pros alike, especially the study of audience psychology, the effect of evoking emotions, and the rules of reasoning.[13] Although practice and experience is still the most important teacher of speaking in public, a student can learn about audience expectations and plan ahead. The term "speech craft" reflects this approach: public speaking is a *craft* that depends on understanding, planning, and doing.

> **?** **What is a *techne*? How is this concept better translated for our times?**

Getting Up There: Fake It Until You Make It

> **You will learn to**
> **EXPLAIN** the importance of positive visualization for public speaking.

Have you ever been told to "fake it until you make it?" The logic behind this statement is that if you pretend to have confidence in what you are doing, you will learn how to do it. Because almost every public speaker experiences speech anxiety, there is a sense in which all speakers "fake it." However nervous we may be, as speakers we want to appear competent and confident. Sometimes demonstrating confidence is hard, but researchers investigating the "fake it until you make it" approach have discovered that pretending does, in fact, work in some contexts.

At Wake Forest University, psychologist William Fleeson and two of his students, Adriane Malanos and Noelle Achille, conducted a study in which they asked students who self-identified as introverts to act extroverted in group exercises. What they found surprised them: introverts who pretended to be extroverted ended up feeling good about their performances. The Wake Forest study suggests that just acting extroverted—displaying an abundance of energy and engaging in frequent conversations, for example—can improve the positive feelings of the speaker and the whole group and lead to more productive or successful interactions.[14] Those who teach and study public speaking have approached the craft this way for centuries by emphasizing two things: the psychology of confidence and the importance of speech preparation. Let us discuss each in turn.

Self-assurance about one's knowledge and abilities, or confidence, is often a hard-won trait of character, especially for the public speaker. Although the exact cognitive and behavioral relationship between confidence and imagining future performance is somewhat unclear,

visualization refers to imagining the outcome of a possible course of action or behavior.

researchers have demonstrated that **visualization** is an important factor in developing feelings of confidence. By imagining yourself doing well at a given task, you are more likely to perform that task well. For example, a study of over two hundred athletes revealed a strong correlation between visualization and confidence in sports-related performance. In other words, athletes who visualize doing well increase their self-confidence and effectiveness in sports.[15] Similarly, researchers have shown that students who imagine doing well on exams tend to get higher grades. Not surprisingly, public speaking researchers have demonstrated repeatedly that imagining giving a good speech gives speakers a confidence boost and actually improves their speaking.[16] In short: visualizing a successful speech has a profound impact on how you give a speech.

Minister and professional speaker Norman Vincent Peale became famous in the United States because of his 1952 *New York Times* best-selling book, *The Power of Positive Thinking*. In his book Peale argued that positive visualization is transformative and that it is best practiced by imagining good or desired outcomes in all parts of one's life. His views about the close relationship between optimism and confidence have now become common sense in North America. Visualizing bad outcomes is sometimes necessary when planning ahead to avoid making mistakes or hurting others, but dwelling on the negative in public speaking situations can—and often will—make your speech worse and probably make you more nervous.

Speakers who envision failure or who get caught up in gloomy scenarios can lead themselves to what sociologist Robert K. Merton termed a self-fulfilling prophecy, "whereby fears are translated into reality."[18] Research by scholars has shown that speakers do better when they visualize making a good speech before they start speaking. Visualizing success is easier to do and can be a powerful asset to you as a speaker. Even when you are very anxious about giving a speech, most audiences won't notice your nervousness unless you tell them to notice it in some way. In other words, pretending that you are *not* nervous and visualizing your speech's success will influence an audience to perceive your speech as a success.

Astrid Stawiarz/Getty Images for Marie Claire

Harvard social psychologist Amy Cuddy argues that "power posing" can increase a speaker's confidence.[17]

Visualizing a positive speech encounter is also easier if you are prepared to speak. Thinking about, researching, and planning a speech before it is given are crucial components to visualization and confidence in speaking. In some speaking situations, you may not have time to prepare, but in most, including those you will experience in the public speaking classroom, you will have time to think about and plan a speech before you give it. Just knowing that you have your speech researched and mapped out will reduce your nervousness substantially.

The rest of this book is dedicated to helping you plan and prepare a variety of speeches—notably those designed to celebrate community (such as a toast or a eulogy) and to inform or persuade audiences. It's likely for this class, however, that you'll be asked to deliver a short speech before you have had an opportunity to study all the chapters that follow. So what do you do? The next section gives a quick overview of some of the basics of speech preparation, which will be elaborated in more detail across the chapters of *Speech Craft*. Because your first speech for this class will be a short one, you don't

need to know much to start speaking; the key to getting up in front of the class is visualizing doing well and having a plan.

Basic Speech Prep and Delivery

> *You will learn to*
>
> **LIST** the four steps of basic speech planning and delivery.

Right away, your instructor will ask you to prepare a short speech, commonly termed "the first speech" or "the icebreaker." It will probably help to know why you are being asked to speak before you've had a chance to learn about the fundamental elements of the craft of public speaking. For your teacher, the reason for getting you to speak in front of the class right away is to help reduce your anxiety about public speaking in general—that is, if you have it (some of us don't, and if you don't, consider yourself a lucky exception). Once you've delivered your first speech, your anxiety will (most likely) be reduced, clearing the way for deeper study into the craft. Researchers have repeatedly shown that the primary source of speech anxiety is a lack of experience.[19] By getting a little experience, the longer speeches that you will be asked to develop and deliver later in the course will seem less daunting.

Following below are the four basic steps of preparing and delivering a speech. Reviewing these steps will help with any jitters you have about giving that first speech in class.

- RESEARCH: research the speech
- ORGANIZE: put your main points into some sort of organization
- PRACTICE: plan how you will present the speech, and rehearse it to yourself
- DELIVER: deliver it to the class

The first step when preparing any speech concerns figuring out what you're going to say. We will call it "research" for now, but really, this might only entail thinking. Originally termed the step of "invention" in the ancient Greek study of oratory, the first thing you have to do is figure out what to say for a particular audience. More than likely your instructor will tell you what kind of speech to give, if only because the point of the first speech is less about what you say and more about getting a little experience. Regardless, note that there is another huge constraint on what you say: your particular audience. Part of your research is anticipating how the audience may react to what you have to say, and planning to say something that will appeal specifically to them. What you come up with must be relevant to the audience you are asking to listen to you, and care should be taken not to offend them. For example, your first audience will consist of other students in the class, and most of them will probably be strangers to you.

When you have time to observe your classmates, you'll be able to understand basic demographic information: gender conformity or nonconformity, fashion sensibility, age, and so on. This part of the research is the step known as "audience analysis," which we will address in much more depth in chapter 3. For this first speech, though, just take notice of who your classmates are and what kind of people they seem to be. You'll learn much more about them over the quarter or semester, but for now, observe them and think about how you might connect with them.

After you understand who your audience is and have a good sense of what you want to say, you must organize your main points into some sort of arrangement. For all sorts of reasons we will discuss in the chapter on organizing speeches (chapter 7), audiences respond well to speeches that have no more than three main points. The magic of three is also reflected in the basic tripartite structure taught for writing essays and speeches: introduction, body, and conclusion. Even for the shortest of speeches, write the structure down on a piece of paper or on your computer. Sometimes you will have an opportunity to write out a speech word for word, but in general, most speeches are delivered **extemporaneously**, or seemingly with little preparation. This is where the "fake it until you make it" motto is built into the craft of public speaking. Although many gifted public speakers may seem to be speaking without preparation, the truth remains that most speakers have planned their remarks in advance. You may be able to use a note card or reference a manuscript, or you may be asked to memorize your speech. Either way, your speech should be organized and planned in advance to appear spontaneous.

extemporaneous speaking is a form of public speaking that appears to require little or no preparation.

In life as well as in your public speaking class, most speeches have time limits, and going under or over time is generally regarded as undesirable. For all of the speeches that you will give in this class, you'll be asked to keep them to a certain length of time. The way to ensure staying within your time limit is simply by rehearsing. When you rehearse a speech, you will discover phrases or points that can be added or eliminated. You'll also notice words that are difficult to say and that might need to be replaced. Rehearsing will also help you to get a sense of how long your speech is, and will also help you to start committing your main points to memory (bonus!). Be careful to practice speaking at an even pace (not too fast, not too slow) and at a volume that your audience will be able to hear.

As previously noted, anticipating the delivery of a speech is usually more nerve-racking than actually delivering it. If you have researched, organized, and rehearsed your speech, however, you will have the confidence to get up there. Try to make eye contact with your instructor and classmates as you deliver your speech; if your instructor allows you to use notes, be careful not to read; only reference your notes if you get stuck or if your memory starts to flag. Speak at an even pace and at a volume that is appropriate for the room you are speaking in.

(?) What are the four basic steps of speech preparation?

Let's Do This!

> *You will learn to*
> **APPLY** the principles of speech preparation to your first speech.

For the most part, you'll be speaking publicly for much of your life in private settings—family gatherings, weddings and civil unions, toasts at parties, and so on. You'll also find yourself speaking or listening to speakers in many career contexts (in boardrooms or courtrooms), perhaps in contexts for political or religious causes (rallies, protests, or

community events)—really, once you are aware of public speaking as an idea, you'll start to see it *everywhere*. As a craft, speaking in public—creating relationships with others—is a lifelong art. Right now, as a college student, you're just beginning, so don't be too hard on yourself. Just remember: visualize doing well, then research, organize, practice, and deliver!

end of chapter stuff

The Purpose of Public Speaking

The primary purpose and function of all types of speaking in public is to establish relationships with others and to create a sense of community.

The Celebrated and Feared Power of Speech

Public speaking has been celebrated and feared throughout history.
As a craft, public speaking has been compared to spell binding.
Public speaking can be used for good or ill, depending on the ethics of the speaker.

Courtesy the Everett Collection, Inc.

High Anxiety: The Fear of Public Speaking

Speech anxiety can be reduced through positive thinking and visualization.
The four basic steps of all forms of public speaking are (1) researching, (2) organizing, (3) practicing, and (4) delivering.

AP Photo/Jim Cole

Public Speaking as a Civic Conversation

Today the conversational and civic models of public speaking are most popular. Audiences and speakers are generally thought to be in a conversational context, with more give and take than in past centuries.

Basic Speech Prep and Delivery

To prepare any speech, you should research the topic first. Then, organize your main points and practice your speech. Finally, deliver the speech to the audience.

CHAPTER 1

ACTIVITY

Raise a Toast!

A toast is a short speech that celebrates a person, a thing, or an event, and typically involves a call for a group of people to drink a beverage at the conclusion. Traditionally the beverage was alcoholic, but today toasts are made with all sorts of drinks; the important point is to hold up a glass indicating that you share in the spirit of celebration and wish someone well. For this activity, you'll be asked to develop a very short toast to a classmate, which means you will *not* have a lot of time to prepare. Your instructor will pair you with someone, or you will pair yourself with a classmate. Work through the four basic steps of speech prep:

RESEARCH: Interview your classmate, and find out why he or she is taking the class. Then ask your classmate to tell you about a recent accomplishment.

ORGANIZE: Toasts are typically very brief and usually have only one point; however, they do model the magic number of three in structure: (1) the opening, (2) the main point, and (3) the conclusion. Briefly write out a plan for your toast. The opening usually asks for the attention of the audience; the main point is usually a reference to why you are toasting; and the conclusion is typically a wish for the person being honored, followed by a sip of a drink.

PRACTICE: Briefly rehearse your toast with your classmate. Get his or her feedback, and revise your speech if you need to.

DELIVER: When asked by your instructor, stand in front of the class and offer your toast. Use a soda or water bottle for your beverage. Please note: Insofar as the whole class will be giving toasts, you should probably *pretend* to drink at the conclusion of each toast; your bladder will thank you.

KEY TERMS

 Videos in LaunchPad describe many of these terms. Go to launchpadworks.com.

communication apprehension 8

▶ speech anxiety 8

▶ techne 12

▶ visualization 14

▶ extemporaneous speaking 17

LISTENING

& THE ETHICS

ETHICS

OF

SPEECH

CHAPTER 2

What do concertgoing and public speaking have in common? Calling and responding. Whether you're at a Jay Z, Beyoncé, or Pixies show, when you go to a concert you are asked to respond to the music based on the many ways in which the musicians "call" out to you with instruments, voices, show lights, and movements. An artist might call for you to "make some noise," and you scream in response. The chorus of a song is also a call, perhaps stirring you to declare, "We're never, ever, ever getting back together!" with Taylor Swift. Although different in goals, purposes, and functions, going to a concert and delivering a speech both rely on call-and-response, which is the communicative foundation of many forms of listening and speaking.

For centuries, people have thought of listening as a passive activity, as if the ear were a sound receiver answering the call of another. Scenes from everyday life, however, quickly dispute any passive conception of listening: you perk up when your roommate says that she has some confidential news; a young man sings along to the music in his headphones on the subway; and a parishioner replies "Amen!" to the shout of a preacher in church. Whether at a concert or talking with a friend, observing others in public or in private spaces, *listening* is a dynamic and interactive process that is anything but passive.

Speaking with an Open Ear

> **You will learn to**
>
> **EXPLAIN** how listening is foundational to all public speaking.
>
> **DEFINE** "listening" in relation to communication and public speaking.
>
> **DEFINE** "noise" and explain its role in public speaking.

Listening is an active response to the call of another. When we answer a call—whether it is from a public figure on a big stage or from our best friend asking us a question—we are actually experiencing something universal to the human condition: responsiveness.[1] There are a variety of everyday examples in which we are "called" to respond and we do so without even thinking about it: while walking down the street, an unfamiliar voice calls to you, and you respond by turning around; you receive a text message and immediately look to see who sent it; a teacher calls on you unexpectedly to answer a question, and you respond before you have time to think about the answer. In each case, someone calls for your attention and you have an *impulse* to respond.

An interesting thing about "the call"—whether it be from a speaker, a singer, or a cell phone—is that *most of us respond without thinking about it.*[2] And in almost every kind of example of calling we can imagine, it is this almost automatic *ability to respond* that makes the call possible in the first place. Without this ability, speakers wouldn't speak and pop stars wouldn't sing. This means that *listening comes before speaking.* This means that listening is prior to speaking. If we understand speaking, especially public speaking, as a form of calling to an audience, then listening is a precondition of speaking. Because any kind of speaking is a form of calling, we are enjoined to understand listening better.

What Did You Say? Understanding Listening

Your public speaking class is designed to help you become more comfortable speaking to a group of others. Even so, the fact remains that for most of your life you will be a listener. As strange as it may seem now, thinking about your life as a listener can be quite helpful to you as a speaker because it will prepare you to adapt to any audience. In fact, to become a better speaker, it is essential that you practice the difficult skill of active listening. Public speaking concerns other people to whom you call and from whom you ask for a response; before you can deliver any speech, you must first listen. If you do not understand how listening happens, it will be difficult to figure out how to speak so that others will listen to you. As we will see, a more robust understanding of listening also involves a set of moral principles that can help you become not only a more skilled speaker, but perhaps a more ethical one as well.

Defining listening

Most of us have a habit of defining listening by comparing it to what listening is not. Common sense tells us that listening is the counterpart to speaking. Because we are constantly observing the responses of others when we speak to them, however, communication scholars suggest that this common distinction doesn't hold up; research suggests that it is difficult to maintain the idea that speaking is not listening and listening is not speaking. In terms of how our brains and bodies work, we tend to speak and listen at the same time (in greater or lesser degrees). For example, when you are speaking, you're often observing the facial expressions of others, "listening" for any verbal and nonverbal cues they send you (such as laughter at a joke, a smile, or a frown), and even hearing the sound of your own voice. You cannot help but "listen" when you speak.

Recognizing the indivisible or intertwined character of speaking and listening, communication scholars tend to define listening by contrasting it with *hearing*, which can be confusing because many of us use the terms "listening" and "hearing" interchangeably. Were you ever told to clean your room or take out the trash and then asked, usually in an angry tone: "Do you hear me!?!!" In such a scenario, what the demander is really asking is, "Are you listening to me?" This gives us a hint about the distinction between hearing and listening: *hearing* is the physiological event that concerns waves of *sound* entering your ear, greeting your eardrum, and firing up neurons in your brain. Hearing is a physical event. We hear things all the time without listening to them. Our brains, in fact, work to "filter out" the sounds we hear every day so that we are not overwhelmed by sensory information. Listening, on the other hand—or on the other ear, rather—typically refers to the way in which we consciously and actively make sense or meaning of sound.

> For our purpose of speaking in public, then, let us say simply that **listening** is the process of actively making meaning of messages.

Listening involves some degree of active attention with which we assign, or begin to assign, meaning to a sound stimulus. The attention part of listening seems to require some degree of self-consciousness: you think to yourself, "I am hearing something meaningful." In this respect, the leading group of listening scholars in the United States formally defines listening as "the process of receiving, constructing meaning from, and responding to spoken and/or nonverbal messages."[3] According to this broad definition, you can listen to a sneeze as much as you can listen to someone's facial expression; what makes either "listening" is the *attribution of meaning* to the message. Many in the deaf community would agree that one can "listen" with his or her eyes or through the sense of touch without ever "hearing" a sound wave. For our purpose of speaking in public, then, let us say simply that **listening** is the process of actively making meaning of messages.

listening is the process of actively making meaning of messages.

Although our culture associates listening with hearing, one can listen without actually hearing.

The challenge of listening: Noise

Although we listen all of the time, the achievement of making meaning of messages is actually quite difficult. Our brains help us do a lot of the work by attending to sensory information that we should notice, but we still have to make meaning of that information by actively interpreting it. The problem with actively interpreting information from any of our senses is there is a lot of "noise" that gets in the way. For example, if you are hungry, you may find it difficult to listen to your instructor's lecture because images of food keep popping up in your head. Sometimes in speaking situations a chatty audience can make it difficult to actively interpret and understand what a speaker is saying. In short: listening is hard because of interference. This interference, or **noise**, is defined as anything that distorts or distracts from a message. Technicians who work on your Internet connection or cable service often refer to interruptions to your carrier signal as noise.

Most people think of noise as only concerning sounds, such as a loud jackhammer, your neighbor's motorcycle, or Norwegian death metal. Because "listening" is a metaphor for attending to all sorts of information, in the public speaking situation we shouldn't reduce noise to *only* sounds. We can experience noise in our own minds as well, such as distracting thoughts, hunger pangs, or even when we get excited or have depressed feelings. *Anything* that gets in the way of attaching meaning to what someone is trying to communicate can be "noise."

> **?** **What is the difference between listening and hearing? Is it possible to listen without hearing, or to hear without listening? Why or why not?**

noise refers to anything that distorts or distracts from a message in the context of communication. Noise can be internal or external to the listener.

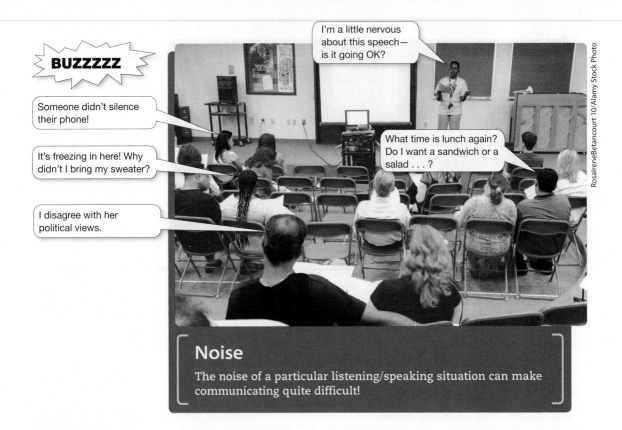

Noise

The noise of a particular listening/speaking situation can make communicating quite difficult!

If you keep in mind that the word "noise" is derived from the term "nausea," it will be easier to remember that it can refer to both environmental distractions and internal states of mind and body. Consequently, we can discern two kinds of noise:

- **external noise:** Anything in a communication environment that one can sense or feel that distracts, or can distract, from a message. This includes everything from room temperature, street sounds, the failure of a microphone, and distorted feedback to applause and laughter, a fire alarm or cell phone ringing, even your own hiccups.
- **internal noise:** Any thoughts, feelings, or bodily disturbances — such as a stomach growl that only you can hear — that distract you from attending to a message. Internal noise includes beliefs, attitudes, and values that get in the way of clearly or more fully listening to what a speaker has to say. "Hearing what you want to hear," as the common phrase goes, is a kind of internal noise.

While external and internal noise can be managed, we tend to think about noise as something that is often beyond our control. Noise will happen, and you cannot always plan for it. We will discuss how you can plan to minimize external and internal noise as a speaker in the next chapter, especially when discussing physical settings and audience psychology. In this chapter, we will focus on what to do about noise as a *listener*.

As a listener, external noise can be a challenge in a speaking situation. More often than not, there is little you can do to prepare for distractions that might occur in a given listening encounter: roadwork outside a building may distract you, or your cell phone carrier may drop you in the middle of a call. If you know that you are easily distracted by environmental noise in a listening encounter, you might plan to sit closer to a speaker. If you use sign language, you might check to see if someone will be interpreting for you. Whether you are going to be at a concert or in a classroom, try to anticipate what the environmental conditions might be and plan ahead.

Internal noise, however, is the strangest kind of distraction to anticipate. For many speaking situations in which we are asked to listen, we do not know in advance exactly what will be said, and consequently, we cannot always predict how our minds and bodies will react. This unpredictability is why managing internal noise is the greatest challenge of listening. Fortunately for us, there has been a lot of research on this challenge. In the next section, we'll examine this research to better understand the importance of active listening for achieving an understanding with others.

> ? What is noise? What are the different types of noise? How can you control for noise?

Communication and Understanding: Listening beyond Noise

> **You will learn to**
>
> **DEFINE** communication.
>
> **DEFINE** active listening.
>
> **LIST** the steps of active listening.

Rethinking Noise: There Are Always Two Messages

The internal noise we experience when communicating with others often has to do with our own self-concept or identity. When you speak to me, I am not only trying to understand or interpret what you are saying (the message) but also thinking about (and feeling) what your message says about me, as a person. In other words, every message sent between or among people is fundamentally about identity. Messages contain both a "content" (or meaning) that we share, as well as information about who we are to each other: I am a teacher, you are a student; you are a listener (or reader), I am a speaker (or author). When you take part in any listening situation, you bring your self-understanding with you, and

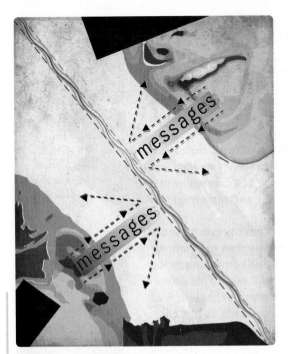

There are always two messages when communicating: what a speaker believes he or she is saying, and what a listener believes he or she is hearing.

communication refers to the coordination of behavior using symbols.

misunderstanding refers to the inability of one or more communicators to apprehend meanings, feelings, or identities, and to coordinate their behaviors.

that self-understanding is often addressed in listening and speaking, even if you're not consciously thinking about it. (Reading this, you might be thinking, "So why is this relevant *to me?*") In short, anything that means something to us implies an *identity*.

Taking the internal noise of our self-identities into account, some thinkers have argued that communication as pure or absolute understanding is impossible. What speakers and listeners actually do when communicating is coordinate their behaviors through language. Whether or not pure or absolute understanding is possible, we do know that people can and do coordinate their thoughts and behaviors and understand each other meaningfully with language. So, instead of thinking about communication as a kind of mind meld, let's think of it as a kind of interaction or dance: **communication** is the coordination of behavior through symbols. For this dance of meaning to be successful, whatever the content of the message may be, speakers and listeners must also navigate their own identities. What such a view of communication implies is that whenever we speak and whenever we listen, we're not simply coordinating what we say but also coordinating who we are to each other.

In light of the internal noise of identity that communicating entails, we can presume a rule or motto for understanding speaking and listening: *there are always two messages*. For example, as a speaker, there are always two kinds of speeches: the one you deliver, and the one the audience hears. As a listener, there are always two kinds of speeches: what the speaker says, and what you actually respond to. We could say, then, that effective listening and speaking reduces to the moments when the two messages line up or overlap. When these two messages misalign or don't overlap, we have **misunderstanding**.

As a listener, accepting the fact that there are two messages means that misunderstanding happens more often than people think it does. Avoiding misunderstanding can be difficult. When we listen to others, we have to navigate both *what* is said as well as what the saying implies about ourselves (e.g., emotional cues about the relationship). Researchers have tended to focus on this identity-related internal noise problem as one of selective perception, and the remedy as one of active perceiving. Let's turn to a discussion of these two concepts as they relate to selective listening and active listening.

Selective and Active Listening: Moving toward Understanding

Read any conflicting reviews of a new album and one thing is obvious: each music critic *listened* to a different album. One reviewer found Kanye West's latest album to be the best hip-hop record of all time, while another found the music unworthy of distribution. What accounts for the different opinions? Many things, including the circumstances in which they listened to the album, with all its accompanying distractions (external noise), but also their tastes, their politics and values, and most certainly their identities as people and as critics.

When we perceive the world, we come to it with a set of beliefs, attitudes, and values that influences our perceptions. In general, these influences inform what is known as **selective perception**, or the ways in which we choose to pay attention to something as meaningful, important, and relevant.

Researchers have found that one of the key perceptual differences between older humans and infants concerns an older person's ability to *selectively* attend to stimuli from the environment. As we grow older, we develop both cognitive and personality-based "filters" for attending to one thing while ignoring other things. Selective perception, in other words, is an observational skill that we develop out of necessity to

selective perception refers to the ways in which people attend to the things they like, ignoring things that they do not.

perceive the world. We cannot help but selectively perceive because we *have to* for the world to make any sense.

For most of us, how we selectively perceive the messages coming from others is highly refined and grafted onto our identities as individuals.[5] Media scholars—and in particular those concerned with cultural differences such as gender, race, and political affiliation—are especially interested in how audiences expose themselves to some messages while avoiding others (also known as **selective exposure**).[6] Although selective perception research extends across all the senses, a great deal of effort has been spent on understanding **selective listening**, or the ways in which people perceive the spoken messages of others. This research supports what you probably already anticipate in your "selective reading": that people tend to listen to what they believe is important or relevant to them, and that they tend to listen in a way that reinforces or is informed by what they already know. For example, cable television audiences have a number of "news" channels that claim to present information about world events in objective terms. And yet we all know that those who listen to the Fox News channel tend to identify as "conservative," and those who listen to MSNBC tend to identify as "liberal." Consequently, the audiences of these different media outlets selectively expose themselves to messages that reinforce their preexisting worldviews.

selective exposure is a psychological theory suggesting that people prefer information that supports their views and avoid information that does not.

selective listening refers to the ways in which a person attends to some auditory information (speech or sound), ignoring other information.

Why They Don't Hear You: Reasons Why We Don't Listen

Listening to others is a challenging skill because of the barriers that block us from active understanding. These barriers include the following:

- **external noise:** Distractions from the environment make it hard to focus on what a speaker is saying, whether it's his or her speech volume, noise coming from the street, or your neighbor chewing gum.
- **selective listening:** You attend to only that information you think is important or relevant to you. Listening only to the parts of a teacher's lecture that may be on an exam is an example.
- **defensive listening:** Defensive listening occurs when you anticipate what the speaker is going to say, especially if it is contrary to what you believe, feel, or value.
- **cultural differences:** If a speaker comes from a different part of the world or belongs to a foreign culture or community, it may be difficult to understand the perspective he or she is coming from. This includes language barriers as well as differing values.
- **pretend listening:** Sometimes when we are distracted we may fake listening to another person by nodding our heads or seeming to understand. Perhaps we cannot concentrate on a speaker because we are hungry, or cold, or worried about something else. People pretend to listen all the time, which is why, as a speaker, it is always good to pause and ask questions like, "Does that make sense?"

Some of these audience members are not actively listening!

You and I are predisposed to ignore others who challenge our identities and assumptions. Few of us are able to listen to others objectively—and thus we cannot help but be selective listeners. Consequently, we have to learn and practice what is referred to as "active listening," and very few of us are taught this skill before college. You have been listening all your life, but have you ever actually been taught how to listen *actively*?

Active listening is a technique of observing and responding to a speaker's verbal and nonverbal messages with the goal of mutual understanding. Listening scholar Graham D. Bodie characterizes active listening as a form of "positive communication," meaning that it is not a passive process but a willed attempt to take a speaker at his or her own words and expressions (including nonverbal messages).[7] As a technique, active listening comes to us from therapeutic settings—picture a psychologist or psychiatrist listening to a patient's concerns and problems.

It would make sense that those who earn a living listening to others—psychologists, psychiatrists, counselors, and therapists—have developed the technique of listening as an active and positive component of understanding. Many communication scholars teach the active listening technique to help communicators work toward more effective messaging. Interpersonal communication scholar Steven McCornack helpfully describes active listening as a series of "steps," which we simplify in four steps here.[8]

active listening is a technique of observing and responding to a speaker's verbal and nonverbal messages with the goal of mutual understanding.

Receiving and attending

In the first step of active listening, you are physically hearing and seeing a speaker craft and deliver a message. "Receiving" is a physiological process involving the ears and eyes, and sometimes other senses (don't forget touch and smell!). When you are conscious that someone is speaking to you, you are attending to what it may be that the person means. "Attending" to another refers to making the speaker's message meaningful. In this step, try not to prejudge what the speaker is saying and avoid making conclusions. Reduce external and internal noise as much as you can.

Understanding

In the next step of active listening, you interpret and assess the meaning of a message a speaker has given you. Interpreting and assessing means that you actively compare the meaning of what was said with what you already know, the context of the message, and other kinds of information you have already learned. When you are aware of your own assessments, you are self-monitoring—or getting meta- with "metacognition." Self-monitoring means simply that you are thinking about *your* thinking about communication.[9] You are asking yourself questions like "OK, so what did she just say to me?" "What does the speaker mean to communicate?" and "Do I actually understand what he just said?" In most speaking situations, understanding is a *continual process* that begins long before and continues well after a speech.

Responding, paraphrasing, and clarifying

In this step of active listening, you indicate to the speaker in some way that you are understanding him or her. If your education was in a classroom, you already understand this step, as many of us have been taught to raise our hand if we have a question about a teacher's message. If you are listening to someone give a long speech, however, you will probably not have an opportunity to raise your hand. In many speaking situations, you might indicate your understanding by nodding or smiling, perhaps laughing at a joke, or saying "Yeah!"; if you do not understand, you may look confused or ask, "What?" Researchers discuss these kinds of responses, verbal and nonverbal, as **feedback**. In a conversation, you have more of an opportunity to clearly respond by paraphrasing the speaker's message and asking for clarification: "OK, José, what I hear you saying is that you would like to go to the amusement park on Saturday. Is that right?" In most public speaking situations, however, the time for verbal responses, paraphrases, and clarifications is either after a speech is given or in a designated question-and-answer session.

feedback refers to verbal or nonverbal responses to a speaker that indicate an understanding or misunderstanding of a message.

Recalling and remembering

The final step of active listening concerns memory, or how to hold on to the meaning of a message. In most speaking situations, you will not remember everything a speaker has said, only those aspects of the message that were repeated or that have importance and relevance to you. For this reason, most speakers in a formal setting will repeat their main points and sometimes even enumerate them. In a conversational setting, you are

The Power of Paraphrasing

Since few of us are taught how to really listen in school, we have to learn and practice how to give helpful responses to others. Most of us have a tendency to respond to speakers immediately in a way that says "I agree!" or "I disagree!" which skips the very important step of indicating you have understood the speaker's message first. Most people like to know that they are understood before they know whether someone agrees or disagrees with them.

Try to indicate in some way that you have understood a speaker's message before responding; understand the message before judging the message! Doing so helps speakers feel welcome and shows that you respect them. A key phrase to use is "What I hear you saying is that . . ." or "If I understand you correctly, you are saying that. . . ." This language acknowledges that you have the burden of listening and care about the other person's message (and identity). Language like "You are saying" or "You just said" is sometimes OK, but it shifts the burden of listening to the speaker. You will be surprised at how much easier it is to reach an understanding when you "own" the responsibility of listening and can paraphrase what you hear.

much more likely to remember relational information (character traits, who the individual is to you, whether he or she has something valuable to teach you, and so on) than you are the word-based content of a message. As listeners, we often take notes to help us remember information from a speaker, especially if the message is a longer one, like a speech or a lecture. In everyday conversations, of course, taking notes would seem strange, even rude—unless, perhaps, you were investigating a crime!

? What are the four steps of active listening?

An Ethics of Speaking as a Listener

You will learn to

DETAIL the relationship between listening and responsibility.

EXPLAIN how speaking and listening implies an ethics.

DESCRIBE the guidelines of ethical speaking.

Responsibility as "Response-Ability"

Earlier in this chapter, we observed that most people have a tendency to respond to the calls of others automatically, without thinking about it. Philosopher Diane Davis calls this tendency to respond to the call of

response-ability is the ability to respond to others, which is the foundation of listening and speaking.

others **"response-ability."**[10] In fact, Davis argues that our self-identities are fundamentally based on our responses to the calls of others, and that the foundation of all communication is response-ability. By thinking about responsibility as based on response-ability, Davis links the condition of listening and speaking to ethics: our ability to respond to the speech of others (listening) is the basis of our responsibility to others (ethics). In short, listening involves an ethical orientation toward others.

In the everyday sense, the term "responsibility" is a set of rules about how to respond to others. Responsibility refers to the guidelines for relationships that we learn as we grow up in a particular community or culture. Obligations or duties to others are taught and learned. The centuries-old Golden Rule—"Do unto others as you would have them do unto you"—specifies a generally accepted responsibility that we share with our fellow human beings: treat others as you would like to be treated. When we refer to the responsibilities of a speaker or a listener, then, we are referring to established cultural or social rules. Over the past century, scholars of public speaking have developed a number of rules, drawn from larger cultural expectations, which we teach to students as guides for moral behavior. We will examine the rules and responsibilities of both listeners and speakers in the following sections.

In most discussions of listening, the question often arises: *Why should I listen?* Or, perhaps: *Why bother?* The answers you have been given to these and similar questions for most of your life are often pragmatic or instrumental, meaning that listening is important because it helps you understand others or because it helps you retain information that is useful for you (e.g., for an exam, to get ahead in a job, to be a better communicator, and so on). These answers may seem obvious, but they are all about consequences: if you don't listen, then something bad will happen or something good will not happen.[11] Consequence-based answers also beg the question because they do not address the more fundamental question of "Why?" at their core: *Why should I try to listen at all?* If a message does not affect me one way or the other, what is the effort worth?

To be honest, you have to answer this fundamental question for yourself, because the reasons for listening (and speaking) to others concern morality and ethics. If you're reading this textbook, you may be taking a course in public speaking because it is required for a credential or a degree, or you may be taking the course because you wish to be a better speaker. For those of us who study and teach public speaking, however, there's more at stake: how to be a better human being. The ability to speak and listen is part of what it means to be human. The author of this textbook considers listening and responding to others, or "response-ability," as the most fundamental human trait, and learning about how to listen and respond to others is really about learning how to be with others. One way to get a better understanding of the human condition is to think about the ethical assumptions of speaking and listening in the concept of making a *pact*.

What is the difference between response-ability and responsibility? How do these concepts relate to ethics? ⑦

An Oath Is a Promise in Speech. Immigrants to the United States take the oath of allegiance to become naturalized citizens.

The Pact of Speech: Accountability and Ethics

Thinking critically about speech or speaking is one way to understand how our (often automatic) ability to respond to others implicates a responsibility. For something to be considered "speech" or "speaking," a speaker must assume a listener. Mere utterance is just vocalization or noise—like a burp or a hiccup. Speech, however, is something that becomes meaningful because listeners are present; for meaning to exist, speech *must assume* a listener. Even when you and I talk to ourselves, we are assuming we are our own listeners, or we are imagining speaking to someone. If you are at home rehearsing a speech that you prepared for this class, you are probably imagining your teacher and classmates. Whether real or imaginary, speech assumes others.[12] It is in this way that we can say that all speaking, most especially public speaking, implies an often unspoken agreement between a speaker and a listener or audience—that is, an assumed "speech pact."

What is this pact? Well, it's a kind of reciprocal deal or unspoken agreement between two or more parties, most especially speakers and listeners. A line from William Shakespeare's famous play *Julius Caesar* sums up this implied speech pact in an opening line from Mark Antony. At Caesar's funeral, Antony gives a speech in which he attempts to persuade those in attendance to hunt down those responsible for Caesar's death. He begins his famed speech with "Friends, Romans, countrymen, lend me your ears," in effect saying, "Hey, folks, I have something to say!" With this, Antony makes explicit what is usually implied by any speaker in the presence of a listener: *Please listen to me!* Whether you ask explicitly or not, whenever you speak you are imploring others to listen and to respond.

When you ask someone to listen, you are suggesting that what you wish to say is important, of value, *and even* at some level that what you have to say is *true* (at least for you). Think about this issue as a listener: when you respond to a call—a phone call, a teacher asking you a question, or listening to someone giving a speech—aren't you also assuming that what they are saying is offered in the spirit of sincerity or truth? If we did not assume that speakers were truthful most of the time, no one would ever bother listening. Of course, there are always exceptions in any speaking or listening situation. For example, as an audience member going to a stand-up comedy show, you do not assume that everything the comedian says will be *factually* true, but you assume some degree of sincerity or genuineness of emotion. Regardless, whenever you choose to listen to someone, the speaker enters into a pact with you to be earnest, be truthful, or say something of value—in other words, to be *responsible*. Similarly, when you speak, you are asking the audience to afford you a certain degree of welcome and trust.

Ethics

Ethics concerns the discernment of right and wrong or good and evil. In philosophy, the systematic study of ethics is sometimes referred to as morality or moral philosophy. In the context of communication, ethics concerns the study of how we should and should not respond to others.

On Character, or Ethical Speaking

The implied pact of responsibility made between speakers and listeners leads us to questions about ethics: "What is my duty to other people?" and "How am I to be held responsible as a speaker or a listener?" In a public speaking context, the question of responsibility is usually phrased in one of two ways: "What is my duty to the audience as a speaker?" and "What is my duty to the speaker as a listener?" Such questions are also associated with the issue of "credibility"—the

> The issue of character extends far beyond audience perceptions of trustworthiness.

quality of appearing to be someone who can be trusted—but the issue of character extends far beyond audience perceptions of trustworthiness. We will bring this chapter to a conclusion with some tentative answers to questions about character and credibility, keeping in mind that duties and responsibilities to others are dynamic and constantly change, depending on the context.

For centuries, scholars and teachers of public speaking have been obsessed with discerning the responsibilities and duties of a speaker. The ancient Greek philosopher Aristotle located the speaker's responsibility in the concept of *ethos*, which translates roughly as "character." It's from the term *ethos* that we get the more contemporary word "ethics" in the first place. We will discuss *ethos* in more detail in the chapters on style and delivery (chapters 9 and 10), but the concept is introduced here as fundamentally *ethical* in scope. Aristotle argued that an ethical speaker must cultivate three character traits to model responsible and credible speaking, traits that we still believe more than two thousand years later: (1) practical wisdom, (2) expertise, and (3) goodwill toward the audience. These traits are not clearly distinct but overlap in ways that touch on ethics. Let's examine each one briefly.

Practical Wisdom.   Most of us are impressed by speakers whom we regard as intelligent or experienced; however, that's usually not enough for us to respect them. We also desire speakers to be prudent in their reasoning, meaning that they care about the implications and consequences of sharing their wisdom. Practical wisdom also entails a degree of common sense. As a speaker, you know, or at least believe, that the information you share with an audience will not be harmful. A speaker with wisdom is great, but a speaker who knows how to share and use that wisdom in a helpful and honest way is more responsible. Sometimes practical wisdom entails knowing what *not* to say or sharing only information that is helpful and useful.

Expertise.   We expect responsible speakers to know what they are talking about, through either formal study or experience. Whatever the speech topic, we usually assume that when a speaker is sharing information, he or she has a personal understanding of it. Expertise is often linked to what a speaker does for a living or a certain role that he or she occupies. For example, would you expect a personal trainer who claims to have worked at a gym to have some knowledge of strength training? Of course you would! Expertise refers to the cultivation of skills and knowledge particular to a practice or role and, consequently, we are less likely to respect a speaker as "responsible" who does not have some first-hand knowledge of his or her topic. Expertise does not necessarily mean you are an "expert" in the topic area you are speaking about; however, it *does* mean that you possess knowledge or have at least taken some time to learn more about a speaking topic (e.g., through research, participant observation, and so on).

Demonstrating expertise as a speaker is ethical because it relies on the assumption of truth at the heart of all speaking and listening encounters. As noted earlier, to speak at all is to announce your truth or sincerity, and to listen is to grant the speaker some claim to truth or sincerity and the acknowledgment that listening is worth your time. Consequently, the easiest way to destroy your credibility as a speaker is to lie or deceive. For example, speaking about the treatment of a disease without having any experience practicing or studying medicine would be a serious violation of the trait of expertise—and could even cause others harm. Credibility is also undermined when you claim to share knowledge or expertise that you took from someone else. When speaking, it is always important to cite your sources, though the ways of doing so can vary widely given the context of your speech. In a speech, credit is often given to others orally through the use of **direct quotations**, in which you say word for word what another person has said: "According to reporters at the *New York Times*, many FIFA officials were arrested in May 2015 because of charges of—and I quote—'widespread corruption in FIFA over the past two decades, involving bids for World Cups as well as marketing and broadcast deals.'"[13] You can also **paraphrase** or summarize the ideas or remarks of others: "As many fans of soccer—or in Europe, 'football'—already know, a number of the top officials in FIFA were arrested for corruption charges in May 2015." Finally, speakers often cite statistics or studies by crediting the person or group who developed and published the information.

Plagiarism, or the representation of someone else's ideas or words as your own, is one of the worst kinds of expertise misrepresentation and should be strictly avoided.

Goodwill. A speaker's goodwill refers to the ways in which he or she addresses an audience with respect and care. Few audiences will listen to a speaker who insults their intelligence or values. You can establish goodwill with an audience by acknowledging their presence and your concern for their well-being as individuals, as an audience, or both. Goodwill is based on the fundamental condition of response-ability, as well as acknowledging your responsibilities as someone with practical wisdom and expertise. There are really no hard-and-fast rules on how to cultivate a sense of goodwill—only a sincere and honest personal conviction that,

direct quotations are word-for-word references to what someone else has said.

to **paraphrase** is to summarize the ideas or remarks of others without directly quoting them.

plagiarism refers to the representation of someone else's words or ideas as your own; plagiarism is intellectual theft.

> **What are the three elements of *ethos* or a speaker's character? How do you cultivate them?** ❓

plagiarism

is just plain nasty

Dishonesty is widely regarded as the most egregious violation of educational integrity. Scholars, politicians, and leaders of all sorts get into trouble when they are caught using information or the ideas of others without giving those others credit. We tend to regard those who claim and use the ideas developed by others without giving credit as immoral and ethically challenged.

A century ago, plagiarism was typically a problem one encountered only in speeches or writing. Even then, however, what counted as plagiarism was not so clear. A similar confusion also arises in art. Many painters borrow ideas and techniques from other painters without giving those painters credit. In the music industry today, it is common for musicians to use samples or previously recorded sounds in their own musical compositions. Where plagiarism ends and creativity begins is sometimes hard to say.

As students and scholars, the rule for avoiding plagiarism is clear: when you use material or information taken from others, you must give them credit in some way. It is better to err on the

Tom Petty believed that the melody of Sam Smith's "Stay with Me" was too similar to Petty's "Won't Back Down." The two reached a settlement in 2015, and now Petty receives royalties for "Stay with Me."
Josh Brasted/FilmMagic/Getty Images

side of giving too much credit than not giving credit at all. For written papers, there are fairly standard guidelines for citing one's sources, such as with a bibliography or a citation at the end of a sentence. For the written work you turn in for this class, your instructor will provide you with instructions on how to properly document your sources.

LaunchPad macmillan learning

Sometimes we have trouble recognizing why and how using the ideas or words of others is wrong. Sometimes we know, intellectually, that such theft is inappropriate, but we do not *feel* that way. To get a sense of how plagiarism can feel inappropriate in emotional terms, visit LaunchPad at launchpadworks.com and link to the video that the Cable News Network (CNN) created of two speeches titled "Comparing Melania Trump & Michelle Obama." Melania Trump's speech honoring her husband, Donald J. Trump, at the 2016 Republican National Convention borrowed phrases verbatim from a speech given by Michelle Obama honoring her spouse, Barack Obama, at the Democratic National Convention in 2008. Trump did not, however, give Obama credit for the stolen phrases until many days later, after repeated denials of plagiarism.

After watching the Web video, consider the following questions:

- How did Trump's "borrowed" phrases make you feel? Why?
- Did Trump violate an assumed sense of trust? If so, where does this sense of trust come from? If not, why not?
- If Trump had given credit to Obama for her words, could her speech have been redeemed? Why or why not?

Television journalist Christiane Amanpour is widely regarded as an ethical public speaker because of her preparedness.

as a speaker, you care about and respect the audience. This may entail explicitly recognizing the values you share with your audience, a topic we will address in the next chapter when we look at audience psychology (Audience Analysis, chapter 3).

Guidelines for Ethical Speaking

Establishing *ethos* or a sense of your character—cultivating a sense of goodwill as someone who also has a measure of expertise and practical wisdom—is done in two ways: over the long term of your life and in the short term of a speech. How you live your life and build your character long term is your choice. In most speaking situations in the West, however, audiences will listen to you with a set of moral expectations that are inherent in our culture. If you violate any of these expectations, you'll probably have to explain to your audience why you are doing so. Try to observe these rules as best you can:

- **Know Your Stuff:** If you are asked to speak on a given topic, it is typically your responsibility to either know or research that topic.

Audiences expect you to have some expertise or understanding of the issues you discuss.

- **Be Prepared:** If you have the opportunity, always think about, plan, and rehearse your speech before delivering it. If an audience has assembled to hear you speak, they are expecting you to be prepared. In consenting to listen, there is a tacit agreement that you will present to them something coherent and organized. Even when you are asked to speak off the cuff, take a moment to organize your thoughts and think about what you are about to say before speaking.

- **Demonstrate Respect:** You demonstrate respect for an audience by thinking of each member as a human being with thoughts and feelings, not an object to be talked at. Respect is also demonstrated by acknowledging common beliefs and values, as well as an understanding of those who may be different from you. Be honest in what you say, try to avoid stereotyping, and do not use language that might anger or polarize an audience.

- **Do No Harm:** Perhaps one of the worst experiences that we have in life is realizing that we have hurt, harmed, or offended someone without knowing it. For most of us, trying to be a good person involves reducing the harm we might cause others. Speakers are unethical, however, when they knowingly share false information, mislead, or intentionally cause harm to others. Before delivering a speech, always take the time to think about whether what you wish to say could cause someone harm.

Ethical Listening

Most of the time, listening ethically is listening *actively*, trying to reflect the goodwill of the speaker. Your concern as an ethical listener is to both actively listen and show in some way that you care about what the speaker has to say. Of course, ethical listening is easier said than done, primarily because of the noise that runs interference through every communicative encounter. When we consider the ethical dimensions of speaking, there are no absolute right or wrong principles. How one responds to others depends on the context. What is important to remember is that active listening is an acknowledgment of an unspoken pact between you and a speaker, that you are response-able and responsible, and that you recognize the speaker as a human being worthy of your consideration. In turn, the speaker makes good on the often unspoken promise to be truthful and sincere as a condition of speaking in the first place.

As a listener, your primary task is to interpret the meaning of what a speaker is saying, and there are some useful tips that apply across many speaking situations. In this class, you are likely to be asked to provide feedback as a listener for a classmate's speech. When doing so, you can

? Why and how are listening, speaking, and ethics intertwined?

RosalreneBetancourt 10/Alamy Stock photo

try to follow a common plan that you already adopt as a note-taking student: (1) listen for the main points, (2) try to determine how the points are organized, and (3) assign meaning to the speech based on both *what* the speaker says and *how* he or she says it (nonverbal cues).

In many speaking situations, you will not be able to take notes, so you should rehearse a mental outline in your head of what the speaker is saying. Good speakers will typically order their main points ("My first point is that . . . My second point is that. . . .") and provide you with brief summaries. Ethical listening does not mean you have to remember and understand *everything* a speaker says—something that is very hard to do when we take internal and external noise into account. Ethical listening does mean, however, that you must try as best you can to understand what the speaker is saying on his or her own terms.

Speaking with an Open Ear

Listening is a dynamic, interactive process. Listening is the foundation of public speaking.

BSIP SA/Alamy Stock Photo

Communication and Understanding: Listening beyond Noise

Listening is the process of actively making meaning of messages. Successful communication and understanding require active listening — despite noise.

RosalreneBetancourt 10/Alamy Stock Photo

An Ethics of Speaking as a Listener

Ethical speaking requires the cultivation of practical wisdom, expertise (including the perception of credibility), and goodwill.

Communication is based on an ability to respond to others.

A tacit pact between speaker and listener in any speech situation is the basis of speaking ethics.

CHAPTER 2

LaunchPad for *Speech Craft* includes a curated collection of speech videos and encourages self-assessment through adaptive quizzing. Go to **launchpadworks.com** to get access to:

 LearningCurve adaptive quizzes

 Video clips to help you improve your speeches

ACTIVITY

The Psychic Powers of Listening!

A psychic or medium is a person who believes or claims that he or she has an ability to communicate with the souls or spirits of those who have died. There have been many television shows over the past two decades featuring psychics, from Sonya Fitzpatrick's *Pet Psychic* and John Edward's *Crossing Over* and *Cross Country* to Theresa Caputo's *Long Island Medium*. Whether or not you believe in telepathy or psychic powers, there is no question that the most successful psychics are very good listeners. With your classmates in a group, use YouTube or Vimeo to find a video of a psychic doing a reading with someone. After viewing, describe how the psychic demonstrates each step of active listening: (1) receiving and attending; (2) understanding; (3) responding, paraphrasing, and clarifying; and (4) recalling and remembering. Can the psychic teach us something about active listening? In what ways is the psychic a bad listener? Why?

Psychics are extraordinary active listeners.
© TLC/Courtesy Everett Collection

KEY TERMS

 Videos in LaunchPad describe many of these terms. Go to launchpadworks.com.

listening 24
noise 25
communication 28
misunderstanding 28
selective perception 29
selective exposure 30
selective listening 30

active listening 31
feedback 32
response-ability 34
ethics 36
direct quotations 38
paraphrase 38
plagiarism 38

AUDIENCE
ANALYSIS

You have probably had a nudity nightmare at some point in your life: everything is fine until you realize that you're naked and standing in front of a large audience. Audience members are pointing and whispering furtively to one another other — some are even laughing. Cold and exposed, you fantasize that if an escape hatch opened up in the floor, you'd jump right into it. Instead, you cover up and slowly slink, inch by inch, toward the exit — until you realize it is a terrible dream and . . . WAKE UP!

The nudity dream is a good allegory for public speakers who have not studied their audience before a speech. In general, what we fear most about public speaking are the negative judgments of an audience. When speaking, we often ask ourselves questions like "Are they following what I am saying?" or "Is this making any sense at all?" or "Can they tell I'm nervous?" or "Do they think I'm smart?" When we let these kinds of questions overwhelm us, we can feel exposed and naked. **Audience analysis,** or the process of studying your audience before, during, and after a speech, is one way to combat metaphorical nudity. That's why the sections in this chapter are designed to provide you with some virtual clothes. By anticipating audience reactions and gathering information about them, you are much more likely to avoid public speaking anxiety. In short, analyzing the audience is like finding the right wardrobe and then putting on some clothes.

Checking Out Your Speech Location

> *You will learn to*
>
> **EXPLAIN** the importance of the space and place of a speech.
>
> **EXPLAIN** how the size of an audience can influence a speech.

Before giving your speech, it's smart to scope out the speech location if possible (many times it will not be possible). In any public speaking situation, you will have to scrutinize the audience and their *physical arrangement* in the space before you can make any decisions about what to do or say. It is a good idea to think about where and when you'll be giving your presentation in order to get a sense of what is and is not possible to say and do. In short: analyzing the speech space and knowing when you will be speaking can give you a lot of useful information for preparing for your speech.

Sometimes the size of your speech location will impose limits on what you can say or do; for example, a small chapel would make it difficult for you to do an interpretive dance as a part of your eulogy. If you have to speak in a large room or auditorium, dramatic body movements would work well, but you will want to find out if you will have access to a microphone. In most cases, it's useful to know the physical possibilities and limitations of *where* you will be speaking before you prepare a speech.

audience analysis is the process of studying an audience before, during, and after a speech.

> ## Analyzing the Speech Situation
>
> When you analyze the speech situation, you should consider where you will be speaking in relationship to whom you are speaking to, including the physical space and the general characteristics of your probable audience.

Physical Location

Where and when you give a speech influence how you will relate to your audience. Suppose you want to give a pep talk to your classmates about a group project you are working on for a sociology class. The only space you can find to talk is a very small janitor's closet, replete with a sink and mops. How would this determine what you can and should say as a speaker to your audience?

Most formal speaking situations will be in spaces created for public speaking: an auditorium, a reception hall, and a boardroom are familiar examples. For this class, you probably have been (or will be) speaking in a

Analyzing the Speech Situation at a Glance

Location: Determine where you will be speaking, as well as the time of day. If the room is small, think about making your speech more personal and intimate. If the room is large, consider a more formal approach. The time of day can also affect the dynamics of the speaking situation. For example, if you are speaking after lunch, your audience might be sleepier than usual; if you are speaking during a busy time of day, you might have to consider outside noise.

Technology: The kind of space you are speaking in will help you determine your technology needs. Are you planning to show slides? If so, does the space have the technology you need to do so? Is the room large? If so, will you have access to a microphone, so that everyone can hear you?

Audience: Who will be watching and listening to you speak? Factors including age, demographics, gender, and diversity of background should be considered.

classroom. This is great news, because classrooms are designed to make it easier to hear and speak. Moreover, if you will be speaking for your public speaking class, the audience size is known in advance, and your audience will consist of the same people you meet with week after week!

Keep in mind, however, that most of the speeches you will give in your life *after* this course will probably *not* be in a classroom, or even in a professional setting, but rather in a restaurant or bar (giving a toast); a reception hall, church, mosque, or synagogue (speaking at a life event); and other places where people assemble. For this reason, it's helpful to scope out your speaking location before your speech if you can, or even to ask the person arranging your speech if you can see a photo of the speech space. If it is not possible to see the space yourself, ask those more knowledgeable about the setting what you should expect. For example, I regularly speak at colleges and universities across the United

States. Before I set out, I always ask the planner what kind of room I will be speaking in, clarify what the size is and what technology is available, and sometimes ask if a photo of the room could be sent to me. As we discussed in chapter 1, because visualization of a successful speech is so important to speech planning, having a sense of the speaking space before the day of the speech makes visualizing success easier.

Finally, it is important to remember that different physical locations place different demands on you as a speaker. The bigger the space (a large auditorium), the more animated you will need to be as a speaker. You will have to gesture more, and depending on how large the space is, you may even have to exaggerate your facial expressions. The smaller the space, the more subtle and subdued your expressions can be.

Technological Needs

Just as the physical space of your speech directly affects how you relate to an audience, so does technology, which usually includes computers, **sound reinforcement** machinery, and any other objects used to present audiovisual aids. To enhance your speech, you might want to present a series of Apple Keynote or Microsoft PowerPoint slides to accompany a speech; if this is the case, make sure the space has a computer, a projector, and the software necessary to show slides. If your speaking space does not have the electronic equipment you need, you will need to supply your own or prepare your speech without visual aids.

sound reinforcement is the use of microphones, sound processors, and amplifiers to enhance the quality or volume of sounds.

If you are asked to speak in a very large auditorium or to a bigger audience outdoors, you may have access to a microphone and a sound amplification system. It is always good to know if you will be amplified, because it will influence the style of your delivery.

Finally, we would be remiss not to mention forms of technology we often take for granted: chalkboards and dry-erase boards, easels for

The Right Volume for Your Location

CLASSROOM: moderate voice tone and volume; technological needs usually easy to meet.

RESTAURANT: louder voice tone and volume; technology is usually not available.

RELIGIOUS VENUE (CHURCH/MOSQUE/SYNAGOGUE): moderate to loud voice; gestures should be animated; amplification technology may be helpful.

ROLLER COASTER: will need to sit in back car and scream as loud as you possibly can; technology usually not available. Technically, this is not a public speaking venue but rather a "public screaming" venue.

posters, and flip boards. For smaller audiences (such as a classroom audience), using a chalkboard or a poster may be just as effective as a Keynote or PowerPoint presentation. When you think about your speaking space, be sure to consider *all* your technological needs—both digital and analog.

Important Tips on Microphone Use

If you will be using a microphone, remember these tips:

1. Stick with your everyday speaking voice; you don't need to raise your volume.
2. Do not yell or scream unless you are at a sporting event or pep rally.
3. When your mic is turned on, remember that it is hot and that anything you say will be heard. A statement like "I can't stand that guy!" may be heard by the entire audience — or, if you're on television, the world!
4. Microphones amplify sound, so yes, they will hear you burp.

Audience Size

If you are giving a pep talk to five classmates in a very small room, the situation demands an informal speech. It is not likely that you would prepare for days, nor is it likely that you would carefully practice the speech for hours before you deliver it. If, however, you are asked to speak to an audience of five hundred in an auditorium, you will want to prepare your speech carefully and formally. *In general, the larger the audience, the more prepared you should be.* Indeed, the larger the audience, the more you must rein in informality, slang, and inside jokes. Of course, there are situations in which a small audience requires a lot of preparation (for example, a sales pitch in a boardroom). But in general, the bigger the audience, the more you should prepare.

For this class, you will probably be speaking to a group ranging from ten to forty students. In your life outside class, however, your audiences will vary widely. At a wedding or civil union, there may be a hundred or more guests listening to you toast the happy couple. If the event will be a small affair with familiar guests, you could craft an intimate speech full of inside jokes. But if the nuptial crowd is going to be large and includes far-flung family members, you will want to avoid inside jokes that most people in the audience will not get.

There is another exception to the general rule that the bigger one's audience, the more prepared and formal one should be. Internet audiences, known as **amorphous** or **unknown audiences**, are a group of

amorphous or **unknown audiences** are groups of individuals who are brought together by a given message who may or may not share common characteristics.

individuals brought together by a given message who may or may not share common characteristics. For large television audiences, a speaker can research an audience's general characteristics and craft a speech accordingly. This is what television executives, politicians, and advertisers do all the time, usually with the help of polls, surveys, and focus groups. With the Internet, however, the audience is more difficult to gauge. Because of the way information circulates online, anticipating a message's eventual audience can be challenging. Think of how hard it is to predict who might end up watching a YouTube video you've posted. For more on presenting to Internet audiences, see chapter 18.

? How does the setting of the speech influence an audience? In general, how does the size of the audience effect the speaker's preparedness?

Who Is Your Audience?

You will learn to

EXPLAIN stereotyping and why people do it.

DESCRIBE the characteristics of an audience that a speaker should consider before developing a speech.

LIST AND EXPLAIN the three basic concepts for analyzing audience psychology and feelings.

So far we've seen that a major component of audience analysis is knowing what the physical setting and constraints are for a given audience. The counterpart to checking out your speech location is, of course, learning about the people in your audience. Even if you know everything about the space you will speak in and the technology available to you, unless you know something about the audience you'll be addressing, you'll be at a disadvantage. Having some sense of *whom* you'll be speaking to will boost your confidence and help you better research and prepare your speech.

It's helpful to consider the basic identities or self-concepts of those who will hear you. How audience members think of themselves will affect how your message is received, and central to that thinking is identity. Scholars who study audiences tend to break down identity characteristics into what is termed "demographic analysis," or "demography." Closely related to demography are the ways in which speakers make faulty assumptions about demographic information, which we tend to discuss in terms of stereotypes. The danger of demography is almost always stereotyping, and so we cannot discuss one without the other. In other words, we cannot study commonalities across group identities without also studying how assumptions about them can go wrong. How can we use demography to get a better sense of our audience without making unwarranted assumptions about people through stereotypes? It's not easy to avoid stereotyping, but it's important to try!

If Demographic Information about Audience Members Was Presented as Online Dating Ads

MARCUS

Relationships: Single, never married

Have children: No

Religion: Christian

Drink: No

Who I Am and What I'm Lookin' For: I am easily delighted by things in my world, such as Christmas morning, roller coasters, and equal pay for equal work, but also by some stuff that isn't exciting to many, like making gelatin casseroles with pineapple bits. I collect stamps and like walks in the park.

SATURNIA

Relationships: Single

Have children: Two girls

Religion: Buddhist

Drink: A few times a week

Who I Am and What I'm Lookin' For: I'm high maintenance but generally an optimist. I enjoy the company of others who can handle being serious every now and again. Why don't you just send me a note to find out more about me?

HECKBENT4LTHR

Relationships: Divorced

Have children: No

Religion: Catholic

Drink: Yes

Who I Am and What I'm Lookin' For: I'm smart, well educated, and adventurous. I have done lots of traveling and want to do more bike rallies. I wear only Brooks Brothers clothing for my day job. I like to read novels by F. Scott Fitzgerald. I'm looking for a lady who has similar interests and who would enjoy starting up a poodle-breeding business.

Demography and Stereotyping

Simply stated, **demography** is the study of the statistical characteristics of a given population. If you've recently filled out an application for college admission or a job, you're already familiar with the characteristics typically studied by demographers: age, sex and gender, socioeconomic status or class, and racial or ethnic identification. Sometimes this information overlaps with what scholars refer to as "group affiliations," which can include anything from age- or sex-based groups and interest groups (generational identification, mommy groups, sports teams) to religious and political affiliations.

Demographic information is useful for speakers because it provides a general understanding of basic facts about an audience. Combined with an understanding of group affiliations and in-the-moment audience analysis, demographic data can help you establish common points of reference and develop a rapport with your audience.

As the parody of personal ads illustrates, demographic information can sometimes tempt us to make inaccurate assumptions (who knew the biker was Catholic and into F. Scott Fitzgerald novels?). A **stereotype** is an overgeneralization about a person or group based on assumed characteristics. For example, a classic stereotype you may recall from your high school years is that cheerleaders and jocks are not academically gifted. If you were a cheerleader or an athlete in high school, you probably resent such a stereotype (and rightly so!), although we see these stereotypes over and over in television shows and films.

As we consider the basic tools of demography and heed warnings about their abuse, let us go ahead and admit that *everyone* stereotypes. While often harmful, stereotypes are used to make quick judgments about others when we have limited information—which is to say, we do it all the time, but we should try to avoid it if we can. So why do we do it? Brain research has shown that we are "hardwired" to make quick assumptions based on identity characteristics. In fact, our affiliation with gender ("masculine" or "feminine")—understood in terms of what researchers call "likeness"—begins before we learn how to speak. Because our brains have developed to group others into categories of "like" and "different," we tend to make assumptions about groups of people without meaning to. Because our brain works by simplifying complex information into categories, and often automatically and unconsciously, we have a tendency to stereotype. But we can learn to be mindful of stereotyping—and we can even avoid it.

demography is the study of the statistical characteristics of a given population.

a **stereotype** is an overgeneralization about a person or group based on assumed characteristics.

All audiences are made up of individuals with different values, personalities, and affiliations.

appealing to **audiences**
of all ages

Thinking about the age of your audience members is important because different generations have different core values and goals. Thinking about how different generations have experiences, values, and goals that are particular to their age group can help you better adapt your speech to them; for example, teenagers have vastly different interests than thirtysomethings. In addition to holding varying values and interests, different generations are likely to experience contrasting challenges in each stage of maturation.

Psychologist Erik Erikson argued that each of us goes through eight stages in life marked by an **identity crisis**, which roughly corresponds to one's age. In our teenage years, our identity crisis concerns gender and sexual identifications, as well as decisions about college and a future career. In our twenties, however, we struggle with career decisions and perhaps relationship decisions. In the so-called midlife crisis of the forties and fifties, we're thinking about retirement, job satisfaction, and — of course! — whether we will be buying a convertible or a sports car (just joshing).

Regardless, thinking about how old your audience is and what stage of life they are in will help you make informed guesses about their values, concerns, and struggles. Knowing something about what your audience may be going though will help you better adapt your speech to meeting them where they are at. The charts that follow this page illustrate how a speaker might adjust his or her speech topic to a given age group.

LaunchPad
macmillan learning

Examples of speakers adapting to the age and life experiences of audiences are not hard to find; however, they are more noticeable when the speech topic concerns a particular age group. To get a better sense of how speakers adapt to audiences of different ages, visit LaunchPad at **launchpadworks.com** and link to the two videos titled "On Bullying."

In the first video, speaker Nick Vujicic attempts to persuade an audience of teenagers to take bullying more seriously and to do what they can to stop it. In the second video, speaker Kevin Jennings attempts to persuade the parents of young persons to take bullying more seriously in order to prevent it.

Consider the following questions:

- In what way does each speaker adapt to his audience?
- How does the tone and pacing of each speech attempt to connect with the audience?
- In what way does each speaker address the experiences and crises of their target audiences?
- How might Vujicic's audience respond to Jennings's speech? How would Jennings's audience respond to Vujicic's speech?

Life Crises: An Overview

LIFE CRISIS	CRISIS CONCERNS	WHAT DOESN'T APPEAL	WHAT DOES APPEAL
Child crisis	Basic needs; craves love, attention, toys, and candy.	Reasoned discourse or arguments; appeals to future consequences.	Bright colors, fun words and language; a focus on the present; promises or displays of love, attention, toys, or candy.
Teenage crisis	Friendships and romantic relationships; career decisions; how to live without parents; sexual identity.	Long-term consequences or goals; chastisement or threats of imminent doom.	Promises of career success and wealth; sex appeals, broadly construed; reasoned arguments that lead to lifestyle or financial stability; appeals to individualism.
Twenties and thirties crises	Starting a family/not having a family; career is not what was imagined; lack of finances; new babies to care for.	Crude or vulgar humor (with the exception of comedy clubs); appeals to immediate gratification.	Reasoned arguments and emotional appeals promising future stability or career achievement; arguments that stress community focus.
Midlife crisis	Aging and the reality of death; declining looks and obesity; rebellious teenagers or empty-nest syndrome; lack of financial or marital stability.	Appeals to extremes in any domain of life (radical politics); references to the latest teen celebrity.	Appeals to wealth and retirement issues; strategies for more control and order; tips for better health.
Old-age crisis	Death and dying; leaving a legacy; losing friends and loved ones.	Sex appeals; any kind of argument that threatens income, retirement funds, or investments.	Arguments for larger, social causes; political and religious appeals; arguments for volunteerism and charity; suggestions for retirement and healthy living; focus on the community.

Age

Over two thousand years ago, the ancient Greek philosopher Aristotle argued that understanding the age of one's audience is tremendously beneficial to a speaker. He maintained that knowing the general age of the audience can help a speaker predict how the audience will react and respond to a message: "In terms of their character," Aristotle wrote, "the young are prone to desires and inclined to do

Speech Topic: Healthy Eating Tips

AGE GROUP	DOS	DON'TS
Elementary school children	State that healthy eating is fun and that kids can create their own healthy snacks. Bring in carrot sticks and other fresh vegetables for the audience to taste.	Do not mention technical terms, like "metabolism" and "lipids."
Teenagers	Recognize that teenagers have a limited income by stressing healthy eating choices that are *inexpensive*. Emphasize ordering salads at fast-food restaurants, and inform teens which dressings are healthy and which they should avoid. Recommend carbonated water instead of soda.	Researchers believe the teen years are among the most stressful of growing up. Consequently, teens are already wrestling with their identities. Do not use scare tactics or try to shame teens into eating better. Stress that junk food is OK *sometimes*, just not as a routine.
People in their twenties	People in their twenties are focused on their careers and their relationships; therefore, focus on healthy eating at work and when out with friends. Suggest healthy recipes that can be easily cooked at home by couples or groups of friends.	Twentysomethings are just getting established in their lives, so avoid stressing expensive health fads, diets, or medical procedures.
People in their thirties, forties, and fifties	By this time, many people will be raising families or becoming more health conscious as individuals. Stress healthy ways to raise children of all ages, as well as healthy eating plans for individuals.	People in these age groups have had some exposure to healthy eating, so don't use condescending language or assume a lack of knowledge.
People in their sixties, seventies, eighties, and beyond	Emphasize heart-healthy eating and using diet to control diabetes. Discuss healthy meals that can be easily prepared.	Don't use technical terms without providing clear definitions. Don't forget to leave time for a question-and-answer session.

whatever they desire."[1] Now, you may or may not agree with Aristotle, but his point is that younger people respond to messages in ways that are fundamentally different from those of older people. In part, this is because of life experiences, the relative strength of hormones, how one metabolizes breakfast, and whether or not one subsists on steamed noodles and macaroni and cheese day to day or a more varied diet of vegetables. In short, the age-group affiliation of your audience influences how they understand and process the world.

Another age-related element to consider is life experience and, in particular, the typical challenges different generations experience in the successive stages of maturation. When you consider the life stage (or crisis) your audience may be going through relative to their age, it becomes easier to see what kinds of messages will probably stick. In general, the younger the audience, the harder it is to convince them to think about long-term goals. Few people in their late teens and early twenties are thinking about their retirement funds when they're trying to figure out how to pay for college. On the other hand, many audience members in their forties and fifties might be more receptive to a speech about saving for retirement. Consider the Life Crises chart (p. 57), based on Erik Erikson's identity-crisis theory, when analyzing a future audience for your speeches.

> ? **What are the key demographic categories? How can a speaker use each to appeal to audience members? How can a speaker avoid stereotypes based on these categories?**

Sex and gender

How a person identifies in terms of sex and gender may influence how he, she, or they responds to messages, and knowing the basic sex and gender of your audience can be important for developing speeches depending on the topic. If you are speaking to an all-female or all-male audience, you can assume they are affiliated with a number of common experiences. We stress *experience* here because whether an audience identifies as male, as female, or in an alternative way, such as trans, varies from community to community and culture to culture.

It's important to distinguish between sex and gender because the two may not necessarily overlap. One's sex typically refers to biology, whereas gender refers to the sociocultural identification of "male," "female," or "trans." In other words, gender refers to whether one thinks of oneself as masculine or feminine or in some other way. As a general rule, when referencing identity you will be more inclusive thinking about gender than you will be thinking about biological sex, if only because the relationship between sex and gender is culturally variable.

social norms are rules that govern what is normal in a given culture.

In any given culture, a number of **social norms** or rules help establish ideas of what it means to be "a man" or "a woman," and these do differ, often dramatically, from culture to culture. In the United States, norms of "maleness" tend to be associated with physicality, strength, and rationality, while those of "femaleness" tend to be associated with empathy, emotional depth, and gentleness. Such associations may not be true, nor do they necessarily hold across cultures, and it won't take long for you to identify men and women who embody masculinity and femininity in ways that are counter to common assumptions. You probably know many self-identified women who participate in culturally "masculine" activities, and many self-identified men who enjoy "feminine" activities. In short: gender is mutable.

Why is understanding sex and gender important for speaking publicly? Put bluntly, knowing the sex and gender identifications of your audience helps you understand how audience members think and feel, especially if you can get a sense of their relationship with social norms of maleness and femaleness and critiques thereof.

Sex and gender stereotypes can be offensive and oppressive. Such stereotypes range from the assumption that your car mechanic is a "he" and your hospital nurse is a "she," to the terms we use to indicate certain people, such as "policeman" versus "police officer." Despite the recognized fact that gender is socially constructed and changes over time, references to gender as absolute, universal, and fixed persist in our culture.

It's vital that you try to avoid stereotyping if you want to connect effectively with your audience. Just because you're speaking to an all-male audience does not mean that everyone will be immediately engaged by a speech on car engines or the big football game. Similarly,

Defying Gender Norms

Aby Baker/Getty Images

American film and television producers often provide us with the most extreme examples of gender stereotypes (just about any action film would suffice), yet they sometimes introduce shows or characters who defy them. Lena Dunham's famed HBO series *Girls* made fun of gender stereotypes. The character Dunham played on the show, Hannah Horvath, was a complex woman who displayed both masculine and feminine characteristics; how she resisted and complied with gender in the show emphasizes just how fluctuating and changeable gender norms can be.

many all-female audiences might be bored by a speech focused on the latest fashion trends.

Sexual orientation and identity

Closely related to gender as a category is **sexual orientation and identity**. Sexual orientation refers to the gender identity of those with whom you choose to be intimate. Sexual identity is how you express your gender and, perhaps, your sexual orientation to yourself and others. The terms "lesbian," "gay," "bisexual," "trans," and "queer" (LGBTQ for short) have become identity categories that are increasingly studied by demographers. Scholars and government officials do not know how much of the U.S. population identifies as heterosexual, homosexual, bisexual, trans, or queer, but it's clear that the percentage is significant enough to consider as a public speaker. Estimates of LGBTQ people in the United States vary from as low as 2.5 percent to as high as 10 percent, but we simply don't know for sure, as many people are not willing to talk about their sexuality to researchers.

North American culture often assumes sexual orientation to be heterosexual. Most films made in Hollywood, for example, feature heterosexual couples, and popular magazine articles assume a "straight" audience. Yet as a public speaker, it is important that you hold yourself to a different standard by considering the possible range of audience members' sexual orientations as you plan your speech. As with gender stereotypes, one should rarely, if ever, assume the audience shares a given orientation or identity. If you are speaking at the annual meeting of Heterosexuals Anonymous or at an LGBTQ rally for civil rights, it's probably safe to assume a more homogeneous sexual identification among your audience. In our time, however, it's probably better to use the language of "partnership" and "your partner" instead of "husband and wife" if your speech topic concerns relationships. Avoiding assumptions of heterosexuality or other orientations will not only keep you from offending listeners but also help you get your message across to a larger portion of your audience.

Racial and ethnic identification

As with an attention to gender and sexual orientation, sensitivity to the racial and ethnic identifications of your audience will make you a more effective speaker. As a speaker, it's vital to remember that most U.S. audiences today are racially diverse and will continue to become even more so. To be an effective and ethical speaker, you must strive to include everyone in your remarks by addressing diverse backgrounds and varied interests while avoiding stereotyping.

What are race and ethnic identification exactly? Race indicates a group of people identified as having the same or similar physical characteristics based on genetic heritage, visible traits, or social relations.

sexual orientation refers to the gender identity of those with whom you choose to be intimate.

sexual identity is how you express your gender and, perhaps, your sexual orientation to yourself and others. Sexual orientation and identity are often, but not necessarily, the same.

Harvey Milk

Robert Clay/Alamy Stock Photo

Harvey Milk was the first openly gay elected official in the United States. Until his assassination in 1978, he was regarded as a masterful public speaker whose impassioned oratory helped change minds about LGBTQ persons. Here is an excerpt from Milk's "Hope" speech, which he composed with the assumption that his audience would consist mostly of lesbian, gay, bisexual, trans, and queer people. How does Milk tailor his message to his audience? Does Milk say things that indicate an awareness of a broader, more sexually diverse audience?

"I can't forget the looks on faces of people who've lost hope. Be they gay, be they seniors, be they blacks looking for an almost-impossible job, be they Latins trying to explain their problems and aspirations in a tongue that's foreign to them. I personally will never forget that people are more important than buildings. I use the word "I" because I'm proud. I stand here tonight in front of my gay sisters, brothers and friends because I'm proud of you. I think it's time that we have many legislators who are gay and proud of that fact and do not have to remain in the closet. I think that a gay person, up-front, will not walk away from a responsibility and be afraid of being tossed out of office."

A related although not completely overlapping concept is ethnic identification, which is understanding oneself to share or participate in the language, culture, style, and history of a given group of people.

It's important to note that standards for the respectful treatment of diverse audiences are constantly changing and dynamic, which is a reason why audience research is always necessary. For example, consider the unintentional prejudiced remarks of the much beloved president John F. Kennedy on June 11, 1963, in his famous address on civil rights. As speech scholars Robert James Branham and W. Barnett Pearce have noted, Kennedy enacted a racial contradiction by limiting the label "Americans" to white people only, unintentionally excluding African Americans and other minorities. In one part of the speech, President Kennedy said,

> We cannot say to 10 percent of the population that *you* can't have that right [to full civic participation]; that your children can't have the chance to develop whatever talents they have; that the only way that *they* are going to get their rights is to go in the streets and demonstrate. I think *we* owe *them* and *we* owe *ourselves* a better country than that [emphasis added].

President Kennedy began his speech by addressing the American people as "we," but Branham and Pearce argue that it is apparent from remarks later in the speech that by "we," Kennedy meant white people. In their discussion of the speech, Branham and Pearce draw attention to

Kennedy's use of the words "we," "you," "they," "them," and "ourselves" to show how he excludes the very people he is arguing are entitled to the rights and benefits of U.S. citizenship.[2]

Kennedy's unintentional remarks teach us that however good our intentions, we cannot assume audience members share our racial or ethnic experiences, nor can we even assume that English is the first language of our audience. A consideration of the audience's racial and ethnic self-identifications can help speakers anticipate how an audience may react to a speech. Because of the well-documented violence toward people of color in the United States (for glaring and painful examples, think of slavery, the removal of Native Americans in the nineteenth century, and Japanese internment during World War II), speakers in the United States should cultivate an understanding of U.S. history, especially if one is speaking about a topic that evokes racial differences or historical consciousness, such as civil rights.

Socioeconomic status

Socioeconomic status refers to the incomes, occupations, and educational background of a given group of people. Knowing these details about your audience will help you better adapt your speech. Let us suppose you were giving a persuasive speech to your classmates urging them to buy something. Based on the people in your class, which of the following would be the better argument? (a) You should buy a used Vespa scooter; (b) you should buy a top-of-the-line Harley Davidson motorcycle; (c) you should buy a Ford minivan; (d) you should buy a Range Rover. Each vehicle is successively more expensive, and the effectiveness of your speech would depend on what most people in your audience can afford. (Many college students could afford a used scooter; most could not afford a Range Rover.)

Sometimes socioeconomic status is related to the concept of class, which refers to the hierarchical ordering of society based on socioeconomic status. In the nineteenth century, political philosopher Karl Marx argued that the best way to understand how society works is to focus on its class system. Marx argued that in capitalist countries like the United States, the working class has been pitted against the wealthy capitalist class, and that many, if not most, of our social problems can be traced back to class struggle. The arguments that you would use to persuade the wealthy (here's how to make more money through investment!) would be very different than those you would use to persuade the working or middle classes (here's how to make more money by fighting the rich!).

Group memberships: God, politics, and beyond

Other categories of belonging can also influence how your audience responds to messages. Two of these categories concern the ones your parents or guardians may have told you were inappropriate to discuss in polite company or at the dinner table: religion and politics.

Unlike the more traditional categories of demography, figuring out the religious and political beliefs of your audience is more difficult. Religious and political beliefs are diverse, and like most of the self-identifying categories we have reviewed, it is often impossible to tell what they might be just from looking at a person. Sometimes the venue for speaking can offer indications of an audience's religious or political beliefs. For example, when speaking to a church congregation, at a synagogue, or at a mosque, it's probably safe to assume the audience believes in deity. In general, however, in most speaking situations you cannot assume the religion or politics of an audience.

Of course, the topics of deity and politics do not exhaust the kind of group affiliations people have. Demographic categories often double as group memberships: people affiliate on the bases of their age, class, and sexual orientation, to name a few. Other categories of group affiliation include membership in civic organizations, causes, social clubs, alumni organizations, sports teams (as players or fans), and unions. In Austin, Texas, where your author lives, there is an LGBTQ bar scene that has become a strong and visible community with political power, influencing how the city is governed. Similarly, there are a number of golf courses in Austin that are almost exclusively used by those with a high socioeconomic status.

Gathering Info about Your Audience

> **You will learn to**
>
> **EXPLAIN** the difference between formal and informal analysis.
>
> **LIST AND EXPLAIN** the three types of formal audience analysis.

So far we've discussed a number of categories that you can analyze as a public speaker to get a better sense of your audience. In most speaking situations, audience analysis is casual and informal. **Informal audience analysis** refers to the way in which a speaker gathers information about his or her audience in an unsystematic way. A speaker can ask the host of the event about the expected size of the audience and who will be present, think about the physical location and get a sense of what is and is not appropriate, and so on. Most seasoned speakers rely on their past speaking experiences to get a sense of their audience—and if they speak often, audience analysis may even become an unconscious habit. For many of the assignments in your speech class, your method of audience analysis may be informal. After the first week or so of class, you will likely have a strong sense of who your audience is for your speeches in this course, their socioeconomic background, and so on. Alternatively, your speech instructor may ask you to perform additional types of audience

informal audience analysis is the way in which a speaker gathers information about his or her audience in an unsystematic way.

analysis, which will provide you with more concrete information about the listeners in your class—or beyond.

You may also want to do a **formal audience analysis**—employing various tools and methods for gathering information about people, such as focus groups, interviews, or surveys. Speakers tend to "go formal" with audience analysis when the audience is going to be large or when relatively little is known about them. Let's say you're the president of a large metropolitan food bank and you've been asked to deliver a speech at a local community group. You know you want to ask for donations, but you are not sure how much to ask the audience for. You decide to mail or e-mail a survey to all community group members asking for basic demographic information. You learn that most members of the group have low to moderate incomes, so you decide to ask for $10 donations instead of the larger donations you might request of those from a well-to-do group. Similarly, advertising firms routinely engage in formal audience analysis to get a sense of audience needs and desires in order to market their products. Corporations, firms, politicians, advertising agencies, and any number of entertainment companies engage in formal audience analysis all the time. In fact, there are whole companies dedicated to doing nothing but audience analysis!

> **formal audience analysis** involves employing various tools and methods for gathering information about people.

There are three basic ways in which formal audience analyses are conducted: interviews, focus groups, and surveys.

Interviews

Interviews are usually conducted one on one, and can be in person, on the phone, or via e-mail, instant messaging, or chat, and so on. Interviewers usually prepare a number of questions in advance to ask the interviewee. The interviewee is usually chosen because he or she is representative of a larger group—a stand-in, as it were, for one's audience.

Focus groups

Focus groups are group interviews in which a given number of people are asked to deliberate on a question or a problem while researchers study the conversation. Focus groups are especially popular among advertisers, politicians, and speakers who craft mass media messages.

Surveys

Surveys usually involve a written questionnaire, distributed to a group of people in order to collect information about their demographic characteristics, group affiliations, and beliefs and opinions about a given question or topic.

In this section we've discussed some of the major categories of audience analysis, which can be reduced to a simple motto: *appeal to audiences based on what ties them together; however, try not to stereotype along the way!* The best way to avoid making bad assumptions about your audience is to think about, formally or informally, who is in your audience and to identify their basic characteristics. Knowing audience characteristics, however, is just one part of audience analysis. To be a compelling speaker, you also have to anticipate how your audience will understand and respond to your speech, and the only way to gauge that is to understand a little bit about audience psychology—which leads us right to Freud and desire.

Audience Psychology: Identification and Core Values

To better understand how to connect with audience members, it's important to understand them as people—how they think, what they care about, and what they believe in. To gain some insight into what makes people tick, let's take a quick look at the work of Sigmund Freud, a key pioneer of looking at the human mind. Back at the turn of the nineteenth century, Freud, a physician living in Vienna, conducted groundbreaking investigations of how people think and feel, which helped shape our understanding of the human psyche today. Along with creating a form of individual talk therapy he termed "Psycho-Analysis,"

Freud and his colleagues developed a key insight: most people share common motives and desires. Although many of Freud's psychological theories have been disproven and critiqued over the past century, many of his key insights have been accepted. When discussing audience psychology, we are concerned with the Freudian ideas that have proven helpful and that have been accepted by scholarly and scientific communities.

Freud argued that deep down, everyone is motivated by unconscious wishes that sometimes surface in our dreams. Ultimately, one way to describe Freud's view about human desire and motivation is that many, if not most, of our wishes can be summed up as one super-duper wish: *we all want to be loved.* In the end, most of our dreams are about wanting the positive recognition of others.[3]

Although not everyone agrees with *all* of Freud's theories (and we don't have to either—I certainly don't!), his concept of love can be very useful to an aspiring public speaker. By "love" we mean that most of us want to be important to someone—our friends, our parents, our romantic partners, *and* our audiences. Most of us, in other words, like to be recognized. We like to hear others speak our name, and we like to get phone calls and texts from people who are important to us. As we will see, understanding this basic desire can help us become better speakers.

Audience Psychology: All You Need Is Love (and Identification)

> **You will learn to**
>
> **DEFINE** *identification*, and explain how to create it with an audience.
>
> **DEFINE** *beliefs*, *attitudes*, and *values*, and explain how they differ.

To borrow a phrase from legendary R&B singer Tina Turner, "What's love got to do with it?" And by "it," Tina and I mean to ask what love has to do with helping us understand audiences and become better speakers. The views of Freud and his followers provide some helpful answers. In their view, all people are inherently separate. We all desire love (and connection, and recognition, and warm fuzzies) because at the most basic level, each of us is divided from everyone else. That is, each of us is a discrete animal with our own brain, blood type, body, and so on. According to Freud and others, at about the age of two or so we each realize this fact. We stop thinking that we're the same as our mothers (or primary parent) and start to understand ourselves as individual persons, independent of our guardians. Once we realize that we are individuals, we experience mixed feelings: on the one hand, it's great to be our own person; on the other hand, it's scary! Freud and others suggest that we experience these mixed feelings—a desire for independence and a desire for connection—for most of our lives. For example, whether you came to college after leaving home for the first time or are returning to school after a period of work or military service, the transition will offer new freedoms along with change and separation from familiar people and routines. At every stage of life, becoming one's own person entails a sense of loss, and the joys of independence often come at the expense of a feeling of togetherness. And in just about any speaking situation, you are revisiting this fundamental tension between independence and the desire for connection. This is why public speaking can be both exciting and terrifying!

Good speakers can harness the power of love and foster togetherness by creating moments of **identification**—moments when both audience and speaker forget the differences between them by recognizing that they are alike in some fundamental way. Aristotle called this the establishment of goodwill, whereas more recent thinkers might describe the connection as establishing "common ground." Ultimately, successful

identification is the shared sense of identity between or among two or more people, usually in reference to a common thing, experience, or event.

speakers transport their audiences to a place of understanding through feelings of love.[4]

Let's look at an example of identification in action. I recently posted the following status update on an online social networking site: "Watching the television show *Naked and Afraid*. Wow!" *Naked and Afraid* is a cable television show that documents two nude people trying to survive in the wilderness for twenty-one days; it is both fascinating and silly. Minutes after I posted my status update, three of my friends responded with messages like, "I know! I can't believe it!" and "This show documents the worst of humanity!" With these messages my friends were telling me that they felt similar to the way I felt about the show. As I watched, my friends and I bonded over our horrified response. This feeling of bonding is "identification," and creating it is one of the keys to success in public speaking.

Burke-ification: Identification and Kenneth Burke

> *You will learn to*
> **DEFINE** *identification*, and explain its importance to public speaking.

In the field of communication studies, the scholar most identified with the concept of identification is Kenneth Burke, a major influence in the study of persuasive speaking today. Burke argued that all compelling speech is established on the basis of identification. Indeed, identification is one of the basic goals of all public speaking.

Burke wrote extensively on the connection between the mixed feelings we all share about our inherent separateness and the process of identification. As Burke argued, you cannot have identification without a prior separateness. If we were not divided from one another as discrete persons, we wouldn't desire to be "connected." This feeling of connection with others is "identification"—the recognition of others and of others recognizing us.

"Here is perhaps the simplest case of persuasion. You persuade a man only insofar as you can talk his language by speech, gesture, tonality, order, image, attitude, idea, identifying your ways with his. Persuasion by flattery is but a special case of persuasion in general. But flattery can safely serve as our paradigm if we systematically widen its meaning, to see behind it the conditions of identification." — Kenneth Burke[5]

Now, Burke also says that identification is related to flattery. He doesn't mean "flattery" in the usual sense; in general, most audiences find pandering insincere and off-putting. Burke's idea is that speaking successfully to an audience requires the speaker to communicate that he or she is fundamentally like the audience in some way. Think about identification this way: you are at a party and hardly know anyone. You're wearing a Bob Marley T-shirt, and a person walks up to you and says, "Nice shirt. I love Bob Marley. What's your favorite album?" Suddenly you feel welcome and interested in talking to this new person. This is exactly what Burke is talking about: a stranger is suddenly no longer "strange" because she pointed out a similarity of taste—in this case, a shared love of Marley's reggae music. Identification therefore concerns a reference to something commonly shared between a speaker and an audience. That something could be as basic as language itself or as obscure as a mutual fondness for anago sushi. It all depends on the context of your speech and the size and character of your audience.

> **?** **What does the concept of love have to do with audience analysis and connecting to listeners? How does it relate to identification?**

Beliefs, Attitudes, and Values

Establishing feelings of affection with an audience is no small feat and often requires a lot of practice. No matter what your topic or message, it is difficult to speak to any audience unless you can establish some point of identification. Yet identifying with your audience is only part of the challenge; you also have to know something about their beliefs, attitudes, and values (BAVs).

Social psychologist Milton Rokeach made a pretty big splash in the 1960s with his model of belief and attitude change. Still widely used by communication scholars today, Rokeach's model is a predictor of how audiences tend to process and respond to messages. In Rokeach's view, what an audience hears is filtered through their system of understanding the world, a system made up of three basic elements: *beliefs, attitudes,* and *values.*[6] In fact, this is true to such an extent that in any speaking situation, it is often observed that there are actually two speeches: one that the speaker delivers, and another that the audience hears. In general, people tend to hear only in a way that is consistent with their beliefs, attitudes, and values—that is, the only messages an audience can really hear are those that line up with the way in which they already understand the world. For this reason, it is easier to inform or entertain an audience than it is to persuade

them, because persuasion often pushes toward a change in these beliefs, attitudes, and values.

Rokeach also observed that in general, an audience's beliefs are easier to change than their attitudes and values. Depending on the topic of your speech, this fact could seriously cramp your style. Let's take a look at each of the three elements.

Beliefs

a **belief** is an idea about reality.

For Rokeach, **beliefs** are the ideas we have about reality. Beliefs vary in strength, too: some beliefs are relatively inconsequential to us, while others are more central. For example, the belief that some people are funny (Key and Peele) is probably more important to someone than whether or not their pajamas match the bedsheets. Beliefs can be factual (the sun sets in the west) or even erroneous (the earth is flat). The important point for Rokeach is that some beliefs matter to us more than others, and the more they matter, the harder they are to change.

Attitudes

an **attitude** is a set of beliefs that cluster around a common object and predispose behavior.

Beliefs are the basic building blocks of a person's "self." These basic beliefs can cluster together and form an **attitude**, which Rokeach defines as a group of beliefs that form around a common object and predispose behavior. Whereas simple beliefs tend to function as truth, attitudes clump beliefs together into feelings, which serve as the glue of attitudes. For example, let's say Jules has a bunch of beliefs about Miley Cyrus: (a) Miley always has the best outfits; (b) Miley is smarter than people give her credit for; (c) Miley takes good care of her health; (d) Miley is attractive. These beliefs combine to form an attitude: *Jules just loves Miley Cyrus.*

Attitudes vary from person to person, of course, but one thing we know for certain is that attitudes couple emotions to beliefs. Attitudes are also, at some level, judgments about something. Because they are made of beliefs, however, attitudes are sometimes difficult to distinguish from beliefs. A good rule of thumb is to think of attitudes in terms of evaluative judgments: "I like X" or "I dislike Y" are the kinds of statements that attitudes are often reduced to.

Values

values are deeply held core beliefs.

The most important component of Rokeach's model are **values**. Values are the core beliefs of an individual and are almost impervious to change. Rokeach argues that values come in two types: terminal values and instrumental values. Terminal values are life goals, or ends toward which we live. Freedom, family security, happiness, and pleasure are examples. Instrumental values guide us in our daily lives and usually toward the achievement of our terminal values. Those familiar with the Boy Scouts will recognize a list of instrumental values in the Scout Law: I am a loyal person, I am a trustworthy person, and so on. Terminal values describe what you consider to be the ends of a good life; instrumental values are those that you think will get you there.

Why should you care about beliefs, attitudes, and values? The answer is easy: it's relatively easy to change inconsequential beliefs, harder to change important beliefs, even harder to change attitudes, and downright impossible to change values. Like Freud, Rokeach believes that people are contradictory creatures who tend to avoid directly confronting their own contradictions. If someone points out a contradiction to us, we feel uncomfortable and will seek to either avoid or resolve the contradiction. In general, this discomfort varies depending on the strength and importance of the belief. If the belief is relatively inconsequential, a speaker can probably get you to change it. If the belief is a deeply held core value, however, a speaker is not likely to make you budge.

The reason attitudes and values are more difficult to change is directly related to the time it takes for them to form and the influences that help form them. If your attitude is "I love to cook," it took some experience in the kitchen or on the grill for you to form that attitude. Values typically develop over a very long period and tend to be informed by influential people in our lives, such as our parents or role models. If one values family life, for example, it is probably because he or she had a strong family upbringing. Political and religious beliefs are also often associated with one's value system, and these tend to be fairly consistent with the political and religious beliefs of one's family. Because role models are so important in the cultivation of values, only certain authority figures tend to be successful in changing the values of others: parents, teachers, and religious leaders are the kinds of figures who can change people's values because they tend to speak with an audience over a long period of time. As we'll discuss in a later section, only in the rarest of circumstances should a speaker try to change the values of an audience.

In which of these speaking contexts are values more likely to be changed? Why?
Left: Jake Lyell/Alamy Stock photo   *Right*: Michael Reaves, The Denver Post via Getty Images

What are beliefs, attitudes, and values? Which is the easiest to change? The hardest? Why?

The better route is almost always to create identification on the basis of commonly shared values.

Finally, we can't mention BAVs without discussing behavior. Like changing values, *changing behavior is very difficult*. Speakers are more successful when trying to influence beliefs or attitudes and less successful when attempting to change values or cause a behavior. Understanding that audiences are psychologically predisposed toward doing nothing is important to keep in mind, if for no other reason than it will help temper your ambition as a speaker into something more realistic.

Feelings: More on Audience Disposition

> **You will learn to**
>
> **EXPLAIN** *audience disposition* and how a speaker would analyze it.

All this business about identification and love and BAVs can lead one to think that public speaking is mostly about feelings. If you're starting to think—or better, feel—that, then you'd be right. Perhaps one of the biggest misconceptions about public speaking in our culture is that it is reasoned and works by appealing to our sense of logic. Since antiquity, there has been a focus on reasoned argument in public speaking, but in the twentieth century, there was a tendency to overemphasize logic and reason. To be a good public speaker in our postmodern times, you should focus on feelings at least as much as you focus on logic.

For starters, doing so will allow you to address the whole human being, not just the rational part. Neurologist Antonio Damasio has made his career arguing that human reason functions in concert with feelings and cannot work without them. If the part of the human brain that processes feelings and bodily sensation is damaged, various forms of judgment—such as ethical reasoning—become impaired.[7]

For a great example of the connection between reason and feeling, we can look at professional football. No football player has to make more split-second decisions than a pro quarterback (QB). In virtually every play, the QB has about three seconds to make a staggering number of calculations while a bunch of competitors try to pound him into the turf. Where is the most dangerous defender coming from? Where are my receivers? Who can I safely throw a pass to? For many years, football coaches thought that a QB's decision making was based on the quality of his logical calculations. Before signing with an NFL team, most QBs had to take a specialized algebra test to assess their computational skills. Eventually, however, coaches realized that the best QBs weren't necessarily the ones who scored highest on the math test; rather, something beyond algebra was shaping the QB's decision making.

Coaches figured out the "X factor" when they began asking the best QBs how they made their decisions during a play. Although the QBs did in fact make countless calculations and decisions during a play, instead of talking about those decisions, the QBs wanted to talk about their *feelings*. When QBs described a play, many of them talked about anxious feelings when they looked one way and happy feelings when they looked another—usually right before they threw a successful pass. The interesting point is that the QBs' feelings tended to line up with the reality on the field—anxious when a receiver was covered, happy when a receiver was open. The decision that led to a completed pass may have been based on the QB's feelings, but it was still linked to logical analysis, even if that analysis happened unconsciously.

Your job as a public speaker is, in some sense, to deliver a good "speech pass," based on in-the-moment impulses about the audience's reaction to you. It's also your job as a speaker to think about and anticipate the audience's emotional response. From a psychological standpoint, audience analysis becomes **psychological audience analysis**, *an anticipation of audience feelings and an attempt to marshal those feelings in order to change beliefs, attitudes, values, or behavior.*

Understanding the demographic characteristics and group affiliations of an audience, as well as the general BAVs they share, can give you a good sense of how the audience will feel about your speech topic. Heck, figuring out who your audience is and what they believe and value should give you a pretty good sense of how they will feel about you.

Now, let's say you've analyzed your audience and have a pretty good sense of who they are and what they likely believe and value. What do you do next? Well, that depends on how the audience feels about you, your topic, and the occasion for which you're speaking—an orientation known as **audience disposition**. In other words, what you do with this information depends on the disposition and attitudes of the audience. See page 72 for a handy audience disposition chart with some dos and don'ts.

In this chapter, we have examined how to analyze and understand your (future) audience as a public speaker. The space you will speak in will influence your audience, as will their basic characteristics and BAVs. Although your speech should depend on sound reasoning, you should also think about ways to create a sense of identification with your audience, as well as the ways in which their and your feelings are an important part of the speaking situation. Now, if you have identified the probable audience for your speech, listed as much about their characteristics as you can, and tried to anticipate how they will react to your message, you are ready to start figuring out *what* you can speak about. Choosing a speech topic is the topic of the next chapter.

psychological audience analysis is the anticipation of audience feelings and an attempt to marshal those feelings in order to change beliefs, attitudes, values, or behavior.

audience disposition is how the audience feels about you, your topic, and the occasion for which you're speaking.

? **What is audience disposition? How will knowing your audience's disposition to you and your topic help you craft an effective message?**

Audience Disposition

SPEAKING SITUATION	DOS	DON'TS
Audience Doesn't Know Anything	Justify for your listeners why they need to hear you out. Proceed gently, presenting material in an easy-to-understand fashion. If the material is complicated, consider using visual aids.	Don't move through the speech rapidly; avoid using specialized language (known as *jargon*) unless the audience is specialized (e.g., if you're a doctor speaking to doctors, some jargon is OK, but if you're a doctor speaking to nondoctors, jargon is bad).
Audience Loves You, the Topic	Try to reinforce existing attitudes toward you or the topic by being charming, being good-natured, and stressing commonalities between yourself and the audience.	Don't assume that you don't need to explain why you are speaking or speak in detail about the topic. Just because the audience is positively disposed toward you or the topic doesn't mean you can cut corners.
Audience Hates You, the Topic (Hostile Audience)	Attempt to identify common attitudes and values, and build from those. Be careful to point out similarities between yourself and the audience, and stress your goodwill toward them.	Don't directly challenge beliefs, attitudes, or values against you or the topic, or insult the audience by insinuating that they are wrong.
Audience Is Captive	Make your speech as short as you can. Tell lively stories, and use vivid illustrations.	Don't assume that the audience will be willing to participate in activities or be motivated to change their beliefs, attitudes, values, or behavior. The captive audience should usually be treated like a hostile audience.
Audience Is Mobile (for example, on the sidewalk)	Simplify for your audience. Use vivid metaphors and energetic examples. Move around and gesture to invite interest among passersby.	Don't deliver an overly long message, use complicated language or jargon, or stay in one place.
Audience Is Up Way Too Early	Arrange to have coffee served, if possible. Donuts are a plus.	Don't scream loudly or brag about how much sleep you got last night.

Who Is Your Audience?

Analyzing the audience of your future speaking situation can help you reduce speech anxiety and help you adapt your speech. Audience analysis is the process of understanding an audience before, during, and after a speech.

Gathering Info about Your Audience

Considering the basic identities or self-concepts of those who will hear you will positively affect how your message is received. To avoid stereotyping, consider such characteristics as the audience's age, sex, gender, sexual orientation, and racial or ethnic identification, as well as their possible beliefs, attitudes, and values.

Beliefs, Attitudes, and Values

Understanding basic audience psychology and feelings can help you create points of identification with audience members. Psychological audience analysis is the anticipation of audience feelings and an attempt to marshal those feelings in order to change beliefs, attitudes, values, or behavior.

 **LaunchPad**
macmillan learning

LaunchPad for *Speech Craft* includes a curated collection of speech videos and encourages self-assessment through adaptive quizzing. Go to **launchpadworks.com** to get access to:

 LearningCurve adaptive quizzes

 Video clips to help you improve your speeches

ACTIVITY

Writing a Horoscope

The horoscope that appears in your local newspaper or online news source is a prediction about what will happen to you based on your zodiac sign, which is in turn based on the position of the stars on the day you were born. Some people believe in astrology and some don't; for many people, however, horoscopes are fun to read because they are vague and subject to multiple interpretations. This is because they tend to be written in a way that will appeal to a wide audience. Horoscope writers are particularly good at audience analysis and psychology, as they often successfully anticipate the hopes and fears of the average person. The principle behind the horoscope is the same as that underlying this section: people want to be loved. For this activity, write a horoscope for a friend or family member based on the principles of audience analysis. Follow these steps:

1. Think of a person whom you regularly have conversations with as your "target audience" or your "mark." Consulting this and the previous section on audience analysis, list as many of the person's characteristics as you can, as well as a number of his or her core beliefs and values.

2. Find out this person's birthday so that you can determine his or her astrological sign. Then, based on your analysis, write a five-sentence horoscope that includes the following: (a) a vague statement addressing this person's workplace or school demands, (b) a statement addressing whether or not this person traveled or will travel, (c) a statement addressing this person's health or age, (d) a statement addressing this person's love life (don't name any names!), and (e) a random lucky number.

3. Once you have composed your horoscope, share it with the person you wrote it for and note how he or she responds. Take careful notice of how this person's response to your horoscope was an indirect result of your background analysis.

KEY TERMS

 Videos in LaunchPad describe many of these terms. Go to launchpadworks.com.

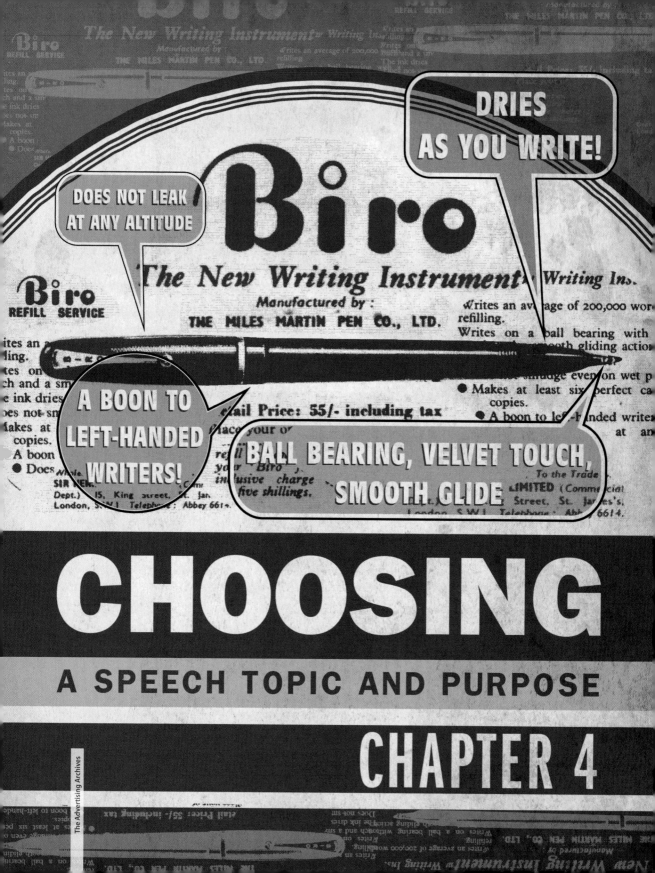

When we are asked to think about "invention," most of us think about a *thing*, like a light bulb or various gadgets like the smartphone that people have created to make life easier. Originally, however, the meaning of the word "invention" was a noun for *an action* or a kind of *doing*. According to the *Oxford English Dictionary*, "invention" originally meant "the action of coming upon or finding . . . [the process of] discovery (whether accidental, or the result of search and effort)."[1] Consider the case of László Bíró, a Hungarian newspaper journalist whose accidental "aha" moment of creativity led to the invention of a tool many of us use everyday: the ballpoint pen.

As a journalist in the 1930s, Bíró found himself continually frustrated with his fountain pen, which would leak in warmer temperatures. Watching printing-press cylinders got him thinking about a cylinder-based pen. While sitting in a Budapest café, however, Bíró reasoned that the problem with a pen based on a rolling cylinder was that it would only be able to write in a back-and-forth direction. To work well for writing, the ink would need to be produced by something that could "roll" in all directions. Then he noticed some children playing with marbles in the street. He observed how one child shot a marble through a puddle, making a streak of water on the dry pavement. Watching the children play led Bíró to his "aha" moment: a tiny ball bearing could do the trick. He went on to invent what we now know today as the ballpoint pen.[2]

Developing an idea for a speech is similar to Bíró's marbles — both in the sense of his creativity and in the sense of the games that children of all ages play: to select a speech topic, you have to let your mind wander and play with ideas until something sticks and you have that "aha" moment. Sometimes topics will come to you quickly, and sometimes you will simply get stuck until some happenstance event or observation inspires ideas to shake out.

Developing a Dynamite Topic

> **You will learn to**
>
> **DISCUSS** how an understanding of the speech situation can help you develop a speech topic.
>
> **DESCRIBE** how an understanding of your and your audiences' interests can help you develop a speech topic.
>
> **EXPLAIN** why having passion or strong feelings about a speech topic can interest an audience.

As noted in chapter 1, the ancient Greeks and Romans termed the process of developing and researching a speech **invention**. Since the time of the ancients, the concept of invention has been taught as the first step of public speaking that concerns the discovery of speech topics and the possible language, structures, and arguments that could be used. How you come up with a topic for a speech can be deliberate or accidental (or, as was the case with Bíró, a little of both). Sometimes your instructor will provide you with a speech topic, but often you will be asked to come up with something on your own. This chapter will help you "invent" a speech topic and related materials on your own, providing you with a number of tips and tricks to help you get your creative energy flowing. It will also help you *narrow* your speech topic once you've figured it out.

invention refers to the process of discovering materials and arguments for a speech.

Selecting a topic is tough if you just start out willy-nilly. Having some rough guidelines or constraints will help you, so let's begin there. When coming up with a topic, your task will be made much easier if you are able to answer three basic questions:

1. What is the speaking situation?
2. What topics are interesting and relevant to me?
3. What topics will be interesting and relevant to my audience?

The first question has to do with your speaking situation, and the answer will inform you about the direction of your speech and get you thinking about the topics that are interesting and relevant to you—and to your audience.

Consider the Speech Situation

The first question—"What is the speaking situation?"—primarily concerns the reason you are giving a speech, but it also includes the constraints we touched on when discussing audience analysis (chapter 3): the location of the speech; the size, age, and other demographic characteristics of your audience; and so on.[3] Your individual **speech situation** is the most important factor to consider when choosing a topic and crafting the mood of your speech. If your supervisor asked you to make a speech at a company picnic, your topic would need to be more lighthearted and community minded than it would if you were asked to present a speech in your public speaking class. The goal of the speech at the picnic would be to celebrate your coworkers,

a **speech situation** refers to both the exigency or reason for giving the speech as well as those things that constrain what can be said. The primary characteristic of the speech situation is the reason and purpose of a speech. Secondary elements include the space and place of a speech, as well as the characteristics of the audience.

whereas the goal of the speech in the classroom would be to demonstrate that you are learning the skills that the course is designed to teach you.

In the classroom setting, your speech situation will probably have different constraints than it would in community or work-related settings. Often in public and professional speaking courses, you will have a lot of freedom to research and speak on a topic of your choosing. Sometimes, however, your instructor will not allow you to speak on certain topics, such as topics that are too common, like why someone should join a sorority or fraternity, or controversial topics. Regardless, it is important to remember this one fundamental fact about choosing topics: *each speaking situation has unique contexts and constraints.*

Consider Your Own Interests

Once you have a clear sense of how your speech situation will influence the topic selection, ask yourself the second question, "What topics are interesting and relevant to me?" If you're a beginning speaker, you may be surprised to learn that audiences are often more interested in speeches when the speaker seems genuinely jazzed about the topic. When you pick a speech topic, you should have a strong feeling about it—whether positive or negative. Are you ambivalent about football? If so, you should probably avoid composing a speech about this sport. Does planning a backpacking trip get you excited? If so, add adventurous outdoor trips to your list of possible topics.

Selecting a topic that interests you has a lot to do with how you *feel* toward the topic. Ideas are infectious, but feelings are often an important part of how ideas catch on. Body chemistry and even unconscious forms of human thought influence what we find interesting or relevant as listeners and speakers.[4] For example, have you ever walked into a party or a stadium and immediately felt a sense of excitement and energy? Or have you ever entered a room full of people and suddenly felt sad or anxious, only to learn seconds later that they had just received very bad news? If so, these feelings have a lot to do with the ways in which our bodies respond to other excited or depressed bodies.[5] Picking a speech topic that excites or interests you is much more likely to interest listeners for reasons that have less to do with what you say than how you say it—especially your body language. Body language (like gestures and vocal tone) can also express how you *feel* about the topic beyond the words you actually say.

David Redfern/Getty Images

It is important to stress that feelings about a topic do convey a message and pique the interest of listeners. Think about it this way: many revered singers and songwriters in Western culture, such as Bob Dylan or legendary bluesman Muddy Waters, are celebrated because their music seems achingly personal and intimate. When Muddy Waters rewrote and recorded a song originally penned by Preston Foster, he made the song his own—so much so that many people believe "Got My Mojo Working" is actually Waters's song.

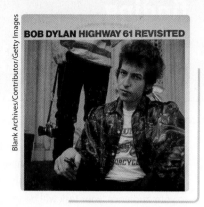

BOB DYLAN HIGHWAY 61 REVISITED

Blank Archives/Contributor/Getty Images

In a famous folk song, Bob Dylan implores, "How many seas must a white dove sail / Before she sleeps in the sand? . . . The answer my friend is blowin' in the wind / The answer is blowin' in the wind." Although Dylan's lyrics are vague—even nonsensical to some—listening to him sing the song gives the listener a strong sense that the meaning is deeply personal and moving. Regardless of the words each artist sings, Waters and Dylan communicate a sense of personal investment in their messages that "touch" the listener. Similarly, when you select a topic for a speech, it should *mean* something to you.

Consider Your Audience

Finally we move on to the third question: "What topics will be interesting and relevant to my audience?" As discussed in chapter 3, when choosing a speech topic you must also consider the interests and needs of your likely listeners. Always keep in mind that when speaking publicly, your fundamental purpose is to build a sense of community with your audience. For this reason, it is important to remember that just because a topic is interesting to you does not necessarily mean that it will be interesting to your listeners. To help in this situation, it is useful to think about how your own interests *intersect* with topics that might be compelling or useful to your audience.

For example, let's say you have to deliver an informative speech to your class and it needs to be five to seven minutes long. Let's also say you're a political science major who is excited about kayaking and hip-hop, and who enjoys taking long walks in the park, cooking extravagant brunches, and playing video games. Finally, let's say that you're at a loss for a speech topic. Any one of your interests could be an excellent starting point for a speech topic simply because you have an investment in them. What topic do you think will interest both you and the audience of your public speaking class? Various types of audience analysis (chapter 3) should help you decide which of your enjoyments, concerns, or hobbies may also be of interest to your listeners.

> ? **What three questions should you ask yourself when selecting a speech topic?**

Mind Storm: Concept Mapping and Other Explosives

> **You will learn to**
>
> **DEFINE** brainstorming.
>
> **DESCRIBE** two techniques of brainstorming.

In order to choose a speech topic, you have thus far asked yourself three questions: (1) What is the speaking situation? (2) What topics

finding inspiration for your speech

DIGITAL DIVE

Coming up with a speech topic can be challenging, but if you keep in mind that any topic that is of interest to you will probably be of interest to your audience, your task will be a little bit easier. One way to generate a topic is to think about your daily life and activities. What blogs, web pages, or magazines do you read and find entertaining? Do you enjoy playing video games? Do you enjoy running, biking, or swimming? Do you sing or play a musical instrument? Is there a popular hangout in your community where you spend a lot of your time? If so, what draws people there? Thinking about what holds your interest in your everyday environment can become a great resource for generating topics.

Whenever I am stuck in the brainstorming process, I always turn to popular music for inspiration. This is because, for me, popular music weds feeling or passion and speech in a unique way that I find infectious: the creative inspiration of musicians can be transferred to their listeners live or even in recordings. Of course, a muse refers to any source of creative inspiration; however, the term is based in Greek mythology, in which the Muses are goddesses who inspire scholarship and art. Perhaps for this reason,

the late musician Jerry Garcia and his frequent writing partner Robert Hunter evoke the Muses many times in their epic Grateful Dead song "Terrapin Station": "Inspiration, move me brightly, light the song with sense and color / Hold away despair, more than this I will not ask."

LaunchPad
macmillan learning

Interestingly, Garcia and Hunter's song lyrics are somewhat mystical and less straightforward than one would imagine, inviting all kinds of creative interpretations. Visit LaunchPad at launchpadworks.com to link to the song lyrics for "Terrapin Station." You might also search for a video or audio recording of the song on YouTube or other video websites.

As you examine the lyrics, consider the following questions:

- What do you think this song is about?
- What images does the song conjure for the listener?
- Do these lyrics evoke any ideas in you for a speech topic?

are interesting and relevant to me? and (3) What topics will be interesting and relevant to my audience? The answers you develop will give you a sense of your topic *constraints*. Once you know your constraints, you can then turn to another technique for developing possible topic ideas: letting your mind explode with ideas, or simply **brainstorming**.

For centuries, students and speaking professionals have used the practice of brainstorming to develop speech topics. The technique consists of simply letting your mind wonder and wander through ideas. When the earliest Western thinkers began formally teaching and studying public speaking in ancient Greece and Rome, they termed the process of coming up with ideas "invention" or "inventory" (both combined in the Latin term "*inventio*"). For the ancients, "invention" referred to both creating something new (a speech!) and discerning what arguments and evidence speakers have at their disposal—the available "inventory" of one's culture. In many ways, invention is the first and most important step in the speech creation process.

Now, there is no right or wrong way to brainstorm topics. However you choose to get stormy, the important thing is to *write your ideas down*—on your computer, your phone, or a piece of paper.

Getting Unstuck with Word Association

Over a century ago, Sigmund Freud developed a technique to help his patients get over their shyness and begin talking about their lives. He called the technique "free association" (or "word association"), and it went like this: Freud would say a single word, such as "apple" or "telephone," and then ask his patients to blurt out whatever word came to mind (such as "banana" or "my mother"). This technique is often used by psychologists to help their patients begin to talk, overcome shyness, and free themselves of anxieties they may have about saying the wrong thing, not pleasing the therapist, and so forth. Subsequently, many scholars and teachers have used the technique for brainstorming in a variety of academic settings, from the laboratory to the public speaking classroom.

If you are trying to brainstorm topic ideas and you find yourself stuck, you can use word association to get "unstuck." First, write down an idea—it could be a favorite hobby, a musician, a leader you admire, anything. Then, write down the next word or concept that comes into your head based on what the first word or idea reminds you of—and then

When starting to brainstorm topics, let your mind go wherever it wants; you can eliminate ideas that don't work later.

Psychotherapists sometimes use the technique of free association to help people break through mental blocks.

a **concept map** is a visual representation of the relationships between different concepts, usually depicted with arrows and lines.

keep going, jotting down terms until you have a page full of words and ideas that are related in some way. Sometimes you'll be very surprised by what you come up with (for example, you begin with "stapler" and end up writing "yacht"). After you have a page of ideas, ask yourself, What do these words have in common? What links them? You may discover that links that were previously "hidden" to you have now become clearer, and suddenly you can discover something that really interests you.

Concept Mapping

One of the tools that I like to use to come up with ideas for speeches is a **concept map**. This visual technique for brainstorming forces you to think about the relationships between different ideas or concepts. It's very similar to word association, except that your focus is more on the *association* or relation between words and concepts, and less on the words or concepts themselves. One of the reasons people get stuck or are anxious about choosing speech topics has to do with obsessing over the concept of a single word or idea. Exploring the underlying *relationships* associated with an idea, a concept, or an object brings to the surface other topics you never considered before but which you perhaps already know something about and may want to use for your speech.

To make a concept map:

- Draw a circle, then write your initial concept inside it.
- Then draw more circles and arrows to indicate related concepts and relationships.

Page 83 shows two concept maps that this book's illustrator and I developed, starting with my love of scrambled eggs. Because I like to cook, I have more interest in their preparation than in some of the related topics, such as the history of scrambled eggs or their biological background. While concept mapping, I got carried away thinking about the ingredient "salt," because salt helps keep scrambled eggs tender by separating proteins in the eggs. So I started a new concept map and then found an article from a cooking magazine that helped me further focus my topic.[6] The bottom image is the new, "spin-off" concept map.

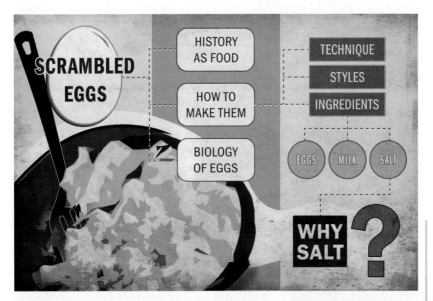

Working through a concept map on a given topic can lead you to surprisingly interesting topics. Here, concept mapping "scrambled eggs" led the speaker to the topic of "salt."

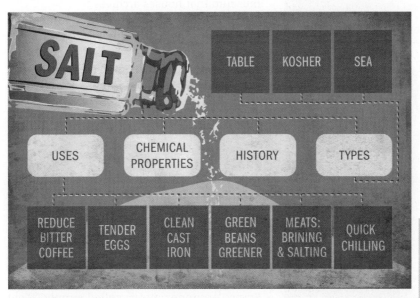

After stumbling upon the unexpected topic of "salt" by concept mapping "scrambled eggs," the speaker was able to generate a lot of information about salt and its uses.

By sitting down with my tablet for ten minutes or so, I was able to think about how my initial love of scrambled eggs led me to an interest in salt. Looking at my new concept map, I now must consider my third question: Would this topic interest the audience? I think so, especially if my informative speech on salt begins with the observation that everyone usually has this product in his or her home or apartment—and its power is underutilized! The reason this would be a good topic for a general audience is because most people have salt in their kitchens and would be fascinated to learn about all the ways they could use this common kitchen staple.

Research

Conducting research is one of the most fun and surprising ways to come up with speech topics. "Research" can mean a lot of things, but here we mean digging through materials, usually printed or online, in search of information, background, and context for something (a person, a war, a technology, and so on) that you want to learn more about. It's likely that your school or local city government has an *archive*, or a collection of materials about a given person or topic, or perhaps even a museum that houses archives.

Sometimes visiting a museum or an archive can inspire curiosity about a topic. Let's say that you are visiting the Rock and Roll Hall of Fame museum in Cleveland, Ohio, and see a dress worn by pop music performer Lady Gaga. If you didn't know much about her, seeing the dress may lead you to do an Internet search to learn more about who she is, which may then lead you to artists who are often compared with her, such as Madonna. Who designed Gaga's costume? Did Madonna ever wear a costume that was wilder than anything Gaga has worn? These are the kinds of thought-provoking questions, here inspired by visiting a museum, that can lead you to begin researching a speech topic further. (Gaga's dress, by the way, was designed by Franc Fernandez and is called simply "Meat Dress"; it was taxidermied before being displayed in the museum.) Research can also include the kinds of discoveries you can make by browsing Twitter or the *Huffington Post* or

Frederick M. Brown/Stringer/Getty Images

Lady Gaga debuts an outfit made of raw beef at the 2010 MTV Video Music Awards.

by reading an article in a magazine. Anything that catalyzes your curiosity is the beginning of research, and actively pursuing the answers to questions that come to mind is *researching*.

Note that along with word association, concept mapping, and research, your instructor may have other suggestions for brainstorming topics. The techniques described here are just a few among many.

? **What are three methods of brainstorming? How can a concept map help you brainstorm your speech topic?**

Narrowing Your Topic: What's Your Purpose?

> *You will learn to*
>
> **LIST** the three types of speech purposes, and explain how they differ.

After you have determined a topic — or at least a topic area — for your speech, the next step in the invention process is narrowing your topic. Because many topics are broad and could be explored from multiple angles — Pies! Fishing! Lawn ornaments! — it's unlikely that you'll be able to cover every aspect of a given topic in a five- to seven-minute classroom speech (or an hour, or even a full day!). In virtually every speech situation, it will be crucial for you to narrow your speech topic.

Let's think about salt again. What is there to say about salt? Assuming that you and the audience are interested in the topic and that it meets the demands of the situation, what you might say about salt depends on the purpose of the speech. And fortunately, we've got a concept map all ready to go. The concept map of salt, however, presents too many subtopics to be adequately covered in a short speech, so we will have to winnow it down to a handful of concepts. One way to do this is by discerning another important constraint by asking the following question: What is the general purpose of the speech we have been asked to give?

The **general speech purpose** answers the question "why" with regard to the topic, audience, and occasion, and is framed around informing, persuading, or honoring a specific occasion. All public speeches can be categorized by one of three general speech purposes:

the **general speech purpose** answers the question "why" with regard to the topic, audience, and occasion.

- to inform or teach (increasing listeners' understanding or awareness)
- to persuade or seduce (altering listeners' beliefs or encouraging specific actions)
- to celebrate, honor, or mourn (bringing a community together in speech on a special occasion, such as a birth, a death, or a toast at a party)

Knowing whether your purpose is to inform your audience about something, persuade them to believe or do something, or celebrate a person or an event helps you narrow your speech topic. If you preview the rest of *Speech Craft*, you'll find an entire chapter dedicated to each kind of speech purpose.

Once you have chosen a topic, narrowed it, and decided on a general speech purpose, you will need to come up with a **specific purpose statement**—a single sentence, often beginning with the word "to"—that explains the specific topic and goal of your presentation. Let's return to our example of salt and look at specific purpose statements geared to each of the three general speech purposes.

a **specific purpose statement** is a single sentence that explains the specific topic and goal of your presentation.

To Inform

Example Setting and Topic: The setting is a reading and discussion group made up of thoughtful people, many of whom also love to cook and learn about food. It is your turn to prepare a short presentation on a topic that interests you. You decide to inform your group about the little-known things you can do with salt, including making the perfect cup of cold-brewed coffee, composting at home, and keeping the green beans you picked up at the farmers' market greener during cooking.

Specific Purpose Statement: To inform a small audience of food enthusiasts about the little-known properties of salt

To Persuade

Example Setting and Topic: You are a nutritionist who is speaking to a retirement community about the health effects of salt. Because people who are fifty and older should be mindful of their salt intake to prevent high blood pressure, you elect to focus on the salt content in foods that is normally "hidden," or not widely known.

Specific Purpose Statement: To persuade senior citizens to use less salt, to be more conscious of their salt consumption, and to be aware of hidden sources of salt

To Celebrate

Example Setting and Topic: The setting is a going-away party for a good friend who is moving to Canada. You prepare a toast in which you discuss the tradition of throwing salt over your shoulder for good luck. At the end of your speech, you invite the other party guests to grab a pinch of salt to throw over their shoulders in order to wish your friend good luck.

Specific Purpose Statement: To bring the community together by wishing a friend safe travels while explaining a good-luck ritual involving salt

How does assigning a specific purpose help you narrow your speech topic?

From Topic to Thesis

> **You will learn to**
>
> **EXPLAIN** the difference between a statement of purpose and a thesis statement.

Once you have identified a topic and narrowed its scope with a specific purpose statement, it's time to create your thesis statement. In general, a **thesis statement** (sometimes also referred to as a *central idea*) is a single sentence that expresses the topic and purpose of the speech. Often the thesis statement overlaps significantly with the purpose of a speech, but not always. For example, if my speaking situation were to inform an audience about salt, then my thesis might be something like this: "Today, ladies and gentlemen, I'm excited to explain to you that there are many uses for salt other than seasoning food." In this thesis statement, the purpose of informing is deliberately *not* mentioned to make the thesis statement more interesting. You could easily write a thesis statement that includes a direct mention of the purpose, but doing so tempts boredom for the audience: "Today I am going to inform you about the many uses of salt." Such a thesis gets the job done; however, it's . . . [yawn].

My thesis about salt would be different if I were trying to persuade an audience to use more salt. Although my purpose is to persuade, I may not want to be so blunt about it. Let's suppose, for example, that I am a representative from Morton Salt, and I am trying to promote my company's product. My thesis would sound silly if I included my purpose: "Ladies and gentlemen, I'm here today to persuade you to buy and use more salt, even if your doctors have warned you to cut down on sodium for medical reasons."

You can still ethically encourage your listeners to use more salt without explicitly mentioning your underlying specific purpose in your thesis statement: "Although the medical community has learned over the past century that for some people, salt can contribute to hypertension, there are several beneficial uses for salt that don't require consumption, and I'd like to tell you about them."

To write your thesis statement, you must be very clear about your purpose or reason for speaking *first*. Once you create your specific purpose statement ("To inform the audience about some nontraditional uses of salt" or "To persuade the audience to use more salt"), you'll be ready to write your thesis statement, which should be more engaging, perhaps

> a **thesis statement** is a single sentence that expresses the topic and purpose of a speech.

Daniel Acker/Bloomberg/Contributor/Getty Images

indicating your purpose only indirectly. A good rule of thumb to keep in mind is that your thesis statement differs from your purpose for only one reason: *The thesis statement is what you will actually say in your speech.* In general, the purpose is what you work out before you start writing your speech; you will keep the speech purpose to yourself. Let's return to our salt example and pair the specific purpose statements with thesis statements; take care to notice how the thesis statements are more arresting than the purpose statements.

To Inform

Specific Purpose Statement: To inform a small audience of food enthusiasts about the little-known properties of salt

Thesis Statement: "For decades people have thought about salt as a seasoning. However, you can use salt in ways that you may have never thought about before!"

To Persuade

Specific Purpose Statement: To persuade senior citizens to use less salt, to be more conscious of their salt consumption, and to be aware of hidden sources of salt

Thesis Statement: "Many people are not aware that salt is hidden in our diets and can be found in foods that we would never suspect. By explaining where salt hides in our food, I hope to show you how to consume less salt for good health and a long life."

To Celebrate

Specific Purpose Statement: To bring the community together by wishing a friend safe travels while explaining a good-luck ritual involving salt

Thesis Statement: "Let's send Sandra on her Canadian adventure by enacting an ancient tradition—throwing salt over our shoulders for good luck!"

For beginning and seasoned speakers alike, coming up with a great speech topic can be a tricky pickle. Paying attention to the speech situation, your interests, and the interests of your audience can provide helpful constraints for you to brainstorm speech topics. Word association and concept maps can help you generate ideas—and can even help you get "unstuck." Once you have a page of possible speech topics, however, the process of invention is not finished: you must further narrow your speech topic by first discerning the speech purpose (to inform, to persuade, or to celebrate) and then writing a thesis statement. Once you have a topic, purpose, and a draft of a thesis statement, you are ready to do further research and begin preparing and organizing your speech—our tasks in the next couple of chapters. Let's go!

What is a thesis statement, and how does it relate to the purpose of a speech?

end of chapter stuff

Image Courtesy of The Advertising Archives

Developing a Dynamite Topic

For the craft of public speaking, invention is the process of generating the materials of a speech based on three elements: the speech situation, your personal interests, and the interests of the audience.

Mind Storm: Concept Mapping and Other Explosives

Developing possible speech topics is a creative process termed "brainstorming." The techniques of word association and concept mapping can help you generate ideas.

Daniel Acker/Bloomberg/Contributor/Getty Images

Narrowing Your Topic: What's Your Purpose?

One can narrow a speech topic by identifying the general purpose of a speech: to inform, to persuade, or to celebrate. A thesis statement is a word-for-word sentence or two that states for the audience a speech's topic and purpose.

LaunchPad
macmillan learning

LaunchPad for *Speech Craft* includes a curated collection of speech videos and encourages self-assessment through adaptive quizzing. Go to **launchpadworks.com** to get access to:

 LearningCurve adaptive quizzes

 Video clips to help you improve your speeches

ACTIVITIES

Choosing Appropriate Topics

On your own or in a group, brainstorm or discuss and then write down appropriate topics for each of the following scenarios:

SCENARIO ONE: You have been invited to speak at a local youth swim club. The club consists almost entirely of ten- to twelve-year-old girls and boys. You are asked to give a speech to inspire them. What topic will you choose?

SCENARIO TWO: You are a student in a public speaking class, and your teacher has asked you to speak on a topic that informs your class about a pressing and relevant campus issue. What topic will you choose?

Practice Concept Mapping

Concept mapping can often lead you to unpredictable ideas and interesting topics. Select one of the following concepts and create a map. Then, create a second concept map using one of the sub-concepts from the primary map (much like the example of scrambled eggs and salt in this chapter).

music festivals	perfume	Alicia Keys
garden gnomes	littering	jelly beans
ballroom dancing	sports stadiums	texting and driving

KEY TERMS

 Videos in LaunchPad describe many of these terms. Go to launchpadworks.com.

invention 77
speech situation 77
brainstorming 81
concept map 82

general speech purpose 85
specific purpose statement 86
thesis statement 87

RESEARCHING
YOUR SPEECH TOPIC

CHAPTER 5

From the "tough love" advice of behavioral scientist John Watson in the early twentieth century, to the softer, kinder recommendations of Benjamin Spock midcentury, parenting techniques have been a hotly debated topic in North American culture.[1] On October 26, 2011, a number of social media and networking sites reported the findings of a study that put the debate to rest. Presumably released by the California Parenting Institute (CPI), the study concluded that "every style of parenting inevitably causes children to grow into profoundly unhappy adults." One of the researchers was quoted as saying that "despite great variance in parenting styles across populations, the end product is always the same: a profoundly flawed and joyless human being."[2] A number of people who read about the study were alarmed; some of them were even employees of CPI, who contacted the director of marketing and development to inquire when the study was conducted.[3]

Although believable to many, the parenting study was actually a hoax created by a satire organization that published the bogus report in their fake digital newspaper, the *Onion*. CPI is a real organization based in California; however, it did not publish the parenting study and has denounced the *Onion*'s joke. So why do people fall for hoaxes like this? Eighteenth-century philosopher Thomas Reid echoes a sentiment still held today: humans are gullible because we are fundamentally trustful in character.[4] In general, people trust before they are led to doubt. Before the days of wireless broadcasting and the Internet, our trusting nature did not so quickly lead us into error. Today, however, we live in a time when speech, images, and words circulate on screens faster than we can absorb or understand them. If we are trustful creatures as human beings, then an initial response to a social networking hoax might be to believe it, because at face value it seems credible (especially if a trusted friend or loved one made us aware of it).

Why Research Matters

You will learn to

EXPLAIN when and why research is required beyond common knowledge.

DESCRIBE the practical and ethical reasons for speaking truthfully.

This chapter provides guidance on how to go about researching your speech, much as a journalist or scholar would do. To this end, we will address questions like, "Why does research matter?" and "Why do you need to fact-check?" Although not all speeches require in-depth research, speeches that provide information or include factual claims that can be proven or disproven require investigation.

Even in more formal contexts, speeches don't always need to draw on research from the Internet or the library. Many of us can simply draw on **common knowledge**, or beliefs that are known and understood by members of a given community, for materials to support a speech. Common knowledge is usually the first place we research, and it requires only thinking or having a conversation with a friend or colleague.

But when is common knowledge not enough? That's a hard question to answer because figuring out when and what to research depends on the kind of speech you are giving and the speaking situation. For example, if you are lecturing on the potentially harmful effects of the sun on human skin, it is common knowledge that too much sun exposure accelerates aging and increases the risk of skin cancer.[5] Insofar as such a lecture concerns people's health, our conscience should goad us to pursue accurate, up-to-date information; there is an additional burden of research because the well-being of the audience is at stake. What is not common knowledge, for example, is *how* sun damage causes or accelerates aging, and what kinds of sun rays (UVA and UVB) are more likely to harm people. These are the kinds of facts you would want to research for a lecture that can influence people's health—perhaps even save their lives.

Did you know, for example, that although we do know that sun exposure increases the risk of cancer, researchers are still figuring out how to predict the harm and what models to use for doing so? Relying too much on common knowledge could lead a speaker to overlook important complexities and details about a topic.[6]

Finally, you may want to research statements of fact that are commonly known if they could be

common knowledge
refers to events, ideas, things, or beliefs that are widely known and understood in a given community.

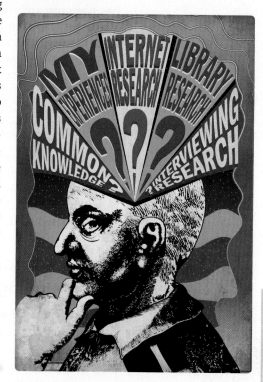

The varieties of research

When does a speech need to be researched? When is drawing on common knowledge appropriate for a speech? When do you know that a speech requires a trip to the library?

viewed as controversial by some audience members. For example, as an educator, I have a tendency to think that the theory of evolution—that human life evolved over time from earlier life forms—is common knowledge. Over the past years, however, some secondary education school boards across the country have decided to discontinue teaching evolution because of disagreements about the specifics of the theory among teachers, parents, and politicians.[7] In other words, what was common knowledge to me turns out to be not so common anymore. The lesson here is simply this: when in doubt about an assumption or claim you would like to make in a speech, you should probably go ahead and research it.

Truth and the Importance of Research

Why is it so important to research your speech? From a pragmatic standpoint, speeches that make claims beyond the reach of common knowledge are more credible when they appear to have been researched or seem to be based on evidence from reliable sources. Moreover, a speech that draws on a variety of sources for evidence can be perceived as more reliable and balanced. In short: if you don't appear to "know your stuff" from a variety of angles, your audience may not take you seriously.

From an ethical perspective, the cultural expectation that a speech has been researched is based on a common trust. Think about it: when a stranger is speaking and you are listening, do you automatically regard what she says with suspicion, or do you listen with the presumption that what she says *she* believes to be true? Most folks listen with the presumption that the speaker believes what she says. Of course, there are always exceptions, but most of us tend to give those we encounter the benefit of the doubt—we'll hear them out.

As discussed in chapter 2, you should speak the **truth**—as best as you understand it—in most speech situations. "Truth" is a charged word and introduces a complexity to public speaking that most of us don't normally consider. We're usually more preoccupied with our nerves about getting up in front of a group and delivering our speech. Indeed, the question "What is the truth?" sounds like something a philosopher would ask.

truth is a fact or belief that is widely accepted by a given community or group of people.

Debunking Hoaxes

You can learn about all sorts of hoaxes and scams by visiting website resources such as Snopes.com. Researchers at the Snopes website, for example, investigate and debunk urban myths, dubious stories, and spurious claims—from the deaths of celebrities to the use of earthworms in the hamburger meat at fast-food chains.

Even so, thinking about being truthful is important. If you consider it, we all tend to assume what truth means at some level of our consciousness. Whether you believe in absolute, capital-T truth (history as settled fact) or relativism (all truths are subject to revision and are contingent), the fact remains that to get on with your day-to-day living you must assume everyday truths. For example, you must assume that it is true your vehicle needs gas to run, that if you don't eat you will get hungry, and that if you don't bathe you will start to stink.

misinformation is false, inaccurate, or misleading information.

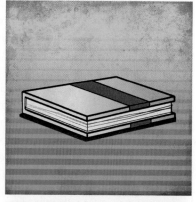

As we encountered in chapter 2, lying or being dishonest in a speaking situation is a bad thing, unless there are circumstances in which deception may be called for (such as protecting the public from imminent danger). In this chapter, we are not going to discuss purposeful deception or lying, because most folks approach the craft of public speaking earnestly. What concerns us as speakers—and the reason research is not to be taken lightly—is the spreading of *unintentional* untruths. **Misinformation** (sometimes termed "disinformation") typically refers to deliberately incorrect statements, but most misinformation in speeches is often the result of carelessness or misguided research instead of outright deceit.

Unintentionally making statements that are not true is more common that we realize. We all do it, even when our intentions are honest, but there are ways to prevent it. If you wish to make claims based on knowledge that is not common, or if you are trying to inform or persuade an audience, it's always a good idea to look more deeply into your topic. What follows are some basic research techniques and resources that are available to you.

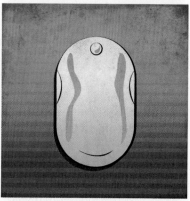

How to Research a Speech

> *You will learn to*
>
> **LIST** the steps of research planning.
>
> **DESCRIBE** how a librarian can help you with research.
>
> **EXPLAIN** the different kinds of digital information you can research.
>
> **DESCRIBE** how to evaluate sources for accuracy, credibility, and reliability.

So far, the reasons for researching a speech that goes beyond common knowledge boil down to this: (1) pragmatically, most audiences expect research, and (2) ethically, as a speaker you want to avoid communicating misinformation.

Research Planning

When embarking on a research adventure, keep these tips in mind:

- **Narrow Your Topic during Preliminary Research.** Perhaps the biggest challenge for researching a speech is picking a topic that is not too big. In general, one can pack more research into a written document than one can actually deliver in the time allotted for a speech.

  Remember to pick a topic that is doable, then narrow your topic during your preliminary sleuthing (looking at books or searching the Internet). Preliminary research refers to the early moments when you are selecting your topic; Google or *Wikipedia* searches, for example, are a good way to start developing your research plan.

- **Give Yourself Enough Time.** Bad speeches are often a consequence of waiting until the last minute to research and compose them. Research entails a lot of reading, and reading always takes longer than you think it will. Give yourself enough time to take a trip to the library, to search for information in databases and online, and to actually read the materials you discover.

- **Develop a List of Possible Sources.** During preliminary research, you'll come across articles about your topic; look up the sources those articles cite, and develop a list of materials to examine more deeply.

- **Take Notes and Print Your Sources.** As you move from preliminary research into more focused, in-depth research in the library or using databases, take detailed notes (either on note cards, in a notebook, or on your computer) that indicate basic bibliographic information (author names, titles, and dates) and reproduce any quotes you might find useful. Print out articles that you think you might use, or keep PDF copies of them on your computer.

Now what? Well, you need to think about what kinds of information you need based on your topic, and then develop some sort of plan (see sidebar on "Research Planning"). In general, the three basic ways speakers research speeches involves going to the library, researching on the Internet, and interviewing.

Libraries (such as the Seattle Library, shown here) offer a substantial wealth of resources that you can read, feel, and hear.

Librarians in Their Natural Habitat (the Library)

In addition to books, magazines, and newspapers, libraries now house everything from records and films to popular culture artifacts, including government documents and rock concert posters. Many libraries today also offer access to computers with a wealth of digital information to

Interviews with Librarians

During the writing of this book, I interviewed a number of librarians and asked them to name the top reasons students ask for their help. Kelly Booker is an information specialist at the University of Texas at Austin Law Library: "People generally come to the library to use the space (it's quiet!) or the equipment (the computers)." She reports that many students will open a live chat window rather than approach a person in the library. Whether in person or on chat, "we are mostly helping patrons find where their questions can be answered." Similarly, a librarian at the University of Minnesota in Duluth has observed a general reluctance to interact with them. "To be honest," said Kate vo Thi-Beard, "students usually come see me because an instructor required it for a class." Another common reason students ask for help is because they found a periodical online but could not retrieve or download it, and so ended up in the library. "Really," says Kate, "most librarians love to interact with people who need assistance with research, but with the ease of the Internet, we just don't get the help requests like we used to." In other words, dear reader, librarians feel neglected and are eager to help, so go see one!

> A librarian can be more helpful than a Google search in determining where to find information.

examine as well as database search possibilities. What a given library offers depends on its collection, and the easiest way to figure this out is to go online and read up about a particular library, or to phone or visit one and ask a curious, knowledgeable person who works there: a librarian!

Ask any librarian who has worked in a library for more than ten years, and he or she will tell you that libraries are changing at a mind-boggling rate. Increasingly, librarians are thought of as "information scientists," or experts who know where to look for information. All librarians can help you find books or periodicals, but they also possess a deep knowledge of other resources—often digital—that you may not know about. Typically, a library will use a searchable database that has a record of every book, periodical, or archive material that it houses. A librarian can be more helpful than a Google search in determining where to find information. Google and other Internet search engines are not able to filter information as specific as you may need it; therefore, if you do a search of a general topic, you may get everything from a personal web page to an opinion piece in a magazine to a conspiracy theorist's blog. Search engines do filter information, but the process is complicated by what researchers term "search bias," which refers to how search engines alter the way user searches are conducted to increase revenue for themselves and their business partners.[8] For this reason, librarians can be much more effective in helping you figure out how to search for credible information.

Research in the Digital Domain

Many speakers today search the Internet to research information that will support their speech. Even if you go to the library, you're more likely to be directed to a computer to search for materials than to a reference shelf or card catalog. In fact, many of the databases in library reference rooms are also available to you on a computer from just about anywhere, as long as you have permission to use the database and a password and user ID. There are sharp distinctions between databases and the Internet in a general sense. Research databases, such as those maintained by EBSCO and Gale Research, the United States government, and academic institutions, are vetted and generally reference reliable sources. Your instructor or librarian can point you to the most trusted and reliable research databases.

Sometimes a speaker can pass along misinformation by trusting unreliable Internet sources.[9] When you conduct a Google search, your search terms are plugged into a complex set of rules and calculations—or algorithms—that determine the results that appear on your screen. As commercial enterprises, search engines like Bing, Google, and Yahoo! keep their algorithms secret, so only those who actually do

Popular Research Databases

DATABASE	DESCRIPTION
EBSCO Academic Search Complete	A multidisciplinary database with full-text articles, essays, and monographs. Provides both academic texts as well as popular periodicals.
Gale Academic OneFile	Searches both academic and general-interest periodicals.
LexisNexis Academic	Searches popular periodicals, newspapers, and magazines. Contains some television and radio news transcripts. Best for information that is of general interest or for current events.
JSTOR	Database of peer-reviewed, academic essays, primarily in the humanities but also in the sciences and social sciences. Many are available as full text (PDF files).

the programming for these companies know how the calculations are made. We do know, however, that powerful economic incentives drive the search results. For example, large corporations might pay a search engine to have their web pages appear before others. And web pages that are clicked more often than others will appear more frequently in search results than less popular pages. This means that you should be careful when determining whether the information you find from an Internet search is useful and the source is trustworthy. In general, databases are more trustworthy research resources than general Internet searches because they index articles that have gone through some kind of editing process (meaning that more than one person has reviewed the work for quality and accuracy).

Busting misinformation

Public figures, especially politicians, are routinely called out for saying things that are not true. Over the last couple of decades, journalists, public figures, scholars, and students have used websites like FactCheck.org to research the claims of prominent public figures and to assess whether they are true or false. FactCheck.org is a nonpartisan project of the Annenberg Public Policy Center of the University of Pennsylvania, which claims to be an advocate for voters by researching the "factual accuracy of what is said by major U.S. political players in the form of TV ads, debates, speeches, interviews and news releases."[10] For example, 2016 presidential candidate Carly Fiorina appeared on a news program in June of that year, arguing against the legalization of medical marijuana: "I remember when I had cancer, my doctor asked me if I had an interest in medical marijuana. I did not, and he said good, because marijuana is a very complex chemical substance now, we don't understand how it interacts with other drugs, we don't understand what it does to your body." After reviewing a number of medical studies, researchers at FactCheck.org concluded that Fiorina's claims were misleading: "There is still much to be learned about medicinal marijuana, but it's not accurate to say that 'we don't understand how it interacts with other drugs.'"[11]

Although they are not as reliable as the database services offered by your library, doing research online using search engines *can* be very useful, and you can find a lot of valuable information by going online and searching. Still, the trouble with doing research on the Internet concerns the reliability of the source of information. This is best understood by comparing web pages with more traditional articles, research papers, and essays. When a journalist or another professional writer composes a story for a magazine or web page, a television newscast, or a radio program, that story is usually read by others before it is printed or posted. Having another set of eyes to read through and fact-check the story helps ensure that the writing is high quality and that the information is accurate. Similarly, when a scholar submits an essay or a paper for publication to an academic journal, it is sent to two or three scholars in the appropriate academic field, who read it over to determine whether it is well researched and high quality; this vetting process is called "peer review." Much of what you find in a library, or through a database hosted by a library, has gone through a thorough editorial or peer review process.

On the Internet, just about anyone can publish anything without having the writing reviewed. Your Uncle Earle can publish a web page about his six cats and their magical abilities. Lady Gaga can blog about how her latest fashion creation—a dress made out of Vienna sausages and canned ham—is a true testament to individual liberation. Conspiracy theorists can publish articles that claim the president is making himself president for life. A revered climate scientist can publish a recent paper as a PDF file.

How can you determine which Internet sources are reliable and which are not? Truth be told, there is no right or wrong answer to this question. We will discuss some helpful guidelines for assessing online sources in the next section; however, the bottom line is that you will ultimately need to trust your instincts about which sources are reliable and which are suspicious. It's likely, for example, that information from a respected institution like the Mayo Clinic or the *New York Times* is more reliable than a personal blog or a Reddit discussion. Remember that you can bypass your uncertainty altogether by going to the library and asking for help from a librarian.

What online information is more reliable and credible? Materials posted by the United States government, sponsored by the Library of Congress or by smaller local libraries, or provided by academic institutions will be more reliable than materials sponsored by a corporate interest. For-profit companies that provide information to the public often make materials available as a form of advertising. Should you trust a fast-food company's sponsored study that argues that trans-fatty acids are not as harmful as previously thought? Should you believe a beverage company when it tells you that its sugar-loaded soda is good for you? Umm, no.

CARS: An Internet Research Checklist

Retired professor Robert Harris has taught students how to responsibly research on the Internet for years. He has created a memorable checklist of questions you should ask about Internet sources, developed around four key terms:

Back to the Future's DeLorean

Credibility: What are the author's credentials? Does the information appear to be edited or peer reviewed?

Accuracy: Is the information timely and comprehensive? Does it appear to serve a general audience or a special interest? Is the information dated?

Reasonableness: Does the information appear balanced and objective? Is the information biased toward a particular worldview?

Support: Does the information provide its sources (a bibliography)? Can you find other resources that corroborate the information?

You can visit Harris's full website at www.virtualsalt.com/evalu8it.htm.[12]

the three "hecks"
of internet source reliability

© Hanna-Barbera/Courtesy Everett Collection

Who the heck wrote it? The most important question we can ask about an online source is about its authorship. In general, Internet sources with clearly discernible authors are more trustworthy than sources that have no author or that are authored anonymously. Let's say we do a Google search for "the Smurfs," which are the little blue mythological creatures created by the Belgian cartoonist Peyo in the 1950s. Now, one of the first web pages that appears in the results list is titled "Who are the Smurfs?" The first text to appear is this:

> The Smurfs are tiny, blue creatures who live in mushroom houses in a village hidden in the forest. Smurfs are blue, three-apples tall, and speak a dialect which makes heavy use of the word "smurf". [sic]. . . . The word "Schtroumpf" (Smurf) is the Flemish equivalent of the English language colloquial "Whatchamacallit."

Can we trust this information and use it as a source for our speech? It seems legitimate, although the incorrect punctuation and double-negative phrasing should make us a little suspicious. After scanning this web page I note there is no mention of an author anywhere. Therefore, it's probably not the best web page to cite in an informative speech on the Smurfs. Among the search results, I also notice an article penned by Leo Cendrowicz for *Time* magazine. Because we now have a clearly discernible author and recognize the publication as a popular, widely read magazine, this article seems more trustworthy as a source. In addition, since the article originally appeared in print, we know that it's gone through an editorial process.[13]

Who the heck paid for it? Sometimes you might find what appears to be an informative article but no author is listed. For example (at the time of this writing), if we do a Google search for "global climate change," we get over 136 million results. The top three links are actually advertisements (denoted by a yellow box that reads "Ad" before the link), so we should not look there for reliable information. The next five links that appear are from a variety of sources. Of these results, I recognize NASA, which is the U.S. government's space exploration and science program, or the National Aeronautics and Space Administration.[14]

Exploring the NASA website, I find dozens of essays and articles on climate change. One article, titled "Causes: A Blanket around the Earth," explains how gases created by humans have helped create a "greenhouse effect" around the planet. Now, here's the thing: no author is listed on this web page. The article *does* list five sources (all scientific papers or reports). That's good, but should I trust this source? Yes, I should. But why? The reason has to do with the *reputation of the institution* that is sponsoring the website. NASA is recognized around the world as a credible source for scientific study.

We're asking the question, "Who the heck paid for it?" in part because financial motives can skew information. Does NASA have a financial motive for providing information about global climate change? Perhaps, to some extent, but part of NASA's mission is to make the information that it collects about the environment and space available to the public. That is, it's NASA's *duty* to publish information about global warming. Notably, in the "global climate change" search, the Global Warming Solutions, Inc. (GWS) website also comes up. These web pages include lots of information about the use of solar energy and how the effective use of solar energy can help reverse the effects of global warming. Yet GWS is a publicly traded company that sells solar power systems. In other words, it's in the company's best interest to publish information that is pro solar power. Consequently, the site's information should be considered less reliable than NASA's. It is important to remember that you should always be wary of information provided by for-profit companies.

When the heck was it published? In general, when you're looking at online articles or blog posts about current events or cutting-edge research and statistics, the more recent the information is, the more reliable it will be. For example, if you were to do a search on the Internet for "Pluto," you'd find some pages devoted to the Disney cartoon character and others devoted to the former planet Pluto. Certain pages discuss Pluto as a planet, which is no longer correct information, as the International Astronomical Union urged the scientific community in 2006 to downgrade Pluto from "planet" to "dwarf planet," as it is in general believed to be a sphere of gases and not an actual planet. Regardless, you do need to do your homework to make sure your information is, to the best of your knowledge, true and accurate.

How good are you at Internet sleuthing? Visit Launch-Pad at **launchpadworks.com** and click on the pages dedicated to chapter 5. There you'll link to two news stories. Using the three heck questions, determine who wrote the story, who paid for the story, and when it was published.

- Which story is more credible?
- How do you know?

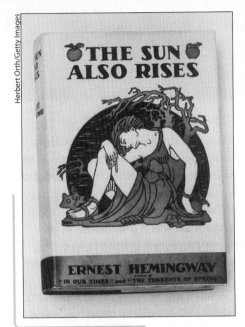

To Wikipedia or Not to Wikipedia? That Is a Good Question

The "free" Internet encyclopedia project *Wikipedia* boasts more than four and a half million articles covering a wide range of topics. But do you know that anyone can edit or write an article for *Wikipedia*? For example, if you look at the entry for Ernest Hemingway's novel *The Sun Also Rises*, you'll see three small tabs in the top, right-hand corner of the page: "Read," "Edit," and "View History." If you hit the "Edit" tab, you will be asked to create an account with *Wikipedia*. You could, if you wanted to, add information to the entry or change it entirely. In just one day, five people edited *The Sun Also Rises*'s entry. Because of this "open source" approach to creating information, it's difficult to know who the author of any given *Wikipedia* entry is and, consequently, whether the information is accurate. Some entries are written by scholars and are well researched, as evidenced in the endnotes, while others are not.

Although some academic studies have shown that information from *Wikipedia* is just as reliable as information one would get from a librarian at a reference desk, other studies have found *Wikipedia* entries to be untrustworthy.[15] Here's the thing about the largest encyclopedia in the world: thousands of people—a worldwide community—are responsible for its content. *Wikipedia* is one of the largest community-building, community-supported repositories of human knowledge, and consequently, it is an invaluable resource to you. So the question is, should you cite *Wikipedia* as a speech source? That's really up to your instructor and your best judgment.

> **What are the three "hecks" of digital researching? How can you determine the credibility or reliability of an online source?**

The Research Interview

Depending on your speech topic, sometimes it's useful to interview an expert. Research interviews can also save you a lot of time. If you interview an expert in a given area, he or she can suggest possible sources of information that you would probably not have otherwise considered. For many reporters and other journalists, interviewing is the primary way in which they discover information that is eventually published online and in newspapers. Interviewing is an art that is not easily taught. As part of the speech research process, the primary goal of the research interview is to get information about a given topic from someone who knows a lot about that topic. Here is the number one rule of all interviewing: do not waste the interviewee's time. The best way to follow this rule is to only ask questions that you cannot answer yourself by other means. For example, students who are learning the art of investigative journalism often ask

> **What are the general guidelines for conducting a good research interview?**

to interview me. Sometimes beginners ask questions such as, "Approximately how many students attend your university?" or "When did you start graduate school?" These students could have easily researched the answers to these questions by going to the university's website or asking for my résumé.

If you are asked to conduct a research interview for your speech project, consult the box that follows for some tips.

Don't Forget to Cite Your Sources!

> **You will learn to**
>
> **LIST** the basic information included in source citations.

When researching and preparing a speech, you must always be mindful to document where you got your information. For the major speeches in your public speaking course, you will be asked to submit a preparation script or an outline documenting your research. At the end of this document should be a bibliography, which lists all the sources you consulted in preparing your speech (some instructors may require a certain number of sources).

In North America, sources are typically cited in one of four standardized formats: (1) MLA style, developed by the Modern Language

Association; (2) APA style, developed by the American Psychological Association; (3) Chicago style, developed by the University of Chicago Press; and (4) AMA style, created by the American Medical Association. This book, for example, follows Chicago style. Your instructor will determine which style you should use, but you should know that all four organizations have guidelines for using their citation style, which are available for free on the Internet. For most public speaking courses in North America, you will be asked to use the MLA, APA, or Chicago format. You can find thorough information about documentation styles on Purdue University's Online Writing Lab website at owl.english.purdue.edu/owl.

Although the requirements of each style can differ substantially, you should typically include the following information:

- The source: the newspaper, magazine, book, journal, online publication, or blog you consulted for information. If the source is monthly, weekly, or yearly, you may need to include the volume and issue number (e.g., an academic journal).
- The author, organization, or group that claims authorship. Very rarely does one ever use an "anonymous" author for information.
- The credentials of the author, organization, or group that authored the information. Sometimes credentials are not important, but if you are relying on an author for expertise, skill, experience, knowledge, and so on, credentials help make the source more credible.
- The date the information was first made available, almost always a year (and sometimes a month and day). Some citation styles also require a date for when you accessed material from the Internet or an online database.

Each sponsoring organization for documentation styles—the APA, the MLA, and the *Chicago Manual of Style*—periodically update and change their rules to keep pace with the dynamic character of information and changing technologies. The online resources on LaunchPad for *Speech Craft* have more up-to-date information on documentation styles, including examples.[16]

In sum, as a speaker you need to research your speech for both practical and ethical reasons. In the practical sense, most audiences generally assume that if you are speaking, you have some expertise on the topic; audiences expect speakers to have "done their homework." Ethically, researching your speech is a good way to avoid passing on misinformation or unwittingly misleading an audience. To be a dutiful researcher, however, you must take care to be critical of your sources, so you can make sure the information you use is credible and reliable. Finally, be sure to cite your research in a bibliography using one of the three dominant documentation styles in North America.

Why Research Matters

In our world of rapidly changing information, one must be careful not to trust everything one hears or sees. Researching your speech topic can help you separate fact from rumor and hoax!

Lambert/Getty Images

How to Research a Speech

Speakers need to research their speeches for practical and ethical reasons, both of which rest on the generally trustful character of audiences. Avoid passing on erroneous and inaccurate information.

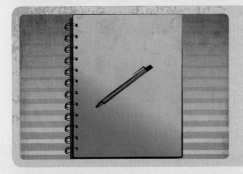

Don't Forget to Cite Your Sources!

Don't forget your librarian! He or she can help you find reliable and credible sources for conducting research. Databases housed or sponsored by libraries often index articles that have been edited and peer reviewed for quality control.

The Three "Hecks" of Internet Source Reliability

When evaluating sources for accuracy, credibility, and reliability, ask yourself these questions: "Who the heck wrote it?" "Who the heck paid for it?" and "When the heck was it published?" Document your sources using the style your instructor requires (MLA, APA, or Chicago).

CHAPTER 5

ACTIVITY

Researching Your Speech Topic

1. Do an Internet search as well as an academic database search on your speech topic. List, skim, and briefly describe the first five results of each kind of search. How do the source results compare? Which appears more reliable? Why?

2. With a topic provided by your instructor, do an Internet search using one of the most common search engines, and find a source. Your task is not to find a credible source but rather *the most unreliable piece of information or web page that you*

can. Be sure to list all the reasons why the source is not to be trusted, and share your terrible find with the class.

3. With a classmate, discuss your impending speech topic. Then, in no more than five minutes, come up with three good questions to ask your classmate about his or her topic that you would not be able to find the answers to yourself. When your instructor gives you the cue, interview your classmate, being careful to practice active listening.

KEY TERMS

 Videos in LaunchPad describe many of these terms. Go to launchpadworks.com.

common knowledge 93

truth 94

misinformation 95

SUPPORTING
MATERIALS
&
CONTEXTUAL
REASONING

CHAPTER 6

Neal Hamberg

Before completing his MBA at Harvard Business School, Casey Gerald helped create a nonprofit organization with three other Harvard students called MBAs Across America. Gerald and his colleagues drove across the country to connect with visionary entrepreneurs for mutual learning and innovation. The group helped promote the work of little-known entrepreneurs and assist them with fund-raising and marketing.[1] Based on the success of the program, as well as his stellar gifts as a student, Gerald was asked by his fellow MBA graduates to deliver the 2014 commencement address. Like many commencement addresses, Gerald's central message was to inspire his peers to go out and change the world.[2]

As is the case with most commencement speakers, Gerald's challenge was to deliver an inspirational speech that resisted clichés ("Oh, the places you will go!"). Bucking a common cultural stereotype about business school graduates, in his speech Gerald said that he wanted to devote his "life to a cause greater than myself." He announced that he was beginning his career in finance by deliberately working for a nonprofit start-up, which for many people would seem an atypical choice. Gerald ended his speech with this explanation:

> Now I see, after all the miles and all the memories of the last two years, now I see the bigger sign for hope: you, my friends, my fellow graduates. Not because of what we've done, because I know we have more work to do. . . . And as we leave this place for the last time, . . . we take up the work not just of making a living but of making a life. For if all we've learned here are four Ps [product, price, place, and promotion, the principles of marketing], . . . [then] we will prove William Faulkner right, that we labor under a curse, that we live "not [for] love but [for] lust, . . . [for] victories without hope and, worst of all, without pity or compassion." That our "griefs grieve on no universal bones, leaving no scars." That we live "not [from] the heart but [from] the glands." No, my friends, we have more work to do. Hard work. Frightening work. Uncertain work . . . but work on which the whole world depends.

Gerald's speech was recorded and posted to YouTube. It quickly went viral and landed him on the covers of various industry magazines, such as *Fast Company*.[3]

Types of Speech Support

You will learn to

LIST the five types of speech support, and define them.

DETAIL the two basic questions one should ask about statistics.

I've opened this chapter with Gerald's speech not only because of its eloquence but because of its exemplary use of supporting material. Gerald's conclusion references a speech by William Faulkner, even though the original context of Faulker's remarks was very different: Faulkner's speech was delivered at a Nobel Prize banquet in his honor in 1950; he was worried about writers who write without *compassion* at a time when the United States and its allies were recovering from the Second World War. Gerald thought Faulkner's words could be applied to himself and his fellow graduates embarking on careers in business, and so he skillfully used them to urge his audience to make the world a better place by helping others. Gerald's use of Faulkner's words is an example of *speech support*, or material that a speaker selects to back up his or her claims. The support Gerald chose for his commencement address was just right for the mood and tone of the moment of his speech: commencement addresses tend to be optimistic and inspirational, and attempt to bring the assembled community together.

supporting material refers to the facts, statistics, testimony, examples, and stories that bolster your claims.

It is essential to think about setting and audience when considering what you will use as **supporting material**—the facts, statistics, testimony, examples, and stories that bolster your claims. The key to understanding what *kind* of supporting material is appropriate for a speech is knowing the *context*, a process that we will describe as *contextual reasoning* in this chapter. To this end, then, the chapter proceeds in two ways: First, we will explore *types of speech support*, including facts, statistics, testimony, examples, and stories. Second, we will discuss the process of contextual reasoning, or how you go about determining when and what kinds of support are appropriate for a speech by considering its context.

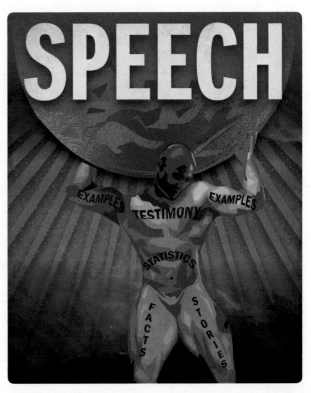

A speech is held together and aloft by many kinds of support.

Three Questions of Speech Support

Knowing what types of speech support to use depends on the context of the speech. Asking yourself these three questions can help:

1. **What kind of speech is called for?**
   The types of support you can draw on for supporting your claims depend on the type of speech. Speaking for special occasions, for example, may call for more artful or poetic types of support — as with Gerald's speech — while speaking to inform or persuade may call for facts, statistics, and examples. Remember that using a variety of types of support will make a speech more interesting.

2. **What is the setting and mood of the speech?**
   Where, when, and why you are giving your speech determines the situation or setting that it will be delivered in. Knowing that setting will help you better discern the tone or mood of the moment and guide your selection of support materials. For example, eulogies can be both somber and humorous. Persuasive speeches about public policy may demand more serious forms of support and quantitative forms of evidence, such as statistics.

3. **Who is the audience of the speech?**
   Knowing who will make up your audience will also help you determine what kinds of support to use in a speech. Do not use overly technical evidence for an audience who may not have an in-depth understanding of the topic. Use quotes that will be interesting and easy for your audience to follow.

The different kinds of support used for speeches span from the casual (commonsense observations and personal stories) to the formal (statistics or scrupulously researched studies on technical topics). For example, celebratory speeches — the most common type of speech — require easily understood examples and stories, as well as clear and digestible facts. When preparing any speech, remember that whether formal or informal, *every* speech requires support.

Types of Speech Support at a Glance

Facts	Verifiable truths or information; often contrasted with opinions and beliefs
Statistics	Quantitative measures of the amount, size, or number of something; statistics are facts delivered in numbers
Testimony	The sharing of viewpoints, perspectives, or opinions of an individual
Examples	The illustration of a claim of fact or opinion
Stories	An account of real or imagined events or people for the purpose of illustration or entertainment

Facts

Facts refer to verifiable truths, or information that is independent of opinion. For example, such things as the height of the Empire State Building (1,453 feet, 8 9/16 inches), the winner of the 2015 NCAA Women's Division I Basketball Championship (University of Connecticut), or the Academy Award winner for Best Picture in 2011 (*The King's Speech*) are all facts—as close as we can come to agreed-upon, objective truths.

Facts are often contrasted with opinions and beliefs. Opinions are conclusions or judgments based on facts, which in speeches are regarded as "testimony." Facts are also often contrasted with "beliefs," which refer to the perception or conviction that something is true. In our culture, we tend to think about "facts" as relatively straightforward and dispassionate, while beliefs are often associated with feelings, attitudes, and values.[4] Despite these common assumptions, facts are actually a subset of beliefs.

For Ben Franklin, "in this world nothing can be said to be certain, except . . ."

As we discussed regarding audience analysis in chapter 3, beliefs are the basic building blocks of thought, and we all have them. In general, a belief is an idea that we hold to be true. Both facts and opinions are types of beliefs, but a fact is the only kind of belief that can be empirically verified. Even so, much of the time we act on our beliefs as if they were facts to simply get along in the world. When in doubt about the difference between facts, opinions, and beliefs, just remember that facts have been, or can be, verified by others. Although both types of beliefs are appropriate for speech support, facts are generally regarded as the most basic and reliable type.

facts are verifiable truths, or information that is independent of opinion.

? What are the five main types of speech support?

Statistics

According to the Pew Research Center, the most recent data on marriage shows that most Americans are not rushing into it: "The median age at first marriage was at a record high [in 2011]—about 29 for men and about 27 for women, according to census data."[5] Based on such a statistic, most new readers of this book are not married. **Statistics**, of course, refer to forms of quantitative evidence, or a kind of measurement based on numbers, like the median age for marriage. Statistics are widely used as a form of factual support in speeches because they can deliver facts speedily.

statistics refer to numerical facts or measurements about a large group or collection.

You're probably already familiar with statistics because of your math classes in high school, where you were introduced to the "average" or the "mean" (such as how your course grades are usually calculated, or how many hours you spend texting in an average week). Other common statistics include the "median" (the middle value of a grouping) and the "mode" (the most frequent number in a grouping).

> The latest census report shows that three out of four people make up 75 percent of the population.

In general, statistics are a powerful and useful form of support for speeches and can help you convey a factual observation quickly. Let's suppose you were giving an informative speech on the popular music star Adele. In order to establish her cultural significance, you might say something like, "Adele is among the most popular music artists of our time. According to the leading music industry magazine *Billboard*, Adele's album *21* was the best-selling full-length album in 2012, selling over 124,000 copies. The last album to achieve this kind of popularity was the soundtrack to the film *Titanic* back in 1998." In this example, basic sales statistics are drawn on as facts to support the claim that Adele is popular.

Statistics are an important part of our culture, our financial well-being, and our educational system.

- Civil engineers rely on statistics to design, plan, and build the places where we live and travel.
- Politicians rely on statistics—especially from polls—to make policy decisions and run for office.
- Economists and businesspersons rely on statistics to determine supply and demand.
- Educators not only teach statistics but also rely on them to assign grades and assess what students are learning.

In addition, the study of statistics is essential to numerous academic fields and professions, including accounting, engineering, health science, psychology, and sociology. Statistics can be exceptionally powerful as tools to convince listeners of your claims. As a speaker, however, you must be aware of the *fairness* and *appropriateness* of your statistics, and be careful in how you use them.

Keep in mind that people put a lot of faith in numbers—even though this faith is sometimes unwarranted.[6] The phrases "seeing is believing" and "numbers don't lie" express a naive trust in pictures

As of 2017, Adele has won 15 Grammy Awards for her music.

and numbers. Just as pictures can be altered and distorted (with tools like Photoshop, cropping, or other forms of digital manipulation), statistics can be misused and abused—and often are. For example, in 1994 the Associated Press reported on a Harvard Medical School study that concluded that angry tantrums can double the chance of heart attacks, based on the statistic that "anger was associated with 2.3 times the usual (heart attack) risk."[7] However, as MIT statistician Arnold Barnett points out, the data for the Harvard study was collected from only those who suffered heart attacks and survived. The AP story was misleading, because it's also possible that those who have angry outbursts could reduce their "overall long-term risk" for heart attacks; there's no way to know because individuals who did not suffer heart attacks were not included in the study.[8] To avoid misleading your audience—however unintentionally—you should always strive to present the proper interpretation and use of statistics.[9]

You don't need to be a statistical expert to draw on and interpret statistical information for a speech. You want to make sure, however, that your source is trustworthy and that the use of statistics is appropriate and fair. You can determine this by asking yourself two guiding questions: (1) What do the statistics measure? and (2) What or who is the source of the statistics? In most cases, answering these two simple questions will help you decide if a given statistic is trustworthy and appropriate to use in your speech. Let's discuss each question in turn.

What do the statistics measure?

When you discover a statistic to use in a speech, the source will typically identify how the number was determined, and this will tell you what the statistic is measuring. Let's return to the example of marriage: according to the Pew Research Center, 51 percent of U.S. citizens eighteen years and older were married in 2011, which is significantly less than the 72 percent reported in 1960.[10] This information was released in a report on the center's website, as well as in a press

The idea that statistics are frequently abused or misleading is not a new one. In his autobiography, the great writer and humorist Mark Twain notes that there are three kinds of lies: "Lies, damn lies, and statistics."

release sent to many news media outlets, in December 2011. In both the report and the press release, Pew researchers identify their source as coming from the survey data compiled by the 2010 U.S. census. From this we can deduce that the marriage rate actually measures, or counts, the *self-reports* of people participating in the census—that is, the number of admissions people have made on a form distributed by the U.S. government in 2010. The measure is a sum or a tally—not an average, median, or mode—of people surveyed in the previous U.S. census. Because the Pew Research Center has taken its data from a highly trusted source, widely regarded as providing accurate data (the U.S. Census Bureau), and because the number is a direct count and not extrapolated or projected, we can trust that the data is solid. Whether or not self-reports are trustworthy is another question, but the figures based on the self-report are sound.

Another example: when we argued that Adele was among the most popular music artists of our time, we drew on a statistic from *Billboard* magazine: more than 124,000 copies of her album *21* were sold in 2012. What, however, does this number actually measure? According to *Billboard*, this number is an aggregate (or combination) of many different kinds of album sales, including physical albums bought in stores and digital downloads from services such as iTunes and Amazon.com. These numbers are not actually compiled by *Billboard*, however, but by Nielsen Media Research—a company it pays to provide the statistics. Nielsen Media Research got its start in the 1950s by measuring the number of households that had television and what these audiences watched, gradually expanding its studies to measuring all types of media consumption.

According to Nielsen, album sales are determined by compiling the sales data shared by major music retailers. It's improbable that the 124,000-plus number reported by Nielsen is an exact measurement of the total number of albums sold. For example, there's no way Nielsen could know the exact number of Adele albums peddled by small mom-and-pop record stores or merchandise booths at her concerts. The number is a rough estimate used by the music industry as a guide. What the 124,000-plus actually represents is an estimate of the number of Adele albums sold from the album's release date until 2012. Even so, the number probably measures what *Billboard* says that it measures; it's a reliable ballpark figure. The Adele album sales statistic is an *estimate*, whereas the numbers relied on for marriage statistics by the Pew Research Center study is based on a *direct count*. The latter is certainly a stronger statistic than the estimated one, but both are reliable as statistics as long as they are used and reported responsibly.

Unfortunately, whether an estimate or a direct count, statistics are routinely used inappropriately and are often reported by speakers to measure something that they do not in fact measure. We are perhaps most familiar with misleading statistical support in political rhetoric.

When and for what should you use statistics in a speech? ?

For example, in its opposition to national health care reform in 2009, a conservative, nonprofit group called the Independent Women's Forum (IWF) ran a television advertisement claiming that if certain health-care legislation passed in Congress, it would establish a national health-care program similar to that of England, resulting in the breast cancer deaths of hundreds of thousands of women. "England already has government run healthcare, and their breast cancer survival rate is much lower. . . . Government control of healthcare here could have meant that 300,000 American women with breast cancer might have died," claims a speaker in the commercial. In the advertisement, the source of this figure is cited as the British medical journal *Lancet* and the American Cancer Society (ACS), a respected U.S. fund-raising and research-sponsoring organization. The ACS, however, denies that the statistic is legitimate.

The researchers at FactCheck.org, a "fact-tank" sponsored by the Annenberg Public Policy Center, report that the figure was arrived at by "applying the difference between the U.S. and England five-year survival rates in a 2008 report to the 2.5 million breast cancer survivors in the U.S., as estimated by the American Cancer Society." In other words, the idea that "300,000 . . . might have died" is based on a crude and unscientific calculation comparing 2008 breast cancer survival data from the United States and Britain; this number came from neither *Lancet* nor the ACS. "The ad implies, intentionally or not, that we did come up with that figure," said a senior director of media relations at the ACS. "In addition to the fact that the figure is not a reliable figure, it's not one that we have ever cited."[11] The 300,000 figure doesn't measure what it purports to measure; in fact, it doesn't measure *anything* real or verifiable because it is the result of faulty calculations.

Most of us, of course, are not trained statisticians and would not have recognized that the IWF commercial used statistics inappropriately. It's possible that the organization simply made a mistake interpreting the data; it's also possible, however, that it deliberately misused the data to advance a political agenda. Individuals, organizations, and companies do, in fact, manipulate statistics to advance agendas or for marketing purposes. As a speaker, you should always try to make sure that when you use statistics, the numbers actually measure what they purport to measure. If you cannot determine with certainty that a statistic is reliable based on the data available to you, there is another question you can answer to help ease your conscience.

What or who is the source of the statistics?

Many of us simply do not have the training or the resources to arrive at our own statistical information, which is why we turn to others for this data. Because we often put our trust in the expertise of others for statistical information, it is vital that the information comes from a reliable or respected source that has made some effort to control for bias.

Is Bias Always Bad or Avoidable?

Why do we stress the importance of controlling for bias instead of finding statistics that are completely unbiased? As human beings, it's difficult for us to avoid **bias**, which can be defined as a preference for something — including beliefs, ideas, and values — that benefits you or others unequally. While many think of bias as unfair, it's hard to say bias is always wrong or unethical. In fact, many scholars have come to adopt the position that one cannot avoid bias.[12] For example, many of us are biased toward our friends and family; we often interpret factual information in ways that reinforce our feelings for, and interests in, our loved ones. The important thing to know about biases is that you have them and that you should keep them in check so as not to mislead others. When using statistics (or any kind of evidence, for that matter), making sure your data both measures what you claim it does and is from a reliable source are the best ways to keep your biases in check.

A similar bias dynamic generally holds true for institutions — companies, political parties, garage bands, and campus clubs — which tend to promote beliefs, attitudes, and values that are biased toward their own continued existence. We can expect, for example, any recognized world government to issue statements about world affairs that are biased toward itself: the United States issues briefings and statements that are biased toward the United States inasmuch as North Korea or Iceland does the same. The question of bias is not whether an individual or an institution has it; it is whether or not that individual or institution distorts the truth, alters facts, or promotes misinformation. Here are some questions you can ask to identify possible bias from a speaker:

- Does the data support the ethical, political, or religious goals of a person or an organization? If so, do those goals stand to hurt or disadvantage others?
- Does the data support the financial gains of a person or an organization? Would such gains hurt or disadvantage others?
- Does the data represent what the speaker claims it represents? How do you know?
- What or who is the source of the information? Is the source trustworthy and reliable?

When using statistics we should always ask what the source has to gain by advancing or publishing the statistical data. Is the source committed to fairness and accuracy? Does the source try to minimize its own bias? Does the source stand to profit, financially or otherwise, by pushing favorable statistics? What, in other words, does a source have to gain from its statistics? For example, in the 1960s, a sugarless gum company began to advertise its product by claiming "four out of five dentists surveyed would recommend sugarless gum to their patients." For decades, various cultural critics and commentators have pressed the gum company to produce the source of this statistic; the company has consistently refused, citing the survey data as proprietary research, presumably because it is part of the company's trade secrets. Perhaps the secret is that the company asked only five dentists—all of whom worked for the gum company? We simply don't know. We do know, however, that the gum company is biased toward selling more gum—a concern less important than the verification of fact. Hence, the "four out of five dentists" statistic is dubious at best.

Visualizing statistical support

Speakers who use statistics often share them with audiences visually, either on posters or with slide software such as Keynote or Power-Point. More detailed guidelines for using visual aids can be found in chapter 11; however, it's helpful to think about how you might help your audience visualize your statistical support as you research and develop your speech. Let us return to the marriage example again, changing it up a bit: According to the Pew Research Center, 57 percent of U.S. citizens opposed gay marriage in 2001. Since that time, support for same-sex unions has grown substantially to

Would you take a piece of sugarless gum from this dentist?

Don't Cherry-Pick!

When a speaker knowingly points to a specific statistic that confirms his or her position while ignoring data that contradicts it, he or she is "cherry-picking," or guilty of what is termed "the fallacy of incomplete evidence." Because statistics require a lot of contextual information for interpretation, they lend themselves easily to biased use. For example, writing for the British tabloid the *Daily Mail*, David Rose writes, "The supposed 'consensus' on man-made global warming is facing an inconvenient challenge after the release of new temperature data showing the planet has not warmed for the past 15 years. . . . Based on readings from more than 30,000 measuring stations, the data was issued last week by the Met Office and the University of East Anglia Climatic Research Unit. It confirms the rising trend in world temperatures ended in 1997."[13] This statistical information sounds convincing, doesn't it? Yet climate expert Dr. Peter Gleick argues that this and similar claims are based on cherry-picking complex, scientific data: "All of the false claims [about global cooling] take advantage of one fundamental truth about the average temperature of our planet: it varies a little, naturally, from year to year. Some years are a bit warmer than average and some are a bit colder than average because of El Niños, La Niñas, cloud variability, volcanic activity, ocean conditions, and just the natural pulsing of our planetary systems. When you filter these out, the human-caused warming signal is clear. But natural variability makes it possible for scurrilous deceivers to do a classic 'no-no' in science: to cherry-pick data to support their claims."[14]

55 percent in both 2015 and 2016, with a significantly lower opposition of 39 percent in 2015 and 37 percent in 2016. Such statistics are impressive when spoken but perhaps a little difficult for an audience to visualize in their heads. A chart such as the one developed by the Pew Research Center (see below) helps us see the dramatic shift in attitudes toward gay marriage at a glance, visually depicting the reversal around the year 2011.[15]

If you are using statistics to support your speech, however, thinking about how you can visually depict them is a good way to go: it's quicker and helps make the abstraction of numbers more concrete.

Testimony

We've noted that beliefs are the bedrock of all thinking. Beliefs concern things that we perceive to be true, right, or factual (they may or may not be actually true, right, or factual). We've also discussed how most beliefs reflect a bias of some sort. Now, when a belief—true or untrue, right or wrong, factual or false—also includes a judgment about something, it tends to be described as an opinion. Speech support based on opinion is more complicated than the use of statistics because someone's judgment or considered viewpoint is central.

opinions are judgments that may or may not depend on facts or knowledge.

An **opinion** is a considered or thought-out conclusion about something, alternatively termed a *stance, viewpoint, or perspective.* We tend to think about opinions as thoughtful decisions about something in the absence of certainty. Opinions are views that someone adopts that can

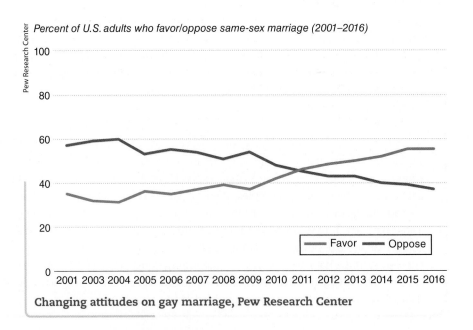

Changing attitudes on gay marriage, Pew Research Center

be based on facts or simply educated guesses, and they will vary in degree of conviction. Opinions can be valued forms of speech support when the person holding or sharing them is trusted or considered an expert.

In the context of public speaking, opinions often take the form of testimony. While the sharing of beliefs and facts can be included in testimony, more often than not testimony is thought of as the sharing of thoughtful opinions based on one's experience, knowledge, or expertise. **Testimony** typically refers to the sharing of an individual's viewpoints, perspectives, or opinions, and is used as a form of support or evidence. There are four basic types of testimony: expert testimony, lay testimony, personal experience, and declarations of faith.

testimony refers to the sharing of an individual's viewpoints, perspectives, or opinions.

Types of testimony

Thinking about magazine ads or television commercials can help you quickly summarize the types of testimony that are often used for speech support: when a medical expert touts a product, it's expert testimony; when a celebrity describes his or her approval of a product, it's lay testimony; when common folks testify to their personal experience of the effectiveness of a product, it's personal experience (and *also* lay testimony; the two often overlap); and when an individual confesses spiritual inspiration or the glories of a deity, it's a declaration of faith.

Expert Testimony.   An expert is the term we use for a person who claims to be, or is widely acknowledged as, an authority in a particular profession or practice. We often see experts in the mass media, especially on television news programs: from professors of economics to legal experts and politically savvy campaign advisers, our mediated culture is awash with experts. As a speaker, you tacitly present yourself as an expert on the topic you are discussing. And you will often need to cite the viewpoints and beliefs of other experts as support for your claims (unless you are already a respected authority on the topic, but let's face it: most of us are not!).

Citing the beliefs and informed opinions of experts can lend a speech you deliver added credibility, especially if you are speaking on a topic that extends beyond basic facts or veers into matters open to dispute. If you want to inform or persuade an audience, making a verbal nod to an expert communicates to the audience that your views are more widely shared by authorities in the area of your topic; in effect, by citing an expert, you're saying, "Don't just take my word for it! Here's an expert who agrees." For example, suppose you were giving your speech about the popular music artist Adele, whom you have claimed is among the most popular artists of our time. To bolster your claim, you could cite a respected

? **When is an expert testimony appropriate?**

music critic who has written or spoken about Adele's popularity: "According to the *New Yorker*'s respected music critic, Sasha Frere-Jones, Adele's album *21* is an 'impeccably sung collection of unperturbing soul.' Frere-Jones humorously muses that Adele's popularity will not waver and that her 'career is likely to be long' because 'she is selling to the demographic that decides American elections: middle-aged moms who don't know how to pirate music and will drive to Starbucks when they need to buy it.' "[16]

Lay Testimony.   In addition to sharing the beliefs and opinions of experts, sometimes a discussion of the experience of everyday folks is also useful support. For example, at a fund-raising event for a foundation dedicated to providing support for cancer victims, you might share the experiences of folks battling with cancer. The experiences of others are used when a speech calls for common, everyday experiences or the unique perspectives of nonexperts, including celebrities.

Personal Experience.   Drawing on expert and lay testimony for speech support is not the whole story, however, because sometimes one's personal experience is good evidence, too. Of course, the things that have happened to you are *facts*; however, when we draw on personal experience, we are typically sharing our beliefs based on those experiences. When toasting the happy couple at a wedding reception, for example, one draws on his or her own experiences with the couple to celebrate their union. At funerals and wakes, one often shares his or her experiences with the deceased. When informing an audience about how to make smoothies at home, a speaker would be expected to share her personal experiences doing so.

The basic guidelines for using personal experience as speech support depend on the particular speaking situation, but in general, one draws on personal experience only very sparingly. Use personal experience as evidence only if it is relevant to your main claims, if it helps establish a sense of rapport with the audience, or if you have expertise and personal knowledge of the subject matter discussed. Personal experience tends to be used as speech support in three ways: (1) when the occasion or speech genre calls for it, especially celebratory speeches (weddings, funerals, award banquets, and so on); (2) when you are speaking as an expert, with special, firsthand knowledge of the topic or event; or (3) when mentioning a personal connection to a speech topic that will help create a sense of interest among the audience, such as in a conclusion or an introduction.

Examples

examples are descriptive representations used to illustrate claims.

In addition to facts, statistics, and testimony, a speech is often supported with examples. Simply put, an **example** is the illustration of a claim.

examining

testimony

Rolls Press/Popperfoto/Contributor/Getty Images

In general, "faith" refers to a strong conviction in a belief without certain knowledge. We can have faith in a person we hold up as a role model, faith that the sun will rise tomorrow, or faith that our beat-up Volkswagen will make it to the next town. When speaking about declarations of faith as a form of speech support, however, faith takes on an *inspirational* or even a spiritual connotation. And frequently we are moved by the spiritual faith of others.

In civic culture, one of the most famous uses of a declaration of faith was by Martin Luther King Jr. in his much studied and quoted "I Have a Dream" speech. The "dream" (or faith) that King shares with his immediate audience on the steps of the Lincoln Memorial in 1963 still has the power to inspire us today. Consider how King ends his speech:

> From every mountainside, let freedom ring. And when this happens, when we allow freedom ring, when we let it ring from every village and every hamlet, from every state and every city, we will be able to speed up that day when *all* of God's children, black men and white men, Jews and Gentiles, Protestants and Catholics, will be able to join hands and sing in the words of the old Negro spiritual: *Free at last! Free at last! Thank God Almighty, we are free at last!*

King was a Baptist minister of the Christian faith; throughout his speech to end racial inequality, he invokes his and his audience's faith in God. Because King does not evoke the specific tenets of his religious faith, the speech has the power to inspire all who listen to it. Whether or not one believes in divine intervention, King's declaration of faith in his speech — faith in God and in the human spirit — helped change the world.

LaunchPad
macmillan learning

The Center for Disease Control created an anti-smoking campaign called "Tips from Former Smokers." The organization uses a variety of speech supports in the videos created to discourage adults from smoking. To get a sense of how testimony (and other forms of speech support) can be used in public health campaigns, visit LaunchPad at **launchpadworks.com** and link to the two videos created by the Center for Disease Control.

Then see if you can answer the following questions:

- What kind of testimony is featured by each public service announcement?
- Is the testimony real or acted? Does this make a difference in the impact of each message?
- Can you imagine an antismoking advertisement that relied on a declaration of faith? What would this advertisement look like? Whom would it feature?

Examples are descriptive representations that speakers can use to make what they mean to say clearer. In the roughly two thousand years that human beings have studied the art of oratory, Aristotle's idea that public speaking fundamentally concerns examples has rarely been disputed. The ancient thinker originally held that public speaking concerned only two things: informal logic (which we'll discuss in depth in chapter 15) and the use of examples.[17] The challenge of using examples—and why we sometimes might not take them as seriously as we should—is that they are so familiar to us that we often simply assume their use as a fact of life.

For example, let's say Andrea is giving a speech about her love for rescue dogs at a fund-raiser for an animal shelter: "All of us here today know that rescues are not for everyone. Rescue dogs can be challenging to train, but that's why so many of us fall in love with them," says Andrea. "For example, let me tell you about how I met my dog Zoë. I was driving home in my neighborhood when I spied a bull terrier snooping in someone's trash, obviously looking for food. I stopped to pick her up, thinking I would feed her and take her to the shelter—you know, because I already had two rescue dogs. As soon as I opened my car door, Zoë bounded into the passenger's seat and promptly barfed into my very expensive Burberry purse. [Laughter] At that point, I knew it was meant to be: I took her in, and we have been best friends ever since." In this example of an example, Andrea created a vivid image of her dog's quirky character as an example of the special bond people forge with their rescued pets.

The primary function of an example is to create a mental image or picture in the minds of audiences. Aristotle considered the example to be a major part of public speaking because he believed—as many do today—that people cannot think without creating mental pictures.[18] Of course, in Aristotle's time they didn't know about those who cannot create mental pictures, a rare condition termed "aphantasia." For most people, however, when we listen to someone we often create mental images to help us grasp the meaning of what he or she is saying. Because we tend to think in illustrations of one kind or another, using examples when we speak is often second nature.

Whether short and anecdotal (as Andrea's example) or longer, examples typically refer to factual events or concrete things. A *hypothetical example* is the description of an imaginary scenario. Hypothetical examples paint a picture of a scenario or an event that invites listeners to mentally participate in a speech. "Imagine you are marooned on a desert island" is the beginning of a clichéd example of a hypothetical (and one you should probably avoid). More artfully, Martin Luther King Jr.'s "I Have a Dream" speech provides us with a number of hypotheticals, such as the one he closes the speech with: King says he looks forward to "that day when *all* of God's children, black men and white men, Jews and Gentiles,

What are the reasons for adding supporting material to speeches? ❓

Protestants and Catholics, will be able to join hands and sing in the words of the old Negro spiritual: *Free at last! Free at last! Thank God Almighty, we are free at last!*" Here King creates the vision of a diverse group of people holding hands and singing together, a powerful image to help illustrate his larger point: that we are all human beings entitled to equality regardless of our respective differences.

Stories or Narratives

Strictly speaking, all stories—even fictional ones—are examples. **Stories** are basically extended examples with a familiar pattern: they have a beginning, a middle, and an end. The stories we tell can be personal, such as when we are a central character, or they can be impersonal, such as when they describe the experience of someone we have learned about. Stories can be short, such as an anecdote, or they can be much longer, such as a narrative of one's life.

stories are extended examples that follow a familiar pattern that includes a beginning, a middle, and an end.

Stories hold a potent appeal for most people, including your audience. The philosopher Alasdair MacIntyre has argued that stories are powerful because they comprise the basis of how we see ourselves and our shared lives together. Stories give meaning to the sequence of events in our lives. A human being is, in his or her "actions and practice . . . essentially a story-telling animal," says MacIntyre.[19] We are all storytellers because, in our attempt to make our lives meaningful and coherent, we organize our experiences into a chronology with a beginning, a middle, and an end—and hopefully an end that doesn't come too soon! And because each of us embodies a collection of the stories we tell ourselves, these stories are compelling to read and to hear.

Consider the speech craft of one of the most gifted speakers of the twentieth century, the late U.S. president Ronald Reagan. Reagan famously used stories as support for his speeches, and this skill at storytelling is frequently mentioned as one of his greatest talents.[20] For example, consider his remarks from a Republican Party fund-raiser in Jackson, Mississippi, in 1983. Until the later part of the twentieth century, the southern United States had been solidly democratic for many years. Reagan, a Republican, makes light of this history:

> But isn't it wonderful to see so many Republicans in Mississippi? [Applause] Times have changed and for the better. Former Congressman Prentiss

Janette Pellegrini/Stringer/Getty Images

"Stories matter. Many stories matter. Stories have been used to dispossess and malign, but stories can also be used to empower and to humanize. Stories can break the dignity of a people, but stories can also repair that broken dignity."—Chimamanda Ngozi Adichie[21]

Walker, who I understand is here today, tells a story about his first campaign. He dropped in on a farm and introduced himself as a Republican candidate. And as he tells it, the farmer's eyes lit up, and then he said, "Wait till I get my wife. We've never seen a Republican before." [Laughter] And a few minutes later he was back with his wife, and they asked Prentiss if he wouldn't give them a speech. Well, he looked around for kind of a podium, something to stand on, and then the only thing available was a pile of that stuff that the late Mrs. Truman said it had taken her 35 years to get Harry to call "fertilizer." [Laughter] So, he stepped up on that and made his speech. And apparently he won them over. And they told him it was the first time they'd ever heard a Republican. And he says, "That's okay. That's the first time I've ever given a speech from a Democratic platform." [Laughter]

Here, Reagan opens his speech by repeating a story that someone told him. As his speech continues, Reagan then reveals the point of telling the story: "Seriously, though, we have to understand the importance of reaching out to Democrats with whom we have fundamental agreement." His opening story is thick with political humor, creating a sense of goodwill among his audience. Once Reagan has used the story to create that feeling, he can then deliver the more serious message: that he believes Republicans should be cooperating more with Democrats. The Reagan example teaches us that because we are born storytellers—and story listeners—a story can often unite an audience despite tensions or disagreements.

Orally Referencing Your Sources

When you read a news article or research in a scholarly journal, sources are often directly referenced. Academic papers—including your written speech materials—frequently have a bibliography or list of works cited that outlines all the sources consulted for support. When you are speaking to your audience, however, they will not have a bibliography at their disposal, so you'll have to refer to your important sources orally. There is no right or wrong way to refer to sources in a speech, and how you do so depends on the type of speech you are giving and the context for it. In general, your goals when orally citing sources are similar to those for a written version; the sources will just appear in a more abbreviated manner. Give your listeners enough information to track your source if they want to, and also to impart a sense of your sources' credibility. When orally citing sources, consider including the following information:

- Author (with credentials if appropriate)
- Type of source (book, article, interview, speech)
- Title or description of source
- Date of source

Depending on the speech situation, you may not need to include all of the source information.

To get a real-world sense of how people generally cite sources orally, listen to how a radio journalist reports a news story. You'll notice that they typically follow the preceding guidelines when they reference facts or testimony, beginning with the author and the source type or source title—a newspaper, a book, a study published in this or that medical journal. If a publication, statistics, or other numerically based evidence is referenced, the journalist will often give the date of the information.

For example, on National Public Radio's *All Things Considered* program on July 29, 2015, a reporter led a story on debt this way: "At some point most of us will face this four letter word: 'debt.' A new study out today by the Pew Charitable Trusts says that 80 percent of Americans carry some form of debt, from student loans to credit card balances." In one short sentence, the reporter alerts the listener to a statistic, its source (the Pew Charitable Trusts), and the date of the information (a "study out today," which was July 29, 2015). Television reporters do not generally cite their sources orally because that information is often given to the viewer in a graphic (an option that is not available to most public speakers). Although your instructor will give you guidelines on how to orally cite your sources during a speech, radio news reports—not television or Internet videos—will provide you with the best concrete examples of how sources are orally cited in our culture today.

Contextual Reasoning

> **You will learn to**
> **DEFINE** contextual reasoning.

You now have a sense of the five major categories of supporting material: facts, statistics, testimony, examples, and stories. But you may be wondering how you can put these materials to best use in supporting your speech. The answer is **contextual reasoning**, which is just what it sounds like: *reasoning* your selection of supporting materials, tailored to the *context* in which you're speaking. Contextual reasoning is thinking about what kinds of support you can use to bolster your major claims in respect to the speech situation, including the occasion, the genre of speaking, the setting, and the mood of the event.

contextual reasoning concerns thinking about the kinds of support you can use for a speech given its contextual demands and constraints.

The kind of reasoning that most people do in public speaking is often said to depend on what philosopher Douglas Walton refers to as "informal logic"—a term for the rules of thinking that you and I simply call "common sense."[22] We tend to think about the rules of thinking in

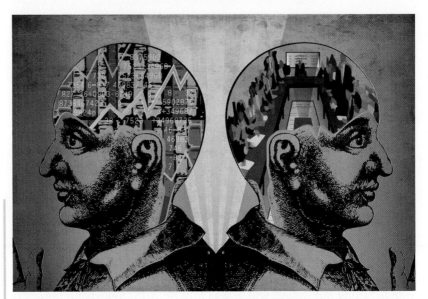

Determining which types of support are appropriate for a given speech depends on the larger context of the speech's delivery.

respect to the logical order of arguments, whether the claims we make are supported by evidence, whether we contradict ourselves, and so on. But judging when it is appropriate to use a statistic or a story is also a form of reasoning. Contextual judgments do not simply concern how you order your main points or avoid contradictions; it is also a matter of choosing support that is appropriate for the occasion. We will examine the logical reasoning *internal* to a speech in more depth in chapter 15. Here, however, it is important to underscore that when you select speech materials based on the *context* of a speech, you are also engaging in a form of reasoning that is as much about figuring out the mood and feeling of a speaking situation as it is about the soundness of what is to be said.[23]

Why is contextual reasoning important? ❓

Because the idea of "context" can include everything from audience expectations to the physical setting of a speech, it is difficult to specify any strict guidelines that will cover all speaking situations. What we can say is this: what may seem like weak support in one context can be strong support in another. A touching personal story would be inappropriate for a policy report in a boardroom but just right in an informal speech honoring a friend at a family gathering. Only by analyzing context—thinking about it in advance, contemplating the type of speech that is called for, and considering the types of people that will be there—can you figure out how to best support a speech. Because there is no correct or incorrect way to reason contextually, we must consider what is appropriate speech support on a case-by-case basis. Consider, for example, these scenarios:

1. **A Persuasive Speech at a Political Fund-Raiser:** You are a political candidate running for a seat in city government and will be giving a speech detailing your platform at a community-center building. The room seats seventy-five people, and you expect about fifty attendees. Your speech goal is to raise money for your campaign by detailing your projects (e.g., building a new animal shelter). Appropriate speech support might include personal anecdotes and stories about who you are to create a feeling of goodwill and familiarity with the audience. The use of facts and statistics (e.g., about the need for a new animal shelter) are also appropriate, as they are common in political speeches.

2. **An Informative Speech during a Cooking Class:** You are a seasoned chef and routinely offer cooking classes. Your class tonight takes place in a cooking kitchen at the local culinary institute. The class will have a total of twelve adults and will focus on making sushi. Appropriate support for your opening speech would include factual information about the history of sushi and the different ways of preparing it, visual examples of sushi you have prepared in advance, and your expert testimony about tips and tricks for making sushi quickly and safely.

3. **An Online Informative-Persuasive Speech:** You recently saw director Lee Hirsch's documentary *Bully* (2011), which chronicles the lives of a number of young people who suffered bullying in secondary schools. After watching the film, you came to realize that you bullied others when you were younger. You were so moved by the film that you want to create a YouTube video that informs others about bullying behaviors that may not seem like bullying but are and that persuades others not to bully. Because online speeches of this sort are typically intimate, appropriate support for your speech might include stories about seeing the film *Bully*, memories of your personal experiences, statistics about the prevalence of bullying, and accounts of its consequences (see chapter 18 for more guidelines for online presentations).

4. **Speech of Introduction at a Sorority Meeting:** You are a sister in your campus chapter of the Alpha Pi Omega Sorority, the oldest Native American sorority in the country. Your friend happens to be the grand president of the national organization, and she is visiting your campus house. Your job is to introduce her as the keynote speaker at your annual chapter banquet. Appropriate support for your speech of introduction might include factual information about your friend's biography, statistical information about the sorority's membership, examples of the kind of philanthropy work

your chapter has done under her leadership, and even personal stories or anecdotes about the kindness and charity work of the grand president.

In each of these scenarios, the occasion, audience, and kind of speech you are giving—not to mention the mood—help guide what types of speech support you use. If you have a specific scenario in mind, you can also quickly determine what would be inappropriate support, too: at the political fund-raiser, overly technical statistics and data would not be appropriate for a general audience coming to hear your policy proposals. At the sorority banquet, funny yet potentially embarrassing personal anecdotes about the guest of honor may not be the best idea (save that for a more informal gathering). Ultimately, the point of contextual reasoning is to keep in mind that the process of selecting speech support is not simply a matter of cold, rational logic. It depends on the physical setting of the speech, the kind of speech one is delivering, and the people who are hearing it. Contextual reasoning is as much about *feeling* as it is thinking. The remainder of this book is designed to help you develop and hone your skills of contextual reasoning.

In this chapter, we have examined the five basic types of speech support you have at your disposal when developing a speech. We also took a closer look at the appropriate use of factual and statistical data, being careful to note that with statistics, in particular, you need to make sure that they measure what you claim they measure and that they are taken from a reliable source or trustworthy expert. We rounded out our tour of speech support by stressing how important the context is for determining what kinds of support are appropriate. Having determined what kinds of support you want to use, the challenge then becomes how to organize it. It is to that topic that we will turn in the next chapter.

Neal Hamberg

Supporting Materials

Speech support refers to the material that a speaker selects to back up his or her claims. Choosing the appropriate kind of support depends on the speech situation, especially the audience and the setting of the speech.

Types of Speech Support

Facts, statistics, testimony, examples, and stories are the five most common types of speech support.

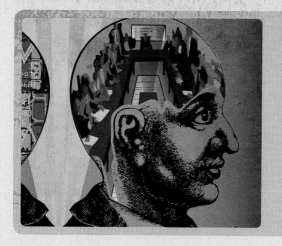

Contextual Reasoning

Contextual reasoning refers to how you select the support for your speech in respect to the setting of your speech, including the occasion, the genre of speaking, and the mood of the event.

CHAPTER 6

 **LaunchPad**
macmillan learning

LaunchPad for *Speech Craft* includes a curated collection of speech videos and encourages self-assessment through adaptive quizzing. Go to **launchpadworks.com** to get access to:

 LearningCurve adaptive quizzes

 Video clips to help you improve your speeches

ACTIVITIES

Supporting a Toast!

Imagine you are asked to give a ten-minute speech at a retirement dinner for an aunt who worked in the dairy industry for thirty years. The audience consists of members of your family, as well as your aunt's colleagues.

What will you say? After identifying your main purpose and writing a thesis statement, list the kinds of speech support that would be appropriate for your speech.

Analyzing a Speech by Ronald Reagan

Examine Ronald Reagan's "Remarks at a Republican Fundraising Dinner." After identifying the main purposes of the speech and Reagan's thesis statement, list the types of support he employs. To find this speech, go to reaganlibrary.gov, then go to the Research tab and select Speeches. The speech was given on May 12, 1983.

KEY TERMS

 Videos in LaunchPad describe many of these terms. Go to launchpadworks.com.

- **supporting material** 111
- **facts** 113
- **statistics** 113
  bias 118
- **opinion** 120

- **testimony** 121
- **examples** 122
- **stories** 125
  contextual reasoning 127

ORGANIZING
AND OUTLINING YOUR SPEECH

WATER IS LIFE!

SENECA NATION STANDS WITH STANDING ROCK

NCAI STANDS WITH STANDING ROCK

NCAI STANDS WITH STANDING ROCK

NO DAKOTA ACCESS PIPELINE

CHAPTER 7

Participating in a social demonstration about an issue that is important to you is exciting and emotional: people carry signs and passionately chant slogans; engaged speakers inspire the audience and capture the attention of the mass media; and you might walk through the streets with dozens or even hundreds of like-minded citizens, strengthening your ties to fellow marchers and helping to raise awareness about your issue to the wider community.

Creating a structured and safe environment for demonstration participants to chant, speak, and march takes a lot of work. As with any public gathering in which a large audience is assembled, a lot of planning goes into organizing a demonstration: someone or a group must select a date and pick a location, permits to assemble must be filed with the local authorities, speakers must be chosen, and so on. After that, the event must be advertised. Someone might create an announcement or event page on social media, and texts and phone calls will inevitably be made.

Even during the event itself, planners might use their smartphones to communicate directions to others quickly about when it is time for a different person to speak, when to chant, and so on. Organizing for social or political demonstration requires pulling together many different elements for the event to be a success.

I've opened this chapter on organizing your speech with reference to demonstrations because an analogy converges over the word "organizing" itself. Fortunately for you, organizing a speech is less complicated and time consuming than organizing a social demonstration. As a speaker you must take on the role of a leader who brings the different elements of a speech together. You have already determined your topic, narrowed your purpose, and researched your subject. You have amassed your evidence, or support, and now you have a collection of papers and files and notes. How do you bring this stuff together into something that will be coherent to an audience? To start, you need to decide on your main points and then make decisions about how to structure them. In this chapter, we will discuss these steps in two parts. First, we'll examine the different ways you can organize your speech materials so that your speech will be memorable for an audience. Second, we'll discuss the primary tool used by speakers to structure speeches for delivery: the outline.

Organizing Your Speech

You will learn to

EXPLAIN how human memory affects speech organization.

LIST the six basic organizational patterns for speeches.

EXPLAIN how speech organizational patterns differ.

In the real world, there are many ways to go about organizing a presentation—or anything else, for that matter, like a closet or a tackle box. When speaking in public, however, there are two things to keep in mind: (1) our individual ways of organizing things, from weekly schedules to books on a shelf, may be different from the way others organize those things, and (2) speeches are *oral*, which means the audience has to remember the main points of the speech primarily by *listening*. The trick, of course, is to balance your own ways of organizing things with the organizing expectations of the audience, especially in respect to the speaking situation, the genre of your speech, and so on. To this end, making sure that you have identified (more or less) three main points, stressed a clarity of purpose, and selected an appropriate organizational pattern will help.

Michael Courtney/Shutterstock

It's easier to hook an audience with a clearly organized speech.

Memory: Three Is a Magic Number

Perhaps the most important thing to consider when organizing speech materials is that most people have a limited ability to remember *without* taking notes. Consequently, when organizing your speech, you want to do so in a way that is manageable to you as a speaker and memorable to a listening audience. Understanding the difference between short-term and long-term memory is helpful for organizing a speech because it helps you discern how much information is too much information.

For centuries, thinkers have described our short-term memories as something that is "written" upon by our senses, like a kind of note pad. Although short-term memory cannot hold a lot of information, it is readily accessible to you in the moment.[1] As a speaker, you are primarily engaging an audience's short-term memory. Unless we have something outside our minds to inscribe a memory onto or into (like a piece of paper, sticky notes, or a smartphone), much of our "note

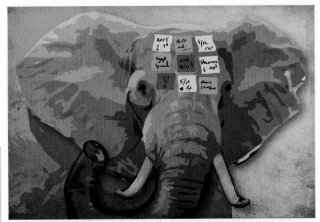

Even elephants will struggle to remember too many speech points.

pad" memory is easily "erased" or written over. By contrast, long-term memory is often described as a kind of archive, or a series of books on a shelf. As a speaker, you should not expect an audience to remember your speech in its entirety over the long term; what you can hope for is that your audience will remember the mood or tone of your message (the feeling part) and a number of your main points. When thinking about how best to communicate a memorable speech, it is instructive to think about what you remember from the last class lecture you attended. Without looking at your notes, what do you recall your instructor saying?

What can you reasonably expect an audience to remember from your speech? How many points should you make? Memory scholars have researched these and related questions for decades. You may have heard the common view that people, on average, can remember *seven* things after seeing or hearing them. This common belief is based on a psychological study by George A. Miller in the 1950s, which suggested that seven was the "magical number" of human memory, "plus or minus two."[2] As Jean-Luc Doumont has explained, however, the Miller study does not mean that people can remember five, seven, or nine items without *organization*. Doumont argues that most people can remember up to nine things if those things are organized into "chunks"; thus, whether someone is asked to remember five or ten items, he or she does so in groupings of *three*, much like a phone number. For Doumont, the more reliable "magic number" for short-term memory is actually *three*, not seven![3]

Your speech instructor will recommend that you use one of the many organizational patterns discussed in this chapter, all of which limit the number of *main points* in your speech based on your speech's purpose. You may have two main points, or four or five, but in general, most organizational patterns seem to aim for three main points. Although every speaking situation demands different approaches, remember that in most speaking situations, *three is the magic number*. Two is terrific, and four is fabulous, but if you can manage it, narrowing your main points to three—or into clusters of three—will serve you well as a public speaker.

Because speeches are *oral*, we have to make them memorable

↓

In order to make them *memorable*, we need to understand how memory works

↓

To describe *memory*, we learn about short-term and long-term memory

↓

Organizing your speech will help listeners *remember* your message

The Speech Overview: On Purposes and Points

Whether owing to the limits of our memories or simply to cultural convention, the norms of writing and speaking are woven around a three-part sequence: beginning, middle, and end. For example, essays typically have an *introduction*, a *body*, and a *conclusion*—and the *body* is usually written first. Before you craft the beginning and end of your speech, try to figure out what the main points of the speech are going to be. Learning to develop your speech in parts, beginning with the body and then moving on to your introduction and conclusion, can help you in just about every future public speaking situation you encounter.

To figure out the main points of your speech, you must first determine the speech purpose and the thesis statement (see chapter 4, "Choosing a Speech Topic and Purpose"). Start by listing your purpose and thesis statement. Remember, the speech purpose refers to the primary goal the speech is trying to accomplish, which is typically to celebrate the community, to inform the audience, or to persuade the audience. The thesis statement sums up the topic and purpose of your speech for a particular audience, and is what you will typically say word for word. Once you have listed the purpose and thesis, you can begin to examine the material you have collected to support your speech and figure out the best way to organize it.

To get a better sense of what a speech overview looks like, let's examine a speech from

The average person can remember seven digits in short-term memory, but those digits must be encoded in "chunks," which is why early telephone pioneers assigned phone numbers into bits of three and four. The eighties pop band Tommy Tutone immortalized this observation in its unforgettable hit, "867-5309."

? Why should a speech generally include three main points? How does this number relate to memory?

Speech Overview

- **Speech Purpose:** what the speech is to accomplish
- **Thesis Statement:** what you actually say to the audience about your topic and purpose
- **Main Points:** the three to five main points that support your thesis

Kevin Costner and Whitney Houston became friends on the film set of *The Bodyguard* (1992).

popular culture. In 2012, actor Kevin Costner was asked to speak at the funeral of his friend Whitney Houston, a singer who died suddenly and unexpectedly of an accidental drug overdose. Although we don't know how Costner actually prepared his eulogy for Houston, we might imagine he started by listing his purpose and thesis:

Speech Purpose: To celebrate the life of Whitney Houston and to help friends and loved ones mourn her death

Thesis Statement: "Whitney returns home today to the place where it all began, and I urge us all, inside and outside, across the nation and around the world to dry our tears, suspend our sorrow—and perhaps our anger—just long enough, just long enough to remember the sweet miracle of Whitney."

Note that Costner did not state his purpose directly in his thesis statement, "I am here to celebrate Whitney and to help you mourn." Instead, Costner announced his purpose in the beauty of metaphor, acknowledging that her death is a return to heaven ("the place where it all began"), the need to bring together the community ("urge us all . . . to dry our tears"), and the goal of celebrating her life ("remember the sweet miracle").

How might Mr. Costner have supported this well-crafted thesis statement? The answers that he developed to this question became his main speech points. Notably, Costner kept his main points to a minimum—only three. Each of Costner's main points conforms to the expectations that audiences typically have about eulogies: to honor the deceased, to assert that the dead continue to live, and to bring the community together in memory (see chapter 13 for more on the eulogy genre).

Here are Costner's main speech points:

1. A shared love of the Baptist church bonds the community that has assembled to remember Houston's life.
2. Houston's death is connected to her worries about not being good enough, a worry we can all relate to.
3. Even though she didn't always know it, Houston was amazing and set the standard for beauty and talent.

Once Costner figured out what his three main points were to be, he could then begin to think about his supporting materials. Because the purpose of a eulogy is most often to bring a community together by celebrating the life of someone who has died, hard facts, statistics, and other more formal kinds of speech support are unnecessary. Contextual reasoning suggests that eulogies should be personal, as they often take place in intimate settings, like a church, a civic space, a funeral parlor, or someone's home. Although, strictly speaking, eulogies do not always concern the deceased (they can be delivered for the living, too), most of us think about eulogies as consisting of stories from personal experience with the departed—and this is precisely the kind of speech support Costner used to make his main points. For each of Costner's main points, he drew on personal experiences with Houston, particularly in the making of their 1992 film, *The Bodyguard*.

Patterning Your Main Points

Once you have determined your speech overview, what your main points will be, and how you intend to support them, you then need to think about the order of your main points. That order will often depend on your topic, your purpose, and your audience.

In most parts of our lives, the most common speech pattern is either spatial or chronological; this is because we tend to order our experience of the world in space and time. When we talk to one another, we tend to describe the concerns and events of our lives in ways that suggest moving across a place, from the past and toward a future. Because of their fundamental rooting in the human ordering of experience, then, spatial and chronological patterning are often powerful aids to an audience's memory. In general, organizational patterns for speeches reduce to six basic kinds: spatial, temporal, topical, problem-solution, cause and effect, and rambling. Let's briefly examine each kind of pattern.

Spatial

The most primary of our sense-making constructs is *space*, which our minds impose on the world so that we can move about within it. When you organize the main points of your speech this way, you are attempting to help your audience visualize moving through a place (e.g., a building) or over an object (e.g., up or down the parts of a tree). This organizational pattern is especially useful for speech topics that concern geography in some way, such as when you are describing the migration of a people across the globe, the length of the Appalachian Trail, or landscape design.

"We make sense of the world by imposing the constructs of space and time onto what we perceive."—Immanuel Kant

Because navigating space in the world is central to human activity, spatial organization is closely related to memory.[4] The ancient orator Cicero, for example, recommended thinking about a speech as moving through a building or house: the entrance is the introduction, the formal sitting room is the body of the speech, and so on. Visualizing the speech as moving through a "memory palace" helps the speaker remember different parts of the speech.[5] Spatial organization also has the added bonus of helping the audience remember the order of your main points.

> Because navigating space in the world is central to human activity, spatial organization is closely related to memory.

The spatial organizational pattern is most commonly used by speakers when describing a physical place or space. For example, an architect might deliver a speech about a proposed building design in which each part of the speech describes what a visitor would see on each floor (on the first floor would be a lobby with marble floors, on the second floor would be meeting spaces, on the third floor would be planned offices, and so on). A speaker could describe how airports are designed by "walking" the audience through each area and its purpose: the check-in, baggage check, and security areas are located in the front; the terminal gates next; and so on.

The spatial organizational pattern is not limited to things that we actually think about as "space," however, because it fundamentally concerns inspiring audiences to visualize moving through or over an external place, thing, or concept. For example, Sigmund Freud's model of the human psyche has three parts: the conscious, the preconscious, and the unconscious.

When introducing Freud's model, speakers sometimes ask audiences to visualize the psyche as an iceberg, with the conscious residing just above water, the preconscious residing just below the water's surface, and the consciousness located underwater. When describing the model, speakers often organize their three parts by moving "up" or "down" the iceberg: "Consciousness, the part of the psyche that we are aware of, is above water. . . . Now, to the second part of the psyche, the preconscious. This part of the mind is just below the water." In short, the spatial organizational pattern is most often used for topics involving physical places or objects; however, it can also be used to help audiences visualize concepts or ideas.

Temporal

Organizing a speech *temporally*, or in a time sequence that the audience anticipates, is as powerful as spatial organization because humans also use time to make

The psyche visualized as an iceberg is an example of spatial organization.

sense of the world. A temporal organization pattern can move *back* in time, but most of the time—pun intended—people think in *chronological* order: the arrangement of a series of events in the order in which they occurred. The most straightforward organizations for time-related topics are twofold: (1) **historical arrangement,** which refers to how a given object or event occurred in documented, historical fact; and (2) **narrative arrangement,** which sequences a speech like a story, moving from the beginning to the end. A historical arrangement is also a narrative arrangement, but you can have a narrative arrangement without a historical one. Whether you pattern a speech in specific, historical dates and events, or simply as a story that moves across time, you are drawing on your audience's inner sense of progression and their anticipation of an end. Indeed, if we could reduce the power of temporal patterning to one phrase, it would be *imparting the sense of an ending*. Speeches that recount the history of an event, detail the biography of a person, or argue for a course of future action almost always draw on a type of temporal pattern.

historical arrangement refers to how a given object or event occurred in documented fact.

narrative arrangement sequences a speech like a story, moving from the beginning to the end.

Topical

When you pattern a speech topically, you present your main points in respect to a series of topics, characteristics, parts, or types. With this organizational pattern, the order of your main points is less important than with spatial or temporal patterns. The challenge of arranging a speech topically is figuring out how to transition from one main point to the next. For example, let us imagine your family is meeting to discuss where to have the next reunion. You want to have it in your apartment complex's clubhouse, but you know others will be arguing for having the reunion at a public park or a resort. At such a meeting you might create a short speech that has three main points: (1) it's free to have the reunion at your complex's clubhouse because you live there; (2) it's indoors, so weather is not an issue; and (3) the place is centrally located and easy for everyone to get to. Your three main points concern economics, weather, and location. What actually determines the order of your main points is up to you, as you could just as easily discuss the weather first, then the location, and finally the economics. Perhaps you know that some of your family members are on a tight budget, so you might want to lead off with the economic point. Or it may be that April is rainy in your part of the world, so you might lead off with the weather point. In a topical speech pattern, you arrange your main points in the way that seems best for the speaking situation.

Problem-solution

The problem-solution pattern of organization is powerful because it is so pervasive in popular culture. One of the major reasons we speak publicly is in response to "problems"; therefore, this pattern of speechmaking is one of the primary patterns speakers use to persuade. Policy makers, business professionals, and teachers—just about every kind of speaker you can think of—use the problem-solution organizational pattern to convince audiences to do or think things they wouldn't otherwise do or think. You are probably most familiar with the problem-solution pattern in online and television advertisements that attempt to encourage you to buy a product.

Typically, a problem-solution pattern (1) names or describes the nature or character of a problem, (2) outlines or describes the effects or consequences of a problem, and (3) advances a way to solve the problem. A familiar problem-solution pattern in our culture today concerns childhood obesity. Speeches about this issue are often patterned in the following way:

1. In the United States, we are experiencing an epidemic of childhood obesity.
2. The effects of childhood obesity are health problems, including premature death.
3. The solution to the problem is
   a. better education about nutrition;
   b. policy reform (e.g., regulation of the food served in schools);
   c. more exercise.

The problem-solution pattern is encountered most frequently in persuasive speaking; therefore, we will investigate the pattern in more depth in chapter 15.

Cause and effect

The cause-and-effect pattern of organization is usually used in concert with temporal or problem-solution forms, and this pattern typically demands that speakers offer well-established or researched support. The issue of childhood obesity is also a good example for cause and effect: when outlining the nature or character of the problem, a speaker will typically suggest that childhood obesity (the effect) is caused by (1) overeating or eating an unbalanced diet, (2) a sedentary lifestyle or lack of exercise, (3) a lack of knowledge about nutrition, and (4) unregulated food merchandising and misleading advertising. Because well-established or researched support is crucial to forging a relationship between causes and effects, this organizational pattern should be used with caution.

Some solutions to the pimple problem are positively shocking!

Rambling

Have you ever taken a course in which the professor seemed to talk endlessly without making a point? If so, you may have experienced a rambling organizational pattern, which is when the main points in a speech appear to be offered at random. On the face of it, a rambling speech doesn't seem organized at all. And often, a rambling speech is simply unorganized.

In general, you want to avoid the appearance of rambling as a speaker because it communicates to an audience that you don't care about the speech or, worse, the audience. There are rare instances, however, when a rambling speech is appropriate or even strategic. We are most prone to rambling when we are asked to speak on the spot and are caught offguard. In that context, audiences rarely expect a neatly ordered speech. Since a rambling speech typically denotes *informality*, some speakers choose a rambling pattern to put an audience at ease.

A deliberate rambling organization can also be used for dramatic effect. This occurs when the speaker makes all the seemingly random points of the speech come together at the end. This *inductive* approach to public speaking is often discouraged because it demands a great deal of patience from an audience. If done well, however, a deliberately rambling approach to speaking can deliver a powerful, and memorable, conclusion. Rambling speeches are more commonly delivered in the context of entertainment (e.g., fictional monologues in film and stand-up comedy routines) or politics (political rallies and conventions) because audiences are more likely to expect impromptu styles of speaking. For the purposes of your public speaking class, however, this organizational pattern is best avoided.

> **?** What are the basic types of organizational patterns for speeches? Which two types are most fundamental or primary, and why?

Outlining Your Speech

> **You will learn to**
> LIST the two types of speech outlines, and explain their similarities and differences.
> DESCRIBE the differences between citations in working and speaking outlines.
> DEFINE extemporaneous speaking.

> When you hear a very good public speaker, her or his comments flow from one point to the next as if they were spontaneous and part of an elegant whole.

When you hear a very good public speaker, her or his comments flow from one point to the next as if they were spontaneous and part of an elegant whole. Regardless of the perception, the speech most likely began with the speaker thinking through the overview and organization of the speech first, and then creating a detailed outline.

Because public speaking concerns oral delivery, outlining is crucial. Developing a speech outline can ensure that you have identified your main points clearly and arranged them in a way that will impress your meaning on the minds of audience members. When an audience listens to a speech, they are often mentally piecing together the outline you prepared in their heads. To help them achieve a mental assembly, speakers typically fashion an outline to reduce their speech comments to the most fundamental and memorable points.

One useful way to prepare for a speech is by working through two kinds of outlines: (1) the preparation or working outline, and (2) the speaking outline. Each type of outline serves a unique purpose. By working from a preparation outline toward a speaking outline, you gradually condense your speech to its most memorable points for delivery, with the bonus of helping you commit your speech to memory.

The working and speaking outlines concern the specific sentences and even words that you want to be sure to speak aloud, and may even be required as a turn-in assignment by your instructor.

What is the purpose of outlining a speech before you write it?

Developing a Preparation Outline

The purpose of a preparation or working outline is to organize your main points and speech support on paper or on your computer or tablet. In the larger scheme of speechwriting, the preparation outline is like a list of driving directions ("turn right there, and then make a left at the stop sign"), along with phrases, sentences, and evidence you intend to share with your audience.

What is the purpose of a preparation outline?

The basic outlining format

A large part of developing a preparation outline concerns the outline form. An outline is usually written in the form of a list, divided into headings and subheadings that distinguish between main points and supporting points. The purpose of an outline, however, is to determine a *hierarchy* among the speech points by alternating between number and letter, from abstract to specific: Roman numerals are the most general (I, II, III) and are followed by capital letters (A, B, C), which in turn are followed by Arabic numerals (1, 2, 3), and so on. Of course, the outline form is easiest to explain with an example:

I. Big Point
   A. Point
      1. Smaller Point
      2. Smaller Point

    B. Point
        1. Smaller Point
        2. Smaller Point
II. Another Big Point
    A. Point
    B. Point
    C. Point
        1. Smaller Point
            a. Even Smaller Point
            b. Even Smaller Point
        2. Smaller Point
III. Final Big Point

In general, the outline form can descend to a fifth level of specificity, denoted by lowercase Roman numbers (i, ii, iii, and so on) before the outline form reverts to previously used item markers (namely, capital letters).

STANDARD SPEECH OUTLINE
Speech Title

I. Introduction
    A. Attention Getter
    B. Thesis Statement
    C. Preview of Main Points
II. Body
    A. Main Point
        1. Support
        2. Support
        3. Support
    B. Main Point
        1. Support
        2. Support
        3. Support
    C. Main Point
        1. Support
        2. Support
        3. Support
III. Conclusion
    A. Summary of Main Points
    B. Closing or Parting Shot

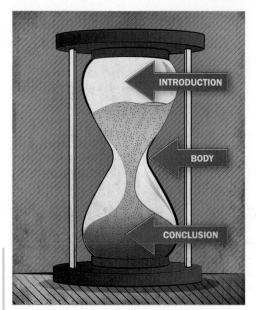

Basic speeches begin wider in scope, narrow to the main points, and then open up again for the conclusion.

That said, if your preparation outline becomes so detailed that you are referring to five or six lines of specificity, then you are getting too specific for a speech. Speeches, in general, should remain at the level of big points, points, and smaller points. If you find yourself dividing your smaller points into even smaller points, what you are planning to say will likely be too detailed or complicated for your listening audience. Keep in mind that three is the magic number. This means that *three levels of abstraction* is about as much as you can ask of a given audience to comprehend and remember.

In the teaching of public speaking over the past century, the popular style of outlining has converged with general cultural expectations to create a standard default, or template, for speechmaking.

Using the standard speech outline to create a preparation outline

Beginning speakers often bristle at the standard speech outline form. They may wonder if it is absolutely necessary to pattern everything in threes, and what would happen if they have four or five main points. The "standard" outline for speeches is simply a guideline and is, consequently, what a general audience tends to expect. Like a road map or a cooking recipe, a speaker certainly has the option to deviate from audience expectations of his or her speech. Keep in mind, however, that whether your audience realizes it or not, the standard outline format is so widespread that it is in their psyche. Consequently, sticking to the basic speech outline will help your audience remember the main points of your speech. Like a recipe, once you learn the basic ingredients and directions, it's much easier to *improvise* without disastrous results (getting lost). To put the same point another way: *before you can rock and roll, you need to learn three chords.*

For your preparation speech outline, you should plot the ideas you have for your speech on the standard speech outline. As you fill in the actual words you would like to say, you can begin to alter the organization in a way that fits your needs and purpose. As you work on your speech by changing, deleting, and adding points, remember that your goal is to arrange the different parts of your speech into a hierarchy that audiences can easily discern from hearing you speak. As you work on the outline, you can begin to write transitions that include phrases and sentences that you want to make sure you say. As you continue to revise your preparation outline, it will gradually get longer.

Depending on the speech situation, you may elect to use your preparation outline for delivering your speech, or you may decide to reduce

AP Photo/Alexander F. Yuan

During the 2016 presidential election, a controversy broke in the national news media over taking photographs of oneself, or "selfies," in the polling place or voting booth. There is no federal law for or against photography in the polls, so rules governing selfies are determined by local and state agencies. Although restrictions on voting behavior at polls vary from one state to the next, some states levy hefty fines for taking photos in or near voting booths; Illinois even makes taking a selfie while voting a felony crime! A number of celebrities and public figures posted photos of themselves or loved ones voting in social media, presumably to encourage fans and followers to exercise their civic duties. Justin Timberlake, for example, received a lot of press while voting early in Memphis, Tennessee, for potentially breaking state law.[6] Owing to the Great Selfie Voting Controversy of 2016, after the election many states have been reviewing, revising, and repealing laws related to polls and photography. Nevertheless, some argue that state laws against photography in the voting booth protect the democratic process from tampering or perhaps (sacred) degradation, while others (such as the American Civil Liberties Union) argue that taking selfies in the polls is a form of protected free speech.

Whatever your personal opinion about taking voting-booth selfies, this intriguing topic provides you with an excellent opportunity to practice speech outlining. Do a quick Internet search to find information about the controversy, then visit LaunchPad at launchpadworks.com and click on the link dedicated to chapter 7, where you will find a collection of speech outlining templates. Practice creating a speech that informs the audience using the basic speech outline.

How would you introduce and conclude such a speech? How could you arrange the following main points into a five-minute speech?

- Defining the "selfie"
- The history of the selfie
- Laws that govern voting booths
- Generational difference and technology
- Arguments for allowing selfies in voting booths
- Arguments against allowing selfies in voting booths

the details of your speech so that they fit on one or two pages (or on note cards) for the *speaking outline*. Either way, you should employ the standard style for preparation outlines as well as speaking outlines covered in this chapter. Because a working outline is better shown than explained, we'll turn to a speech that student Victoria Filoso delivered as an example.

A PREPARATION OUTLINE EXAMPLE

Originally from Toronto, Victoria Filoso moved to Texas to study economics and communication at the University of Texas at Austin. Victoria is passionate about art and international issues, and she loves to debate. She enthusiastically agreed to share the following speech, which she composed and delivered for a course in professional communication skills during the fall semester of 2015. Her speech, which she titled "The Science of Dreams," is about research on the function and meaning of dreams. Note that the speech is organized both topically and chronologically. Also note that while *Speech Craft* itself is documented in Chicago style, Victoria's instructor required the MLA style of formatting.

Freud argued that dreams are the "royal road" to unconscious wishes and memories.

The Science of Dreams

Victoria Filoso

Visit LaunchPad to see a video of "The Science of Dreams," delivered by student speaker Meagan Robertson.

Purpose: To inform the audience about the science of sleeping and dreaming

Thesis: Studies have proven not only that our dreams significantly resemble our reality, but that they can also affect our reality.

I. Introduction

  A. **Attention Getter**

    1. How many of you remember your dreams from last night? How many of you remember your dreams every night? Why do we remember some of our dreams and not others?

    2. Something all college students are passionate about is sleep, but most of us do not take the time to consider the impact or meaning of our dreams on our reality.

    3. In my high school psychology class, we did a segment focusing on the science of dreams, and ever since then I have been interested in it.

  B. **Thesis:** Studies have proven not only that our dreams significantly resemble our reality, but that they can also affect our reality.

  C. **Preview:** Today I will take us through some theories about

    1. how dreams form in the mind,

    2. how they affect our sleep cycles, and

    3. their impact on our reality.

II. Body

  A. **Main Point:** Dreams form out of our unconscious mind into what is called the preconscious mind. Over the past century, there have been and continue to be many theories about why we dream.

    1. In 1899, famous psychoanalyst Sigmund Freud, in his book *The Interpretation of Dreams*, claimed that "a dream is a (disguised) fulfillment of a (suppressed or repressed) wish" (194).

    2. In 1902, another dream theorist, Carl Jung—who was mentored by Freud until they disagreed about the purpose of dreams—claimed that dreams served as a necessary "hidden door" to one's unconscious, and that they can lead us to discover our true personalities in a way that we cannot know solely through consciousness (304).

    3. (**Transition**) These are both examples of some of the original, classical theories about the function of dreams.

B. **Main Point:** Today, more general "commonsense" theories about dreams have emerged that are not tied to the theories of classical dream analysts.

   1. Contemporary dream analysts have come to a general consensus that there is probably not a specific reason for why we dream, due to the fact that we remember so little of our dreams; if they are so important, why don't we remember them?

   2. In 2010, psychologist Kelly Bulkeley, coauthor of the book *Children's Dreams: Understanding the Most Memorable Dreams and Nightmares of Childhood*, commissioned a demographic study of approximately 3,000 U.S. adults; 68% of them remembered only 2–3 dreams each month (para. 9).

      a. Only about 10% of women and 7% of men said that they recalled a dream almost every morning (Bulkeley para. 11).

   3. Although there is no clear evidence for why people dream, most analysts agree that dreams do contain meaning.

      a. Some people believe certain symbols or events that happen in dreams can correspond to things that have happened in everyday life (this is what "dream dictionaries" are used for). For example, teeth are a common dream symbol. Dreaming of losing your teeth can symbolize anxiety or even a fear of public speaking (Vigo paras. 3–4; "Dreams of Teeth," para. 5)!

C. **Main Point:** In addition to the meaning of dreams, researchers have long known that dreaming corresponds to rapid eye movement—or REM—during sleep.

   1. So what is REM sleep? Rapid eye movement sleep is when your eyes flicker about while your eyes are closed, usually 90 minutes into your sleep cycle. Intuitively, argues researcher Yuval Nir, it would seem that our eyes flicker as "we scan an imaginary scene" in a dream, "but it has been very difficult to provide evidence for it" (Hamzelou 12). This difficulty is due to the fact that the dreamers in research studies are asleep!

   2. In a well-known 1957 study, two experimental psychologists, William Dement and Nathaniel Kleitman, argued that REM corresponds to dreaming. Since that time, there have been numerous studies.

      a. For example, today Dr. Nir at Tel Aviv University has come very close to proving that REM corresponds to eye movement by monitoring the sleeping patterns of volunteers with epilepsy. These volunteers had "electrodes implanted deep into their brains to help with treatment," reports the *New Scientist* journal (Hamzelou 12).

      b. Nir and his colleagues "found that activity seemed to spike around a quarter of a second after an eye flicker, just as it does after seeing an image when awake" (Hamzelou 12).

      c. Dr. Nir reports he and his research team "are sure that the brain is alternating between different imagery" (Hamzelou 12).

  3. Because the theory of REM sleep and dreaming was so widely accepted, it was also believed that we could *only* dream during REM sleep. Today we know that is no longer the case.

      a. For example, according to psychologist G. William Domhoff, "children under age 5 in the sleep laboratory reveal that they only report dreams from REM sleep awakenings 20–25% of the time, so REM sleep does not automatically equate to dreaming" ("The 'Purpose'" para. 8).

      b. In his book *Dreaming: A Cognitive-Psychological Analysis*, dream psychologist David Foulkes argued that dreams are a "cognitive achievement," which means that we basically learn how to dream (or at least remember dreams) over time (Domhoff, "Dreams Have" para. 8; see also Foulkes). Just because we experience REM sleep does not necessarily mean we dream. (Many mammals also experience REM sleep, but there is no hard evidence that they dream.)

  4. Many sleep researchers believe that REM sleep is the most desirable way to sleep because it is the deepest sleep humans can achieve.

      a. In a 2005 study by Tore Nielson, director of the Dream and Nightmare Lab at the Sacré-Coeur Hospital in Montreal, "losing 30 minutes of REM sleep can lead to a 35 percent REM increase the next night" (Nicholson para. 10).

      b. According to *Scientific American*, "Nielson also found that dream intensity increased with REM deprivation. Subjects who were only getting about 25 minutes of REM sleep rated the quality of their dreams" much higher on a 9-point scale (Nicholson para. 11).

D. **Main Point:** Although scholars and researchers disagree about whether dreams have some adaptive purpose, G. William Domhoff argues that "human beings gradually invented uses for dreams. In more technical terms, dreams have an 'emergent' function that develops through culture" ("Dreams Have" para. 14).

  1. Domhoff reports that "dreams are used by shamans to diagnose illness," and in this sense "shamans were the first psychoanalysts, and Freud and Jung are modern-day shamans" ("Dreams Have" para. 15).

  2. Domhoff also suggests that dreams give therapists and their patients a common thing to talk about.

3. Domhoff's observation is useful because it points out a common misunderstanding about dream interpretation: the content of a dream is less important than how a person *describes* the dream. In Freud's approach to dream analysis, the therapist learns as much about a patient from how he or she *describes* the dream; this is because Freud believed that the content of dreams was a disguised wish (311–12).

4. Neurologist Patrick McNamara argues that dreams affect social relationships. In his book *An Evolutionary Psychology of Sleep and Dreams*, as well as in essays in other publications, like *Psychology Today*, McNamara suggests that the narratives in dreams can help us develop feelings about people, even if we don't mean to (McNamara para. 2).

   a. There is strong evidence that dreams—especially bad ones—have a significant influence on waking life. In a 2004 study by Mark Blagrove, Laura Farmer, and Elvira Williams, "anxiety, depression, neuroticism, and acute stress were found to be associated with nightmare distress . . . and the prospective frequency of unpleasant dreams" (129).

   b. Their study concluded there was a strong correlation between the number of nightmares participants had and their perceptions of well-being in the daytime.

5. So, even if there is no strong conclusive evidence that dreams have an impact on reality and our daily life, most of the researchers I have consulted suggest the two are related. It's simply tough to study dreaming because researchers must rely on indirect data (e.g., electrical activity) or the self-reports of dreamers.

III. Conclusion

  A. **Summary**

    1. **Review of Main Points:** Dreaming, although still a mysterious event and process, is a fascinating achievement of the human brain. Both practicing analysts and psychologists and scientific researchers have been studying dreams since the end of the nineteenth century. Much time has been spent to understand how dreams impact and affect our relationships and reality.

    2. **Restatement of Thesis:** In my time with you today, I have explained how the psychoanalytic analysis of dreams provides us with a more intuitive understanding of the meaning of dreams, and how scientific research suggests a correlation between dreaming, REM sleep, and well-being.

  B. **Closing:** Thank you for your time and hearing me out. I hope I have inspired you to reflect on your dreams and perhaps do more research on your own about this fascinating topic.

Works Cited

Blagrove, Mark, Laura Farmer, and Elvira Williams. "The Relationship of Nightmare Frequency and Nightmare Distress to Well-Being." *Journal of Sleep Research*, vol. 13, 2004, pp. 129–36.

Bulkeley, Kelly. "Dream Recall: The Highs and Lows." *Huffington Post*, 8 May 2013, www.huffingtonpost.com/kelly-bulkeley-phd/dream-recall-the-highs-an_b_3232765.html. Accessed 17 Oct. 2015.

Dement, William, and Nathaniel Kleitman. "The Relation of Eye Movements during Sleep to Dream Activity: An Objective Method for the Study of Meaning. *Journal of Experimental Psychology*, vol. 53, 1957, pp. 339–46, www.holah.karoo.net/dementstudy.htm. Accessed 15 March 2016.

Domhoff, G. William. "Dreams Have Psychological Meaning and Cultural Uses, but No Known Adaptive Function." *Dreamresearch.net*, www2.ucsc.edu/dreams/Library/purpose.html. Accessed 15 March 2016.

---. "The 'Purpose' of Dreams." *Dreamresearch.net*, www2.ucsc.edu/dreams/Articles/purpose.html. Accessed 15 March 2016.

"Dreams of Teeth." *Dream Interpretation Meaning*, 2008, https://sites.google.com/site/dreaminterpretationmeaning/teeth-1. Accessed 15 March 2016.

Foulkes, David. *Dreaming: A Cognitive-Psychological Analysis*. New York: Routledge, 1985.

Freud, Sigmund. *The Interpretation of Dreams*. Translated by James Strachey, New York: Avon Books, 1965.

Hamzelou, Jessica. "Eyes Dart about a Dream Scene in REM Sleep." *New Scientist*, 15 Aug. 2015, p. 12.

Jung, C. G. *Civilization in Transition*. 2nd ed. Edited by Gerhard Adler, translated by R. F. C. Hull, Princeton: Princeton University Press, 1970.

McNamara, Patrick. "The Impact of Dreams on Your Social Life: Dreams Are Always about Other People." *Psychology Today*, 7 May 2011, www.psychologytoday.com/blog/dream-catcher/201105/the-impact-dreams-your-social-life. Accessed 17 February 2017.

Nicholson, Christie. "Strange but True: Less Sleep Means More Dreams." *Scientific American*, 20 Sept. 2007, www.scientificamerican.com/article/strange-but-true-less-sleep-means-more-dreams. Accessed 17 Oct. 2015.

Vigo, Michael. "Common Dream: Teeth Dreams." *Dream Moods*, 2001, www.dreammoods.com/commondreams/teeth-dreams.html. Accessed 15 March 2016.

Citations: Sourcing your speech in the preparation outline

You'll notice that Victoria's preparation outline includes a works-cited list and parenthetical citations referring to these sources. Because the preparation outline marks the point at which you are *formalizing* your speech, you'll need to indicate the sources for the information you collected, as well as the authors of any passages or quotations that were not written by you. Although we have covered the issue of authorial credit and citation in the chapters on ethics and speech support (chapters 2 and 6, respectively), it bears repeating that ethical and professional speech drafting demands that you credit your source material. Using one of the three source citation styles (APA, Chicago, or MLA), or the one specified by your instructor, parenthetically note in the outline your source or insert a note reference (per Chicago style), and make sure to append a list of works cited or a bibliography at the end. When actually delivering your speech, you should orally indicate your source for information because you will not be able to provide your audience with the written list of references (for tips on oral source citation, see chapter 6). Sometimes an audience member may ask you for more detail regarding a particular source (reporters regularly ask this of public speakers), and it's helpful for you to have that list handy.

> Ethical and professional speech drafting demands that you credit your source material.

The Speaking Outline

Once you have created your preparation outline, you'll quickly come to the conclusion that it is *too* long to actually consult for notes when delivering your speech. A speaking outline is a reduction of the working outline into something short enough to refer to—whether on a few pages or on note cards—during your speech. A speaking outline is dramatically shorter than a preparation outline. Like making a fancy sauce when cooking, your task when preparing a speaking outline is to boil down or reduce the verbal volume of your speech to a number of key phrases, words, and behavioral cues (e.g., "slow down") that will be an aid to your memory. Having worked on a preparation outline, you have already begun to commit your speech to memory; the speaking outline acts as a stimulus to that memory.

For the speaking outline, you do not have to write out your speech word for word—with one important exception: quotations from others, statistics, and other important facts or details that need to be precisely reported should be written word for word. Everything else can be collapsed into words or phrases that are helpful *to you*. Pick words or phrases that you find useful or memorable, since no two people's memory works the same. The working or preparation outline is a professional document that puts on paper your hard work; the speaking outline is a tool for you and you alone (your instructor may ask to see it, but in most real-world speaking situations, no one sees the speaking outline but you). The speaking outline should include any "cues," or reminders to yourself to speak a certain way or to show a visual aid or slide, as well as the phonetic spellings of any difficult-to-pronounce words or names.

What is the purpose of a speaking outline?

In many speaking situations, it is helpful to cite one's sources in some way (for techniques, see chapter 6), especially in speaking contexts that are designed to persuade audiences. (In some speaking situations, one doesn't cite sources or only mentions them indirectly—unless there is a direct quote.) Note that in our example from Victoria Filoso, she cites multiple sources and statistics; her use of evidence both builds her credibility and communicates to the audience that she has researched the topic. When transitioning from a working or preparation outline to a speaking outline, you may find yourself reordering your material simply because it is easier to read (for example, two points may become three so it is easier to glance at when speaking). Again, a speaking outline is better shown than explained.

A SPEAKING OUTLINE EXAMPLE

The Science of Dreams

Victoria Filoso

I. Introduction
   A. **Attention Getter**
      1. How many of you remember your dreams from last night? Every night?
      2. Most of us don't take the time to consider the import of dreams
      3. High school psychology class
   B. **Thesis:** Studies have proven not only that our dreams significantly resemble our reality but that they can also affect our reality
   C. **Preview:** Examine theories of how dreams form, affect sleep, impact reality
II. Body
   A. Dreams come from unconscious, enter into preconscious
      1. 1899 Freud's *The Interpretation of Dreams*: "a dream is a (disguised) fulfillment of a (suppressed or repressed) wish"
      2. 1902 Carl Jung: "hidden door" to one's unconscious, way to true personality
      3. Both classical theories of function of dreams
   B. Today, more "commonsense" theories abandon classical theories
      1. Consensus: no specific reason for dreaming because we don't remember

2. 2010, psychologist Kelly Bulkeley, coauthor *Children's Dreams: Understanding the Most Memorable Dreams and Nightmares of Childhood*:

   a. commissioned demographic study of approx. 3,000 adults

   b. 68% remembered 2–3 dreams a month

   c. 10% of women, 7% of men, recalled a dream every morning

3. No clear evidence for why, but most agree dreams are meaningful

   a. symbols correspond to everyday life

   b. losing teeth common dream; anxiety or fear of public speaking

C. Dreams correspond to rapid eye movement (REM) during sleep

   1. REM sleep = eyes flickering, 90 minutes into sleep cycle

   2. Sleep researcher Yuval Nir: our eyes flick as "we scan an imaginary scene" in a dream, "but it has been very difficult to provide evidence for it"

      a. Why? People are asleep!

   3. 1957 famous study, experimental psychologists William Dement and Nathaniel Kleitman argued REM corresponds to dreaming

      a. Dr. Nir at Tel Aviv University has come close to proving by monitoring volunteers with epilepsy, "electrodes implanted deep into their brains to help with treatment," reports *New Scientist* journal

      b. Nir and colleagues "found that activity seemed to spike around a quarter of a second after an eye flicker, just as it does after seeing an image when awake"

      c. He and team "are sure that the brain is alternating between different imagery"

   4. Previously thought REM sleep necessary for dream; that's no longer the case.

      a. Psychologist G. William Domhoff: "children under age 5 in the sleep laboratory reveal that they only report dreams from REM sleep awakenings 20–25% of the time, so REM sleep does not automatically equate to dreaming"

      b. David Foulkes's book *Dreaming: A Cognitive-Psychological Analysis*: dreams are a "cognitive achievement," we learn how to dream over time; REM sleep does not mean you will dream

      c. Many mammals have REM sleep, but no hard evidence of dreaming

   5. REM sleep most desirable because deepest sleep possible

      a. 2005 study by Tore Nielsen, director of Dream and Nightmare Lab at Sacré-Coeur Hospital in Montreal: "losing 30 minutes of REM sleep can lead to a 35 percent REM increase the next night"

      b. *Scientific American*: "Nielsen also found that dream intensity increased with REM deprivation. Subjects who were only getting about 25 minutes of REM sleep rated the quality of their dreams" much higher on 9-point scale

  D. No agreement about adaptive purpose; G. William Domhoff: "human beings gradually invented uses for dreams. In more technical terms, dreams have an 'emergent' function that develops through culture"

    1. Domhoff: "dreams are used by shamans to diagnose illness"; in this sense "shamans were the first psychoanalysts, and Freud and Jung are modern-day shamans"

    2. Domhoff: dreams give therapist and patient something to talk about

    3. Freud: original dream analysis was about how the patient reported the dream, because dreams are disguised wishes

    4. Neurologist Patrick McNamara: dreams affect social relationships

      a. His book, *An Evolutionary Psychology of Sleep and Dreams*, also essays in venues like *Psychology Today*: dream narratives help us develop feelings about people, even if we don't mean to

      b. Bad dreams have influence on waking life; 2004 study by Mark Blagrove, Laura Farmer, and Elvira Williams: "anxiety, depression, neuroticism, and acute stress were found to be associated with nightmare distress . . . and the prospective frequency of unpleasant dreams"

          i. strong correlation between number of nightmares and perceptions of well-being in day

    5. No conclusive evidence, most researchers agree in correlation between dreams and our reality/daily life

III. Conclusion

  A. **Summary**

    1. Mysterious but fascinating achievement of human brain

    2. Both analysts/psychologists and scientific researchers studied since 19th century

    3. Today I have explained how early psychoanalytic analysis provides more intuitive understanding; scientific research suggests correlation between dreaming, REM sleep, and well-being

  B. **Closing:** Thank you, hope I have inspired reflection, more research on your own

The speaking outline is for extemporaneous speaking

When delivering her speech, Victoria referenced her notes more frequently during the parts when she shared research or quotations from others. This is because she needed to be precise with the data and words of others; when sharing her own ideas, she could speak more conversationally. When a speech is particularly important or concerns a controversial issue, sticking closely to written notes allows you to say words more precisely and carefully. At other times, relying too heavily on notes can keep you from making enough eye contact with the audience. The difference is best gleaned from the two types of outlines speakers typically use: the preparation or working outline and the speaking outline. As noted earlier, the preparation outline is a much more extensive and detailed organization of the speech materials you have collected, while the speaking outline is a shorter, phrase-based outline that is used as a quick, at-a-glance cue for memory or for reading quotations and statistics.

When working with outlines in a speaking situation, your challenge is to find a balance between precision and eye contact. You can, and should, lean on one side or the other depending on the speech situation. Even so, the more eye contact you can make with the audience, the more likely you will be perceived as a credible speaker and the better your speech will be received.[7] For precision, you'll rely more steadily on a working outline or even a formal, written-out speech text, such as politicians often deliver using a teleprompter. For your public speaking class, however, your instructor will most likely ask you to use a speaking outline for what is known as an **extemporaneous delivery**—that is, delivery using a speaking outline. Few speeches are truly extemporaneous. Most speakers strive to create the appearance of little to no preparation, when in reality a lot of work has gone into preparing and practicing delivery of the speech.

extemporaneous delivery refers to a speech that is delivered with few notes or that *seems* to be delivered with little or no preparation.

In this chapter, we have explored a number of ways in which you can organize the main points of your speech into a memorable pattern, keeping in mind that audiences have the easiest time remembering three main points. When you commit your chosen organizational pattern to the page or screen, you are embarking on the process of outlining. Initially, your preparation outline will be very basic, but as you begin adding specific sources and details, your outline will become longer and more detailed. You can then transform your preparation outline into a speaking outline, which will guide you as you make your speech. What we have yet to discuss, however, are the details of the preparation outline. How do you craft a good introduction? What makes for a good transition? How do you conclude a speech in a memorable way? These are the kinds of questions we will take up in the next chapter.

Saul Loeb/AFP/Getty Images

Organizing and Outlining Your Speech

Organizing and outlining a speech helps you impart a sense of order for the audience, coordinating with them to recognize your main points.

Organizing Your Speech

Organizational patterns assist audiences in imagining the flow and structure of your speech, helping them remember your main points.

Outlining Your Speech

When preparing a speech for delivery, begin with a preparation or working outline, then reduce the working outline to a succinct speaking outline. This process helps you commit your speech to memory.

LaunchPad for *Speech Craft* includes a curated collection of speech videos and encourages self-assessment through adaptive quizzing. Go to **launchpadworks.com** to get access to:

 LearningCurve adaptive quizzes

 Video clips to help you improve your speeches

ACTIVITIES

Kevin Costner's Eulogy for Whitney Houston

Consider Kevin Costner's eulogy for Whitney Houston. Although the speech is a model speech in many ways, it deviates from the standard speech format in a number of ways. How would you answer the following questions?

1. What is the organizational pattern Costner used for the speech? What other kind of organizational pattern could he have chosen? Would other patterns have been more or less effective? Why?

2. The introduction of Costner's eulogy ends with the thesis statement and not with the typical preview.

Why do you think Costner put the preview before the thesis? What effect do you think this "switch-up" achieved?

3. Costner's eulogy lacks a summary of his main points. Why? Is a summary necessary? If he had included a summary, in what ways would the eulogy be different?

Kevin Costner's eulogy for Whitney Houston is available on YouTube.

Developing Your Outline

By the time you have read this chapter, there's a good chance you will have chosen a topic for your next speech and conducted at least some preliminary research on the topic. If you have done these steps, begin to develop a preparation outline for your speech using the basic speech template. Discuss this outline with a classmate. What organizational pattern are you using, and why? How could you further develop this preparation outline into a speaking outline?

KEY TERMS

 Videos in LaunchPad describe many of these terms. Go to launchpadworks.com.

▶ **historical arrangement** 141

▶ **narrative arrangement** 141

▶ **extemporaneous delivery** 158

TRANSITIONS, INTRODUCTIONS, & CONCLUSIONS

CHAPTER 8

Whenever you start taking classes at a new school or begin a new job, you may find yourself in social situations in which you know very few people. You may be invited to attend an orientation meeting or a social mixer with many strangers from your new school or job. For many of us, the task of introducing yourself and meeting new people at these kinds of events inspires *anxiety*, which is the general term for unease or nervousness about something.[1]

In many ways, speaking to an audience is a kind of self-introduction. Part of the anxiety we feel as speakers comes from a worry that the audience will not be interested in what we have to say.[2] One way to navigate speech anxiety is to think well of the audience before you meet them, imagining them in a positive light.

For Aristotle, the most famous ancient teacher of public speaking, the key to engaging an audience is something termed *eunoia*, which literally means "well mind or beautiful thinking" in the original Greek. The term is better translated as "a beautiful state of mind toward others" — or, simply, "goodwill." As we discussed in chapter 2, Aristotle suggested that having a favorable engagement with an audience requires the speaker to have a positive disposition toward them, which communicates that the speaker cares about the audience *as people* rather than mere objects.[3] The moral here is that successful speaking is *other oriented* — or *audience oriented*.

Unlike meeting a new person at a social event, introducing yourself to an audience as a speaker usually occurs with advance notice, which is very good news. In most cases, a speech is planned in advance, and the speaker has time to prepare. The most effective way a speaker can reduce speaking anxiety and cultivate goodwill is by planning what to say and how to say it. A speaker demonstrates goodwill toward an audience by introducing, ordering, and concluding a speech in a manner that has the audience's level of comprehension and interests at heart. In other words, goodwill toward an audience is best communicated by preparedness. Building on the ways to organize and outline your speech we examined in the last chapter, we will now examine how you can make a more powerful impression for an audience by crafting introductions, transitions, and conclusions.

Introducing Your Speech

> **You will learn to**
>
> **LIST** the three purposes of a speech introduction.
>
> **LIST** three parts of a traditional speech introduction.

Speaking to a group to establish a sense of goodwill comes down to a familiar and crucial moment: the first impression you make with your introduction. For decades, scholars have been trying to understand what makes a favorable impression on others, especially in terms of "first impressions" (both informally and with formal addresses). Research on the process by which people perceive and create mental images of one another is termed "impression formation," and generally supports claims first advanced by psychologist Solomon Asch in the 1940s: the first impressions you have of someone tend to influence your future impressions of that person.[4] Following this insight, many scholars of public speaking would agree that the first impression made by a speech introduction helps frame how we think about the speaker and her or his speech.[5] Consequently, crafting the introduction to your speech is arguably the first thing you can do to impart a sense of goodwill and encourage a good impression.

Introductions create first impressions.

Even before you begin to speak, your audience forms impressions based on your appearance. We will discuss strategies you can use to guide and manage those impressions in chapters 9 and 10. A well-crafted introduction, however, is the most effective way to orient your audience to listen to your speech and find interest in what you say. To this end, keep in mind the three basic purposes of an introduction in a public speaking situation:

1. **To establish goodwill:** An introduction should establish a general sense that you care about the audience and have thought about them in advance of the speech.

What are the three functions of an introduction? ?

2. To establish credibility: Along with the conclusion, the introduction is the part of your speech in which you establish authority as a speaker. It is a place where you say, either directly or indirectly, that you are qualified as a speaker and can be trusted. As we discussed in the chapter on ethical speaking (see chapter 2), your credibility refers to the *ethos*, or the character-based focus, of public speaking.

3. To explain why you are speaking: The introduction is when the audience learns about your purpose (expressed in a thesis statement) and how you will speak toward this purpose, with a preview of your main points.

The purpose of an introduction is to establish goodwill and credibility, and to explain one's purpose. A speaker usually works toward this end by observing the three traditional parts of a speech introduction: an attention getter (or opener), a thesis statement, and an overview (or preview) of the main points of the speech. The thesis statement and preview are usually directly stated and planned out word for word.

The Attention Getter

There is no right or wrong way to garner the attention and invite the goodwill of your audience. The following chart lists a number of the most common techniques for opening speeches.

An attention getter is like the ringmaster of your speech.

Attention-Getting Techniques for Speech Introductions

TECHNIQUE	DESCRIPTION	EXAMPLE
Quotation	Opening a speech with a memorable quotation from a respected speaker or writer is a quick way to gain credibility and frame a speech. Although widely overused, opening with a quotation can be successful — especially if the quote is widely known, memorable, or from someone respected by the audience.	"'We the people, in order to form a more perfect union.' Two hundred and twenty-one years ago, in a hall that still stands across the street, a group of men gathered and, with these simple words, launched America's improbable experiment in democracy. Farmers and scholars; statesmen and patriots who had traveled across an ocean to escape tyranny and persecution finally made real their declaration of independence at a Philadelphia convention that lasted through the spring of 1787." — Barack Obama, "A More Perfect Union (the Race Speech)," March 18, 2008, Philadelphia, Pennsylvania
Acknowledging the Speaking Situation	If your reason for speaking is a special event that is honoring a person or persons, celebrating an occasion, or explaining the complexity of an event, making reference to the person, occasion, or event can unite you and the audience in a common purpose.	"Today we are launching a campaign called 'HeForShe.' . . . This is the first campaign of its kind at the [United Nations]. We want to try to mobilize as many men and boys to be advocates for change." — Emma Watson, "Speech on Gender Equality," address to the United Nations on September 20, 2014, New York, New York
Rhetorical Question	A rhetorical question is a question that is voiced, although it is presumed that the speaker already has an answer. A rhetorical question can also be an invitation to the audience to think about an answer but not to say the answer aloud.	"A variety of factors influence our lives to help shape within us a belief system. And our belief system determines our perspective on every issue, especially those issues in life which are most complex. Is there a God? . . . Is there an afterlife? Where will we go when we die?" — Pastor Randy Smith, "The Blessing of Grace," sermon delivered to the Grace Bible Church, October 7, 2007, Allenwood, New Jersey

(continued)

Attention-Getting Techniques for Speech Introductions (*continued*)

TECHNIQUE	DESCRIPTION	EXAMPLE
Visualization	Closely related to the function of a rhetorical question is visualization, which asks audiences to imagine a scenario or scene in their minds. A common visualization in our culture is the "desert island," in which audiences are asked to imagine themselves alone on a desert island. For example, a speech about popular novels might begin, "Imagine you are alone on a desert island. If you could have only one novel with you, what would it be?" Visualizations are particularly effective because of the way they ask audiences to actively participate in the construction of a speech. Visualizations can also be strikingly moving because of their vivid imagery.	"This is where they fought the battle of Gettysburg. Fifty thousand men died right here on this field, fighting the same fight that we are still fighting among ourselves today. This green field right here, painted red, bubblin' with the blood of young boys. Smoke and hot lead pouring right through their bodies. Listen to their souls, men. . . . If we don't come together right now on this hallowed ground, we too will be destroyed, just like they were. I don't care if you like each other or not, but you will respect each other. And maybe . . . I don't know, maybe we'll learn to play this game like men."—Coach Boone (played by Denzel Washington), pregame inspirational speech in the film *Remember the Titans* (2000)
Telling a Story or Joke	As we discussed in the previous chapter, you can organize an entire speech around a single story, but sometimes you can just begin a speech with a story. Using humor also works to draw people into the speech.	"Good morning, good morning. I am Stephen Colbert and I want to thank the class of 2013 for inviting me here today. . . . And now, then, it is an honor to speak at your 2013 Valedictory Exercises—I believe that means I am this year's valedictorian, and I am as shocked as you are, because I didn't make it to many classes this year. You guys must've really tanked your finals, thank you for that."—Stephen Colbert, "University of Virginia 2013 Commencement Speech," May 18, 2013[6]
Startling Fact or Statistic	Another way to get an audience's attention at the beginning of a speech is to tell a fact or relay a statistic that is not widely known but supports the purpose of your speech.	"Sadly, in the next 18 minutes when I do our chat, four Americans that are alive will be dead through the food that they eat. My name's Jamie Oliver. I'm 34 years old. I'm from Essex in England and for the last seven years I've worked fairly tirelessly to save lives in my own way."—Jamie Oliver, "Teach Every Child about Food," TED Prize speech, February 2010

The Thesis Statement

As discussed earlier, your goodwill and credibility as a speaker are established during the introduction, and making sure your speech topic and reason for speaking are clear constitute an important part of your task. The most efficient delivery device for your speech topic is the thesis statement, which is an expression of what your topic is and why you are speaking about it. Your attention getter has probably already cued the audience about your topic. Your thesis statement establishes the parameters of your talk and is an oral cue for audiences to help them organize your speech in their heads. Notice how celebrity chef Jamie Oliver gets the attention of his audience, establishes goodwill and credibility, and then brings it all home with a clear statement of his thesis in this introduction to a speech on childhood obesity:

❶ [Sadly, in the next 18 minutes when I do our chat, four Americans that are alive will be dead through the food that they eat.] **❷** [My name's Jamie Oliver. I'm 34 years old. I'm from Essex in England and for the last seven years I've worked fairly tirelessly to save lives in my own way. I'm not a doctor; I'm a chef. I don't have expensive equipment or medicine. I use information, education.] **❸** [I profoundly believe that the power of food has a primal place in our homes that binds us to the best bits of life. . . . Your child will live a life ten years younger than you because of the landscape of food that we've built around them. Two-thirds of this room, today, in America, are statistically overweight or obese. . . .] **❹** [We need a revolution. . . . I came here to start a food revolution that I so profoundly believe in. We need it. The time is now. We're in a tipping-point moment.[7]]

The Preview and the Payoff

The final component of a speech introduction is the place or moment in which you give a preview about what the audience is going to hear. Think about this part of the introduction like you would the promotional preview for a movie: the highlights are shown with the hopes of enticing audiences to want to see the movie. You want to strive for the same sense of anticipation in your speech preview. Consider the introduction

---

? **What devices or techniques can you use for attention getters?**

❶ In this one-sentence attention getter, Oliver both acknowledges the speaking situation and presents the audience with startling facts.

❷ Oliver establishes his credibility by providing background information and, interestingly, by telling the audience his expertise is based on his experience as a chef.

❸ Here Oliver establishes goodwill with the audience by acknowledging his conviction in the power of food, as well as his desire to help others overcome obesity.

❹ Finally, Oliver ends his introduction with a thesis statement: he is calling for a "revolution" of beliefs, attitudes, values, and behavior regarding food.

to a November 1, 2011, speech by former Utah governor Jon Huntsman on U.S. energy policy:

> It's an honor to be back at the University of New Hampshire; a university that has distinguished itself as a leader in academics, research and innovation. A few minutes ago I visited your cogeneration plant, which has earned national accolades. Using processed landfill gas, it serves as this campus's primary energy source—powering your gymnasium, your dorm rooms and to the dislike of some, your lecture halls. By taking more control of its energy supply, the university benefits from a stable energy source and predictable energy prices. The need to make our nation itself energy secure is what I'd like to address today.
>
> We are all too familiar with the statistics. Fifty years ago, President Eisenhower warned we should import no more than 20 percent of our oil. Today we import 60 percent. . . . Ladies and gentlemen, for the sake of America's economic and national security, we must unshackle ourselves from the scourge of foreign oil. So how do we do that?
>
> There are three basic steps that need to be taken. First, America is drowning in energy resources. So we must remove the regulatory constraints on the production of domestic energy. Second, we need to break oil's monopoly as a transportation fuel, and create a truly level playing field for competing fuels. Third, we need to build an environment that will incubate the next generation of energy technologies and ensure that America leads the global energy economy in the decades to come. So number one, we must increase domestic production.[8]

Notice in this example Huntsman's artful use of referring to the situation, startling statistics, and rhetorical questions in his attention getter. He has a clear thesis statement that announces his topic and purpose. And the payoff is also indicated in the preview of his three main points.

Transitions

> **You will learn to**
>
> **EXPLAIN** the purpose of transitions.
>
> **LIST** the three common kinds of speech transitions.

The example of Huntsman's energy policy speech shifts us to the topic of verbal bridging, or transitions. In public speaking, a transition refers to the way in which a speaker indicates the movement from one main point or part of a speech to another. A good speech transition is like good salsa dancing: the dancer to watch is the one who goes from one move to the next *effortlessly*. Note how Huntsman has a slow groove going on

Transitions are connections that bring two things together.
Left: Glowimages/Getty Images   *Right:* kali9/Getty Images

as he transitions from the introduction to the body of his energy policy speech:

> Third, we need to build an environment that will incubate the next generation of energy technologies and ensure that America leads the global energy economy in the decades to come. So number one, we must increase domestic production.[9]

Here, Huntsman transitions by using a common transition technique: **enumeration** ("So number one"). In writing, transitions can often be subtle because the reader comprehends what is written at his or her own pace, or can go back and reread something; an audience for a speech does not have the same luxury. As a speaker, you are creating the pace of comprehension, which means the audience has to go along with you. Moreover, your job as a speaker is to help create a mental outline in the heads of your audience members. In doing so, it's most helpful to signal to the audience in a clear way that you are moving from one point to another.

Along with enumeration, speakers often use **internal previews** and **internal summaries** to transition from one main speech point to another. An internal preview is similar to the preview speakers provide in the introduction, but it is shorter and comes in the body of the speech. For example, in a speech about electric car engines, you might say something like, "Having described for you how electric car engines depend on magnets, we are now ready to examine two topics: first, how magnets influence where the engine is placed, and second, the location of the charging point." Internal summaries, on the other hand, remind the audience what the speaker has recently discussed. For example, "So far I have examined the role of magnets in electric car engines and how magnets influence the placement of the engine and charging point in the car body." Internal previews and summaries can sometimes be combined as well.

enumeration concerns composing transitions for oral delivery and the creation of mental signposts, which are verbal indications of the direction the speech will take; many terms and phrases are handy for this purpose, for example: "first," "second," "third," "one," "two," "next," and "finally."

internal previews and **summaries** are more detailed forms of transition that review major points to come or that summarize points that have been said, respectively.

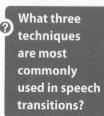

? **What three techniques are most commonly used in speech transitions?**

DIGITAL DIVE

The Mystery of Dreams

As speakers, we hope to make a positive impression on our audience. For this reason, we have a tendency to work harder on composing the introduction of a speech. In addition, there has been some research to suggest that audiences are more likely to commit points that you make early in a speech to long-term memory, which is sometimes termed the "primacy effect."[10] However, there is also research to suggest that how we end a speech is important to an audience's retention of our ideas or arguments in short-term memory, which is called a "recency effect."[11] Although speech teachers may disagree over whether an introduction or a conclusion is more memorable, the scholarly consensus is that audiences remember the introduction and conclusion of a speech more than the body, or middle.

Whether you believe primacy or recency is more memorable for an audience, there is a way to both have your memory-cake and eat it too: compose your speech introduction and conclusion in a mirroring manner. Because the conclusion leaves the audience with the final impression of your remarks, use it as an opportunity to remind them of something you mentioned in the introduction (perhaps your attention getter, but certainly your thesis). Summarize the major points of your remarks, thereby reinforcing the structure of your speech. Finally, end your conclusion with another example or vivid statement that engages the audience and encapsulates the sense and spirit of your address.

LaunchPad
macmillan learning

Beginning public speakers sometimes forget the important role of recency when delivering speech conclusions. A great conclusion, however, can reinforce the main ideas introduced in a speech and can encourage memory. Conclusions are also an excellent opportunity to reinforce the thesis and structure of a speech. To better understand the effect a good conclusion can have on an audience, visit LaunchPad at **launchpadworks.com** and view the two videos provided for chapter 8.

After viewing both videos, attempt to answer the following questions about each conclusion — without having heard the rest of the speech:

- What is the topic of each speech?
- What is the thesis of each speech?
- What are the main points of each speech?
- Which conclusion is stronger? Why?

Concluding Your Speech

How many times have you fallen asleep while watching a movie, only to awaken right at the very end? How did you know it was time to wake up? Chances are that there was some sort of shift in the soundtrack—music or an explosion or a dramatic turn of dialogue—deliberately used by the filmmaker to prepare viewers for the coming credits. This sound-induced sense of an ending used by filmmakers is deliberate because movie audiences respond positively. We derive a sense of pleasure from narrative form, and endings and conclusions represent the closure of a form that's familiar to us. Concluding a speech works similarly by signaling to the audience that you are closing the form, a kind of dotting of the "i" and crossing of the "t."

Creating oral cues signals that a speech ending is important because audience attention is heightened. Except for the most gifted listeners, most of us wander mentally when watching a film, listening to music, or listening to someone speak. An audience is usually very good at attending to the beginning of a presentation. But as the story, song, or speech develops, minds tend to weave in and out of attention and then fade back

During what is commonly referred to as the "golden age" of animation, Warner Brothers ended many of its cartoon shorts with a chummy good-bye from Porky Pig.

Introductions, transitions, and conclusions are the three parts of a speech that most audiences expect to hear. Consequently, you can rely on these expectations to create a sense of rhythm with how you structure your speech, signaling to the audience each part with an internal preview, enumerations, and—when you are coming to your conclusion—an internal summary.

out to associated thoughts.[12] As speakers, many of us assume that listeners generally attend to introductions closely (which is why we spend so much time on composing them). Transitions during a speech function as calls to come back and hear what the speaker is saying, which is another reason enumeration and internal previews and summaries are handy in a speaking situation. Finally, conclusions are the ultimate call to attention. They say, in effect, "Hey, everyone, I'm wrapping up. Pay attention!" The conclusion is the perfect place to insert the things you want the audience to remember from your speech. And a conclusion is also the place where you can inject a final provocation or challenge.

Summary and Signal

The most common and effective way to end a speech is to summarize your main points and reiterate your thesis. Be a bit creative and change up the phrasing you used in the introduction and body of the speech. Let's continue with the example of former governor Huntsman's energy policy speech, looking at the preview and comparing it to the summary of his conclusion:

> **Preview:** So how do we do that? There are three basic steps that need to be taken. First, America is drowning in energy resources. So we must remove the regulatory constraints on the production of domestic energy. Second, we need to break oil's monopoly as a transportation fuel, and create a truly level playing field for competing fuels. Third, we need to build an environment that will incubate the next generation of energy technologies and ensure that America leads the global energy economy in the decades to come.

> **Summary:** America cannot afford the status quo any longer, nor can we afford half-measures, nor can we allow reform to be derailed and delayed once again by powerful, entrenched interests. On my first day in office, I will take three immediate steps to launch a sea change in energy policy. I will direct my administration to clarify rules that ensure the safe and rapid expansion of offshore drilling and fracking. I will move to open our fuel distribution network to all forms of energy, biofuels, natural gas and electricity. I will systemically begin to eliminate every subsidy for energy companies, whether it be oil, natural gas, wind or solar. Under my presidency, the United States will get out of the subsidy business. And if necessary, I will use my executive authority to act unilaterally.[13]

Note that the preview of the main points of Huntsman's speech formally parallels the three points of his summary, but not exactly. He uses enumeration again, but the exact wording has changed to reflect the fact that *he* will be able to enact change as president, making the main points into actual policy. However one stands on the issue of U.S. energy policy, Huntsman's speech is a well-crafted example of a good summary and signal to the audience that the speech is coming to an end.

The Closing or Note of Finality

If you've crafted your speech summary well, your audience has been put on alert to expect the last sentence. Most of the time, this means that your last sentence should be powerful and memorable. In general, keep in mind that people expect and like endings—even if they are not happy ones.

The closing, or "final note," of a speech is often the most memorable part and can be an opportunity to ask the audience to do something or to remember something. In speaking to persuade, this is typically the moment when you can tell the audience to do something specific, or issue a *call to action* (in Huntsman's energy policy speech, for example, it would be to vote for him). To help your speech linger in the minds of your audience members, use the techniques also used in attention getters: quotation, acknowledging the speaking situation, asking a rhetorical question, visualization, telling a story or joke, or offering a startling fact or statistic. Because the closing of a speech is likely the most memorable, it sets the tone for how audiences will remember you.

E. M. Forster takes a bow on stage following a performance of *A Passage to India*, April 1950/ (b&w photo)/Photo © Brian Seed/Bridgeman Images

Consider, for example, how Oprah Winfrey ended her speech honoring civil rights crusader Rosa Parks on October 31, 2005. On December 1, 1955, Parks refused to give up her seat for a white passenger on a bus in Montgomery, Alabama, and was arrested. Recall that African Americans were often asked to move to the back of buses to make room for white passengers at that time (notably, Parks was already sitting in an area of the bus designated for blacks).[14] Shortly after the incident, her refusal to move from her seat became a symbol of the civil rights movement, and

Should You Say "Thank You"?

When giving a speech, it is common—sometimes even customary—to conclude one's remarks with "thank you." However perfunctory the phrase has become, the "thank you" at the end of a speech functions as a cue for the audience to respond. We can think about the "thank you" as an oral period (linguists term it a "lexical chunk"), signaling the end of a very long sentence, or as credits or a "the end" title appearing at the end of a film. Many speech teachers suggest that closing with a "thank you" is an easy way out; their thinking is that if your final note is stark, well crafted, or memorable, you won't need the "thank you." Even so, concluding with a "thank you" is a common and polite final phrase; whether you use it or not, the key is to make your ending effective.

What are the two parts of a traditional speech conclusion? How can we explain the psychological appeal of conclusions? ②

What is an alternative to ending a speech with "thank you"? ②

to this day, she is regarded as the mother of the freedom movement. At her funeral, Winfrey delivered a brief eulogy with only one main point, which was to reiterate Parks's refusal to give up her seat as a much larger conviction in the equal rights of all U.S. citizens: "And in that moment when you resolved to stay in that seat, you reclaimed your humanity and you gave us all back a piece of our own. . . . You acted without concern for yourself and made life better for us all. We shall not be moved."[15]

In this chapter, we focused on further developing your speech outline to include engaging introductions, transitions, and conclusions. Paying careful attention to how you open, move through, and close your speech communicates to your audience that you came prepared, thereby helping to generate goodwill. An introduction crafted particularly to the audience you will address is like an engaging handshake, and using enumeration, internal previews, and internal summaries is akin to offering a guiding hand through your address. Finally, a good closing reminds the audience what your main points are, and leaves them with something to think about—or possibly something to do. Once you have composed your speech, you're ready to start thinking about how to *deliver* it, which is yet another dimension of public speaking that establishes goodwill.

Introductions, Transitions, and Conclusions

Carefully planning and crafting introductions, transitions, and conclusions is a powerful way to connect with audiences and generate a sense of goodwill.

Introducing Your Speech

Good introductions begin with an attention getter, have a clear thesis, and preview the main points of a speech.

kali9/Getty Images

Transitions

Transitions between the main points and parts of a speech are an opportunity to help the audience develop an outline of your speech in their heads.

Courtesy Everett Collection

Concluding Your Speech

Good speech conclusions summarize the main points of a speech, mirroring in some way the preview in the introduction. Ending with a memorable "note of finality" gives the audience something to consider.

LaunchPad
macmillan learning

LaunchPad for *Speech Craft* includes a curated collection of speech videos and encourages self-assessment through adaptive quizzing. Go to **launchpadworks.com** to get access to:

 LearningCurve adaptive quizzes

 Video clips to help you improve your speeches

ACTIVITY

Bruce Springsteen's Keynote Speech at SXSW

On March 18, 2012, musician Bruce Springsteen delivered the opening address, or keynote speech, for the annual South by Southwest (SXSW) Conference & Festivals in Austin, Texas. Springsteen's hour-long speech was well received and widely reported by journalists as setting the perfect tone for the festival.[16] "Bruce Springsteen . . . offered the most thoughtful, poignant and humorous speech over the last 15 years of the event," reported journalist Ed Condran.[17] The immediate audience for Springsteen's speech consisted largely of journalists and music professionals, as well as music fans attending the festival lucky enough to get a seat in the auditorium. Using the key terms "Springsteen," "keynote," and "SXSW," find a video or transcript of the speech online. Read or listen closely to his introduction and conclusion, and then, with a classmate, try to identify the attention getter, thesis, and preview in Springsteen's introduction, and the summary and parting shot in Springsteen's conclusion. Now, see if you can answer the following questions:

- In what way does Springsteen attempt to establish goodwill among his audience?
- What do you think were the goals of this music festival keynote speech? Did Springsteen identify those goals in his introduction or conclusion?
- Springsteen deliberately uses profanity in his speech, but no reporter at the speech remarked on it. Why would profanity be appropriate in this context?
- How does Springsteen establish his credibility as a speaker?

KEY TERMS

 Videos in LaunchPad describe many of these terms. Go to launchpadworks.com.

enumeration 169

▶ internal previews 169

▶ internal summaries 169

STYLE AND LANGUAGE

CHAPTER 9

On the successful cable show *Project Runway*, fashion designers compete against one another by creating clothes that are scored by a panel of judges. Supermodel Heidi Klum is the show's famous host, but the breakout cultural celebrity of the program is Tim Gunn (sadly, no relation to the author) — the impeccably dressed fashion consultant who mentors contestants and advises them on their design choices. Gunn's stylistic judgments are widely recognized in the popular press as tasteful and insightful. Examining a dress designed by one contestant, Gunn remarks, "This is so clean, sophisticated, polished, it's very elegant — it's high spirited!"[1] Gunn's quick wit and discerning eye led to his own show, *Tim Gunn's Guide to Style*, in which he advises a variety of guests on their lifestyles or ways of being in the world, for which fashion is only a part.

What does Tim Gunn's stylistic sensibility have to do with public speaking? A lot! First, he is a great public speaker. Second, and more importantly for this chapter, Gunn's understanding of style does not reduce to clothing choices; Gunn insists that style concerns how you present yourself to others overall, as a human being. Contestants who do well on *Project Runway* are often those who understand that style is not simply about design but also about confidence: how you speak, the vocabulary you use, all the things that make you unique to others. Style concerns having a strong sense of self and knowing how to share that sense with others.

In public speaking, style is traditionally discussed in two ways: (1) in terms of the selection and use of language, and (2) in terms of the delivery of a speech. In keeping with this tradition, this chapter will focus specifically on language choice, and chapter 10 will focus on delivery. Once you start thinking about style more holistically, you will begin to see how the way you present yourself to others connects to *what* you say and *how* you say it. Although language choice and delivery are covered in separate chapters, the two go hand in hand. To get a better sense of why this is the case, let's briefly examine the origin of the concept of style.

What Is Style?

Those first scholars of public speaking, the ancient Greeks, had a somewhat narrower understanding of the concept of style than we do today. Aristotle collected his remarks on style under the Greek term *lexis*, which literally means "word," but what Athenians (including Aristotle's teacher, Plato) specified was the way or manner in which one said something, otherwise known as "style." Aristotle informally used the word to denote one's manner of speaking in general, but more formally he said that the subject of style specifically concerned word choice and diction.[2] Centuries later, the renowned Roman orator Cicero held a more expansive view of style, which he and his colleagues termed *elocutio*, arguing that one cannot easily separate what one says from how one says it.[3]

Style is having a strong sense of self and knowing how to share it.

Perhaps in the world of the ancient Greeks, in which the human voice was the dominant mode of communication, it was easier to separate *what* one said from *how* one said it. In our time, speech, writing, and image all compete for our attention, and the image—photographs, streaming videos, television broadcasts—seems to dominate. If the cliché that "a picture is worth a thousand words" is true, then what do we do with a thousand pictures streaming across our screens on a daily basis, sometimes with accompanying words *and* voices? That old cliché seems to have been replaced with a new one: "Image is everything!" Even so, as long as human beings rely on the voice to communicate, public speaking will remain an important mode of communication. We might say that image is *something*, but speaking is just as important. In fact, knowing that image is *not* everything is what distinguishes the good public speaker from the superficial one.

Defining Style for Our Time

The ascent of the image as a dominant form of communication in our time has complicated the ancient Greek view of *lexis*. Style has become a much bigger, more encompassing concept, which explains why there are so many different definitions of the term, ranging across manners of speaking to genres of musical performance to the clothes that people

Aristotle and Cicero ride in style!

wear. Rhetorical scholar Barry Brummett helps us make better sense of style by anchoring the concept to personhood.[4] He argues that style is no longer limited to the words we use to express our ideas and feelings, nor is it isolated to the image, but it has expanded to include how each of us presents *our person* to the world.[5] If you think about style as concerning *how* you present yourself—including your speaking—then style seems to encompass not simply what you say and how you say it but also how you look and even how you move.

For Brummett, style is intimately caught up in our individual identities, no longer simply referring to how we dress up ideas with words or how we clothe and groom our bodies; style is the *core* of self-understanding: "Style is a complex system of actions, objects, and behaviors that is used to form messages that announce who we are, who we want to be, and who we want to be considered akin to," says Brummett. Becoming conscious of how others will perceive you, and how you wish to be perceived, is the primary task of attending to style in the context of public speaking.

> ## Style
>
> In the broadest sense, **style** refers to the way in which a person presents himself or herself to others. In the context of public speaking, style refers to the relationship between what one says and how he or she says it. Traditionally, the focus on style in public speaking concerns word choice and delivery.

Style as a Meeting of the Body and Language

If we think about style as not only saying something meaningful but also saying something about who you are and with whom you wish to associate, then style is implicated in your **disposition**, or perceptions of your character. Your disposition refers to what others perceive to be the inherent qualities of your person. Many of the signs we use that communicate our character to others are often beyond our own conscious awareness, including the way we move, the way we say things, and the words we use to say those things. You can, however, become more aware of your style and, to some extent, even craft and control it. Becoming more aware of our dispositions in the public speaking situation is part of the task of being a mindful public speaker—and, let's be honest: this is hard to do.

Why is focusing on style so hard? And why is our style often unconscious to us? One of the reasons has to do with the way in which meaning and feeling are combined in speech. When you say something, you

disposition refers to a person's mental and physical orientation toward the world and others. In the context of public speaking, audiences perceive your disposition through your style.

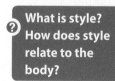
What is style? How does style relate to the body?

Denotation and Connotation

DENOTATION
"A prickly bush or shrub that typically bears red, pink, yellow, or white fragrant flowers."

CONNOTATION
"I love you!"

Meaning is based not only on the difference between our words for ideas and the ideas themselves but on the feelings that words can cause in others and provoke in ourselves. This distinction is captured by the concepts of denotation and connotation. **Denotation** refers to the literal and primary meaning of a sign, what you would expect to find in a dictionary. **Connotation** refers to the feelings one associates with a sign. Understanding the difference between these two meanings is important, especially because one can accidentally evoke connotation when one means denotation, and vice versa. Take, for example, the sign "rose." Denotatively, a rose denotes a colorful, fragrant flower that grows on a prickly bush. Connotatively, however, we tend to associate roses with feelings of love or friendship (a red rose connotes romance, while a yellow rose connotes friendship, and so on). In the world of public speaking, style often concerns how a speaker attempts to control not only the denotative meaning of what she says but also the connotations—the feelings associated with words.

are attempting to communicate meaning to others, but how you say it also imparts feelings. This is because your body is implicated in the process of speaking. The body is what issues forth a voice, the body is what we dress up, and the body is what moves and gestures. The body is that part of a human being that feels. When you speak to an audience, you're not only appealing to their mental processes but also asking them to adopt a disposition toward you—to orient their bodies to your meaning and your person and, most significantly, to feel a certain way.[6]

Impression Management

impression management refers to the way in which a person navigates his or her self-presentation in body and language.

Those who are particularly good at attending to their style are aware of not only the words they use but also their body language. A high awareness of one's style is described by sociologists as **impression management**, which refers to the way in which one navigates his or her self-presentation in body and word. In our time of highly stylistic communication, managing the impressions of others has become increasingly prominent. Whole industries have emerged to manage impressions and predispose or orient bodies and minds in specified ways: public relations firms are hired to promote a product or perhaps a political candidate, advertising firms are in the business of creating impressions about products, the Hollywood film industry promotes impressions of its films, Tim Gunn's television show coaches us on style, and so on. In many ways, the anxieties we share about public speaking have to do with the knowledge that we are creating and managing impressions not only about what we say but also about who we are as bodies that speak in movement, gesture, and dress.

Style can be characterized as a form of impression management. This implies that style attends to both language and the body, both meanings and feelings. And although much of our personal style is unconscious, scholars of public speaking have provided us with a number of tools to grapple better with our dispositions as speakers. The most helpful tools or techniques that have emerged are word choice and delivery. For the remainder of this chapter, we'll focus on word choice.

Choosing Your Words

You will learn to

DISCUSS questions that you can ask about the audience to help with your word choice.

LIST the kinds of language choices that will assist you with perceptions of expertise and credibility.

We might think about one's linguistic style in terms of DJing a party. As a DJ, your primary job is to play music that encourages people to dance and enjoy themselves. Part of this job involves choosing what songs you want to play and when you want to play them. DJs often develop a track list ahead of time in order to have a game plan, but during the party itself, DJs often deviate from their plan based on how the crowd is responding. Unfamiliar music will disappoint dancers, but too many overplayed songs can bore them as well. The analogy here is that in choosing words and adapting language to your audience, you can think about yourself as a kind of public speaking disc jockey, selecting the words and phrases that will get the audience to metaphorically dance with you.

Patti McConville/Alamy

DJs make changes to their playlists in real time according to the responses from the crowd.

Adapting Your Language: What Do You Play?

The most important factor in choosing the words, figures of speech, and general vocabulary that you will use is knowing your audience. What is appropriate to say to one audience may be entirely alienating to another one. In the chapter on audience analysis (chapter 3), we discussed elements of audience psychology and preparing your speech in respect to beliefs, attitudes, and values. In selecting language for a particular audience, however, you must also think practically about audience familiarity and expectations of formality. In adapting language to an audience, ask yourself three questions: (1) Is my audience familiar or unfamiliar to me? (2) Am I an outsider or an insider? (3) Should I be formal or informal?

Is my audience familiar or unfamiliar to me?

If the audience you will be speaking to knows you—and you know them—your language choice can be more relaxed. This is because the prior information the audience has about you—their knowledge of your *style*—will help you anchor the meaning that you wish to communicate. Misunderstanding is less likely because the audience will know where you're coming from. If you're giving a speech at a wedding reception, even if many members of the audience are not personal friends or family members, you have mutual knowledge of the couple you will be speaking about and probably share many similar experiences with them. The language you use can be less formal. If you are speaking before an audience you do not know well, consisting mostly of strangers, the general rule is to use more formal language.

> ? How can you adapt your word choices to your audience?

Am I an outsider or an insider?

Closely related to determining the familiarity of your audience is the question concerning whether you are included in the community you are speaking to. If you're making a speech to your public speaking class, you can safely assume you're an insider: you are all required to present speeches to your class, you all identify with one another in terms of the anxiety you feel while giving speeches in this setting, and you all know you are being judged on your speech by your instructor. You don't necessarily need to mention your insider status or your shared experience, but you *can* assume your classmates will not be hostile to your speaking in general.

If you are an outsider to the group you are speaking to, word choice is a little trickier — even if the audience knows who you are before you speak. In general, if you are an outsider to the audience, you will need to be more formal and carefully select words that you know from your audience analysis will resonate with most of them. A common example of incorrectly adopting the style of an insider is using "y'all" — a contraction of "you all" frequently used in the southern United States as a gesture of familiarity. "How y'all doin'?" is a common rhetorical question speakers *from the south* use to address southern audiences. When a speaker from, say, New York uses the phrase "y'all" to address a southern audience, it can come off as inauthentic or stylistically inappropriate.

Perhaps the most important thing to keep in mind when determining familiarity with an audience is the use of inclusive language. Terms like "we" and "us" are signatures of an inclusive style. As a speaker, when you say phrases like "when we get on our bikes and ride to the park" or "when we watch a series on Netflix," you rhetorically place yourself, the speaker, in the same group as the audience. Care should be taken that "we" and "us" phrases are contextually appropriate and that you are justifiably a member of the group you include yourself in.

Should I be formal or informal?

Use contextual reasoning to help you determine the degree of formality required for your speaking situation. In general, a formal speaking situation (a history report for class, a student volunteer meeting, and so on) requires more formal language. "How y'all doin'?" is probably not the best opening remark in a formal setting. "How is everyone doing?" is more formal. Informal settings — such as a party, a celebration, or a brainstorming session at your job — provide you with a lot more leeway in your choice of words. If you are scheduled to speak somewhere and do not know how formal or informal the audience will expect you to be, ask the person or people who asked you to speak about the audience so that you can better prepare your speech.

One related question you can ask is, "How will the audience be dressed?" Perhaps no other question helps you to zoom in to an appropriate style of speaking more directly: matching words with attire is one of the more interesting ways in which word choice can be adjusted in public speaking situations. As a general rule of thumb, the more formally an audience dresses (suits or jeans?), the more formal the speaking style. A good example of this rule is the award shows seen on national

Which of these audiences would respond more positively to informal language?
Left: monkeybusinessimages/Getty Images   *Right*: Doug Murray/Icon Sportswire/Newscom

television every year. If you've watched the Academy Awards, you know that it is considered a formal affair, with the attendees wearing sophisticated dresses and suits or tuxedos. The speeches—mostly introduction, tributes, and thank-you speeches—are formalized and tightly timed. Sure, there are thank-you speeches that seem overly long or perhaps even too sentimental, but the language is generally formal, bereft of slang and informal terms like "y'all." In contrast, MTV's Video Music Awards is a less formal affair, with speeches to match: some thank-you speeches are formal, but the dressing styles and often flamboyant behavior of many of the artists in attendance mirror the rambling, sometimes incoherent speeches of the award winners.

Expertise and Credibility through Word Choice

One element of style that has been discussed since the time of ancient Greece is **expertise**, an idea many associate with credibility.[7] In his treatise on public speaking, Aristotle identified the difficulty of the "expert" speaking to audiences that were "inexpert" as one of the key challenges of the public speaker—and word choice makes all the difference. In most of the public speaking situations you will encounter, you'll be speaking to family and friends; in others, however, the problem Aristotle pointed out will become an issue, especially in your professional life. As a student in a public speaking class, "speaking to the inexpert" is one of the problems you are going to be asked to address in your informative and persuasive speeches. In both of these speeches, it is assumed that you have knowledge or expertise that your classmates do not, and it will be your task to communicate that expertise in a way that your audience can understand. In speaking to inform, you present yourself as an expert on a topic that most of your classmates do not know about; in speaking

expertise refers to having knowledge or skills particular to a given field. In the context of public speaking, expertise is closely associated with credibility.

to persuade, you present yourself as an expert on a topic that you hope your audience will change their minds about—and perhaps even act on. In both informing and persuading, your expertise is established through credibility, or the audience's perception that you can be trusted as someone who knows his or her stuff.

What is expertise, and how does it relate to style?

Assuming that you will at one point or another need to adopt the position of an "expert" speaking to an audience that is "inexpert" or at some level uninformed about your topic, you should keep the following guidelines in mind: (1) use simple and concise language, (2) be accurate in your use of language, (3) avoid jargon or specialized language that only the expert understands, and (4) strive to use concrete imagery. Let us discuss each guideline briefly in turn.

Use Simple and Concise Language.   In public speaking situations, sticking to shorter words is easier to follow. Concise words that state exactly what you mean to say will also help an audience follow your message. Remember that when you speak, audiences are primarily concerned with comprehension, and you're trying to help them create a mental image of your speech in their heads. Big words, or too many words, can confuse people. Using words that are unfamiliar to your audience— foreign words or Latin phrases like *in situ* or *prima facie*—can confuse an audience too (perhaps you are confused right now, reading the terms *in situ* and *prima facie*; they mean "in position" and "based on first impression," respectively).

Be Accurate.   When speaking publicly, try to say precisely what you mean in order to convey to an audience that you mean what you say. Inaccurate or vague terms and phrases are often off-putting to audiences. For example, how many times have you heard a public official say something like, "Mr. Franken will have a statement at a future time." Well, *when?* "Mr. Franken will have a statement on the matter next week" is more satisfying. "Mr. Franken will have a statement next Tuesday at noon" is even more satisfying because it is not vague but specific—and hopefully accurate!

Avoid Jargon.   **Jargon** refers to specialized language of a clique or group of experts that only they can understand, often closely tied to a given profession. If you are a social scientist and work with statistics, you might be familiar with "regression analysis" and "Cronbach's alpha." Unless your audience is composed entirely of social scientists familiar with these kinds of terms, however, it's best to avoid them. In general, you should avoid specialized terms and language unless you have the time to define them or unless your audience is highly specialized. One of the main goals of public speaking is to communicate

jargon is the specialized or peculiar language of a particular community or group.

clearly and effectively and to evoke a clear mental picture in the minds of your audience members. Unless the audience is familiar with it, jargon does precisely the opposite.

Use Concrete Imagery. Words are abstractions because they represent something that is not present. If I say "dog," I evoke a mental image of a dog in your head because as a writer I cannot plop a dog into your lap. Language serves as a mental placeholder, so that people can discuss and refer to things that are not present. In this respect, when choosing words for a speech, remember that you are creating mental pictures in the minds of your audience. Concrete words, terms, and images are much more likely to put the image of your speech into focus than are vague ideas, which create a blurry mental picture at best. Even so, illustrating abstract ideas—such as *justice* or *love*—with concrete examples will be more satisfying to an audience: "Should Mr. Johnson continue to be shackled behind bars when we have DNA evidence proving his innocence?" concretely anchors a discussion of justice with the vivid image of shackles and jail bars.

On Rhythm and Word Choice

> **You will learn to**
>
> **EXPLAIN** how vivid language engages an audience.
>
> **DESCRIBE** how repetition and rhythm can interest an audience.
>
> **DEFINE** what a trope is and list two examples.

Because public speaking is fundamentally about oral delivery, keep in mind that you cannot speak to an audience in the same way you would write to a reader. As noted in the chapters on outlining and organizing your speech, you are striving as a speaker to create a mental map of your speech in the minds of your listeners. Enumeration and the repetition of phrases are ways that you signal to your audience the structure of your speech. To enhance or amplify your speech's meaning and feeling, you also need to think about evocative or vivid language, which refers to word choices that evoke vivid images and vibrant feelings in the minds of your audience. Jargon and overly abstract, technical language is flat. In this sense, style concerns what we might call word painting, imparting a sense of vivid imagery, melody, and rhythm with words. Most people enjoy vibrant mental pictures and respond bodily to verbal rhythms; being aware of this fact will help you develop a speaking style that encourages memory and audience interest.

Vivid Language

Gorgias of Leontini, one of the most famous orators of all time, stressed the importance and impact of vibrant language in public speaking as early as the fourth century BCE. He said that a colorful description of an oncoming army can be almost as powerful as "the sight" of "hostile persons" wearing an "array of bronze and iron." A particularly colorful army of words may even inspire "people [to] flee in panic when some danger is imminent as if it were present."[8] Using vivid language helps paint images in the audience's mind, which can not only create a mood or stir feelings but also help your listeners remember your speech.

> Simply stated, **vivid language** concerns words that are sensuous, cuing the mind to the experiences of touch, taste, sound, smell, and sight.

Repetition and Rhythm

Repeating important phrases not only assists audiences in remembering what you said but also helps establish a pleasing sense of rhythm. Children's book author Dr. Seuss is famous for the rhythm of his prose, which is achieved through the repetition of words—as he does with "Thing 1" and "Thing 2" in *The Cat in the Hat*—as well as through the rhyming of words. Note, however, that rhyming words tend to connote deliberate artistry, such as in poetry and rapping; therefore, you may want to use that technique sparingly. **Alliteration**, or the recurrence of the same sound in a series of words, is another artful way to make your message memorable. By repeating words, phrases, sentences—even sounds—in key moments throughout a speech, you can capture the attention and imagination of your audience.

vivid language concerns words that are sensuous and evocative.

alliteration is the recurrence of the same sound in a series of words.

Tropes

Perhaps the most studied elements of speaking style are figures of speech—or, more simply, **tropes**. There are literally hundreds of tropes, but among the most common to public speaking are metaphor and irony.

The most familiar tropes are **metaphors**, which concern using a word, an idea, or a concept to represent something else. Typically, a metaphor is a comparison of two things that initially seem dissimilar but are shown to be similar in some way. For example, consider this common cultural phrase: "You've got to jump if you want to fly!" The meaning of the phrase is that success requires taking risks; however, it's told in language that evokes bird flight. Creating vivid images to assist audiences with memory and encourage enjoyment is the primary reason for using metaphors in public speaking.

Metaphors can be large and elaborate, such as describing the government of a state as the steering of a ship, weathering the winds of economics and the seas of international strife. When metaphors are smaller

tropes are figures of speech. Popular tropes include metaphor, simile, and irony.

metaphors are tropes or figures of speech that compare two seemingly dissimilar things.

the effect of
repetition and rhythm

The use of repetition and rhythm in choosing language for a speech can be powerfully effective for an audience, encouraging their emotional and intellectual engagement and memory. Choosing one's words and structuring the rhythm and pacing of sentences for oral delivery often constitute the last part of drafting a speech. We might compare one's language style to the icing on a cake: the structure is exceedingly important, but how you dress it really does influence how it "goes down." Language choice is not merely icing, though; it influences the experience, and therefore the meaning, of a speech.

Artistry in public speaking is often subtle when speaking to persuade or inform, but it is usually more explicit and encouraged in celebratory speaking. For an especially eloquent example of repetition and rhythm in a speech, consider the closing remarks of President Barack Obama for a eulogy he gave in honor of South Carolina state senator Reverend Clementa Pinckney, who was one of nine people hatefully assassinated during a Bible study at his church in June 2015:

Amazing grace. Amazing grace.

(Begins to sing) — Amazing grace — (applause) — how sweet the sound, that saved a wretch like me; I once was lost, but now I'm found; was blind but now I see. (Applause.)

Clementa Pinckney found that grace.

Cynthia Hurd found that grace.

Susie Jackson found that grace.

Ethel Lance found that grace.

DePayne Middleton-Doctor found that grace.

Tywanza Sanders found that grace.

Daniel L. Simmons Sr. found that grace.

Sharonda Coleman-Singleton found that grace.

Myra Thompson found that grace.

Through the example of their lives, they've now passed it on to us. May we find ourselves worthy of that precious and extraordinary gift, as long as our lives endure. May grace now lead them home. May God continue to shed His grace on the United States of America. (Applause.)[9]

LaunchPad
macmillan learning

Having read the text of Obama's speech, now compare your experience of the written page to how Obama actually delivered his eulogy by visiting LaunchPad at launchpadworks.com to link to the video titled "Clementa Pinckney Eulogy."

Consider the following questions:

- How do the written text and the video delivery compare? Which gives you more information, and why?
- Does Obama's word choice influence the meaning of his statements? Why or why not?

Win McNamee/Staff/Getty Images

- After both reading and hearing Obama's speech, which version is more memorable to you? Why?

in scope, we tend to call them **similes**. A simile is a specific metaphor that almost always uses or implies the word "like." Taylor Swift's title track on her 2012 multiplatinum album *Red* is driven by a long list of similes comparing a former boyfriend to a fast car: "Loving him is like driving a new Maserati down a dead-end street." Loving someone can also be like settling into a big old beanbag chair, although such an observation is perhaps best left unsung.

similes are metaphors that use or imply the word "like."

A more complicated figure of speech that is very common in our culture today is **irony**, which refers to saying one thing but meaning something else. Irony is almost always a form of humor that is meant to make audiences laugh or, at least, smile. The most familiar kind of irony takes the form of satire or sarcasm, such as humorist Stephen Colbert's remarks about then president George W. Bush at a 2006 roast—an event that involves the formalized, good-natured ribbing of someone:

irony is the trope for saying one thing but meaning another.

> Now, I know there are some polls out there saying this man has a 32 percent approval rating. But guys like us, we don't pay attention to the polls. We know that polls are just a collection of statistics that reflect what people are thinking in "reality." And reality has a well-known liberal bias. . . . Sir, pay no attention to the people who say the glass is half-empty . . . because 32 percent means it's two-thirds empty. There's still some liquid in that glass, is my point. But I wouldn't drink it. The last third is usually backwash.[10]

Note that Colbert means to be humorous here. His use of irony makes something relatively abstract (poll numbers and what they actually mean) into something concrete (drinking a glass of water). Irony often functions to bring what seems abstract or hard to grasp into sharp focus.

One must be careful when using irony because it involves communicating meaning indirectly. Whenever you are indirect in public speaking, you always run the risk that some people in your audience may not get the joke or, worse, will be offended. When you are reasonably sure that a use of irony will be both understood and appreciated by an audience, go ahead. But if there is any chance that someone will not get your ironic sense of humor or possibly be offended by sarcasm, rethink it.

Common Tropes at a Glance

TROPE	EXAMPLE
metaphor: using a word, an idea, or a concept in order to represent something dissimilar	"Gah! This algebra problem is a bear!"
simile: a smaller metaphor that uses or implies the word *like*	"Love is like an ATM machine, and you've overdrawn."
irony: saying one thing but meaning something else	"That was as fun as getting kicked in the rear end!"

Using Language That Uses Us: Cultivating Awareness

> **You will learn to**
>
> **EXPLAIN** how a speaker can communicate something he or she doesn't intend.
>
> **LIST** three types of language use that speakers can avoid to prevent misunderstanding or possible offense.

The inherent risk of using irony is that someone may not get it, mistaking your attempt at humor as a declaration of conviction. This kind of misunderstanding points us to a difficult but nevertheless important dimension of word choice: the *unconscious of language*. Language can have meanings beyond our intention. For this reason, one of the most important components of style is cultivating an awareness of what words may mean regardless of what you or I intend them to mean. The task of a cultivated style is trying, as best we can, to make conscious those meanings that normally escape our notice.

As public speakers, we are able to direct the possible meanings of what we say. Even so, this dimension of saying more than we know we are saying persists throughout our lives. For this reason, rhetorical theorist Kenneth Burke famously asked: "Do we simply use words, or do they not also use us?"[11] Many scholars of public speaking have answered Burke's question positively by arguing that we communicate meanings that we do not intend all the time. For example, a number of political communication scholars have argued that key terms used by politicians — such as "politics," "government," "media," "people," and "president" — control the speakers and writers more than they think they control them: a left-leaning politician may say "government" in a speech and mean something positive to be developed, while a right-leaning person in the audience may hear "government" as something negative that must be stopped.[12]

Admittedly, when we start thinking about how much we are not in total control of the meaning of what we say, it's easy to get anxious. Because meaning is co-created by people using language, most of us are quite generous to one another. As symbol-using animals, we have to be charitable to one another when speaking and try to meet

Janet and Brad have decided to get a dog!

Malapropism

Malapropism is the accidental confusion of ideas or similar-sounding words, sometimes referred to as a "Freudian slip." Malapropisms are excellent examples of how language "uses us" and often inspires laughter. The late Yankee's legend Yogi Berra, for example, was famous for his malapropisms: **"Baseball is 90 percent mental. The other half is physical."** Malapropisms, however, can also be as simple as using the wrong word, such as saying "for all intensive purposes" instead of "for all intents and purposes." Freud believed these kinds of slips of the tongue show how language works unconsciously through us, expressing feelings and desires we may not be consciously aware of — such as feelings about one's parents: **"Psychoanalysis means saying one thing and meaning your mother."**

others halfway — indeed, this charity is another name for listening. Even so, there are a number of unfortunate word choices that can discourage audiences from listening, causing them to offer less charity and attribute meanings to your words that you may not intend. Cultivating an awareness of language in these specific areas is crucial for encouraging listening. Ignoring these areas of language choice will put you at risk of alienating your audience. These areas include the use of biased language, the use of sexist language, and the use of slang.

Biased Language

Simply stated, biased language refers to the use of words and phrases that indicate unfounded assumptions about others based on personal experience. All human beings have a tendency to be biased, thinking in words and a language that references our individual experiences of the world. For example, we often have stereotypes about groups of people to which we do not belong: older people and younger people; people from different parts of the world; people of different religious backgrounds, class affiliations, racial identifications, gender roles, sexual orientations; and so on. Part of growing up, as you may recall from your youth, is learning not to universalize your individual experience of the world as if it were everyone's experience of the world. If you have grown up in a rural or country area, for instance, you may believe that people from the city are rude and fast talking; if you have grown up in a city, you may believe that people in the country are slow and uncultured. The country hick and city slicker are among the more familiar stereotypes of American life, parodied in countless Hollywood films. As you meet people from places where you did not grow up, you come to realize that they do not resemble your stereotypes at all. We tend to learn, as we grow older, that people are more alike than they are different.

Biased language takes many forms, but all of them rest on unfounded assumptions about others. Consider how biased language can occur when a speaker without disabilities discusses people with disabilities (PWD). For example, "Mr. Smith's autistic son Daniel helped me clean the house" may seem like nonbiased language, but for many PWD and their families, the phrase is unpleasant. This is because the disability is mentioned *before* the person, which implies that the person is defined by his or her disability. People-first language is more appropriate: "Mr. Smith's son Daniel, who has autism, helped me clean the house" is a respectful way to refer to Daniel.

As a public speaker, you need to keep your assumptions in check. When speaking, avoid choosing words that assume that those different from you share your limited experience of the world. When trying to avoid bias in speaking, the so-called Golden Rule can be modified as a guide: speak to others as you would like to be spoken to. Respect the real differences of people in your audience while building on the human experiences you share in common. Remember that public speaking is ultimately about building or celebrating community, and one of the best ways to do that is to ensure that everyone feels included by your language.

Sexist Language

From a very early age, most of us were raised to identify with a biological sex: either you are male or you are female. As you grow older, you may identify with a different sex, both, or neither. Regardless, in our culture all sorts of gender assumptions are made about our supposed natures based on that initial biological assignment, and the messages about how to be a "man" or a "woman" are powerful and often constraining. The tension we all experience to become a "man" or a "woman" is an issue of gender, and it will persist throughout our lives. We simply have to learn how to navigate the assumptions about our characters based on our biological assignment as best we can. As a speaker, you should strive to include everyone, regardless of how he or she defines and navigates his or her gender, sex, and sexuality.

If assumptions about our person based on our gender identity are often beyond our control, there is one thing we can control as speakers: how each of us makes assumptions about the character of others based on gender. In just about every speaking situation, we cannot assume that the experience of those identified as women is the same as the experience of those identified as men, and vice versa. Even so, you will hear speakers refer to people in the abstract as "he" or "she," even though people can be one, the other, or in some cases both or neither. Speakers also mistakenly use gendered pronouns in respect to social roles and professions (for example, nurses are women; firefighters are men). Paying attention to your use of pronouns can help you avoid these kinds of mistake. Making very simple word substitutions can help you avoid

Rosie the Riveter

We Can Do It!

During the World War II, millions of women were recruited to do the jobs of men conscripted for the war effort. In 1942, the artist J. Howard Miller was asked to paint a poster for the Westinghouse Company challenging gender stereotypes in support of women moving into jobs previously done by men.

MPI/Getty Images

alienating or offending members of your audience. For example, "A good dentist is trained to attend to the pain of his patients." Whoops! Not all dentists are male. The better phrasing would be, "A good dentist is trained to attend to the pain of her or his patients." Saying "he or she" or "her or his" is more inclusive and encourages every member of your audience to imagine himself or herself in your example. At the time of this writing, many people in North American culture are moving toward using "they," "them," and "their" as a generic pronouns to be more inclusive.

Slang

A final area of word choice you should be aware of concerns the use of slang, which refers to the informal language of a group of people. In popular culture, slang is often associated with groups that identify in respect to class, race, or profession. You may even have a slang that is particular to your group of friends. The advent of texting over the last two decades has generated a written slang that those less familiar to texting may find off-putting in a speech: "JK" and "LOL" are meaningful to many, but some older audiences unfamiliar with these terms would be baffled if a speaker used these acronyms in a speech.

Despite some exceptions, you should generally avoid the use of slang because, by definition, slang is an insider language. To use slang denotes a membership in some sort of community, and in many speaking situations, you will have no clear indication that everyone in the audience is also a member of the community from which your slang hails. This

How do you become more aware of your language use? What kinds of word choices should you avoid? Why?

On Political Correctness

In our time, the concept of political correctness has become a hotly debated one. In general, political correctness refers to the attempt to avoid expressions or behaviors that marginalize, exclude, or insult people who are different from ourselves—which would include the use of biased and sexist language and, in some cases, slang. A popular example of politically correct language would be using "humankind" instead of "mankind," or using "he and she" instead of simply "he" as a generic pronoun. Until the twentieth century, the use of "mankind" and "he" as generic terms for human beings was relatively commonplace. Some believe that political correctness can go too far, becoming extreme. Others argue, however, that striving to be politically correct does more good than harm, encouraging people to be more mindful of their word choices.[13]

What do you think?

means that slang is likely to alienate at least some audience members. The point of speaking publicly is not to alienate but rather to include.

In popular culture, many people think of style in terms of appearance or fashion. In the tradition of public speaking, however, style refers broadly to how you present yourself to others in a variety of ways: in words, in deeds, in your confidence, and yes, in how you look. Style indicates the place where the body and representation meet. In this chapter, we focused most pointedly on style in respect to language choice: Based on your speech situation, purpose, and goal—including the audience and their expectations—what kind of words and language choices better represent you and what you mean to say? In chapter 10, we take up style as it more directly implicates our bodies, considering the following types of questions related to delivery: How should one dress when speaking to an audience? At what rate and volume should a presenter speak? What gestures should a speaker use?

Tips on speaking style

- Dress appropriately for the speaking situation.
- Present your best and most confident self.
- Choose words that not only reflect your expertise but also relate to the audience.
- Select words that help you establish a rhythm appropriate for the occasion.
- Use vivid language, repetition, and other artful language choices when appropriate and possible.
- Avoid technical jargon, biased language, and slang.

> **What is the relationship between jargon and slang? Are either ever appropriate in public speaking?**

end of chapter stuff

(Portrait reference photo) REUTERS/Fred Prouser

What Is Style?

Rather than simply being about fashion, style refers to the way in which a person presents himself or herself to others. In the context of public speaking, style refers to the relationship between what one says and how he or she says it. Traditionally, the focus on style in public speaking concerns word choice and delivery.

Choosing Your Words

Choosing the right language for a speech requires contextual reasoning about the speech situation and the audience. You need to know where you stand with the audience as either an insider or an outsider, whether the situation is formal or informal, and what expertise they do or do not have. In general, strive for clear, concrete, and vivid language, employing repetition and rhythm to assist memory and encourage interest.

Using Language That Uses Us: Cultivating Awareness

Language is slippery because meaning is made by two or more people. Audiences can often interpret a meaning from your words that you did not intend. Care should be taken to avoid biased and sexist language, as well as slang. Consider how you can be more inclusive with your language, bringing your audience together as a community by avoiding language that excludes or discriminates.

CHAPTER 9

ACTIVITY

Martin Luther King Jr.'s "I Have a Dream"

Speaking from the steps of the Lincoln Memorial in Washington, D.C., on August 28, 1963, Martin Luther King Jr. delivered one of the most famous speeches of all time. King's "I Have a Dream" speech was delivered during the historic March on Washington for Jobs and Freedom, whose 200,000 to 300,000 participants constituted one of the largest rallies for civil and economic rights in the history of the United States. The speech is almost unanimously regarded as one of the most stylistically savvy and eloquent in the history of oratory because of its skillful use of metaphor, repetition, and inclusive language. To better understand how style relates to one's message, find a transcript of the speech online and attempt to answer the following questions:

1. What is the purpose of King's speech?
2. What is King's thesis, and what are his main points?
3. Is King's speech formal, informal, or both? How can you tell?
4. What concrete imagery does King use in the speech? How does vivid language relate to this imagery?
5. Identify the ways in which King establishes a sense of rhythm with repetition. What other devices does King use to impart a sense of melody and rhythm?
6. What metaphors does King use? Does he use irony?
7. Does King's speech betray bias? sexist language? If so, is this appropriate, and why? If not, how does King avoid biased language?

KEY TERMS

 Videos in LaunchPad describe many of these terms. Go to launchpadworks.com.

style 181
disposition 181
denotation 182
connotation 182
impression management 182
expertise 186
jargon 187

vivid language 189
alliteration 189
tropes 189
metaphors 189
similes 191
irony 191
malapropism 193

Style and Delivery

Chapter 10

Many people associate hip-hop with music, but the ardent fan knows that hip-hop is a *culture* that includes a variety of expressive elements involving the body, gesture, dance and fashion.[1] The popular South Bronx block-party scene of the eighties is credited with naming this culture "hip-hop," which is a term that captures the body movement and dance so central to the emerging form of human expression. Artists like Grandmaster Flash helped popularize hip-hop in the early 1980s as a musical culture that depended as much on dance — at the time, break dancing — and fashion as it did on music.[2]

Although many hip-hop artists feature dancers, the vocalist in hip-hop groups — the "mic controller," or MC — typically doesn't dance. Instead, MCs and rappers have developed a rather expansive repertoire of gestures using the hands and arms.[3] One hand holds the microphone while the other expressively punctuates the lyrics or moves to the beat. Hip-hop gesturing by MCs is now a central component of how lyrics are delivered; it's simply difficult to imagine a hip-hop artist who doesn't gesture.

As a public speaker, you have to do more than just craft the right words; you also have to deliver them with your body through voice and gesture. Of course, in most public speaking situations, your gestures and body movement will not be as pronounced as those of a hip-hop artist; however, it is similarly difficult to imagine an engaging public speaker who does not dynamically deliver his or her speech with a pleasing voice and appropriate body movements.

This chapter is about the power of *the way* we say things with our bodies. In chapter 9 we focused on that part of style that the ancient Greeks isolated to *word choice*: how the words one uses in a speech help create impressions. In this chapter, we take up the *manner* of speaking, or what scholars of oratory and public speaking term "delivery": the way a speaker uses the body to convey a speech, including the voice, gesture and movement, eye contact, and fashion.

Nonverbal Communication and Tone

You will learn to

DEFINE nonverbal communication and list the elements it includes.

EXPLAIN the relationship between nonverbal communication and tone.

As noted in chapter 9, **speech** is the meeting place of the body and language. Speech can refer to the physiological event of air passing over the vocal chords, the content or meaning of what one says, or the notion of speaking in the abstract (e.g., free speech). Communication scholars study both the verbal and nonverbal aspects of speech, or both *what* one says and *how* one says it.

Nonverbal communication encompasses all the ways in which we communicate in addition to, in opposition to, and independent of the spoken word. Nonverbal communication usually concerns bodies, as with the study of touch (haptics) or how close we stand to one another (proxemics) or how we use visual cues with our bodies to say things (body language). We have studied the use of repetition and rhythm in chapter 9; here our focus is on body language and elements such as vocalics (qualities of voice), gesture, and facial expression.

One memorable way to think about nonverbal communication in public speaking is with the concept of **tone**, defined as the overall emotional quality or character of a human expression. Tone is emotional because it concerns mood, something that is at once bodily (because it has to do with feelings) and symbolic (because it concerns meaning). As a child, a parent may have warned you with "Don't use that tone with me!" or "Watch your tone!" What do these warnings really mean? The demand underlying "Watch your tone!" doesn't concern *what you say* but rather *how you say it*. When thinking about your nonverbal communication as a speaker, then, imagine the appropriate bodily cues for the speaking situation to help you create the right tone. Planning your speech delivery entails working toward adjusting the emotional character of your nonverbal communication, a process that we can simply term "**tonework**." Tonework simply refers to all the things speakers do to control or manage how they communicate to an audience without words—the work that goes into crafting one's tone.

speech is the meeting place of the body and language, typically understood as meaningful, vocal expression.

tone refers to the emotional quality or character of human expression; in public speaking, tone references the feelings of the speaker as they are expressed in delivery.

tonework references the labor of the speaker to craft, control, or change the expression of feeling in public speaking.

Darren Quinton/Mirrorpix/Newscom

What does the body language from these audience members communicate to you?

Elocutionary Movement

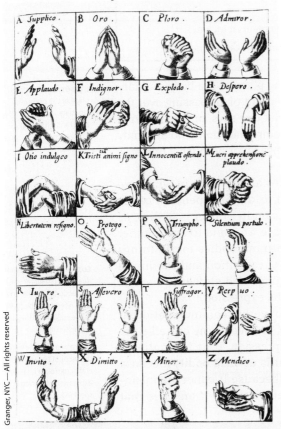

The elocutionary movement refers to the study of public speaking as an art concerned primarily with delivery. It thrived in the eighteenth and nineteenth centuries in the United States and the United Kingdom and largely reflects an overall obsession with the pronunciation of words and their appropriate, corresponding body gestures. The key figures of this movement were Irish actor and educator Thomas Sheridan (1719–1788) and Irish clergyperson Gilbert Austin (1753–1837). By the nineteenth century, the study of elocution was how individuals studied public speaking (mostly privately, in their homes or with a tutor).[4] For elocutionists like Sheridan, one's tone in speaking is related to strong, instinctual emotions, like hunger and jealousy. He believed that tones could even bypass language and communicate through feelings (e.g., laughter is "wordless," yet the sound of it can be infectious).

The way that public speaking is taught today eventually replaced elocution and reduced the concern with vocal delivery and gestures to only a part of the art.

What is nonverbal communication? How does it relate to tone? ❓

As we use it here, then, tone refers to the emotional character of a speech and the kinds of adjectives an audience might use to describe the overall impression of our speech. Eulogies are often given at funerals in a somber tone; wedding toasts are joyful; and presidential speeches are often direct, measured, and serious in tone. Tone doesn't just refer to the vocal elements of style but to how you carry yourself as well, and it includes body movement, eye contact, and how you dress (e.g., a casual outfit would help communicate a casual tone). The work that tone does can also be easily felt or sensed with musical examples. Tones are often associated with musical genres: so-called gangsta hip-hop is bold, macho, and aggressive, and the lyrics and music combine with dance

New York hip-hop trio Salt-N-Pepa versus smooth jazz artist Kenny G. How are different tones communicated by the body language and fashion choices of these artists?

Left: Janette Beckman/Contributor/Getty Images   *Right:* Neil H. Kitson/Contributor/Getty Images

and body movement to create an exciting, rebellious tone. Smooth jazz, on the other hand, is slow and sensual, and the relaxed gestures and body movements of performers help create a more sedate and easy tone.

The way we use language and the words we choose are parts of tone because they help create the emotional character of our speech. Scholars have developed a number of concepts to help us examine more closely the tonal dimension of our speech, or the ways in which delivery can inspire feelings and meanings in addition to the words we say. We can divide these concepts into two basic categories: how we use the body to communicate and express ourselves, and how we adorn the body to communicate and express ourselves (e.g., what we wear). We now examine each in turn.

> **?** What is tone? As a speaker, how do you manage tone in delivery?

Body Language

> **You will learn to**
>
> **LIST** the two primary foci of the study of body language.
>
> **EXPLAIN** how gesture and body movement can help or hinder one's message.

When speaking publicly, your body is its own megaphone, helping to amplify—literally and figuratively—what you say with words. There are two ways this is accomplished: (1) the use of the human voice, or

"vocalics"; and (2) the use of body movement, including gesture, facial expression, and eye contact.

Vocalics

vocalics is the study of the nonverbal character and expressiveness of the human voice.

The study of the way people use their voices, including volume, pitch, articulation, pronunciation, rate, and modulation, is called **vocalics**. Because we tend to adjust our volume, rate of speech, and pitch without thinking about it, these dimensions of the voice are often difficult to notice. It is common for beginning speakers to speak too fast or too low to be heard, as most of us are not taught about vocalics until college. Becoming conscious of one's vocal qualities gets easier with practice, just like a singer can improve her or his voice with rehearsals and training.

Vocalic Elements

VOCALIC ELEMENT	EXAMPLE	TIPS
Volume: The loudness of a speaker's voice	Audience members suddenly jolt or cover their ears when you speak (too loud); audience members lean forward or cup their ears (too soft).	Adjust the loudness of your voice based on the size of the room you are speaking in and whether or not you have a microphone. Without a microphone, you must speak more loudly when talking outdoors or in a larger room filled with more people. In a smaller, intimate space, you should speak with a normal volume. When in doubt, ask the audience if they can hear you.
Pitch: The sound frequency of a speaker's voice, from low to high; the rising and falling of pitch in speech is called "intonation"	Placing different emphases on words creates different moods: "*What* did you just say?" expresses excitement or annoyance, while a plainspoken "What did you just say?" is more of a request.	The pitch of your voice expresses mood. Varying your pitch when speaking conveys interest and excitement, while a sustained pitch can seem monotonous.
Articulation: Pronouncing words in a clear manner	"I think we should go tomorrow" (articulate) versus "wah-wah wah wah wah wah" (the teacher character in *Peanuts* cartoons).	Articulation concerns how you move your lips and tongue when speaking. Articulate speakers are usually easy to understand. Muttering and mumbling should be avoided. A tried-and-true method of practicing articulation is the pen-in-mouth exercise: read something aloud while holding a pen between your teeth. This forces your lips to overcompensate for the obstruction and articulate individual words. Be sure not to keep the pen in your mouth for an actual public speaking situation!

Vocalic Elements (*continued*)

VOCALIC ELEMENT	EXAMPLE	TIPS
Pronunciation: The correct or accepted way a word sounds	The word "timbre": "That song has a funky TIM-bra" (wrong) versus "That song has a funky TAM-ber" (right).	Audiences are unnerved when words are pronounced incorrectly. Bad pronunciation can cause negative assumptions. Remember to look up the word in question, or ask how to pronounce someone's name if you are uncertain.
Rate: The speed or pace of speaking	Imagine the difference between an auctioneer speaking at an auction (fast rate) and a psychotherapist hypnotizing a patient (slow rate).	Speaking quickly communicates excitement and interest, while speaking slowly conveys a serious or thoughtful mood. Strive to vary your rate of speaking to the rhythm of the content of your speech. Closely related to rate is the pause, or the moment of silence between the things you say. Some pauses are fine and connote either emphasis or thinking. Too many pauses can indicate that you are unprepared or distracted.
Modulation: The attempt to vary the volume, pitch, rate, and general character of one's voice	When delivering his "Remarks by the President in Eulogy for the Honorable Reverend Clementa Pinckney," Barack Obama varied the volume, pitch, and rate of his voice in a pleasing manner that almost resembled singing.	Speakers who consciously modulate their voices are considered dynamic, and those who do not are described as monotone. More serious and somber speaking situations generally require less modulation than less serious, celebratory situations.

Verbal Fillers

In our world of continuous stimulation from sound speakers and screens, many of us have become uncomfortable with silence. In speaking, however, silence can be useful: a pause in speaking can give both you and your audience some time to think. Be wary of trying to fill pauses in your speaking with "ums" or "ahs" or the ubiquitous "you know" and "like," which are known as "vocalized pauses," or **verbal fillers**.[5] In casual conversation, we use verbal fillers to create a sense of informality and comfort, but in more formal speaking situations, these filler words can distract from your speech and should therefore be avoided.

The most important vocalic element is volume. If the audience can't hear you, then most of your speech's meaning will be lost. For many speaking situations, you'll have to use **voice projection**, which refers to the way in which speakers increase their vocal volume and adopt a confident tone in order to command attention (much like your instructor does when he or she is lecturing). Be sure to project your voice to the audience with enough volume for those in the back row to hear (or, if signing, be sure everyone in the audience can see). If you are unsure whether those in the very back can hear or see you, it's sometimes helpful to simply ask: "Can you hear me in the back row?" or "Can you see me?"

In some cases you'll be asked to use a microphone, whether clipped to your jacket, blouse, or shirt (a lavalier); handheld (a baton); or fixed (on a podium or microphone stand). Before you speak, either you or your hosts will need to perform a sound check in order to adjust the volume; care should also be taken to correct for **feedback**, which is the unpleasant sound a microphone can make when it is too close to a speaker or playback device. Use microphones with care, and remember that everything from your throat to your voice is mechanically *enhanced*; sudden sounds (like coughing) can be startling. And, most importantly, never say anything when your microphone is on that you would not want the whole room to hear.

Hands, Shoulders, Knees, and Toes

As speakers, we rely on our voices, but we unconsciously employ our bodies in ways that reinforce what we are trying to say in order to help stabilize meaning. Sometimes, however, our bodies are not in sync with our speech. For example, if a concerned friend asks you if you are all right and you respond angrily, "I'm just fine!" while furrowing your brow and crossing your arms over your chest, your friend would notice a mismatch between your language and your bodily expression. Rather than trust *what* you said, your friend would probably put more trust in *how* you said it.

Some people are naturally better at using the body and gestures to reinforce what they say in a speech, but it's also a skill that we can develop. The goal is to become aware of what our body is doing when we speak to make sure our expressions and gestures match up. The quickest way to do this is to watch yourself giving a speech in front of a mirror; however, watching a video recording of yourself is even more helpful.[6] Research by communication scholars has repeatedly shown that speakers who review recordings of themselves speaking have decreased anxiety and more readily develop effective speaking skills.[7]

In addition to watching yourself practice your speech, another way to establish better control over what your body and voice are communicating is to focus on those elements of the body identified by scholars as the most important symbolically: gesture, facial expression, and eye contact.

voice projection refers to the way in which speakers use the strength of their voice to control volume and express confidence in a speaking situation.

feedback refers to the unpleasant sound created when an audio input is too close to an output (e.g., a loudspeaker).

> **What are vocalics? Name the main features of vocalics.** ❓

from where you say it:
feeling accents and dialects

The late Ann Richards, former governor of Texas, spoke with a discernible Texas accent, which she often referenced to impart her authority as a political leader for Texans. Ken Geiger/KRT/Newscom

Adopting appropriate vocalics varies by venue, community, and the background of the speaker. In general, the more formal the speaking situation, the more proper one's vocalics should be. The most obvious example of vocalic diversity is one's **accent**, which refers to the way a person's voice *sounds* and how they pronounce words. A **dialect**, on the other hand, can reference both an accent *and* certain turns of phrase, speaking styles, and grammatical conventions particular to a community, class allegiance, or geographical region. For example, many Americans born in the Deep South speak with a melodic "southern drawl" or accent, which not only has a particularly "twangy" sound, but also has grammatical inventions that specify a regionally specific dialect, such as the term "y'all." If you are speaking to an audience that may be unfamiliar with your accent or dialect, consider speaking more slowly and articulating words more clearly than you normally would. If you're listening to a speaker who has an accent or speaks in a particular dialect, be generous as a listener and try to accept his or her ways of pronouncing things as simply *different* rather than wrong, bad, or uneducated.

LaunchPad
macmillan learning

For a striking example of how one's vocal tone, accent, and dialect influence the perceptions of listeners, visit LaunchPad at launchpadworks.com and listen to an audio clip featuring a speaker delivering a speech by Ann Richards. The speaker reads Richards's speech in what is termed a "north central" or "midwestern" dialect, which is routinely adopted by radio and television personalities. Next, link out to the video of Ann Richards delivering her speech.

After listening, consider the following questions:
- Trying to ignore the actual words spoken, which speaker is more appealing to you? Why?
- In what ways do the speakers' accents and dialects differ? Do these ways influence how you *hear* the speech? How?

High-Context and Low-Context Cultures

davidf/Getty Images

In high-context cultures, such as that of Japan, communication is less direct and more dependent on nonverbal expressions and references to culture.

Anthropologist Edward T. Hall introduced the concept of "high-" and "low-context" cultures to explain how interaction among people differs across various parts of the world.[8] High-context cultures — identified with parts of the Middle East, Asia, most of South America, and Africa — are more community oriented and place more value on bodily expression. In these cultures, the environment and context of speaking — the physical area, as well as the social class and roles of the people speaking, status, and so on — are more important to meaning than the words people actually say. In low-context cultures, which include most of North America and Western Europe, the words people say are given more priority than how they say them; the focus is on the individual instead of the group, and thus the body is de-emphasized (a U.S. citizen in Japan would need to be very aware of his or her nonverbal messaging, taking care to bow appropriately during introductions). Consequently, tonework is more challenging in the United States and Canada than it is in high-context cultures, because we are often asked to "watch what you say" as young persons more than we are instructed to think about how others will interpret our body language. Wherever you are from, when speaking in another culture you should take care to study the body language norms of that culture. Did you know that in parts of Yugoslavia, nodding does not mean "yes" but "no"?[9] Attending to small body-language issues like bowing and nodding can make a very big difference!

Gesture

gesture refers to the movement of the head, hands, or arms to communicate an idea or a feeling.

The elocutionists of the nineteenth century focused on **gesture** and voice and were concerned with making sure that what one said corresponded to the proper hand gesture. International gesture expert Jürgen Streeck has challenged this approach to gesture, however, arguing that our gestures actually connect us to our world.[10] Using our hands does not simply convey a symbolic meaning but articulates our whole persons to the world around us. This view holds that gestures are just as significant to our social world as speech.

It is easy to overlook just how much gesture plays a role in how we think and relate to others.[11] Sit on a bench in a crowded public park and watch people walking by, talking on their smartphones. How many of them are gesturing when they talk, even though the person they are talking to is not present? This example demonstrates that the ways we use our hands and bodies are intimately tied—if not "hardwired"—to

Gesturing can communicate as much or even more meaning than speech.

our speech and to our environments. The consequence is that you should attend to the importance of gestures and the body when speaking in public (and most especially when speaking on a screen!).

Because gesture is such an integral component of being human, for many of us gesturing will come naturally when we speak. Forcing a gesture can often seem staged and unnatural, even awkward. It is important to only use gestures that seem appropriate and unique to your normal, habitual manner. That said, you can often consciously use gesture to embellish what you are saying as long as it's not outside your normal repertoire. When asking a question of the audience in North America, for example, holding one's arms out and turning the palms upward is a welcoming gesture, encouraging participation.

American Sign Language

ZUMA Press, Inc./Alamy Stock Photo

The mayor of New York City communicated news of a hurricane using an American Sign Language interpreter.

Many of those who identify as deaf or hard of hearing use American Sign Language (ASL). ASL was developed in the early nineteenth century at the American School for the Deaf in Hartford, Connecticut, and has gradually become the most popular language for the deaf and hard of hearing in the United States. The language is predominately visual, using the hands, torso, face, and body to communicate ideas and feelings. ASL depends on a large repertoire of gestures, movements, and expressions, yet it is a complex *language* with a unique grammar and syntax, different from those of spoken English.

Although gestures are most commonly associated with the hands, moving other parts of your body—especially your arms—and making facial expressions can also be a form of gesturing. When you move closer to the audience by leaning or walking toward them, this is often perceived as a gesture of intimacy, of wanting to be closer—both literally and metaphorically. When speaking, it's also a good idea to move around and to not remain chained behind a podium. As a public speaker, you often have much more freedom to move around, and you can do so as long as you're not obstructing a visual aid or tethered to a corded microphone. However, care should be taken not to pace or to sway back and forth, as these kinds of movements can make you appear nervous or anxious. Moreover, moving too much can make the audience seasick and detract from your message.

Facial expression

When people speak to us, we usually focus on three sections of the face: the eyes, the eyebrows, and the mouth. Raised eyebrows can communicate interest, intrigue, or excitement. A furrowed brow can indicate intensity, confusion, or even anger. Eye contact can communicate interest, sincerity, or—if held too long—intensity. We also know that no single facial expression is more universal and inviting than a smile. Have you ever interacted with a baby? Often if you smile at an infant, the baby will smile back at you, almost automatically. This has to do with something called mirror neurons, which are mechanisms in the brain that assist with understanding and empathy. In this sense, it seems that humans are "hardwired" to take on the feelings of others.[12] Research has even demonstrated that smiling more frequently can change one's mood.[13] Give it a try the next time you find yourself in a bad mood.

In some cultures and contexts, smiling can be unpleasant. Imagine, for example, how a beaming smile might not be appropriate during a eulogy. Even so, in general, smiling while public speaking is a gesture of goodwill toward the audience and indicates you are happy to be with them. If you are nervous, smiling can often help, making you feel more comfortable and charming the audience into listening more closely to your speech. When in doubt, smile!

Eye contact

Finally, there are the eyes, those proverbial windows to the soul. In general, looking other people in the eyes is an intimate gesture of sincerity, trust, and even caring. In Western culture, making eye contact signifies a human connection and interest. In some contexts and cultures, however, making

Courtesy Everett Collection

Because the human animal relies so heavily on facial expressions to communicate, the "dummies" used by ventriloquists have deliberately exaggerated facial characteristics and movements.

eye contact is governed by rigid rules that one must learn. Eye contact can be read as an inappropriate failure to recognize power in some cultures (e.g., Japan),[14] so care should always be taken when you are speaking outside a Western cultural context.

Research has demonstrated that making eye contact with listeners is important for public speaking because it enhances the speaker's credibility.[15] But the larger the audience is, the more challenging the practice can be. If your audience is larger than a small group, there's no possible way you can remember to make eye contact with every single person in the room. Instead, you should practice scanning, as if your eyes were a searchlight panning back and forth across the audience. Make sure your eyes move back and forth across the room to indicate that you are addressing the entire audience. It's often helpful to identify a handful of people in different areas of the room (one in front, one in back, and one or two on each side) who seem particularly attentive or interested in your speech.

For larger groups, scan your audience instead of attempting to make eye contact with every individual.

Creating the Illusion of Eye Contact

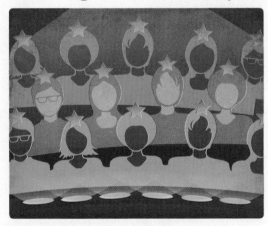

Create the illusion of eye contact by staring at the tops of folks' heads.

As a general rule, when speaking publicly you should attempt to make eye contact with your audience and vary how you do so. If actually meeting the eyes of a listener in your audience makes you nervous, don't fret. Many public speakers use the "head-top method" to create the illusion of eye contact. Because of the way our eyes are situated in our heads, the farther a person is from you the more difficult it is to tell if he or she is making eye contact with you. We have a tendency to assume people looking in our direction from farther away are looking at us. As a speaker, you can use this assumption to your advantage by looking at the tops of people's heads, where the stars are on the heads of this generic audience. From the audience's perspective, it will appear that you are looking them in the eyes, when in reality you will simply be checking out their hairdos.

. . . And a Good Pair of Shoes: Grooming and Dressing to Speak

> **You will learn to**
>
> **DESCRIBE** how a speaker's appearance could be noticed by an audience.
>
> **EXPLAIN** the matching approach to dress and grooming for public speaking.

What are the two basic rules of grooming and dressing for public speaking? What are the reasons for these rules?

When audiences are preparing to listen to a public speaker, they do what most of us do when meeting someone for the first time: check out his or her looks. Before you open your mouth to speak, your audience will be assessing your appearance. Inasmuch as creating the right tone concerns syncing your body and voice with the content of your speech, you should strive to similarly match your grooming and clothing with the context of your speech and the setting. The general rule for appearance that seasoned public speakers follow may surprise you: *Avoid standing out from the crowd!* Speakers adopt this rule because they want the audience to focus on their speech, not their clothing.[16] There are exceptions, of course, such as when a movie or Broadway star wears a zany outfit to an awards show. Clothing can be a statement and a way to garner attention. For most speaking situations, however, you want the focus to be

Even after surviving a tornado, speaker Dorothy is impeccably dressed.

on what you say and how you say it, not on how much makeup you are wearing, why you didn't shave that morning, and so on.

There are two basic ways your appearance is noticed: (1) you appear unkempt and slovenly, or (2) your dress and grooming style is unusual or flashy. Appearing unkempt communicates that you do not care about how you are perceived, which can translate to an audience assuming you do not care about them. Appearing over the top or awkwardly dressed can distract from your message and even eclipse it. You do not want audiences so distracted by how you are dressed that they ignore or cannot remember your message. In short: the goal is to blend in with your audience as much as possible when speaking.

Most of the time, using contextual reasoning can help you decide what is and is not appropriate to wear for a speaking engagement. As a general rule, you want to prepare in a way that you anticipate most of your audience prepares, and dress within the general fashion sensibility of the time, place, and event. If the speaking engagement is formal, dress formally; if the event is casual, dress casually.

There is one important caveat to this matching approach to speaking fashion: make sure to dress one step up. This is to say, once you have an idea of how your audience will appear, wear what they might wear, but do it a little bit nicer. If most people in the audience are dressed in business casual, which usually means a blazer or sport coat, a sweater or classic shirt, and a skirt or slacks, dress similarly but put on a tie or a simple necklace or scarf. The one-step-up rule is tricky, because it can be easily overdone. Dressing one step up shows your audience that you thought about what you would wear beforehand. This subtle gesture communicates your interest in your audience.

Even though the general rule of speaking fashion is to downplay your appearance, keep in mind that the whole point is to communicate consideration and goodwill to your audience.

Finally, a word about shoes. Yes, I said shoes. Many experienced public speakers—and especially those who teach public speaking—will testify that some audience members are keenly interested in footwear as an index of personality.

Justin Sullivan/Staff/Getty Images

Late Apple pioneer Steve Jobs believed that his unpretentious fashion choices helped audiences focus on the new technologies that he introduced, not what he wore.

What shoes are you wearing right now? What do you think they say about you as a person? Would it be appropriate to wear them for a speech in your classroom? Why or why not?

Whether or not there is any correlation between what you put on your feet and who you are, the fact remains that at least some audience members, especially those who take an interest in fashion, will make judgments about you as a speaker based on your footwear. Researchers at the University of Kansas have demonstrated that—at least to a limited extent—people can and do make accurate assumptions about others based on their footwear.[17] If you are wearing tennis shoes, this might communicate that you are athletic or enjoy being comfortable. If you are wearing combat boots, what this communicates will vary from one audience to the next, but in general it would be received as a statement of strength, ruggedness, or punk sensibility.

Observing the rule of avoiding notice, the shoes you wear to a speaking engagement should generally mirror the footwear of your audience. Observing the rule to dress one step up also applies to your shoes, which should be a little nicer, perhaps a little newer, than what you imagine will be on the feet of those in front of you. And with footwear, you can add a little signature of individuality if you want, because the feet are the last thing that gets noticed about appearance.

As an expression of style, delivery is about how you present yourself to others nonverbally with your body. In this chapter, we examined a number of dimensions of nonverbal communication that contribute to establishing an appropriate and effective tone, from the different components of body language to grooming and dressing yourself for the speaking event. We will now move from how you embody your speech and dress yourself to how you can style your speech with visual aids.

Style and Delivery

As the counterpart to word choice, delivery is the component of style that has to do with how we use our bodies to communicate to others.

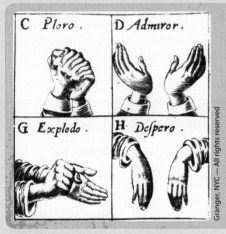

Nonverbal Communication and Tone

Delivery largely concerns nonverbal communication, including haptics, proxemics, vocalics, and various aspects of body language. In public speaking, many of these dimensions are addressed in striking the right tone in delivery.

. . . And a Good Pair of Shoes: Grooming and Dressing to Speak

Grooming and clothing choices should try to match those of your audience and the demands of the speaking situation.

CHAPTER 10

LaunchPad
macmillan learning

LaunchPad for *Speech Craft* includes a curated collection of speech videos and encourages self-assessment through adaptive quizzing. Go to **launchpadworks.com** to get access to:

- LearningCurve adaptive quizzes
- Video clips to help you improve your speeches

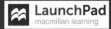

ACTIVITY

Tone and the Adjective

In public speaking, tone is often difficult to describe in words because words detach feelings from specific bodies and put them into language. Yet making this move is the only way we can actually talk about tone. Using adjectives is a typical way to translate the tones of the body into discussions. For this activity, find and watch a video online of Martin Luther King Jr.'s "I Have a Dream" speech. Make three columns on a piece of paper, labeled "Voice," "Body," and "Adjective." As you watch the speech, describe what King does with his voice in the first column, record King's gestures and mannerisms in the "Body" column, and list any adjectives you can think of that describe the things you notice in the third column. Compare your adjectives to those of a classmate. Are they similar? Are they dissimilar? How do you account for the similarities and dissimilarities of your adjectives?

KEY TERMS

Videos in LaunchPad describe many of these terms. Go to launchpadworks.com.

- **speech 201**
- **tone 201**
- **tonework 201**
- **vocalics 204**
- **verbal fillers 205**
- **voice projection 206**
- **feedback 206**
- **accent 207**
- **dialect 207**
- **gesture 208**

PRESENTATION AiDS

CHAPTER 11

From the legendary *I Love Lucy* to the contemporary *Big Bang Theory,* recorded — or "canned" — laughter has been a component of sitcoms for decades. The reason for the laugh track is that it functions as a presentation aid for audiences on both sides of the screen (in the studio and at home). In the early days of television, live audiences were unpredictable and often laughed inconsistently at a joke or gag — or, worse, not at all. In the 1950s, CBS sound engineer Charles "Charley" Douglass decided to remedy the problem with the invention of the "Laff Box," a machine that housed looped recordings (audiotapes) of audiences laughing. During a television filming, if the audience did not laugh at the right moment, Douglass would augment the show by punching keys on his Laff Box, much like one would an organ (the Laff Box looked like a large, mutated typewriter). By the 1960s, Douglass had helped transform television comedies almost completely with his "canned laughter," enhancing the television experience for audiences watching from their living rooms to this day.[1]

The interesting thing about canned laughter is that most of us don't notice it. Once you are used to hearing it, canned laughter on a television show is relatively unobtrusive, yet the laughs can enhance what you're watching.[2] In many public speaking situations, presentation aids should be designed to work similarly: to help enhance the experience of an audience during a speech in a manner that is not too conspicuous and does not detract from the speaker and his or her speech.

By showing your audience objects, images, text, and graphs, as well as incorporating sounds or music, you are enhancing your speech. Aids make presentations lively and help encourage understanding.[3] In this chapter, we discuss many of the elements you can draw on to aid and enhance a speech, including the now pervasive use of presentation software, such as Apple's Keynote, Microsoft's PowerPoint, and Prezi. We'll also discuss the general rules for preparing and presenting visual and audio aids, taking care to note how aids can go wrong. The key to using audio and visual presentation aids is to remember that they are used to support and assist *you* during your speech. In fact, the most important presentation aid is *you!*

Enhancing Your Speech Using Presentation Aids

> **You will learn to**
>
> **UNDERSTAND** the three reasons why speakers use presentation aids.
>
> **DESCRIBE** four kinds of presentation aids.

Speakers often choose to use presentation aids for many reasons. One of the most important reasons is that they can help your audience think more clearly and assist them in grasping complex or abstract ideas. The reason why aids help audiences process and remember speeches is because they engage multiple senses. Owing to the influence of television and the Internet, we also know that younger generations appear to learn and comprehend better when information is received through many kinds of audio and visual media; in our time, our minds have become accustomed to engaging with many types of media for information, sometimes in a very short time span (e.g., we might tweet and watch television at the same time).[4] By displaying charts, passing around objects, or playing music and other sounds, the same principle of engaging multiple senses is at work: the more modes of sensory engagement you stimulate, the better people will be able to engage, understand, and retain information.

Closely related to the cognitive reason for using presentation aids is the emotional one. Hearing and seeing visuals during a speech is more engaging and enjoyable. If you were giving an informational speech about how a car engine works, an audience would find a diagram or model of a car engine more interesting and helpful than hearing you discuss the function of a piston in the abstract. When you use visual or audio aids, audiences usually feel more engaged and tend to believe that they are getting more information. Because visual and auditory presentation aids are so common with public speakers today, most audiences have come to expect them.[5]

Finally, presentation aids have the advantage of bringing efficiency and concision to your speech. For example, when speaking about music you could avoid elaborate descriptions by playing a sample of the music. Similarly, a complex process is more easily described with a visual illustration. Visual aids are especially helpful for presenting abstract information like statistics, which are harder for the mind to grasp without representation.

Before we discuss the kinds of presentation aids you can use in public speaking situations, it's helpful to discuss briefly *why* speakers use them. Edward Tufte — a pioneer of "information design" (or "analytical design") and professor emeritus of political and computer science at Yale University — has spent his career studying visual aids and their use. It may seem unusual to think about visual and audio

? What are some of the reasons why speakers use presentation aids? In addition to the reasons examined in this chapter, can you think of other reasons?

What are the five functions of presentation aids? ⑦

a **prop** is any physical object that helps you illustrate a point in your speech.

Using props can help to contextualize your speech.

aids — photographs, charts, sound clips, computer-assisted slides — as *evidence*, however, Tufte argues that anything that assists an audience in comprehension and understanding is a form of corroboration: "Evidence should not be differentiated by the mode of production," says Tufte. "Word, number, image — it is all evidence."[6] If one begins to think about presentation aids as forms of evidence in public speaking, then by definition, aids are supplementary, or *secondary*, to the primacy of the speech itself as the claim bearer. This means that presentation aids should be used and crafted in ways that affirm, support, or corroborate what you're saying. If your aids overshadow your speech or become the central focus of a speaking situation, then you have reversed the priorities of public speaking. One way to keep your presentation aids from overshadowing your message is by selecting the right *kinds* of aids — that is, making sure that your auditory and visual cues match the simplicity or complexity of your speech's message.

Varieties of Presentation Aids

Props

A **prop** is any physical object — living or inorganic — that helps you illustrate a main point of your speech, a "thing" that you show your audience, much like you may have done during a childhood show-and-tell activity. Whether or not a prop is appropriate depends, of course, on contextual reasoning: Who is the audience? Where will you be speaking? and What kind of object is appropriate? Perhaps the most crucial question to ask about using a prop is this: *Will my audience be able to see it?* If you're giving a speech to your class on biking safety, you may or may not be able to bring in an actual bike; however, you *could* bring in a helmet. When using a prop as a presentation aid, make sure it is appropriate for the speech and that the audience will be able to see or hear it.

Pictures

In public speaking, the most common types of pictures include photos, illustrations (drawings, paintings, graphic arts), diagrams, and maps. In general, you can use an image to assist you during a speech if it helps to explain, depict, or otherwise clarify whatever it is you are trying to communicate to the audience. Using pictures in slide presentations is a common practice. As with using props, the key to using pictures is to make sure they are big enough for all audience members to see.

Library of Congress Prints and Photographs Division

A striking visual, whether it's historical or current, adds interest to your speech.

Data and statistical information

Research often depends on information that reflects size or magnitude (such as percentages), trends over time, organization and structure, or processes. As thinkers, we often rely on tables, graphs, and charts to visually represent this type of information. Most people benefit from visual representations of numerical data, especially when the point of showing the data is to compare and contrast different groups or classes of things.[7] Representing data and statistical information visually is often an attempt to communicate the "big picture." Speakers also use tables, graphs, and charts to reduce complexity, providing a simplified visual representation. Tables organize information into columns and rows. Graphs almost always concern a representation of numbers. Flowcharts, pie charts, and organizational charts are the most common types of charts used in public speaking situations. Let's have a look at each in turn.

Flowcharts detail a process.

Pie charts visually display distributions or percentages as part of a circle.

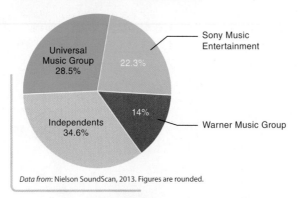

Data from: Nielson SoundScan, 2013. Figures are rounded.

Organizational charts almost always show a hierarchical arrangement of people or groups of people.

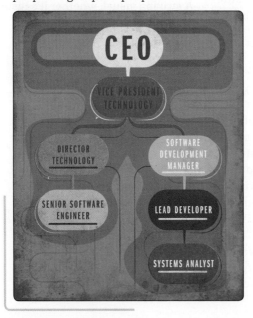

Multimedia: Sound and the moving image

Because increasing numbers of people have greater access to communication technologies, public speakers are more frequently turning to the use of audio and video clips to share information and embellish their ideas. If you have a smartphone, you have the ability to record sound and video on a device that fits in your pocket.

Today, the most common form of audio and video aids is digital, which means that the use of sound and the moving image involves, in one form or another, a computer or other electronic playback device (such as a digital video player) and a screen or a projector. Often audio and video components are incorporated into slide presentations using a software program like Apple's Keynote or Microsoft's PowerPoint. Because using audio, video, and presentation software requires an attention to practical, technology-bound issues, we'll engage sound and the moving image in more detail in the section devoted to presentation software. First, it's helpful to get a sense of the general principles that apply to most presentation aids.

Preparation and Presentation Guidelines

You will learn to

DESCRIBE four tips for preparing aids.

How you prepare and present your presentation aids are closely related, because you must know the interface of your medium (poster, chalkboard or dry-erase board, projection screen, digital display, handout) before you can determine how to prepare it, and what you prepare can determine how you present it. Because props, pictures, charts, graphs, and multimedia aids have unique characteristics, it is difficult to specify guidelines that apply equally to each kind of aid. We can, however, discern a few principles of preparation and presentation that are valid for most—but be sure to consider both preparation and presentation concerns together.

Tips for Preparing Your Presentation Aids

In general, the most important guideline to observe when preparing a presentation aid is that *the aid should assist you and not be the main focus of your speech*. There are exceptions to this guideline, of course. You might be speaking to introduce a product, such as a new vehicle or an electronic device you are selling, and in this case your aid would be the main attraction. Alternatively, in some speaking situations the presentation aid might be a piece of art (e.g., an image of a painting) or

A ventriloquist's dummy is an interactive visual aid that, when used well, creates the illusion of a dialogue.

part of a performance in which you are interacting with your aid (such as a comedian talking to a puppet or a musician playing an instrument). When developing presentation aids, it's a good idea to know in advance what kind of space you are speaking in and how large the audience will be (bigger rooms and audiences require bigger or louder aids). Assuming that your aids are designed to corroborate and reinforce your speech as forms of evidence, you should also consider the following tips.

Clarity and Simplicity. It is possible to communicate a lot of information, both intellectual and emotional in character, with our voices and gestures. Unfortunately, some speakers try to provide the same amount of information on their slides as they do in their speech. This practice can overwhelm an audience and cause information overload. Putting too much information on a poster or a slide can end up distracting the audience from what you are saying. When designing presentation aids, keep in mind that the audience is already receiving a lot of information from the speech itself, so your aids should be limited to only the larger points you want to reinforce or illustrate. Avoid clutter, and strive toward clarity and simplicity when creating your aids.

Bigger Is Better. Perhaps the biggest mistake public speakers can make with their visual aids is making them too small (or, if playing audio, playing it at too low of a volume). Whether you use an image, text, or some sort of graph or chart, it is important to make sure that your audience can easily see what you are presenting. To this end, it is helpful to know beforehand what kind of space you will be speaking in. If you have this information, imagine what an audience member sitting in the very back of the room (or farthest away from you) would see (and hear). If you will be using electronic equipment or a computer, see if you can test these out before you speak to make sure your audience will be able to see and hear both you and your aids.

A cluttered aid (left) and a simple and clear aid (right).[8]

Keep Text Easy to Read. Closely related to simplicity and size is the issue of your text, or any words that you present on a board, poster, or screen. If you are writing on your aid by hand, make sure that your letters are printed, straight, and sufficiently large enough to be easily read by the audience member who is the farthest away from you. Hand lettering (such as on a poster) benefits from the use of a ruler or a straight edge of some sort. Of course it goes without saying that any text appearing as a part of your visual aid needs to be spelled correctly.

If you are using software to make a poster or slides, make sure your font is easy to read and appropriate for your speech. Some fonts communicate a whimsical feeling (e.g., Comic Sans), while others come across as straightforward (e.g., Helvetica, Calibri, or Gill Sans). In general, observe three basic guidelines with fonts: (1) stick with a less playful, more straightforward font, which allows you to use your voice and gestures to communicate the tone and feeling that you want; (2) select a font that is more consistent with the tone and mood of your message; and (3) use only one font, or a limited number of fonts, to tie your aid together.

Lettering is important! Clear, bold lettering makes this sign easy to read.

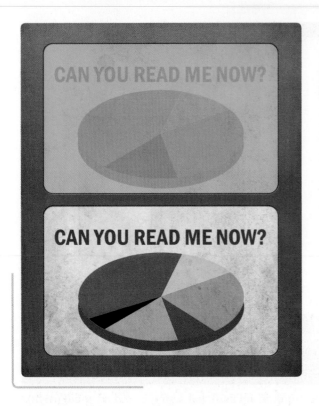

Tips for Using Color. Using bold colors in visual aids, or a variety of colors, is exciting to the eye and visually stimulating. However, too much of a good thing can be tough to interpret. Moreover, as any fashionista would be quick to quip, some colors clash and are difficult to see when they appear together, such as the colors blue and green.

Another important element to consider is **color vision deficiency** (CVD), which is the inability to see certain colors or to distinguish particular colors, most frequently the colors red and green. Although CVD affects less than 10 percent of the population, it brings to light another truth about the use of color in general: the more color you use in a presentation, the more of a risk you'll be taking in terms of your audience's ability to actually *see* it. In addition, some projection systems are incapable of reproducing vivid colors at the extremes of the color spectrum; as the optics of projection systems naturally

color vision deficiency is an inability to see certain colors or to distinguish particular colors.

deteriorate, their ability to reproduce color also steadily declines. To be on the safe side, you may want to use the colors red and green sparingly, or avoid using them altogether.

Someone with color vision deficiency may have difficulty distinguishing the colors in this bar graph.

Tips for Presenting Your Aids

The size, legibility of the text, and choice of color is only worthwhile if you also pay attention to how you present your aids. Because the types of aids available to you vary so widely, there are no universal rules for using aids; however, there are some elements of presentation that are common to most speakers.

Watch Your Back. Because all presentation aids are designed to attract attention, even you, as the speaker, can find it tempting to look at the aids. The problem with focusing on your presentation aids is that it may appear to your audience that you are more interested in speaking to the aids than to the audience. To avoid this perception,

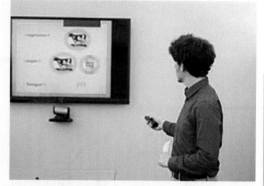

Speakers should avoid turning their back to their audience during presentations.

practice using your presentation aids, making sure to look at them only *briefly* (just to check that the audience can see or hear them).

Watch Your Audience. Avoid reading the content of an aid to the audience. This is a common mistake of new speakers who use presentation software. If you have prepared your aids clearly, you can trust your audience to comprehend their messages without your assistance. To ensure

What to Do If Your Aid Cannot Be Seen

I have been in situations in which I had planned to use Apple's Keynote slide program as part of my presentation, but the projection system was incapable of showing a certain color. What should you do if this happens to you? First, don't panic. If you are already in the middle of a speech, there is simply nothing you can do — you have to go on with the show. Second, remember that the primary focal point of any speech is, in fact, you and the speech itself. All you need to do is quickly acknowledge the situation ("It appears that the display cannot handle some of the more vibrant colors of my slides") and then describe what the audience would see if the aid had appeared correctly. In other words, give the audience the visual information they need by translating it into quick verbal descriptions. Most audiences are sympathetic in these types of situations and will forgive the glitch.

In the event of a technological failure, you can describe what the audience should have seen or heard. What else could you do to assist the audience?

The amount of time Goldilocks spent showing the audience her porridge was not too long, not too short, but just right.

that you will focus on the audience and not your aids, practice using your aids before your speech. If a presentation aid is especially complex and you will need help referencing it, you can reproduce the content of what appears on the aid in your speaking notes. Finally, only use a particular aid when it is relevant to your discussion. When the aid is no longer helpful, remove it or hide it from view.

Timing. Practicing with your aids before your speech will help you determine how much time you need to spend referencing them. Care should be taken to not spend too much time showing or playing your aids to your audience, but you also want to make sure your audience has time to engage with them as well. Observe the Goldilocks Rule: "not too hot and not too cold" translates to "not too fast and not too slow."

Beware (of) the Handout! Handouts are notorious for distracting audiences from what speakers have to say. If you distribute a handout at the beginning of your speech, you can be sure that at least some audience members will not be listening to you but will be reading what is in their hands. If you must distribute something for the audience to handle, such as a prop (e.g., a product or sample), a brochure, or an information sheet, it is usually a good idea to wait until the end of your speech to do so.

What four tips should you follow when designing and using presentation aids? ❓

Presentation Software: Slides, Slides, Slides!

> **You will learn to**
> **LIST** examples of the most commonly used presentation software.
> **EXPLAIN** why presentation software is controversial.
> **DEFINE** the four basic components of a slide.

presentation software are programs that allow speakers to present visuals.

Perhaps no other form of presentation aid has been discussed and debated more than **presentation software** (or "slideware"). The most ubiquitous presentation program in North America is Microsoft's Power-Point (according to researchers, by the end of the twentieth century, as many as 94 percent of professional speakers in one survey reported using Microsoft's PowerPoint when speaking).[9] Since the turn of the century, many other programs have gained in popularity as well, such as Apple's Keynote and freeware programs such as Prezi.

Although many speakers use and enjoy slides, others deliberately avoid them because they believe they are overused—or even abused.[10] There is no consensus among those who study speaking, teaching, and learning about whether slides should or should not be used when speaking, and there are good arguments on both sides of the issue. What is relatively undisputed, however, is that slide software is an integral part of speaking culture in North America and that at some point in your life you will probably be asked to either give or watch a slide presentation.

The Great PowerPoint Debate

Before we examine some general guidelines for using slides in a traditional public speaking situation, you should become familiar with the larger cultural controversy surrounding this software so that you can anticipate any problems your audience may have about the use of slides. In 2003, visual-aid expert Edward Tufte self-published a wry critique of PowerPoint that was widely read. Titled *The Cognitive Style of PowerPoint*, Tufte's monograph claims that Microsoft's slide software encourages speakers to distort their data in order to make it fit into preformatted slide constraints. PowerPoint prompts speakers to use bulleted lists, which present the illusion of analytic rigor but allow the speaker to skip explaining how the points of the list relate to one another. Tufte argues that PowerPoint suggests a cognitive style, or way of thinking, that encourages the "foreshortening of evidence and thought, low spatial resolution, a deeply hierarchical single-path structure," the fragmentation of narrative into slides, and ultimately a "preoccupation with format" over content, reflecting an "attitude of commercialism that turns everything into a sales pitch."[11] Tufte famously argued that the misuse of PowerPoint slides during NASA briefings may have led to the *Columbia* disaster in 2003.[12]

Slideware has also been criticized by some top U.S. military leaders, who believe it is overused in military briefings. Retired general Stanley A. McChrystal, the former leader of NATO forces in Afghanistan, once joked about a particularly complicated slide image showing the counterinsurgency strategy in that country: "When we understand that slide, we'll have won the war."[13] Some commanders have taken to calling thirty-slide briefings "death by PowerPoint," referring to "serious concerns that the program stifles discussion, critical thinking, and thoughtful decision-making."[14] Even so, engineer and consultant Jean-luc Doumont defends slide software as an effective presentation tool for most public speakers, especially when the purpose is to inform or persuade without the kind of detailed, technical data necessary for written reports.[15] Communication scholar Dale Cyphert has also argued that, like it or not, the "fluent use of presentation software is now expected by audiences raised in a media era."[16]

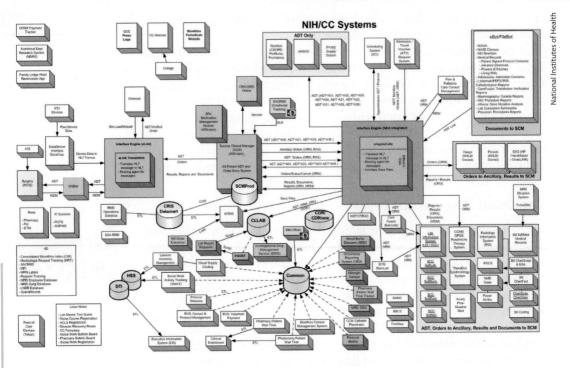

National Institutes of Health

The complexity of this graphic hinders audience understanding.

Why do aids help audiences comprehend speeches better? In what ways can presentation aids hinder a speaker? ?

For most of the speeches you will be delivering in your public speaking class, slide software can be used effectively. Our focus has been on basic skills, and having a familiarity with presentation software can serve you well in your future speaking endeavors. In general, you can use contextual reasoning to determine whether or not slides are appropriate for your purpose and the audience's expectations. If you plan to use slides during your speech, consider the following tips.

The Text. There are two basic kinds of text in slides: the title text, or heading, and the main text or content, often presented as bullet points. Most slideware programs include a slide template that features both a title and content. As with any visual aid, observe the general tips for using text and fonts when composing slides: make sure the text is large enough to read, and use fonts that are straightforward and that communicate the appropriate tone. Choose a slide-show template that includes colors that are appropriate for your speaking situation and topic.

The Object. An object is typically any non-text element in your slide, most frequently a picture, chart, or graph. Make sure your objects are easy to see

understanding
the slide

Most of the tips and guidelines offered about different kinds of *visual aids* apply similarly to the use of slides. Even so, let's briefly examine a few targeted tips particular to using presentation software. The basic building blocks of a slideware program are the slides themselves, the text used in the slides, the objects used in the slides, and transitions — or how one slide "advances" to another slide.

The basic unit of any slide presentation is the slide itself — what will appear on the computer or projection screen. The general principle of layout of a slide is balance. Again, the Goldilocks Rule should guide you here: do not put too much information on a slide, but do not underutilize the slide either. You want the different elements of your slide to be "just right." A typical slide will feature the following:

- A "title," or a short phrase or bulleted list that describes the main idea or theme you are discussing
- An object (a photo, an illustration, a chart, or a graph)
- Text that elaborates your main points

You should use color thoughtfully, keeping in mind that some computers and projection equipment cannot reproduce vivid colors (red or green).

This is a basic slide. Note that the slide title, the bulleted points, and the picture are "balanced" into a kind of invisible triangle.
Getty Images/National Geographic Creative

To see some examples of speakers using slide shows, visit LaunchPad at **launchpadworks.com** and look at two clips. After viewing the clips, consider the following questions:

- Which slide show was easier for you to read and understand?

- Which speaker presented their slide show more effectively?
- How could each speaker improve his or her delivery?

and comprehend. Care should be taken not to use objects that are copyrighted or that violate public use laws. Many images available to you on the Internet are actually the private property of the person who created them; when in doubt, e-mail the owner of the image and ask his or her permission.

In some instances, you may wish to use a film, video, or sound clip in your slide. Moving images and sound are the most difficult types of objects to embed in a slide, and some software programs are more adept at handling them than others. For example, Apple's Keynote program was designed specifically to handle multimedia objects such as video and sound, while competing software has been noted to crash or be uncooperative with their use. When using multimedia clips in your slide presentation, always practice ahead of time to make sure they work.

The Transition. Most presentation software programs feature a number of different kinds of transitions that advance from one slide to the next. Unlike text and objects, however, the transitions available on one software program do not translate across programs—or even versions of that program. For example, Apple's Keynote program and Microsoft's PowerPoint include animated transitions that give slides a unique, even whimsical appearance as they move from one to another. The online presentation program Prezi has a transition that zooms from one element in a slide to another—a style that is self-contained and unplayable on other software programs. Special care should be taken to use only those transitions that are available to you in the software program that you will be using in your public speaking situation. If you will be able to use your own laptop or tablet to display your slide show, you can be reasonably sure that what you create at home will translate to your speaking setting.

Beware of Internet Links in Slide Presentations!

Many a public speaker has been embarrassed by an embedded hyperlink or Internet address in a slide software program that just didn't work. Assuming that your venue will have an active Internet or Wi-Fi connection can get you into trouble, and sometimes connections can be broken. As a general rule, you can avoid embarrassment by making sure all your media objects are on your computer, hard drive, or flash drive with your presentation. If you want to use a video clip taken from the Internet, download the clip to your hard drive and embed it independently into your software presentation. Most software programs have directions for doing this in their help menu.

If you want to show your audience a web page from the Internet as a visual aid but know you will *not* have an Internet connection during your speech, what can you do?

Speaking While Using Slides: Practice, Pacing, and Performance

Using a slide show while speaking is one of the most challenging *and* rewarding skills of public speaking. Not only must you carefully compose your speech, but you have the added task of using slides at key points in your speech and timing how long to keep a slide on the screen. The best way to prepare is to practice delivering your speech while using your slide show.

Use Visual Cues in Your Speech Notes. When using a slide show in a presentation, it is very tempting to look at your slides or perhaps even *read* the content of your speech from your slides during your speech. This is a no-no. You shouldn't read your slides to your audience, as this would require you to stop looking at your audience and, however unwittingly, ignore them. Make sure the content of your slides is included in your speaking notes so that you will not be tempted to look at your slides. If you are speaking from an outline or note cards, you might decide to put visual cues in your speech notes to indicate to yourself when to advance your slides. Use a notation such as "<SLIDE>" or "<ADVANCE SLIDE 3>" so that you will know when to advance to your next slide. It's OK to look at your display to make sure that you are, in fact, showing the slide you want, but don't do that too often. Pretend that you are a swan, elegantly gliding on top of the water; meanwhile, in the speaking notes that only you can see, you can write out all your furious paddling moves.

Time Yourself While Using Your Slides. Many programs feature a practice mode that will display a timer. Use this feature to figure out how long you are displaying a slide in relation to how long it takes you to discuss its content in your speech. Adjust the visual cues in your speaking notes to match up with the time you want to spend displaying each slide. It may take many practice run-throughs to adjust the timing. The key to a good slide presentation is establishing the right *rhythm*.

Use Blank Slides to Help You Pace. A common mistake many speakers make is keeping a slide up too long. If a slide is up before or too long after a speaker covers the material it was designed to address, the audience may get distracted. To avoid this, show a slide for only as long as it is relevant to the point you are making. When the slide is no longer relevant, remove it. One useful technique you can use is simply *to use a blank slide*. If you are speaking about a topic that is supported with a slide, and then move to a topic for which you do not need a slide, simply advance to a blank slide. A blank slide communicates to your audience that they should pay attention *only to what you are saying*. Think about it this way: When you are watching a movie, what happens when there is suddenly no soundtrack music? Typically, it causes you to focus on the action on-screen more closely. You can use this technique to shift attention to the speech itself in a way that emphasizes an important point.

Be Ready for Equipment Failure. As most of us who use computers know, sometimes things simply stop working. If you use slide software frequently, you will at some point encounter an equipment failure. Here's an important observation about equipment failure: audiences are often impressed as much by how you handle failure as how you handle success. Thus, being prepared for equipment failure can be seen as simply another opportunity to delight, inform, or persuade your audience "in the moment."

In the event of software or equipment failure, most of us will experience feelings of panic. One way to alleviate those feelings is by having a backup plan. Here are some things you can do to ease the panic:

- Handouts: Although in general handouts are best saved for the end of a speech, if your speech requires references to important technical information, data on graphs and charts, and so on, you can distribute handouts of your slides. Most software programs have a feature that allows you to transform your slides into printable files, which you can have on hand if you need them.
- Create Alternative Versions: You may discover that the presentation venue does not have the software you want to use. Many presentation software programs, such as PowerPoint and Keynote, allow you to "save as" or "export" your show in alternative formats. Create different versions of your slide program and have them available to use just in case.
- Create a PDF Version: Most computers have the ability to display a PDF (portable document format) file, which is an image-based document. PDF files can be displayed in most word processing programs, and PowerPoint and Keynote can also play PDF files as if they were slides. Having a PDF version of your presentation could save the day.
- Describe Your Slides: If all else fails—you have no handouts and you cannot display anything on a screen—you can simply describe the necessary content on the slides you would have used to your audience. Smile, and then say something like, "I would have shown you a slide featuring a diagram of the instrument I am proposing, but my computer isn't cooperating." Most audiences are forgiving of equipment failure.

> **What can you do in the event of a malfunction with your presentation aid? What can you do in the event of equipment failure?**

In this chapter, we have examined the use of presentation aids for speeches. Of course, the most important presentation aid is *you!* In general, however, aids can be anything from physical objects to posters to slide presentations. The goal of using any presentation aid is to help the audience understand and remember your message. When using presentation aids, care should be taken that your aids do not outshine you or your message. A successful use of presentation aids requires practice before your speaking event and a backup plan in the event of equipment failure.

Enhancing Your Speech Using Presentation Aids

Presentation aids are used by speakers to help audiences better understand and remember the speaker's message. Aids are a form of evidence, and can be physical objects, pictures, graphs and charts, or multimedia (slides, music, film clips, etc.).

Preparation and Presentation Guidelines

The key to creating and using presentation aids is balance: your aid should be clear and simple, be big enough for your audience to see, be easily readable, and use color sparingly. When using a presentation aid, avoid turning your back on your audience, remain focused on the audience and do not read from the aid, and spend an appropriate amount of time referencing it. Care should be taken when using handouts, as they can distract the audience from your speech.

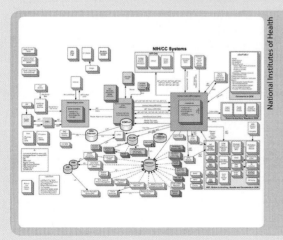

National Institutes of Health

Presentation Software: Slides, Slides, Slides!

While the use of slide software in public speaking is common, it is also controversial. If you use slides, strive to make them balanced with readily digestible information. Make sure the text and font not only are clear but also mirror the mood and tone of your message.

CHAPTER 11

ACTIVITIES

Create a Balanced Slide

For this activity, your instructor will ask you to work in groups with someone who has a slide software program on his or her computer. Using a newspaper, find a factual story (not an opinion piece) that describes a complex event, policy, or invention. With your group, develop a slide that would appear in the body of an informative speech about the story; the slide should assist an audience's understanding using three elements: a title, a three- or four-point bulleted list, and an image. Share both your story and the slide you developed with the class. What does the slide do well? What about the slide could be improved?

Create a Terrible Slide

Sometimes deliberately doing something poorly is as instructive as doing something well. Working in teams created by your instructor, find a factual story in a newspaper or magazine that describes a complex event, policy, or invention. Using slide software with your group, create the most unhelpful and confusing slide that you can muster for use in an informative speech about the story. Share the slide with your class. What is particularly terrible about this slide? What would you have to do to the slide to make it usable in a speech?

KEY TERMS

 Videos in LaunchPad describe many of these terms. Go to launchpadworks.com.

UNDERSTANDING

SPEECH GENRES

Many human art forms are categorized into genres to make them easier to talk about. When talking about Hollywood movies, we might describe them as "dramas" or "horror films" because these are labels for recurring patterns that capture the gist of a film quickly. Most movies labeled "romantic comedies," for instance, follow a familiar plot: two people meet, they recognize a mutual attraction, humorous obstacles keep them from getting together, and by the end of the film they are united in love. In *Say Anything* (1989), a mediocre student and aspiring kickboxer named Lloyd attempts to woo an attractive academic superstar, Diane, shortly after they graduate high school. Despite numerous obstacles—the most significant of which is that Diane's father is prosecuted and convicted for tax evasion—Lloyd ends up "serenading" Diane with a boom box held outside her window, the two fall in love, and they are united as a couple by the film's end.

Movie genres are not fixed, however, and can change over time while still preserving the basic pattern they name. In *Crazy, Stupid, Love* (2011), for example, Emily Weaver asks her husband, Cal, for a divorce. Devastated, Cal meets smooth pickup artist Jacob, who vows to teach Cal how to get his manhood back with a new wardrobe and modern techniques for dating. By the end of the film, however, Emily and Cal realize they are soul mates and reunite. In this way, the basic formula of a romantic comedy is maintained but with surprise modifications: the couple is already married at the beginning, and both are older than the stars of more traditional romantic comedies. Whether straight (*Love, Actually*), queer (*Better than Chocolate*), or unconventional (*Harold and Maude*), all rom-coms follow the same plot with creative variations.

What Are Speech Genres?

> **You will learn to**
>
> **DEFINE** "form" and "genre."
>
> **LIST** and **DEFINE** the three ancient speech genres.
>
> **LIST** and **DEFINE** the three contemporary speech genres.

Movie genres create expectations in audiences *before* they see a given film, and to be successful, the film must meet those expectations in some way (romantic comedies *almost always* have a happy ending). Similarly, public speaking has a number of familiar genres that create expectations in audiences before a particular speech is delivered. Of course, speaking publicly for an audience is different from communicating to audiences in a film, but they have something in common. The perceived success of a speech, just like a film, is often determined in reference to the *expectations* of an audience: audiences usually expect speakers to do and say certain things depending on the kind of speech given and the context for the speech. At a wedding, we wouldn't expect a friend giving a toast to ridicule the newly married couple. At a funeral, we wouldn't expect a speaker to criticize the deceased. We typically refer to these sets of expectations in speaking contexts as *speech genres*.

Ever since the formal study of public speaking began in the West over two thousand years ago, scholars of public speaking have argued that public speaking can be categorized into three types: speeches that

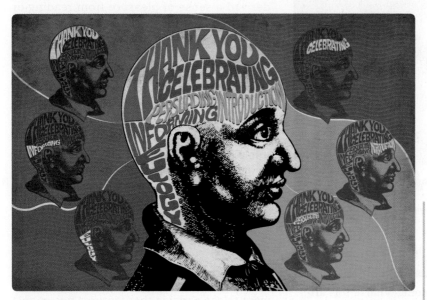

Speech genres are names for sets of expectations that we carry around in our heads.

> ## Three Common Speech Genres
> - Celebratory Speaking
> - Informative Speaking
> - Persuasive Speaking

celebrate or commemorate special occasions (weddings and funerals), speeches that inform (opportunities to teach or explain something), and speeches that persuade (calls for changes in belief or action). In chapters 13–16, we will examine each of these three genres of public speaking in depth—celebratory speaking, informative speaking, and persuasive speaking. In this chapter, however, we will closely examine how speech genres work generally, exploring why they are so powerful and learning how they work to both enable and constrain your speaking.

Culture and Form

While working as a music critic for the literary magazine the *Dial* in the early twentieth century, rhetorical critic Kenneth Burke tried to figure out why some audiences responded favorably to certain literary works and not others.[1] Drawing on observations about people's enjoyment of music, Burke concluded that people derived a sense of pleasure from reading or hearing things repeated. He argued that an audience's sense of *form* led them to either enjoy or reject a work of art. Form, he believed, satisfies the expectations of the audience: "*Form is the creation of an appetite in the mind of the [listener], and the adequate satisfying of that appetite*" (emphasis added).[2] When an audience listens to a musical work, goes to see a movie, or hears a speaker give a speech, their hunger for something they have experienced before—a pattern—is stimulated. If the music, film, or speech satisfies that hunger in some way by following through on expectations, it is usually a pleasant experience. In this way, form is both a mental and a bodily experience because the satisfaction depends on an intellectual as well as emotional response. If we went to see a movie that features two people who are attracted to each other yet separated by obstacles, we would *expect* these two to get

Form Inspires Expectations. What is this artist drawing? Your answer largely depends on your understanding of "form."

Figuring Out Form

Not all forms are easy to name, especially if people have not thought about the patterns of expectation they are experiencing. New forms of music or avant-garde film often emerge without handy labels when initially introduced. For this reason, innovative or otherwise new forms are often criticized as unsatisfactory or incomprehensible by those who cannot fully anticipate the pattern. Think of your experience watching an unusual movie (e.g., *Scott Pilgrim vs. the World* or something by the director David Lynch) or listening to music that seemed like sheer noise. Or think of a relative's or friend's disdain for the music you blast on your stereo. A form is often incomprehensible to people until they have a name for it. If a form is comprehensible, it often becomes a genre.

Think of a film or musical piece that you recently experienced, and then ask yourself: Does it have a pattern? How would you describe the pattern? What name would you give the pattern, and why?

? What is form?

form is the activation and satisfaction of expectations in audiences.

genre is a label for a widely recognized form of a given culture.

together by the end. If they do not, we might experience dissatisfaction. The same response holds true for speeches. It is because of this that we can define **form** as the activation and satisfaction of expectations in audiences.

When a form is named and becomes known to a large community, it is called a **genre**, a label for a widely recognized form of a given culture. Those who study genres, especially academics, will be quick to tell you that genres are complex, and that the ways in which we discuss them differs depending on the medium.[3] Even though music genres, film genres, and speech genres are different, they share a formal function based on expectation. Music genres change quickly because the underlying forms they name are constantly transforming due to the creativity of musicians. The musical genre of hip-hop, for example, began as an offshoot of disco and was first labeled "rap." Film genres, on the other hand, do not change as quickly: horror, romantic comedy, action thriller, and so on, remain relatively stable genres.

Because it is an oral tradition and relies heavily on the memories of audiences over a lifetime, speech genres are among the slowest to change and have remained largely the same for centuries. Although

Genres Are Labels. A genre is the name for a set of formal expectations in the minds of audiences.

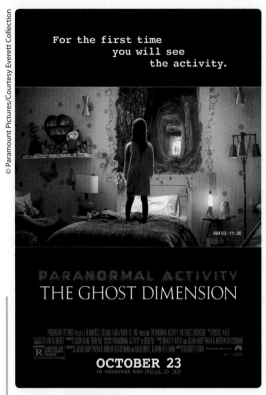

The haunted house genre has changed over time, but the basic plot remains the same.

What is a speech genre? How would you define it to a friend who is not in your class?

this book outlines a great number of speech genres, in ancient Greece, Aristotle argued that most of them could be handily reduced to three types. Because the speech genres have not changed much, knowing their general patterns will help you as a speaker for the rest of your life, enabling you to anticipate what audiences expect. We now focus our attention on these three ancient genres of public speaking and how they differ from today's genres.

The Genres of Public Speaking

At the birth of the formal study of public speaking in ancient Greece, only the wealthy and powerful male citizens of Athens could speak publicly; these elites used public speaking to govern the polis. In contrast, most of us will be expected to speak publicly at some point in our lives, though probably not for governing the nation. For most of us, opportunities for public speaking include a toast at a wedding, a eulogy for a relative, a sales presentation at work, and perhaps speaking up at a community board or township meeting. In the ancient Greek context, Aristotle argued that the types of speeches could be boiled down to three repeated forms: *epideictic* (celebratory), *forensic* (judicial), and *deliberative* (political). He made these distinctions based on the kind of judgments audiences were asked to make, as well as on how the audience was expected to respond to the speeches. Let's go through each form of speech and examine how it has evolved.

Epideictic (Also Celebratory).   For Aristotle and his contemporaries, celebratory speaking, also known as ceremonial speaking, referred to forms of speeches that praised or blamed someone or something. For example, speeches at funerals or weddings usually praise the deceased or newlyweds. Speeches at an event—such as at a rally for a sports team or at a political event—may focus on an unworthy opponent. For Aristotle, celebratory speeches did not ask audiences to do anything but sought to amplify the beliefs, attitudes, and values that many people share. Consequently, the focus of such speaking is to strengthen community bonds and to celebrate the present moment. Celebratory speaking is the most common form of speaking in our culture today and is the topic of chapter 13.

Judicial (Also Forensic or Legal).   Back in Aristotle's time, Athenians didn't have lawyers. If a person was accused of a crime or wished to accuse someone of legal wrongdoing, he (and it was usually a he) had to make a speech of guilt or innocence in court himself.[4] Aristotle suggested that this kind of speaking asked the audience to make a judgment about a deed done in the past and find the person guilty or innocent. Today we refer to this kind of speaking as legal oratory or rhetoric, and it is usually the province of lawyers and court commentators. Although legal speaking is certainly its own genre, public speaking scholars today include it under the genre of persuasive speaking, which we will address in depth in chapters 15 and 16.

Deliberative (or Policy). The most important speaking genre for Aristotle and his peers was the deliberative—that which concerns persuasive argument, or deliberating about what folks should or should not do. Deliberative oratory differs from legal speaking because it concerns an *uncertain future*, while the judicial concerns something that has already taken place.[5] All deliberative speeches ask audiences to consider the future and typically call for audiences to do something. Aristotle placed profound significance on this genre because it was the most risky kind of speaking. Because we cannot predict the future with any certainty, speaking to convince an audience relies heavily on trusting the speaker. The most direct line that can be drawn between ancient Greece and our contemporary form of deliberative speaking is political speaking, because the role of a politician is to persuade colleagues and constituents that a given policy should be supported. Today, however, deliberative speaking is not limited to politicians: you and I speak deliberatively when we try to persuade others to do or think something about the future, which is typically the province of "persuasion."

The Roman orator Cicero addresses the Roman Senate.

Hulton Archive/Handout/Getty Images

? What were the three basic genres of public speaking for Aristotle and his colleagues in ancient Greece?

Ancient Greek Genres at a Glance

GENRE	PURPOSE	TIME ORIENTATION	EXAMPLE
Epideictic	Speaking to celebrate community	The present	A funeral oration
Forensic	Speaking about guilt or innocence	The past	Speech defending oneself in court
Deliberative	Speaking to induce change	The future	Speech in favor of invading Sparta

Supreme Court justice Sonia Sotomayor is a gifted public speaker.

What are the three genres that are most basic for us today? How are they similar? How do they differ?

Genres in Our Time

Over thousands of years the speech genres have evolved and changed, as all genres do. Early theorists of public speaking categorized oratory based on professions, and consequently, genres were highly specialized. Today the study of public speaking has become open to many more people, so the genres have been renamed, despite their origins. Notably, the judicial genre has been absorbed by the persuasive genre, and a new genre focused on the presentation of information or teachings has replaced it. Today we refer to the speech genres as speaking to celebrate (special occasions), speaking to inform, and speaking to persuade. However, the Greek focus on the purpose and time orientation of each genre is still helpful to us. Here are the genres that we will discuss in depth in the next four chapters:

Contemporary Genres at a Glance

GENRE	PURPOSE	TIME ORIENTATION	EXAMPLE
Celebratory Genre	Speaking to celebrate community	The present	A eulogy to honor a deceased relative
Informative Genre	Speaking to inform	The past or something known	A speech that explains how to start an organic garden
Persuasive Genre	Speaking to induce change	The future	A speech that argues that people should adopt animals from rescue shelters rather than buy them from breeders

Earlier I noted that unlike contemporary forms of human expression, such as music and film, speech genres have remained relatively stable for centuries. Comparing the ancient genres to the contemporary genres is useful for understanding just how powerful and deeply ingrained public speaking genres are in Western culture.

Which *contemporary* genres correspond to the past, present, and future?

On Breaking the Rules: Genre Violation

You will learn to

EXPLAIN why genre patterns are comforting to audiences.

DESCRIBE the limitations of genres.

Sometimes audience expectations can feel constraining, and audiences are often surprised if a speaker does not meet their expectations. Whether learning to write poetry or composing a speech, students encountering genres and their tacit rules for the first time can find them both comforting and challenging. Learning the expectations certain genres imply can be comforting because it gives you a road map of sorts, making it easier for you to compose a speech that audiences expect. As human beings, however, some of us delight in breaking the rules and violating expectations, which is often the job of creativity. Part of your success as a public speaker demands that you pay attention to speech genre expectations, but take heart: rules can be broken if done artfully and with respect. The key to this kind of freedom as a speaker—and knowing both when you do and when you do not have it—is learning the rules or expectations of a speech genre in the first place.

Consider a commencement speech delivered by high school teacher David McCullough at Wellesley High School in Massachusetts in June 2012. Typically, a commencement speech, which is part of the celebratory genre, honors graduates' experiences, congratulates them on their hard work, and urges them to move on to do great things in their lives. Mr. McCullough surprised high school graduates and their parents with his unusual *thesis*:

> Contrary to what your . . . soccer trophy suggests, your glowing seventh grade report card, despite every assurance of a certain corpulent purple dinosaur, that nice Mister Rogers and your batty Aunt Sylvia, no matter how often your maternal caped crusader has swooped in to save you . . . you're nothing special.

As you might imagine, such a thesis startled the audience and caused them to reflect on the violations of the norms of a commencement speech. The speech ended with a surprise twist that returned the speech to the proper, formal conclusion: "selflessness is the best thing you can do for yourself. The sweetest joys of life, then, come only with the recognition that you're not special. Because everyone is." Although Mr. McCullough's speech was not met with universal applause, it became a sensation in the mass media, as many commentators of the speech praised its unconventional message. (See the appendix for the full text of this speech.)

In this chapter we have examined the concept of "genre," which is the name or label of a cultural "form" or pattern that has become familiar over time. When you speak at a pep rally, for example, audiences will expect a commemoration of the present and a celebration of the community. For this reason, it is helpful to learn the formal expectations of the most basic kinds of speeches. For the ancients, the main genres were epideictic, forensic, and deliberative. For us, the three basic speech genres are celebratory, informative, and persuasive.

What should you know before you decide to violate the expectations of a speech genre? ⑦

Whether or not it is appropriate to violate an audience's expectations of a given speech genre depends on your familiarity with the conventions. In the public speaking classroom, your primary goal should be to understand common speech genre conventions and model them appropriately. Only after mastering the basic speech genres will you be able to determine how and when it is appropriate to be playful with them. It is to the basic expectations of the three speech genres, then, that we now turn.

What Are Speech Genres?

Genres are labels or names for recurring patterns in forms of human expression, such as film, music, and speeches.

Culture and Form

The recurring patterns of genres are called "forms." A particular form activates and then satisfies audience expectations.

AP Photo/The Deseret News, Tom Smart

Genres in Our Time

The ancient speech genres include epideictic, forensic, and deliberative. Today, our three basic speech genres are celebratory, informative, and persuasive. A speaker should not be playful with the expectations of genres until he or she has a firm understanding of them.

CHAPTER 12

ACTIVITY

Trying Out Different Speech Genres

Following are two speaking-situation scenarios. In class with a partner or in a small group, brainstorm three speech topics for each scenario: one that is primarily celebratory, one that is informative, and one that is persuasive. Care should be taken to identify how each topic meets the purpose and addresses the time orientation of each genre.

SCENARIO ONE: You work with a local animal group, Pups-R-Thriving, rescuing dogs from animal shelters and trying to find them homes in your city. A frequent benefactor to your organization, a local religious community (a church, mosque, synagogue, Hindu temple, or Buddhist group), has invited you to speak to its members.

SCENARIO TWO: A family relative of yours is retiring from a window manufacturing corporation, Streak-Free Window Associates. Your parents have asked you to give a speech at the retirement dinner next Saturday evening.

KEY TERMS

 Videos in LaunchPad describe many of these terms. Go to launchpadworks.com.

form 241

genre 241

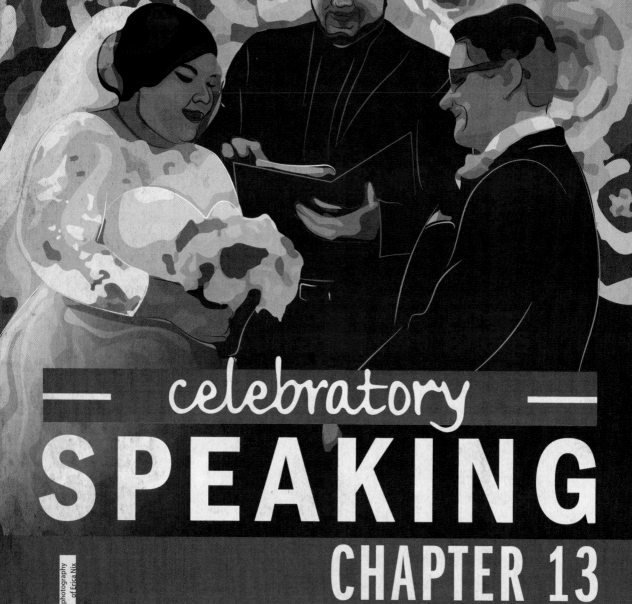

celebratory

SPEAKING

CHAPTER 13

Based on the photography of Erica Nix

For many years I have officiated at weddings for my friends. Before each ceremony, I take the time to sit down with the engaged couple to discuss what kind of ceremony they would like. My friends Kendall and Erika (featured in the chapter title illustration) wanted a medium-length ceremony with speakers, and asked me to open with a quote about love from the philosopher Jean-Luc Nancy. My friends Mirek and Tanner, on the other hand, asked for something "short and sweet," funny, and lighthearted.

Because Tanner, Mirek, and I all came of age in the 1980s and love popular music, when composing their ceremony I decided to layer eighties song lyrics throughout. For example, I began my opening and invocation this way:

Dearly beloved, we have gathered here today to get through this thing called life. Electric word—"life"—it means forever, and that's a mighty long time. But, I'm here to tell you that there's something else: marriage. Although it is not for everyone, for many people marriage is the added power we need to make it through the world together.

Welcome, family and friends, and thank you for joining Mirek and Tanner on one of the most important events of their lives. You have come together to witness a very important event and possibly one of the most noble things human beings can do for each other. We're all here to witness this public promise and to celebrate it. And as witnesses to this public promising, it is our collective supportive gaze that will help to seal the deal.

DEARLY BELOVED, WE ARE GATHERED HERE TODAY TO GET THROUGH THIS THING CALLED LIFE

Celebrating Your Community

You will learn to

EXPLAIN the purpose of celebratory speaking.

In this way, then, a familiar ceremony opened with a slight twist: I began with an allusion to Prince's 1984 hit song "Let's Go Crazy." Although some members of the audience didn't get the musical reference, most people in attendance could sense that the wedding between Mirek and Tanner was exciting or "electric"—especially because same-sex marriage was only recently legalized in the United States. After I thanked the audience for being there, I quickly identified the audience's role as witnesses to their union. In this way, I acknowledged the well-known *form* of the wedding genre, meeting expectations while also saying something unique.

For most readers, a union ceremony is familiar because we have seen them on television and in film and will attend more than a few over the course of our lives. As we become increasingly familiar with the patterns of speaking associated with weddings, we intuitively learn the patterns for officiating and toasting. Even if you don't envision yourself giving a formal speech after this class is over, it is likely that you *will* be asked to speak at a celebration, such as a retirement party, a birthday bash, a wedding, or an anniversary. In this chapter, we will examine the genre of speeches that emphasizes the present and that attempts to bring a community together: celebratory or special-occasion speeches.

As social creatures, we celebrate communities in both happy and sad times. We can experience the joy of birthdays as well as the sorrow of saying good-bye to a person who is moving away. There may be a time in your life when you are asked to speak at a retirement party or at a memorial service for a deceased friend or family member. In between these celebrations of life and memorials to the dead, there are a host of related speeches that are given on special occasions. From introducing a person at a meeting, speaking at a rally to praise a sports team or political candidate, or giving a speech of thanks when accepting an award, speeches of celebration are among the most common in our culture. Although we might not become presidents or politicians, business pioneers, or celebrities, many of us may be asked to toast a friend at a party. Celebratory speaking is also the most personal kind of speaking. For these reasons, some scholars argue that celebratory speaking is the primary speech genre to learn about, study, and master. Celebratory speaking is, in fact, a reflection of the events that make you who you are.

Types of Celebratory Speeches

> **You will learn to**
>
> **RECALL** the two commonalities of all celebratory speeches.
>
> **LIST** the four basic categories of celebratory speeches.
>
> **DESCRIBE** the kind of speaking that occurs at weddings and unions.
>
> **EXPLAIN** the parts of a toast.

Celebratory speaking was originally termed "epideictic" speaking, derived from the Greek word meaning "show" or "display." Aristotle noted that the various speeches of celebration have two things in common: (1) they are fundamentally designed to bring a community together, and (2) they are focused on the present. Although celebratory speaking today includes more kinds of speeches than epideictic speaking did, celebratory speeches still have these two qualities.[1]

The aims of celebratory speaking differ depending on how the community for the speaking occasion is understood. What constitutes a community depends on the context. If one is speaking at a work-related event, the community refers mostly to coworkers, and if one is speaking at a college commencement, the community is that of students, faculty, friends, and family. In any context, one celebrates the community by highlighting mutual histories, shared values, and common commitments. Perhaps one of the biggest mistakes a speaker can make when giving a speech of celebration is neglecting to focus on community. While speaking to celebrate, you may wish to inform the audience of something new or persuade them to do or believe something, but your primary focus should be on what you and the audience share as a community.

There are many different categories of speeches that celebrate community; the most common of these are the following:

- Speeches of recognition
- Speeches of praise or blame
- Speeches of inspiration or encouragement
- Speeches that mourn loss

What are the two main reasons for celebratory speaking?

Speeches of Recognition: Introducing, Presenting, and Accepting

A speech of recognition highlights a person's accomplishments or character. There are three basic kinds: speeches of introduction, presentation, and acceptance. The purpose of this kind of speech is to honor another person. Even if you are being honored, it's often a good idea to express gratitude and honor the community, organization, and event recognizing you.

Introduction Speech. In an introduction speech, your role is to make the audience feel welcome and to get them excited about the person you are introducing. These speeches are typically short because the intent is to prepare the audience for the main speaker. Typically, a speech of introduction requires you to explain who you are and acknowledge the upcoming speaker's interest in the topic. Most audiences expect introduction speeches to describe the speaker's background, including a brief biography, a list of accomplishments, and an explanation of why he or she is speaking to the community. In most cases, you should preview the speaker's topic after relating his or her background.

A Boy Scout and Girl Scout making an oath.

Speeches of introduction tend to close by asking the audience to welcome the speaker. If you are the speaker being introduced, it is customary to thank both your introducer and the audience and to express gratitude for the speaking situation ("I am delighted to speak to you today at this conference on crowdfunding").

Presentation Speech. A presentation speech is one in which you present an award or honor to a worthy recipient. Sometimes a presentation speech will involve an introduction as well—a mention of an individual's background and accomplishments. The most important part of a presentation speech is an explanation of what the honor is and why the recipient is receiving it. Take care to underscore how the award and recipient reflect the community. In general, when presenting a person with an award there is an object to present: a plaque or a trophy. If you are the person to physically present the award, be sure to rehearse how it will be given.

Acceptance Speech. An acceptance speech is given when receiving an honor or award. If the award is a surprise, there's not much you can do to prepare except try to remember the three basic parts of this kind of speech: (1) express gratitude for having received the honor or award, (2) express how much the award means to you or to those for whom you are accepting it, and (3) recognize others who helped you along the way. If you have advance notice that you or your organization will be honored, you can more fully prepare an elegant and graceful acceptance speech.

Many of us are familiar with acceptance speeches because we have seen them given on various awards shows, such as the Grammys, the Academy Awards, and MTV's Video Music Awards. Readers might recognize one of the most important constraints for accepting an award or honor is time. Make sure you know exactly how much time you should take for your acceptance speech, and plan accordingly. Most audiences will not mind if you refer to your note cards or a brief script for your speech, but they will mind if you go on and on. If you can, keep your notes handy.

Speeches of Praise or Blame: Weddings, Toasts, and Roasts

Although most celebratory speeches concern praise at some level, some of these speeches are longer or more important. Monumental celebratory speeches are those that take place at typically once-in-a-lifetime events, such as weddings or roasts, the latter often to honor someone's career or retirement from it. The smaller speeches taking place at these events are toasts, and they are usually delivered while hoisting a beverage into the air. Of all the speeches you will give or hear in your lifetime, you will likely encounter the toast the most.

Wedding and Union Ceremonies. As recently as fifty years ago, most wedding ceremonies were led by speakers who had a special recognition from a given state and county as a religious authority or justice of the peace. Today, in most of the United States and many parts of Canada, anyone can officiate a wedding or union, recognized by the local and federal governments, provided he or she has obtained a credential.[2] The nondenominational Universal Life Church offers online ordination for free and proof of the credential in writing for a nominal fee.[3] In other words, it is easier to unite or marry people than it used to be. Perhaps one day you might be asked to officiate the union of friends or relatives!

The pattern and structure for a wedding or union differ widely and dramatically across traditions, faiths, and cultures. In fact, the norms and expectations differ so dramatically—for example, between a Hindu wedding (Vivaha) and a Southern Baptist wedding—that you must really perform an extensive audience analysis for *whatever* tradition is in question. If asked to officiate at a wedding service, you will need to spend some time with the couple to determine what they would like, presenting them with the basic parts of the service and discussing their vision for each. Moreover, you may want to spend some time talking to family and friends about their experiences at weddings, discussing what they would like to see and hear. Finally, you'll want to spend some time either in the library or searching online for examples of speech scripts that others have used for weddings and union ceremonies.

You can find a link to a chart on LaunchPad that presents the basic parts of a wedding ceremony.

the toast:

the ubiquitous speech of honor and goodwill

Kirn Vintage Stock/Corbis via Getty Images

A toast is traditionally a short speech of praise, and the genre is the most pervasive one in Western culture. Toasts are often given at festive, celebratory gatherings and almost always to express goodwill toward the community or to honor a person, although one can toast to an event or an achievement, too. Scholars are not sure where this tradition came from; some speculate it concerned religious rituals and honoring a god or gods with libations.[4]

Because you may be inspired to offer a toast, or asked to make one on the spur of the moment, you may not have time to prepare.

However, if you think you might make a toast at an event, it is always wise to prepare ahead of time. Observe these guidelines: (1) Keep your speech short; no one likes a toast that seems to go on forever. (2) Use no more than two or three main points; determine quickly what quality, trait, or achievement of the person, community, or event you wish to honor and recognize. (3) Keep the mood cheerful; toasts are by definition uplifting.

Toasts can be planned or "on the spot." Here are some tips that are helpful:

1. Raise your beverage.
2. Express your feelings of appreciation to the audience. If someone asked you to deliver a toast, thank him or her for the opportunity.
3. Open your toast by introducing yourself briefly: What is your name? Why are you present?
4. Share something—an anecdote, an experience—that reflects your admiration for the community or the person you are toasting.
5. Close your toast by saying, "To _____," naming the person, event, group, or achievement that you are toasting. Then take a sip of your beverage.

LaunchPad
macmillan learning

Over the course of your adult life you will likely be a witness to numerous toasts. Learn to recognize the difference between a good toast and a problematic one by visiting LaunchPad at launchpadworks.com and listening to the "A Retirement Party Toast: Who Has the Toast with the Most?" audio example for chapter 13.

You've been invited to the retirement party of your aunt, Mi-young, who is stepping down as the executive vice president of Zippy Coffee, a successful brand of highly caffeinated coffee based in Tacoma, Washington. After dinner, two colleagues who worked closely with your aunt deliver toasts in her honor.

Listen to Sang-chul and Jung-hee's toasts in honor of Mi-young, and consider the following questions:

- Who delivered the better toast? Why?
- Which speech better exemplifies the elements of a toast?
- How might you improve the less successful speech?

Comedian Stephen Colbert roasts President George W. Bush at the 2006 White House Correspondents Dinner.

Roasts. Closely related to toasts are roasts, which are humorous, teasing tributes to an individual. A roast is usually a more formalized event in which the participants and honoree realize the tribute is meant in good fun. Unlike toasts, roasts often take place over a longer period of time, with a series of speakers who offer up stories, jabs, playful insults, and other forms of humorous repartee that celebrate a person among his or her community. If you are asked to participate in a roast, you should check with the planner about norms and expectations. Be certain that your planned remarks do not cross the line into things that would be perceived as offensive or hurtful. Also, it is very important that the individual who is to be roasted knows that he or she is going to be roasted and is not an overly sensitive person. In general, roasts are meant in good fun but can be perceived as mean if everyone—the honoree, the roasters, and the audience—is not in on the joke. As a roaster, please remember that your primary purpose is to honor and celebrate the person in a humorous and ironic matter. True or real meanness violates the unspoken norms of roasting and will damage the fun and humorous atmosphere they are designed to create.

Speeches of Inspiration or Encouragement: Sermons, After-Dinner Speeches, and Commemorations

All the types of celebratory speaking discussed so far are meant to inspire and encourage in some way or another; however, some occasions may call for a more extended speech designed to rouse or energize a community in a more sustained, future-oriented way. Sometimes termed **motivational speaking**, these kinds of addresses attempt to motivate us to feel good about our communities and our future endeavors. Although these speeches can also seek to inform or persuade, their primary purpose is to inspire. Inspirational speeches come in a variety of forms. The most common are (1) sermons, jeremiads, or lectures; (2) after-dinner speeches or keynote addresses; and (3) commemorative speeches. Let us address each briefly in turn.

motivational speaking concerns speeches that are primarily intended to inspire an audience to feel something about their community.

Everett Collection, Inc.

Former U.S. vice president Al Gore wrote and starred in the critically acclaimed film *An Inconvenient Truth* in 2006. Both the film and the book on which it was based were described as an environmental jeremiad.

Sermons, Jeremiads, and Lectures. If you've been to a service or liturgy at a place of worship, you are likely already familiar with a **sermon**, a speech that relies on religious or spiritual texts to inspire listeners to do or think in accord with religious teachings. **Jeremiads** are specialized speeches that both admonish an audience for straying from a religious teaching or failing to live up to moral goodness in some way and suggest a solution.[5] Traditionally, jeremiads were formalized sermonic forms; however, these kinds of speeches have become increasingly common in nonreligious contexts. Many speeches given by politicians about the perils of global warming, for example, are contemporary versions of jeremiads.

Stripped of overt religious or moral trappings, a sermonic form may simply become a **lecture**, such as when a parent attempts to inspire a child not to steal or shoplift after having been caught, or when a basketball coach admonishes her players to focus and work harder, inspiring them to play better in the second half of the game.

After-Dinner and Keynote Speaking. Delivering a speech after a meal is a tradition that stretches back centuries. In the nineteenth century, for example, it was customary for fraternal orders—such as the

a **sermon** is a speech by a religious leader or spiritual person; sermons often include references to religious or spiritual texts, such as the Hebrew or Christian bibles or the Koran.

a **jeremiad** is a prophetic speech of woe and moral or spiritual shortcoming. Jeremiads typically admonish communities to repent or change their ways to avert doom.

a **lecture**, in the context of celebratory speaking, is a speech of blame or admonishment; in the context of informative speaking, however, a lecture is simply educational speech.

Freemasons—to gather at an annual or a monthly "festive board," which featured songs and formalized toasts while food courses were served.[6] At the conclusion of the meal, a guest or fraternal brother was asked to deliver a speech to amuse and entertain diners as they ate their desserts. Today, after-dinner speaking engagements are less formal and ritualistic, and they do not always follow dinner, but they are still common at such gatherings as company banquets, professional and academic conferences, and family reunions. If the speech following a meal is more serious in tone or purpose—for example, if it sets an agenda for a political group or corporate enterprise or shares academic research—it may be termed a **keynote address**.

a **keynote address** is a featured speech at a convention, meeting, or political gathering that is designed to highlight the tone and purpose of the gathering; sometimes keynote speeches advance a collective goal or agenda.

In general, these speeches are more lighthearted, humorous, and uplifting. Here are the keys to delivering a good keynote or after-dinner speech:

1. Know exactly how long you have to speak, and plan for your speech to be shorter. Because these events usually involve a meal for a large crowd and possibly other speakers, it's best to plan for a slightly shorter speech than your allotted time so that you don't keep everyone too late if events are running behind.
2. Start off by thanking the group hosting the event and the individual who introduces you.
3. Acknowledge the reason you are speaking and the occasion that brought the group together.
4. Deliver a speech that relates to the occasion or that highlights the general tone or reason for the event. Because most after-dinner speaking is designed to entertain and inspire the audience, telling stories and the occasional joke—if it is funny!—is a good idea. Avoid gloomy remarks and depressing topics.

Commemorative Speeches. As the word's Latin roots remind us, to commemorate someone or something is to bring it into memory. Most commemorative speeches honor a person, a place, or an idea in a way that not only relates information (such as biography or history) but also inspires deep feelings of anticipation, respect, reverence—even joy. The commemorative speeches perhaps most familiar to readers are **rally speeches** (or pep talks) and **commencement speeches**. At political rallies held in town halls or stadiums, or sports rallies held in high school and college gymnasiums or stadiums, speakers often try to stir positive feelings toward future successes. Even if you are not into politics or sports, you will most likely have participated, or will participate, in a graduation ceremony for a high school, military academy, or college. Commencement speeches are almost always given at graduations. Typically a well-known speaker is invited to commend a graduating class of students for their accomplishments and inspire them to do great

a **rally speech** is an enthusiastic oration designed to inspire and motivate a community, delivered at an event for a social or political cause.

a **commencement speech** is an inspirational speech delivered to graduating students at an educational institution, such as a university.

Speaking to Inspire: Some Tips

When giving a speech of inspiration, your primary goal is to honor the present moment in a way that emotionally motivates your audience. Think about it this way: you are trying to get an audience to collectively smile and feel good. Here are some of the most common things speakers do to inspire audiences:

- Focus on the audience's mood. Recognize what their collective mood is, acknowledge it, and push them toward feeling positive about the present moment.
- Be creative with language and delivery. Think about your inspiration speech as if it were a song. What phrases could you repeat? How can you move audiences into a rhythm of inspiration? Can you paint vivid images in their mind with words?
- Tell stories. Good inspirational speakers often tell stories to encourage audiences to live vicariously. You could tell a relevant story from your own life to communicate your sincerity and generate interest from the audience.
- Be energetic. Make sure you communicate the inspiration and excitement you want the audience to feel by role modeling liveliness. It's very hard to inspire others if you do not appear inspired.
- End memorably. Perhaps the most important part of any kind of inspirational speech is how you end it. Always end on a high note, with a memorable or dramatic statement. Spend time crafting your ending, as it sets the tone for the moment you are celebrating and will be what your audience remembers.

Name three things, events, or people that inspire you. Why do they inspire you? Do you think you can infect others with your inspiration? How?

deeds and work in the future. Studying commencement speeches can offer much insight into successfully inspiring audiences in just about any kind of celebratory speaking—even toasts!

Speeches That Mourn Loss: Eulogies

The most challenging kind of speech you will encounter in this book—and in your life—is the eulogy, or a speech that honors the deceased. At first glance, it may seem strange that a eulogy is included in a chapter on celebratory speaking. However, speaking to honor the departed is not only an acknowledgment of a passed life but also a celebration of that life. When you speak to honor a loved one, friend, or colleague, you are speaking to praise the life he or she lived, call attention to his or her redeeming qualities or deeds, and bring the audience together *in the present* as a community in their memory of the deceased.

Eulogies can be a challenging speech genre to discuss, since many people find it difficult to think about death and dying. When someone we love

> Eulogies can be a challenging speech genre to discuss, since many people find it difficult to think about death and dying.

or admire dies, we not only mourn his or her absence but also think about our own fears of dying. The central truth of eulogies concerns this double structure of reckoning: eulogies are designed to help the living both mourn the passing of a person and grapple with their own mortality. If you keep it in your mind and heart that by delivering a eulogy you are also helping yourself and others think about their mortality, you can give a better eulogy.

Unlike many forms of speaking since antiquity, the expectations and format for eulogies have changed very little in the West. Knowing the basic functions of eulogies that have persisted for thousands of years can make your task of composing one less daunting. Public address scholars Kathleen Hall Jamieson and Karlyn Kohrs Campbell have summarized the functions of eulogies as follows:[7]

1. **Acknowledge the Death.** Even though the passing of a loved one is known at the time of the funeral, acknowledging his or her death helps the audience mourn by actually naming it. Naming someone's death helps audiences begin to move the death from a present event to the past.

2. **Move Death from the Present to the Past.** When someone we love dies, the event of the death seems to occur over and over. When giving a eulogy, you are attempting to help mourners heal by situating the death in the past.

3. **Help Mourners Reflect on Their Mortality.** The passing of a loved one stirs up fears of our own deaths. Eulogies, either directly or indirectly, should acknowledge these fears. "One of the difficult parts of mourning Diana," you might say, "is that her death reminds us of our own." Acknowledge the audience's fears as well as their sadness.

4. **Indicate That the Deceased Lives On in a Different Way.** Eulogies almost always identify the ways in which the deceased continues to "live" in a new way, ultimately celebrating the present moment. In religious services, the continued life of the deceased is often discussed in terms of an immortal soul or being with a higher power. In secular services, the deceased is often discussed as "living on" in terms of his or her good works and deeds, and the memories of the audience.

5. **Reconstitute the Community.** As with all celebratory speeches, the fundamental purpose of a eulogy is to bring the community back to unity—that is, to bring them together over the memory of the deceased. Your fundamental goal in a eulogy is to tell the audience, "We're in this together," however you wish to do that. Helping others mourn is, in part, convincing them that they are not alone in their grief and suffering. By giving a eulogy, you are speaking to comfort the audience.

Tips for Giving Eulogies

How you compose a eulogy depends on the character of the person who has passed, his or her life story, and the rhetorical situation. If the deceased was a religious person and the funeral service is in a church or synagogue, spiritual references are appropriate. If the deceased was not a religious person, you should avoid making spiritual references to a belief system the deceased did not share. And despite our common conceptions of funerals as sad events, humor, happiness, and even a mood of celebration is appropriate for a eulogy if an audience is open to it. Take care to analyze the audience for a eulogy carefully.

- **Write It Down.** A eulogy is the most emotional speech one can give. Consequently, you want to plan your speech ahead of time and know what you are going to say. Plan your eulogy and write it out word for word, or prepare an outline. Use a manuscript or note cards when you speak. You may not need your notes when you start speaking, but you will be glad that you have them.
- **Keep Your Emotions in Check.** It is difficult not to cry or feel upset with the passing of a loved one. When you are giving a eulogy, however, your role is to be composed and strong so that others can cry. Try to avoid losing control of your emotions when speaking. If you start to lose your composure, take a deep breath and perhaps review your notes. Audiences are very understanding at funerals and wakes.
- **Acknowledge Your Relationship to the Person.** If you are speaking at someone's funeral, wake, or memorial service, it is likely that you personally knew him or her. Even so, many in the audience may not know the character or extent of your relationship, so it is important to mention who you are and why you are speaking. You may also take this opportunity to express your gratitude for being invited to speak or for the audience's attention.
- **Acknowledge Important Attendees.** In your speech, acknowledge the family and close friends of the deceased in some way.
- **Recall Stories, Accomplishments, and Deeds of the Person.** Most eulogies recall the life events, accomplishments, and character of the person who has died. Your job is to remind the audience about the person's life and character, and to highlight his or her virtues and positive qualities. Serious life events can be mentioned, as well as humorous stories.
- **Remind the Audience That They Are United as a Community.** Telling the audience "We're in this together" is perhaps one of the most important goals of a eulogy. Grief is often associated with a sense of loneliness, so it is meaningful for audience members to know that they are not alone in this but have one another for support.

Can you think of an occasion for a eulogy in which unifying the community is not a central goal?

ILLUSTRATION: EULOGY FOR OPAL JEANETTE GRESHAM (1920–2011)

What are the five functions of a eulogy? ⊘

I open the eulogy by telling the audience who I am and how I am related to the deceased. This establishes my authority and credibility as a speaker.

In U.S. culture, one does not "speak ill of the dead." Granny was indeed stubborn, but here I recast the quality as a virtue of consistent love.

Here I transition to the body of the speech with a preview. I also acknowledge Granny's death and the purpose of moving on from the present to the past.

This line functions both as a thesis and as something of a refrain that I will use throughout the speech. The repetition of a particular phrase not only reminds the audience of the purpose of your speaking but can also take on a poetic quality.

Here I advance a kind of biography of my grandmother for the audience. By going through family items and interviewing my relatives, I tried to learn stories that some of the audience might not know.

SATURDAY, APRIL 30, 2011

My name is Joshua Gunn; I am the youngest of Jeanette's three grandchildren. As my cousins Kelly and Kathy will tell you, we grandkids were especially close to granny. And it's not like she would have let us be distant, because she insisted on this closeness in her typical unyielding way. Some of you will smile when I say that Jeanette could be a stubborn woman. But she was also stubborn in her loving; she loved us with a relentless consistency.

I wanted to say a few things about my grandmother—a few things about your sister, your mother, your aunt, your friend—I wanted to say a few things about Jeanette so that we can let her body go, so that her body can finally meet mercy in rest.

Jeanette lived a hard life. She lived a good life.

Jeanette was the fifth of six children born to Nathaniel Sepias Freeman and Ila Maude Campbell on December 3, 1920. She was raised—and lived most of her life—in Centerville, Georgia. Before Jeanette came, there were her sisters Illa Mae, Easter Lois, Lucy Belle, and Susie Marie, and after her was born the trickster of the family, Nathanial Morris.

Uncle Morris: Did you know for most of my life I thought you were my uncle Marce, spelled M-A-R-C-E? "Marce!" That's Granny's way of saying Morris! Your sister lived a hard life. She lived a good life.

Along with her brother and sisters, Jeanette picked cotton as a youngster in the hot Georgia sun. The family was poor and worked hard for everything they had. They farmed their own food. I remember Granny telling me that on her most memorable Christmas she got an orange and some pencils, and that she was thankful. I thought she was making that up so that I wouldn't keep begging her for toys. Now I know the lesson of gratitude she was trying to teach me with her stories.

Jeanette said that, as kids, they had no idea about the great depression of the thirties. For them, nothing changed: they were not in want of food because they grew it. They still got their pencils and fruit every year from Santa Claus.

At eighteen she moved to the big city and took a job at a factory, where she became a seamstress. She worked tirelessly for decades ever since. She worked long beyond retirement age, and even worked part time after her retirement. It may seem strange, but [Jeanette loved to work and was happy to have work.] She was proud to work. She was proud to be a woman working, even during a time in our country when it was not fashionable to be an independent woman.

> Here I take care to point out another virtue of my grandmother: she worked very hard, and enjoyed it. As a child of the Depression era, she always expressed gratitude for having a job.

[Your aunt lived a hard life. She lived a good life.]

> Here the refrain of the eulogy returns, but I have replaced Jeanette's name with "your aunt." In subsequent mentions I will change my grandmother's role for different members of the audience because she had many different roles. I wanted to be sure to include everyone's experience. This is also a move toward celebrating the community.

On September 2, 1939, Jeanette married Robert Gresham. With the Second World War looming, they got right to work and had Hilda Ann in 1940. Shortly thereafter, Bob was off to the European theater to help beat back the forces of fascism. Upon his return, Jeanette carried and gave birth to my mother, Nina Jane, in 1946.

Mom, your mother lived a hard life. She lived a good life.

Everyone here will carry with them their own cherished memories of Jeanette, and I will admit most of what I know about Granny happened after 1973, when I was born. So I'll let those of y'all who were around in the fifties, sixties, and seventies tell that part of her story.

Here's what I will remember about Jeanette: She liked peanut butter and Diet Coke and chocolate and black coffee. She liked the pianist Floyd Cramer, and her favorite Christmas Song was "O Holy Night," especially if it was played by Liberace. She adored the ceramic art that my cousin Kathy made for her, because she'd never let me play with it when I was a child. She relished the sweets Kelly made for her.

[She was prideful about her "wheels," especially that ugly beige Nova. She kept her cars in good shape and associated her sense of independence with the open road, even when she was just driving three miles and back from Rockbridge Baptist Church.

She talked to her daughters on the phone almost every day.

She liked soap operas.] She liked them *a lot*. I remember when she looked after me we watched those soaps—and nothing, I tell you *nothing*, is more boring to a seven-year-old than the slow and plodding pace of *General Hospital*. The only reason I watched them with her is because, well, I was with her. I enjoyed her enjoyment, even if I was bored.

> Three paragraphs in a row deliberately began with "she," to create a rhythm for the speech.

Granny made the most amazing buttermilk biscuits. Over the course of many years I have tried to replicate her recipe. I cannot. I wish I could. I've come pretty close, though, and I'll tell you I figured out the secret ingredient: It's not love, although I know that's what I'm supposed to say. It's not love, people, it's Crisco. Lots and lots of shortening. Slopping handfuls of Crisco!

[I remember sitting on the carport with Granny as she told stories and talked to visitors sitting in those uncomfortable metal chairs.

I remember that if Granny ever got tickled about something, she'd laugh until she infected everyone else with laughter so that no one could breathe.

I remember Granny taking a switch to my behind. More often than I'd like to admit.]

> Again, the repetition of "I remember" is to impart a sense of rhythm.

I remember the long ritual of saying good-bye to Granny when I left her house with Mom. We would pile in the car and we'd wave good-bye and Mom would crank the car. And then Granny would say something, and so Mom would roll down her window. And then Mom and Granny would talk some more and say good-bye. Then, as soon as Mom put the car in reverse, Granny would ask a question. Mom would stop, and there would be more talking. The almost-going-then-not-going good-bye ritual could take upward of twenty minutes! But you knew it was over when Jeanette said her familiar parting words: "You be good, now."

[Your friend lived a hard life. She lived a good life.]

> This phrase punctuates the ending of the biographical part of the speech. This part was intended to achieve the function of moving the death from something in the present to something "of the past": Jeanette's life is over. To this end, I deliberately use past-tense verbs throughout.

Yesterday I learned there would not be a preacher or a homily at the service today, in part because Jeanette's cherished preachers have also passed on but mostly to keep things short, as she would have wanted. Even so, as y'all know, it must be said that Jeanette was a deeply religious person who believed Jesus Christ was her lord and savior. In honor of Jeanette's profound and lifelong faith, I thought it would be important to close my remarks with a meditation on deity.

> This is a transition from the biographical section of the speech to key functions of (a) reflecting on mortality, (b) indicating how Granny lives on differently, and (c) reconstituting the community.

No matter what your religious beliefs are, I think most of us can agree that our faiths comfort us for three reasons. [First, our religions teach us that to live—to be human—is to suffer. To reckon with suffering is to know what it is to live.] Second, our religions teach us that there is joy in suffering, that there are moments of happiness together that we need to recognize. Religions teach us to recognize our joy even when we are mourning. [And finally, religions teach us that we are not alone in our joy and suffering. We have each other, and our having each other is the most important thing about this hard life.] This is to say, recognizing our togetherness is love. Love unites us here.

> I mean to name and acknowledge everyone's grief.

> Here I am deliberately attempting to constitute community.

We should be reminded of the song of the degrees of David—Psalm 133 from the Hebrew Bible:

> Behold, how good and how delightful it is for brethren to dwell together in unity! It is as the precious oil upon the head, which descends upon the beard, the beard of Aaron, which descends upon the hem of his garments! It is as the dew of Harmon, which descends upon the mountains of Zion!

There is, strangely, a gift in death. [The gift of death is a reminder of how good it is for us to dwell together today in unity over our love for Jeanette, and over our love for each other.]

Most of the audience was composed of Christian friends and family; the gesture of reading a verse from the Bible was expected. The gesture also brings the audience together over a cherished religious document. Finally, I chose a passage from the Bible that would not offend non-Christians. This is a psalm that celebrates being in a community.

I said our religions give us affirmation that to live is to suffer, our religions teach us where to look for joy, and finally, our religions remind us that we have each other, that we are not alone. We might summarize all of these teachings into one spiritual imperative: our different faiths teach us to recognize the gift of death. Death is anything but clear, and that's why we are all here—to try to see more clearly what Jeanette's passing means for us. No one can witness her own death. No one can invite it or control it.

Here I try to acknowledge death and a reflection on our mortality, but also use it to celebrate those who remain.

We can expect death, we can plan for it, that much is certain. But we cannot die by our own efforts. [This means that we the living have a collective responsibility to bear witness to those who have passed on. My grandmother did not witness her own death.] That is our job. And in our witnessing, in our mourning, we love her beyond her death. In our promise to witness her dying, as well as the passing of others who go before us, [we make good on the eternal promise of love, we make certain that there is love without end, and we ensure that there is love beyond death.]

Here is my attempt to suggest that by being witnesses to Jeanette's death, she continues to live on in a different way.

Although most of the audience were religious people, there were some who were not. Here I tried to write a passage that could be heard as either spiritual or secular, depending on a given audience member's preferences.

My grandmother lived a hard life. She lived a good life. Her hard, good life on this planet has now come to a quiet close. Opal Jeanette Gresham is now—as she always has been—with God. She is now, as she has always been, with us.

We give her body to the earth. But you can know with certainty that her life continues in a different way because of what we are doing right now. We too often think of deity as somewhere up there, in the sky, or in some other place. But I want us also to recognize that our witnessing and our mourning is also a part of our deity. That is to say, God is our love right now, in this moment, in this place. Jeanette is here because God is here, because we are here. Because God is this love.

Celebratory speaking, or speaking on special occasions, occurs at moments when it is important to bring a given community together. Whether honoring a person, a group, or an event, celebratory speeches aim to encourage an audience to recognize the common bonds in the present. Celebratory speeches can recognize others or events, praise or blame people or things, inspire or encourage, or even mourn loss. Despite the differences between toasts and eulogies, most celebratory speeches are personal in tone and attempt to celebrate the community in intimate ways.

Mourners assemble at a memorial service for senior pastor and former South Carolina state senator Clementa C. Pinckney, who was murdered with nine others in a 2015 hate crime.

Based on the photography of Erica Nix

Celebrating Your Community

Celebratory speaking brings together the community in a celebration of the present.

Kim Vintage Stock/Corbis via Getty Images

Types of Celebratory Speeches

There are four basic types of celebratory speaking: speeches of recognition; speeches of praise or blame; speeches of inspiration or encouragement; and speeches that mourn loss.

LaunchPad
macmillan learning

LaunchPad for *Speech Craft* includes a curated collection of speech videos and encourages self-assessment through adaptive quizzing. Go to **launchpadworks.com** to get access to:

✓ LearningCurve adaptive quizzes

 Video clips to help you improve your speeches

ACTIVITY

Introduction Speech for a Classmate

Interview a classmate and discover his or her name, where he or she is from, what he or she is in school studying, and his or her favorite hobby. Then compose a one-minute speech of introduction. After you have had time to interview your classmate and compose your speech, give the speech in class. Unless your teacher gives you an alternative, you can base your speech on the following outline:

I. Introduction
   A. Attention-Getting Statement: Get the audience's attention in a memorable way.
   B. Preview: Tell the audience you are introducing a classmate, and briefly state the main parts of your speech.
II. Body
   A. Biography: Tell the class basic information about your classmate, including his or her name, where he or she is from, and what he or she is studying in school.
   B. Hobby: Relate to the class the hobby or hobbies of your classmate. Illustrate the hobby with a short story you learned from your classmate.
III. Conclusion
   A. Summary: Summarize the main points of your speech.
   B. Closing: Tell the audience what they can learn from knowing the person you introduced.

KEY TERMS

 Videos in LaunchPad describe many of these terms. Go to launchpadworks.com.

motivational speaking 256

sermon 257

jeremiad 257

lecture 257

keynote address 258

rally speech 258

 commencement speech 258

INFORMATIVE

SPEAKING

CHAPTER 14

Because of her personal experience with autism, animal science professor Temple Grandin has built a successful speaking career on her expertise and unique insights into nonhuman animal behavior. "Being a visual thinker was the start of my career with animals," recalls Grandin, "because animals are visual creatures too. Animals are controlled by what they see," not words.[1] Because of her visual thinking style, Grandin eventually established a successful career as an animal behavior expert who designs humane equipment for managing livestock in North America. Today, almost half the cattle on the continent are handled by the processing systems Grandin envisioned and designed.[2]

Today she is also widely sought after as a public speaker and compassionate spokesperson for autism. Diagnosed with "brain damage" at an early age, Grandin would not learn that her hypersensitivity to sound and picture-based thinking were symptoms of autism until she was in her forties. Since that time, she has spoken and written publicly about her experiences as an autistic person, working very hard to explain to neurotypical (non-autistic) audiences how her mind works:

> When I lecture, the language itself is mostly "downloaded" out of memory from files that are like tape recordings. I use slides or notes to trigger opening the different files. When I am talking about something for the first time, I look at the visual images on the "computer monitor" in my imagination, then the language part of me describes those images.[3]

Here Grandin uses an analogy to express her meaning: her mind *is not really* a computer, but the image of one *is like* what Grandin is trying to describe to her audience. Grandin is a particularly gifted public speaker because of her ability to adapt to audiences who think differently than she does. Remarkably, she can *translate* the images she sees in her mind's eye into words, which convey the image, in turn, to the minds of her audience.[4] She is a successful public speaker not only because of her use of spoken language but also because of her visual aids (such as slide software), which also act as a prompt for her memory while speaking.[5] When speaking to inform, the primary challenge you face is one of translation.

The Informing Genre

> **You will learn to**
>
> **DESCRIBE** the primary task and goal of informative speaking.
>
> **EXPLAIN** the difference between informing and persuading.
>
> **LIST** and **DESCRIBE** the five strategies of informing.

Your principle task as an informative speaker is to convey *information* in a way that is clear to understand but that doesn't talk down to or insult your audience. By finding out how much general background knowledge your audience has about your topic—and their interest in it—you will have a better sense of how sophisticated your speech should be and what angle to take. Along with holding your audience's interest, when you are speaking to inform you have one primary goal: to provide a new point of view or new information on a topic. To achieve this goal, you need to know what kinds of things people tend to inform others about, as well as the ways in which they discuss those things.

> The primary goal of speaking to inform is to provide a new point of view or new information to an audience.

We speak to inform all the time, from telling friends about our vacation in Idaho to describing a fantastic lecture to family members. Although there is some crossover between that kind of everyday informing and the kind you are expected to do in a more formal speech situation, this chapter will focus on those formal situations—speeches that attempt to provide a new perspective or information. As noted in chapter 12, informative speaking entails a set of expectations that are different from other genres, like celebratory and persuasive speaking.

Informing versus Persuading

To understand **informative speaking** a little better, we'll first take a look at how it differs from persuasive speaking.

Speaking to inform and speaking to persuade are different in two main ways:

- Speaking to inform is about imparting knowledge—giving audience members new information or novel ways of thinking about a topic. Speaking to persuade, by contrast, aims to change beliefs, attitudes, and values—and sometimes behavior.
- Speaking to inform is usually considered *easier* than speaking to persuade because it's much less challenging to give the audience new information or knowledge than to try to change the audience's behavior or mind about something.

informative speaking attempts to introduce or impart new knowledge and information to audiences.

Another way to think about this is that the role of an informative speaker is usually that of a reporter or a teacher. By contrast, the role of a persuader is similar to that of a politician or other leader. Whenever composing a speech to inform or to persuade, ask yourself, "Do I sound more like a reporter or a politician?" Alternatively, you could ask, "Am I primarily describing and explaining, or am I asking the audience to change or do something?" These types of questions can help you discern the boundaries between informing and persuading and help you better achieve your speech goals.

Another important and helpful difference between informing and persuading concerns *objectivity*, or the presumption of the impartiality of an informative speaker. In Western culture, audiences expect an informative speaker to be objective; audiences tend to assume that when someone is informing us—especially celebrated informers like teachers, reporters, historians, and various experts—the information conveyed is not biased or skewed (recall the discussion of biased language in chapter 9). After all, the goal is to gather the best and most unbiased information available in order to better understand our world and make informed decisions. In contrast to informative speaking, persuasive speaking is purposely *not* objective because it tries to get an audience to see, think, feel, or act in a way the speaker suggests. In short, persuasion always has a specific point of view on an issue.

An informative speech is similar to a teacher's lecture.

is there any speech that is not **persuasive?**

Drew Angerer/Staff/Getty Images

When studying public speaking for the first time, it is sometimes difficult to make sharp distinctions between speaking to inform and speaking to persuade. In part, this is because the goals of informing and persuading are often combined in our culture—even deliberately mixed. For example, news that we receive on the Internet, on television, and in newspapers is often presented as "informative."

At the same time, however, we know that certain news outlets attempt to present information in a way that persuades us to adopt certain political values: MSNBC presents information from a liberal perspective, FOX News presents information from a conservative perspective, and so on. Even in the classroom, where most of us expect teachers to present information objectively, persuasion is at work, because whatever the subject, the teacher is communicating that *the information presented is important*; education as such imparts the persuasive claim that you should value knowledge.

These and similar observations have led many communication scholars—and even some public speaking teachers—to argue that all forms of speaking are persuasive at some level, an idea that speaks to the foundational ethics of communication. As we discussed in chapter 2 on listening and ethics, all speaking is a request for someone to listen to what you have to say. Therefore, anytime you open your mouth and a sound comes out, you are attempting to convince others to listen to you. One might argue, of course, that the suggestion that all speaking is persuasive is a bit simplistic, and that there is at least a pragmatic distinction between speaking to impart new information and speaking to deliberately ask for change. The key to discerning this distinction lies in the *conscious* goal of the speech: if you are primarily aiming to provide the audience with new information or a new perspective, you are informing.

How do you know when a speech is primarily informative or persuasive? Challenge yourself by visiting LaunchPad at **launchpadworks.com** and linking to the video lecture by astrophysicist Neil deGrasse Tyson titled "The Pluto Files."

Consider the following questions:

- **What is Dr. Tyson's primary goal with this lecture?**

- **Based on the primary goal, is this speech fundamentally informative or persuasive?**
- **If the speech is primarily informative, how do you know?**
- **If the speech is primarily persuasive, how do you know?**

Because of the expectations of the genre (see chapter 12 for more about genres and audience expectations), aiming for objectivity when informing is a good thing. For many, the very term "informing" has the notion of objectivity built into it, in the sense that anyone who claims to be informing (or teaching or reporting) has a responsibility to uphold this unspoken promise. As an informative speaker, if you strive for objectivity, you will more than likely enhance your credibility; if your speech seems biased, you will risk dismissal by the audience.[6]

So where does this leave us? It's important to remember that because every speaker has a unique mind and approaches speaking from a particular perspective, objectivity has its limits—and some listeners may be aware of those limits. In any case, when you are giving an informative presentation, it is vital that you do your best to be as objective as possible. Think of objectivity as an ideal to strive for every time you speak to inform. As a listener, you would expect nothing less; as a speaker, you owe that much to your audience.

What is the primary difference between speaking to inform and speaking to persuade?

Informative versus Persuasive Speaking at a Glance

	INFORMATIVE	**PERSUASIVE**
Expectations	A speech that educates or explains, providing new information or a new perspective	A speech that deliberately attempts to influence or change beliefs, attitudes, values, or behavior through appeals and arguments
Example Topic	How the autistic mind works	Autistic people have rights that need protection
Example Topic	Nonhuman animals are sentient creatures with complex neurological systems	Nonhuman animals deserve legal protection against pain and suffering[7]

Choosing an Informative Topic

If the primary goal of speaking to inform is to provide an audience with new information or a new point of view, then you might be asking, "Well, new information about what?" What you speak about should be determined by the reason for your speech.

You have already learned about brainstorming topics (see chapter 4) and perhaps worked with your teacher to generate ideas for an informative speech. If you're still stumped, you could try an approach pioneered by the ancient Greeks that is still used by public speaking experts today: generating informative speech topics by selecting a generic "commonplace," or topic, and then winnowing the topic down to something you're interested in (see chapter 4 for general guidelines for choosing speech topics).[8] The following chart illustrates how topics might be selected in this way:

Types of Informative Speeches

TYPE	DESCRIPTION	EXAMPLE
Objects	A speech about a specific thing, either abstract or concrete	Doping controversies in the Olympics; the history and uses of safety pins
People	A speech about a person or group of people	Abraham Lincoln; Young Money recording artists; Brandon Stanton
Events	A speech about an important event from the past or possibly something in the future	The U.S. women's suffrage movement; the invention of the Frisbee; D-Day
Processes	A speech about how things happen or how to do something	How to practice yoga; how to make a stuffed omelet
Concepts	A speech about a philosophical or intellectual idea, typically abstract	Fuzzy mathematics; the idea of beauty
Issues	A speech about a current situation or problem; a briefing	The future funding of Social Security; reducing the dangers of nuclear power

Considering these categories in your search for possible speech topics can be an effective way to go. But you have another powerful tool at your disposal. When selecting a topic for an informative speech, begin by asking yourself one simple question: *Why have you been asked, or why have you volunteered, to speak?*

In most public speaking classes, you will be asked to deliver an informative speech. Your instructor may provide you with the topic, or he or she may let you determine your own topic. Yet even in this situation, the single, simple question—Why have you been asked, or why have you volunteered, to speak?—can be of service to you. In a classroom setting, you've been assigned an informative presentation not only to give you a chance to demonstrate and practice your speaking skills but, more importantly, to share with your classmates your expertise and research on a topic that is new to them. For this reason, you will want to keep your peers engaged.

Once you know the context and guidelines for your informative speech and have chosen a topic to speak on, you will need to prepare a presentation that will inform your audience. To do this, you'll need to employ a number of the specific informative strategies discussed next.

> When selecting an informative speech topic, ask yourself, "Why have I been asked to speak?"

> **What are two ways to choose an informative topic? What are the advantages of each?**

Informative Strategies

How one informs the audience can vary widely. There are several strategies you can use to help your listeners imagine, envision, or otherwise

Speak for a Reason!

Informative speech topics should always be chosen with your specific reason for speaking in mind; merely *looking for* a reason to speak often results in the kind of empty speech many would dismiss as malarkey. When you speak outside the classroom, it's more likely that the occasion for your speech will actually determine your topic for you. Let's say you are at a party, and the guests want to play a party game. You volunteer to explain how the game works. This impromptu speech at a party is really an informative speech, since you're providing new information about the fine art of pinning the tail on the donkey—a *process*. Or let's say your supervisor at Jitters Coffee asks you to conduct a morning workshop for your colleagues concerning how to use the new espresso machine. This planned, thirty-minute speaking opportunity is really a "how-to" informative speech about an *object*. Or you've just taken a job as an on-location television news reporter, and you've been sent to cover recent flooding in your local community. Your subsequent report for the evening news, in which you detail how local businesses and roadways have been affected by the flooding, is an informative speech about an *event*.

understand your topic and message. The following section covers five strategies: description, definition, explanation, demonstration, and narration. In some cases, the strategies can work in combination to get your ideas across.

Description

> **description** gives audiences a mental sense of an event, a process, or an object, evoking sights, sounds, and smells.

The purpose of **description** is to give an audience a mental sense of an event, a process, or an object. Description evokes sights, sounds, even smells. You are probably most familiar with this kind of speech from watching reporters on television or YouTube, since they describe events for a living. Description is not reducible to reportage, however, because the language you use for description is typically more vivid and sensuous.

Speeches that are primarily focused on description are rarely about abstractions, like concepts, because these are difficult to imagine. Description is often used to create mini-speeches, or parts of larger informative presentations. For example, an interviewer once famously asked pop-rock musician Rickie Lee Jones, "What were the skies like when you were young?" As with many musical artists, Jones is an artistic reporter, and she answered her interviewer with a vivid example of an impromptu speech of description:

> [The skies] went on forever. . . . We lived in Arizona, and the skies always had little fluffy clouds in 'em. . . . They were long and clear and there were lots of stars at night. . . . They were beautiful, the most beautiful skies as a matter of fact. The sunsets were purple and red and yellow and on fire, and the clouds would catch the colors everywhere.[9]

Rickie Lee Jones describes poetically the skies of her youth in Arizona. Her trippy description of her childhood skies presents us with so much sensory information that we can easily imagine those little fluffy clouds.

Definition

The purpose of **definition** is to explain or describe the meaning of a term or concept. Typically, speakers define terms or concepts that the audience is unlikely to have much knowledge about. And, like description, definition often makes up a smaller section of a larger speech. For example, if you are giving a speech about the history of the U.S. Social Security program, you might benefit from spending some time defining the term *social security* itself. For example, you might say, "The *Oxford English Dictionary* defines *social security* as 'a state-run system providing financial support for people who are unemployed, sick, retired, or otherwise in need.'"[10]

definition is used to explain or describe the meaning of a term or concept.

Speakers use definitions for a variety of reasons, from adding precision to correcting a misunderstanding to clarifying a potentially complicated idea or technical term. Speakers also typically employ different types of definitions, including dictionary, etymological, example, and functional/operational. The following chart provides an example of each type, used to define the term *courage*.

Types of Definitions

TYPE	EXPLANATION	EXAMPLE
Dictionary	Cites the meaning of a term or concept as given in a dictionary.	*Merriam-Webster's Collegiate Dictionary*, 11th edition, defines *courage* as "mental or moral strength to venture, persevere, and withstand danger, fear, or difficulty."[11]
Etymological	Defines the term by showing the development of its historical meaning in one or more languages (the origin of the term).	The word *courage* may ultimately derive from the Latin *cor*, meaning "heart," which remains a common metaphor for inner strength.[12]
Example	Defines the term by giving one or more concrete examples of it.	Examples of courageous people include firefighters, soldiers, war reporters, and single parents.
Functional/ operational	Defines the term by showing how it works or operates.	Courage is feeling tremendous fear while facing a task and getting the task done anyway.

Scholars believe that goats were domesticated by humans over nine thousand years ago.

Explanation

When using explanation, you position yourself as an educator. With this strategy, your job is to explain how or why something is the way it is. Along with demonstration (discussed next), this is a common strategy of informative speaking. An example of an explanatory speech topic would be to describe the history and function of the rotary engine, or to explain the domestication of goats by humans over nine thousand years ago.[13]

Demonstration

Demonstration is another term for "how-to." Just think of an infomercial or a television cooking show, and you've got a good sense of this technique already. Entire presentations are often structured around a how-to topic, usually incorporating both definition and explanation. A sample speech of demonstration about how to cook on your car engine appears at the end of this chapter.

Narration

Public speakers frequently tell stories in their speeches, and the technical term for this strategy is **narration**. Fundamentally, a narrative is a story, or a verbal account of an event or series of events. As communication scholar Walter Fisher puts it, narration concerns telling stories that have "sequence and meaning for those who live, create, or interpret them."[14] Narratives fundamentally tell audiences about something, whether an event, a person, or a deed. Fisher has argued that because telling stories is so universal—common to all cultures around the world—using them in speeches is a great way to connect with audiences and draw them into the speech.

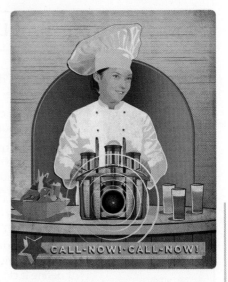

A cook demonstrates how to use the HAL 5000 Juicer.

Tips for Informing

> *You will learn to*
>
> **LIST** three tips for creating a great informative speech.

narration is a verbal account of an event or series of events.

> ? **What are the five strategies for informative speeches?**

Now that you understand how to consider the context of your informative speech and the five basic types of informative strategies, it's time to start developing your presentation. As you start this process, keep in mind that in addition to finding an appropriate topic, two key challenges in informative speaking are (1) getting your audience to find your topic interesting, and (2) encouraging them to remember your speech.

This chapter opened with the example of Temple Grandin, who is a widely sought-out speaker because of her unique talents. An eager audience, of course, is the best-case scenario when speaking to inform, and Grandin often has that advantage when she speaks in public. Even though as informative speakers we are in a position to help the audience learn, most of us are not famous like Grandin and will need to do things to encourage and interest the audience. The following three guidelines should help:

1. **Keep it simple, students.** Otherwise known as the "K.I.S.S." rule in popular parlance (and you may know it by a slightly different name), keeping your speech clear and easy to follow is the first step to encouraging audience interest. To keep it simple, you can do a number of things.

How to Observe the K.I.S.S. Rule

DO THIS...	BECAUSE OF THIS...
Avoid overly technical language and jargon.	Audiences dislike it when a speaker talks over their head, causing them to lose interest.
Reduce the quantity of information.	Audiences can become overwhelmed with too much information and will tune out if you present too much.
Do not over- or under-estimate the audience's knowledge (see chapter 3 for tips).	Assuming that your audience does not know anything about your topic may create the perception that you are talking down to them. Assuming that your audience knows more than they do, however, can create confusion and encourage disinterest.
Use visual aids.	Visual aids, such as posters, objects, or slide shows, can reinforce your message by adding a new way to experience your information.
Keep things concrete.	When informing, it is important to use lots of examples and to avoid abstractions. If you need to use an abstract term or concept, be sure to define it clearly.
Teach, don't browbeat.	Informing too forcefully can turn off an audience. Remember, your goal is to inform, not persuade.
Rinse, repeat.	Even if you use a visual aid, it is always important to repeat your major points to reinforce retention.

2. **Make your speech unique.** Many informative speeches, especially of the how-to variety, include similar information and duplicate the structure of speeches that have gone before. This is because as participants of our culture, we have learned the genre (watching cooking or home-renovation shows has accustomed us to the rhythms of "how-to" speaking). Ask your friends or perhaps even your instructor about the topic you have in mind: Have they heard about it before? If so, what did they hear? Simply talking to others about the topic you have in mind can give you a better sense of its uniqueness and whether an audience would find it of interest.

In addition to selecting an informative topic that is unique, you should present your speech in a way that sets it apart from the way a similar speech has been presented: seek out YouTube videos about your topic to see how others might have discussed it, and then try to present your topic with a different organization. For example, let's say you were to give an informative speech about the first president of the United States, George Washington. Beginning your speech with a reference to the legend of Washington being caught by his father chopping down a cherry tree is not a good idea. Why? We've all heard this legend before, and it's predictable that someone would begin an informative speech on the first president in this way. Instead, it would be much more interesting to begin your speech by stating that Washington was an active Freemason, by noting that he bred dogs and treated them like family, or by debunking the claim that Washington was tall for his time (he was about six feet tall, not unusual for men of his time—or ours). Even familiar topics can seem fresh to audiences when you avoid information that is common knowledge.

The topic "how to make a peanut butter and jelly sandwich" has been used throughout the ages.

3. **Make your speech personally relevant.** If you are not interested in your speech topic, it's going to be difficult to convince your audience that it's worth their time to listen to your speech. Speakers who are genuinely interested in their topics give the most compelling informative speeches because audiences can sense and feel that interest. Nothing is worse than having to endure a speaker who is disconnected from his or her topic, or disinterested in what he or she is saying.

Making your speech personally relevant does not refer only to your interests. As a speaker, you need to make sure your speech relates to the audience, too. Let's say you are a farmer, and you want to deliver a speech about your hay-baling tractor to your public speaking class. You are fascinated by how the tractor works and are excited to talk about your experiences. None of your classmates are farmers, so how will you make your interest in baling hay personally relevant to them? You could begin your speech by saying that your listeners' enjoyment of dairy products—from ice cream to the half-and-half they use in their coffee—all depends on well-baled hay. Introducing your speech this way makes a connection to your audience, allowing them to see how your topic is relevant to them.

? Describe the three guidelines that can encourage audience retention of your informative speech.

SAMPLE INFORMATIVE SPEECH

CAR COOKERY: THE REAL FAST FOOD

> The speaker begins by creating an imaginative scenario, tacitly asking for audience participation. This helps create a sense of personal relevance.

Imagine that your partner has asked you on a dinner date for this Friday night. The restaurant is a surprise, but you are told not to worry about dressing up. Your partner promptly picks you up at 6:00 p.m. and says that the restaurant is about forty-five minutes away, so you have plenty of time to catch up on the week's events.

Soon you and your partner are driving far outside the city into the countryside, and you start to get concerned. When your partner says you have about five minutes to go, you demand to know where you are going. It is then that your date pulls a homemade menu out of the glove box. To your surprise, you're apparently having "Exhaust Eggplant Parmesan" with a side of "Cruise Control Buttered Carrots" and a "Go-Go Greek Salad." As you contemplate the fact that you are miles away from civilization, your partner pulls into the entrance of a park. "Aha!" you think. "We're having a picnic!" Imagine your surprise when your partner lifts the hood of his or her Subaru, only to reveal a series of tinfoil packets arranged on top of the fuel injector housing!

That's right, friends—the meal for your romantic evening was cooked in the car as you were driving.

> The speaker has a straightforward thesis statement.

Today I would like to inform you about the fine art of car cookery, both what it is and how to do it. Although we don't know exactly when engine cooking began, we do know that truckers have been heating their meals on their engines for decades.[15] Regardless, cooking on your car makes planning picnics on road trips a blast! Almost every moving vehicle on the road is propelled by burning fuel, and burning fuel creates heat. That means that car engines get hot, allowing you to cook on them. Doing so requires patience and practice as well as pretesting your own car.

> The speaker's preview is helpful to the audience, as it helps them envision the different parts of the speech to come. Offering a preview of the speech's main points also helps audiences remember the speech.

I will first explain the history of car cooking. Second, I will describe the general techniques of car cooking, including a few sample recipes. Finally, I'll conclude with a few dos and don'ts.

You might be wondering where the idea of car cooking came from. Stories have circulated in popular culture about folks cooking on their cars for decades, from truckers heating cans of beans in their rig engines to hunters using the engine block to cook venison. According to Chris Maynard and Bill Scheller in their definitive guide to car cooking titled *Manifold Destiny*, we can probably trace the practice back to the fourth and fifth centuries. Apparently the Huns made use of a form of combustion—friction—to prepare their food.

"When a Hun wanted to enjoy a hunk of unsmoked brisket," reports Maynard and Scheller, "he would take the meat and put it under his saddlecloth, and the friction between the Hun and the horse would have a tenderizing and warming effect."[16] Sounds delicious, doesn't it?

Although it is not known who started the practice of car cookery or where it began, we can thank Maynard and Scheller for writing a book-length series of guidelines to help us do it. As someone with many years of car cooking experience—first as a Boy Scout and later as a car-camping enthusiast—I think we can reduce their 150-page book on car cookery to three basic steps: get to know your engine, plan your menu, and prepare your food.

Car Cooking Basics

- Get to know your engine
- Plan your menu
- Prepare your food (drive!)

The speaker's slide is not cluttered, highlighting only the three major points to come. This helps the audience remember the speech but does not encourage them to focus on the slide instead of the speaker.

First, you have to figure out the layout of your car engine—or as engineers put it, your engine configuration—to know where the hot spots are. In the 1950s, cars had large, relatively uncluttered engines that were ideal for cooking.[17] Simply put, in the 1950s cars ran hot. Today, car manufacturers design engines that are more efficient, make less heat, and look like spaceships.[18] Manufacturers are increasingly replacing metal parts—the ones that are great for conducting heat from the engine—with plastic. And with the advent of the hybrid electric car, a gas engine is now paired with an electric one, making it a challenge to figure out which is which.

The best way to figure out how suitable your engine is for cooking is to drive it around for about a half hour, then pull over, open the hood, and carefully feel for heat. Quickly touch the metal parts in your engine to see where the heat is. Plastic parts won't get hot enough, so don't worry about those. Unfortunately, if you have one of those fancy futuristic cars in which everything is covered in plastic, you're just going to have to borrow a friend's car to cook on. This is especially true if your car is a hybrid or exclusively electric, as it will not get hot enough to heat hamburger buns.

Once you have determined the hottest spots under your hood, you're ready for step two: planning your menu. As Maynard and Scheller note, planning your menu should be determined by two simple questions: (1) "How far are you driving?" and (2) "When do you expect to be hungry?"[19] You see, cooking on your car uses distance as well as time to determine what's possible for you to eat. If you have 140 to 200 miles to drive, you can pull off baking some chicken wings (anything with a bone in it takes longer to cook). These longer-distance foods are ideal for things like road trips—and, I would add, are much better than the drive-through. But if you have only about 40 miles to go, you'll have to stick with something like "Tube Steak Surprise." Of course, "tube steak" is another word for a hot dog, and the surprise is stuffing it with cheese and wrapping it with bacon. Another shorter-distance dish is salmon, which will poach relatively quickly on the average car engine.

I should mention that you don't necessarily have to cook your meal entirely on your car. I have often precooked my meal at home—which is especially advisable for something like, say, a whole fryer chicken or Cornish hen. You can use your car as a basic food warmer as well, which is ideal for picnics close to home.

Once you have located the hot spots on your car's engine and determined your menu, you are ready for the third step: food preparation and placement. The trick to car cooking is quality tinfoil, and the no-stick variety is especially helpful. Everything you cook will be wrapped in tinfoil three times. Wrapping your food in three layers of foil will protect it from getting dirty, as well as protect your engine from smelling like chicken.

If your car is in good shape—which means you have it serviced regularly and fix anything that needs repair—you do not need to worry about your food taking on exhaust fumes. [All fumes from the engine should be coming out of your muffler; if exhaust is coming from your engine, you got trouble.]

> Note that the speaker uses everyday language and turns of phrase like "you got trouble" to impart a sense of humor.

Once your food is wrapped well, the key is finding a nook or cranny in which to place it. Although engines are much more complex and less hot than they were twenty years ago, they are also full of wires and strange contraptions that can help hold food in place. You just need to experiment, but do so carefully. Don't be yanking and pulling on wires and hoses, folks—be gentle. [And you need to observe three no-no's.]

THE NO-NO'S OF CAR COOKERY

- AVOID ACCELERATOR LINKAGE
- DON'T BLOCK AIRFLOW
- AVOID THE FAN BELT

 NO-NO

> The speaker lists the no-no's of car cooking on a slide to reinforce his message and commit it to the audience's memory.

First, never ever interfere with the free movement of the accelerator linkage. This is the line that runs from the gas peddle to the engine. Now, today many cars are using electronic throttle bodies that make this line obsolete. Nevertheless, if you have a line, stay clear of it. Second, never ever block the airflow to the engine's air intake. The intake refers to all the parts of your engine that suck in air, including the largest tubes going into the engine (and often connected or near the vents on the front of your car), any visible air filters, and so on. To combust, your engine needs air. Finally, stay clear of the belts and moving parts; if you don't, you might be having a little finger with your scalloped potatoes.[20]

If you respect your car engine, it will yield warm, delicious goodness on your next road trip or visit to the park. To be successful at car cookery, I've suggested you first need to learn about your engine and discover where the hot spots are. Then you must plan a food menu based on how far you are driving and when you suspect you will want to eat. Finally, good car cookery requires that you wrap your food not once, not twice, but three times, and that you place it on your engine carefully, avoiding the accelerator linkage, the air intake, and any moving parts, like belts.

As I noted earlier, I started using cars to cook as a Boy Scout, but I have carried the practice into my adult life. I opened my speech today with a hypothetical discussion of a romantic dinner. I confess this was a true story taken from my own dating past. My date was amused by the unique way I made our evening special, and to this day it is among the most memorable romantic evenings of my life. After I cleaned the juice from the baked squash off the top of my fuel injector assembly, we relaxed and finished our bottle of wine as the sun set over Austin.

Sample Speech Sources

Maynard, Chris, and Bill Scheller, *Manifold Destiny: The One! The Only! Guide to Cooking on Your Car Engine!* Rev. ed. New York: Simon & Schuster, 2008.

Michael, Paul. "Cooking Great Meals with Your Car Engine: The Heat Is On." Wisebread.com, May 17, 2007. www.wisebread.com/cooking-great-meals-with-your-car-engine-the-heat-is-on.

Newhardt, David, and Robert Genat. *American Cars of the 1950s.* St. Paul, MN: Motorbooks, 2008.

Peters, Eric. "Hybrid Cars: The Hope, Hype, and Future." *Consumers' Research* 83 (2000): 10–14.

Ulrich, Lawrence. "The Internal Combustion Engine Is Not Dead." *Popular Science*, May 6, 2010. www.popsci.com/cars/article/2010-04/most-advanced-engines.

LaunchPad
macmillan learning

Visit LaunchPad to hear this speech delivered by a student speaker.

In this chapter, we examined the basic expectations, as well as some tips, for informative speeches. In doing so, we have distinguished speaking to inform from speaking to persuade in terms of purpose. When making an informative speech, your primary aim is to create a new perspective or to provide new information. You can do so by adopting one of five informative speech strategies:

1. description
2. definition
3. explanation
4. demonstration
5. narration

Sometimes an informative speech may incorporate more than one strategy, depending on the context and your topic. We also discussed that the primary difficulty you face as an informative speaker is encouraging audiences to retain the information you give them. You can do so by keeping your speech simple and avoiding jargon; by making sure your speech is unique or not typical of what one would expect you to say; and by making your speech personally relevant—both to yourself and to your audience. We'll tackle speaking to persuade in chapters 15 and 16.

end of chapter stuff

Jerod Harris/Getty Images

Informative Speaking

Speaking to inform requires the speaker to "translate" information and knowledge into terms that are clearly communicated to an audience. The purpose of informative speaking is to impart new information or perspectives to audiences.

The Informing Genre

Informative speaking is different from persuasive speaking because it imparts knowledge or viewpoints to audiences in an objective manner that does not seek change. Strategies for informing include description, definition, explanation, demonstration, and narration.

Tips for Informing

To engage audiences while informing, keep your message clear and simple; speak about something that is unique; and only address topics that are personally relevant and interesting to you (first) and your audience (second).

CHAPTER 14

LaunchPad for *Speech Craft* includes a curated collection of speech videos and encourages self-assessment through adaptive quizzing. Go to **launchpadworks.com** to get access to:

 LearningCurve adaptive quizzes

 Video clips to help you improve your speeches

ACTIVITIES

Identifying Informative Strategies

Search YouTube or a similar video website for an informative speech on a topic that is interesting to you. Outline the speech's structure, then answer the following questions: Which informative strategies does the speaker predominately use to present information in his or her speech (description, definition, explanation, demonstration, or narrative)? How many of these strategies do you see present in his or her speech, and where? If the speech had to be delivered to real people in two different venues—a classroom like yours and a church group meeting—how would the speaker need to modify his or her speech?

Informing with Sizzle

With your instructor, identify two cooking programs (the kind in which a cook or a chef shows viewers how to make a dish, not a cooking competition show). Watch both shows, then answer the following questions: How does each cook present his or her recipes? How are their styles similar? How are they different? What does each cook do, specifically, to make his or her speech style unique?

Key Terms

 Videos in LaunchPad describe many of these terms. Go to launchpadworks.com.

- informative speaking 271
- description 276

- definition 277
- narration 279

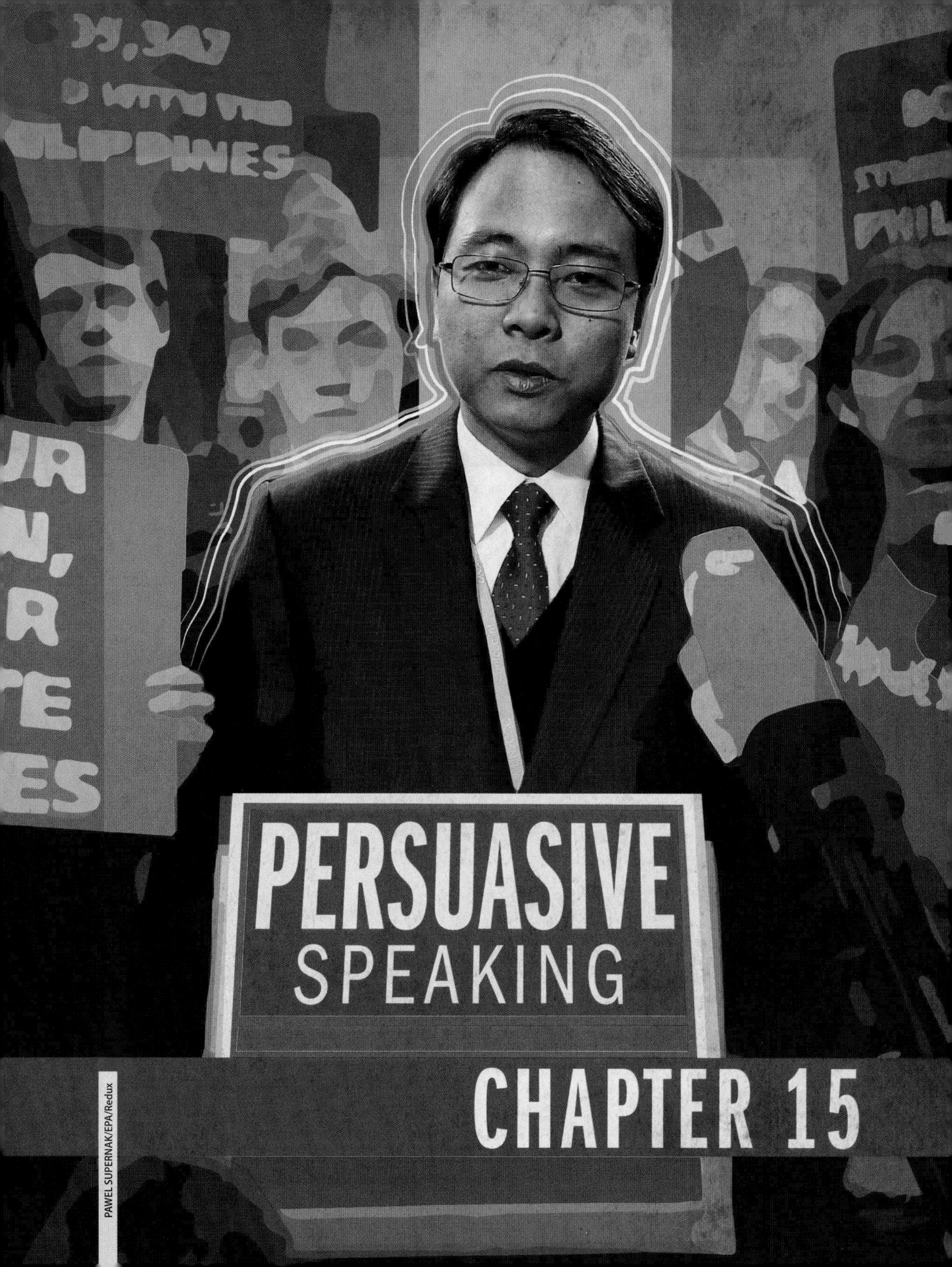

CHAPTER 15

PERSUASIVE SPEAKING

PAWEL SUPERNAK/EPA/Redux

O n Earth Day, April 22, 2015, Naderev "Yeb" Saño resigned as a commissioner of the Philippines' Climate Change Commission to continue his life's work as a champion of environmental protections with private, faith-based organizations.[1] Saño's environmental advocacy came to international attention because of two impassioned persuasive speeches he delivered to the United Nations at climate change conferences in 2012 and 2013, and these in the wake of a series of deadly typhoons that devastated his country. During his 2012 speech in Qatar, he said, "Madam chair, I speak on behalf of 100 million Filipinos. . . . I am making an urgent appeal, not as a negotiator, not as a leader of my delegation, but as a Filipino." Saño began to cry, and then pushed back his tears to deliver his most persuasive lines:

> I appeal to leaders from all over the world, to open our eyes to the stark reality that we face. I appeal to ministers. The outcome of our work is not about what our political masters want. It is about what is demanded of us by 7 billion people.
>
> I appeal to all, please, no more delays, no more excuses. Please, let Doha be remembered as the place where we found the political will to turn things around. Please, let 2012 be remembered as the year the world found the courage to find the will to take responsibility for the future we want. I ask of all of us here, if not us, then who? If not now, then when? If not here, then where?[2]

What was Saño attempting to do with his persuasive speeches? His stated goal was to get the United Nations to help secure resources for the Green Climate Fund, a UN-sponsored program to assist developing countries in adapting to, and preventing, climate change.[3] Because of the power of his words and the impact of his public feelings, Saño brought attention to the urgency of the consequences of climate change to audiences far beyond the bodies of the United Nations.

Understanding Persuasion

As speakers, most of us will not have an opportunity to speak to an international audience about global problems, but Saño's example does teach us something about the scope of the art of persuasion: success is not always discerned by immediate impact or changes in policy but in the *moving* of the hearts and minds of others to consider your appeals. Persuasion occurs both in the moment and over time. Persuasive speaking can certainly be about urging leaders to change a law, but it can also be about making others aware of a need that can only be addressed over a long period. The aims of persuasion are not always so lofty: when you ask your employer to let you leave work early so that you can take your

> **persuasion** is the process of influencing others to do, think, or believe something through speaking and writing.

pet to the veterinarian, you are persuading; when you attempt to convince your friend to attend a concert on campus with you, you are persuading. Whether a speaker is attempting to change the world or simply to get you to change your clothes, the effort is persuasive. In this chapter, we examine the basic components of persuasion: how persuasion has been understood and studied for centuries; the ethical and psychological dimensions of persuasion; and the most basic concept at persuasion's core, the appeal.

Persuasion is the process of influencing others to do, think, or believe something through speaking and writing. Although persuasive speaking is the most complicated speaking genre, it is not necessarily the most challenging simply because most of us persuade

Ximena persuades her family to adopt a puppy.

and are persuaded on a daily basis. You might recall a time when you and your family were deciding on a restaurant for dinner. How did you decide where to eat? Perhaps you are a vegan, and you argued that a certain restaurant had more options for you than other places your family was considering. Another example: Consider three roommates discussing how to divvy up various cleaning responsibilities and chores. One roommate suggests she could clean the bathrooms, while another could do the dusting. Once you start thinking about the daily moments in which you *call* on others to do something or think a certain way, the examples of persuasion are potentially endless. Such everyday examples nevertheless rely on the same basic principles as an elected leader urging Congress to vote on health-care legislation: we persuade in auditoriums as much as we do in kitchens.

We can begin approaching the complexity of persuasion by identifying the two basic building blocks of the persuasive process: appeals and arguments. An **appeal** is a request made to another person with the intent of influencing him or her. A long time ago the word *appeal* meant "to call" or "to address" in the original Latin and French, and it still carries with it the connotation of a request. In terms of persuasion, an appeal refers to a broad array of "calls" on others:

> an **appeal** is a request made to another person with the intent of influencing him or her.

- Writing a letter of recommendation is an appeal.
- Asking your professor to extend the deadline for your speech draft is an appeal.
- Urging the United Nations to do more to address climate change is an appeal.

In other words, all forms of persuasion concern appeals, which are calls on others to do, think, or believe something.

The other building block of persuasion is the **argument**. You may think an argument is a heated exchange between two or more people about some disagreement. Although we should not dismiss this common understanding, it does give the term "argument" an unwarranted reputation. In the formal study of persuasion, an argument is described as the way an appeal to influence others is *structured*. In other words, an argument is how you and I attempt to influence others in a reasoned and orderly manner, usually with a series of statements or claims. For the purpose of public speaking, we can define an argument as a reasoned claim, or series of claims, supported by evidence.

> an **argument** is a reasoned claim, or series of claims, supported by evidence.

The reason that persuasion is complex, however, is that *all arguments are appeals, but not all appeals are arguments*. The difference is one of scope and order. An appeal refers to the general attempt to influence someone (to "call on them"), while an argument refers to the structure of the statements you make. For example, imagine that you and your best friend have decided to take a vacation. You would like to go to the beach and stay in a hotel, but you know your friend wishes to camp in the mountains. In discussion, you say, "Let's go to the beach!" With this statement, you intend to influence your friend, and that is an *appeal*. If you say,

Rick Nielsen of the band Cheap Trick penned one of the most memorable appeals in rock music.

however, "I think we should go to the beach because I haven't been in over a year, and the weather forecast for next week is marvelous!" you have begun to make an argument. The difference is that an appeal by itself is a call or request based on your desire, whereas an argument concerns a statement of reasons.

Because there is a lot to learn about both appeals and arguments, we will separate their discussion into different chapters. For the remainder of this chapter, we will explore the ethical and psychological dimensions of persuasion and the different types of appeals that are involved. In the next chapter, we will examine the process of argumentation and the structure of arguments.

The Ethics of Persuasion

Whenever you address another person, you are making an appeal. Regardless of what you say, you are asking them to *listen*—to let you *influence* them with your words in some way. This implies that all forms of speaking are, at base, a form of persuasion. As discussed in chapter 2, appealing to others also entails a certain responsibility to them, which is the concern of ethics. Because conscious, deliberate persuasion makes a request of others to change their minds, feelings, or behaviors about something, it is important to briefly revisit the ethical dimensions of public speaking in the context of persuasion.

Because persuasion asks a person or an audience for trust, ethical persuasion concerns influencing others through *conscious* choices. For

> ⑦ How is the academic study of persuasion defined? How and why does this definition differ from the influence we experience in everyday life?

example, you may have noticed that at your college or university there are job and career fairs in which potential employers attempt to recruit students for positions and internships. Most universities have guidelines and policies for ethical recruiting on campus.[4] At a career fair, potential employers can try to persuade you to apply for a position or an internship by touting the merits of the company, but they are prohibited from pressuring you to apply or from providing inaccurate information. Persuasion is only fair if you are asked to make conscious and informed choices.

Ethical persuasion concerns more than simple honesty, however. It also concerns power and, in particular, *empowering* an audience to make choices concerning what you are asking them to think, feel, believe, or do. If a job recruiter says to a student, "If you don't apply for our unpaid internship, I will tell the internship director of your college that you are simply not a go-getter!" he is relying on his power to take away the student's capacity to choose. As persuasion scholar Charles Larson has argued, when a speaker attempts to persuade by obscuring the actual choices he or she is posing to an audience, it is unethical persuasion — or, simply, **coercion**.[5] Coercion is influencing others through threat or force, and often in ways that do not make choices conscious or clear. For

Whenever parties agree to meet on a television court show, such as *Judge Judy*, they are agreeing to make ethical appeals. Judge Judy's job is not simply to determine the legality of a case but also to judge the soundness of each side's ethical reasoning.

coercion is influencing someone to do or think something by threats, unwarranted emotion, or force, which includes distorting, hiding, or preventing conscious choices.

simplicity, we can say that speaking to influence ethically is *persuasion*, while speaking by threat, force, or deliberate deception is coercion. From an ethical perspective, persuasion is the process of changing the beliefs, attitudes, values, and behavior of an audience by asking them to make a conscious choice.[6]

The Psychology of Persuasion

Persuasion concerns influencing an individual or a group to change their beliefs, attitudes, or values (BAVs) about something, usually by building on those that you already share (as discussed in chapter 3). Influencing someone's BAVs is usually done to inspire action or change behavior. The difficulty in influencing others to change their BAVs has to do with the fact that they are inextricably linked to people's identities. When you try to persuade someone, you're not just providing good reasons for the person to trust you or what you say; you're also attempting to elevate or amplify feelings in a way that supports your viewpoint. Persuasion is a psychological process that works at the level of *both* reasoning (or logic of thought) and feeling.

Changing beliefs is easier than changing attitudes, and changing attitudes is easier than changing values. Values, which represent the innermost core of an individual's identity, are almost impossible to change unless it is done over a very long period of time through constant reinforcement (values are influenced by parents and religious leaders, teachers with whom you work for a long time, life partners and friends, and so on). When we speak to persuade, we usually do so by enhancing or building on commonly shared values, aiming toward changes in belief, attitudes, and behavior.

Both appeals and arguments have psychological dimensions; however, appeals are broader, general expressions that more directly inspire feelings, whereas arguments are designed to inspire thinking and reasoning. This is not to say that feelings are not involved with reasoning or that reasoning does not appeal to our emotions; in fact, appeals and arguments are not so easily separated in actual speaking practices. In order to study persuasion, however, we need to break these into different areas of study: appeals, which align with feelings and the body, and arguments, which focus on the mind and reasoning.

> **?** In what ways do appeals and arguments align with feelings and thinking?

The Persuasive Appeal

> *You will learn to*
> **LIST** the three types of persuasive appeals described by Aristotle.
> **EXPLAIN** Maslow's hierarchy of needs and how it can be used in a speech.
> **DEFINE** an emotional appeal and provide an example.

In the study of persuasion, appeals are discussed in terms of their history as a field of study in ancient Greece, and then in respect to the most common types of persuasive appeals made today. We begin our elaboration of the appeal in the theory of oratory first advanced by Aristotle, and follow with a discussion of appeals to needs and emotions.

Aristotle's Rhetorical Triangle

Aristotle comes up frequently in the academic study of public speaking because he is often credited with providing the first systematic account of the subject in his fourth century BCE treatise *On Rhetoric*, which is principally concerned with persuasive speaking. Aristotle studied with

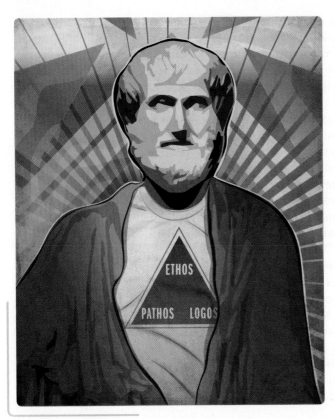

Plato for a long time, and you'll recall from chapter 1 that Plato believed that the dominant form of public speaking during his time was deceptive and immoral. When Aristotle started his own school (he called it "the Lyceum"), he was careful to distinguish his teaching about persuasive speaking from Plato's by arguing that "rhetoric" was an art that could be used to either moral or immoral ends. Ethical rhetoric, Aristotle argued, depended on the character of the speaker and whether or not the speaker used the techniques of persuasion responsibly. Or, to put his perspective in terms from our time, **rhetoric** doesn't hurt people; people hurt people with rhetoric!

Many subsequent studies of persuasion in the West, over thousands of years, are either extensions of or responses to Aristotle's theories on the subject.[7] There are many theories that are advanced in Aristotle's treatise on persuasion, but the most

rhetoric is the study of the ways in which speaking and writing influence people to do or think what they otherwise would not do or think.

famous one concerns the three means, or ways, of persuasion that a speaker can use to appeal to an audience: appeals to reasoning and structure (or *logos*); appeals to feelings (or *pathos*); and appeals to character traits, such as qualifications and trustworthiness (or *ethos*). Aristotle observed that a speaker can persuade an audience by emphasizing any one of these three appeals, and that all of them will be present to some degree in a given speaking situation. For example, when a company creates an advertising campaign, it might use a famous athlete or actor as a spokesperson, suggesting that consumers should buy the product because the athlete or actor likes it. Although rational reasons may be offered—for example, to buy a car because it has good fuel economy (*logos*)—the dominant appeal would be *ethos* (the character of the celebrity) and secondarily, *pathos* (positive feelings toward the celebrity). Depending on our goals and situation, we tend to rely more heavily on one kind of appeal, even though all three kinds are present in any speaking situation.

Logos. The appeal to reason is called logos. Scholars of Aristotle's classic treatise believe that logos is the most important component in the study of persuasion. Logos pertains to the rules of reasoning and how to use those rules to structure arguments that appeal to an audience's thought processes. Logos concerns what we refer to today as logic. In the case of most persuasion today, informal logic is a less technical and more causal way of making claims. We will discuss logos in greater depth in chapter 16.

Pathos. In addition to logos, Aristotle introduced pathos and ethos, appeals that are commonly used to strengthen persuasive speeches. Pathos, or appeals to feelings and emotions, concerns that dimension of persuasive speaking that can arouse a sense of love or hatred, or make us fearful or assertive, proud or ashamed, or peaceful or angry. For this reason, Aristotle included a focus on word choice, illustrations, and other forms of evocative language within the domain of pathos.

Aristotle suggested that while emotional appeals work, they are frequently ineffective unless coupled with a good, reasoned argument. Think, for example, of television shows in which contestants compete to win recognition from a panel of judges. Whether preparing a meal, singing a song, or performing a dance number, contestants on these shows are dismissed during each round of the competition. It is now commonplace to hear a dismissed contestant say, "But I worked so hard!" or "I was born to do this!" appealing to the judges' sense of compassion and feelings toward them. It is usually the case that the dismissed contestant fails to argue convincingly for why their performance was misjudged.

Aristotle was wary of emotional appeals and cautioned against their abuse, preferring to emphasize the importance of reasoning and sound character instead. In part, Aristotle was biased against pathos because of the tendency for speakers to use emotion to deceive or manipulate audiences. Today we see a similar distrust in the common assessment of political leaders. When hearing a political speaker we do not like, we may think, "He's just appealing to the audience's fear!" or "She's just promising something she cannot deliver!" Our feelings about the speaker—which concern both pathos and ethos—can sometimes even keep us from understanding what the politician is actually trying to argue. In general, dismissing a speaker on the basis of our feelings or intuition alone can often lead us into error. We can often detect the misuse or abuse of emotional appeals through the rules of reasoning. In chapter 16, we'll learn more about fallacies, which are often heard in speeches that misuse emotion.

After ten moviegoers were shot—and two killed—in a theater during a screening of her film *Trainwreck* in 2015, Amy Schumer has spoken passionately and emotionally against gun violence.

Despite a long-standing distrust of pathos by public speaking scholars since antiquity, appealing to the emotions of an audience is not necessarily bad—and since we are all emotional beings, it is inevitable. As humans, we feel emotions, and it is as unrealistic as it is undesirable to avoid them in public speaking. If you are speaking to effect change, you want to make an audience react emotionally; otherwise, they may not envision the circumstance in the way you wish them to. If you are arguing for civil rights, you want the audience to feel a passion for social justice and equality. If you are trying to persuade others to buy a product or service you are selling, you want them to feel as if it is in their best interest to do so. Part of the way that you get an audience to feel along with you, and achieve identification and a sense of community, is by conducting yourself in a way that encourages trust and respect, which is also known as ethos.

Ethos.   Ethos, or appeals to your wisdom or character as a speaker, is the glue that holds both rational and emotional appeals together. Why? Because perceptions of your character and reputation usually guide how audiences will judge your arguments and influence how they will feel about what you are saying. In his system of persuasion, Aristotle was primarily concerned with how a speaker makes appeals to character in a given speaking situation. All the things a speaker does or projects— including how he or she delivers an argument (voice and speaking style), his or her appearance, and how he or she demonstrates knowledge of the topic and the rules of reasoning—contribute to the audience's perception of his or her character. Whenever you give a speech, you are helping to create an audience's perception of you as a person, in addition to what you say. Aristotle suggested that if an audience does not develop a sense of you as a good and trustworthy person when delivering a speech, no skillful argument or appeal to emotions will help you persuade them.

In a speaking situation, we can identify at least two ways in which ethos comes into play. The first way concerns how your character emerges while giving a speech, and the second way concerns your reputation with the audience before and after the speech. In his teaching on public speaking, Aristotle emphasized the things a speaker does while delivering a speech. We know, however, that how our reputation precedes us before giving a speech may influence how an audience perceives our character. For example, we know that an audience about to hear Justice Sonia Sotomayor give a speech will hear her words differently than an audience about to hear Katy Perry give a speech because each speaker has reputations for expertise in different vocations (e.g., we might find a Perry speech on the Constitution less trustworthy than a speech on the music industry). Consequently, the elements of ethos detailed by Aristotle can apply not only to the speaking moment but also to our reputations as people in general.

When persuading others, Aristotle suggests that a demonstration of our character, or ethos, is created and maintained in three ways: a

Tips for Developing Ethos as a Speaker

- Know what you are talking about: Research your topic and cultivate expertise in the area. If you do not have a reputation with the audience before you speak, explicitly mention why you are qualified to speak on the topic.
- Demonstrate common sense: Wear clothing appropriate for the speech context; develop your speech in ways that the audience can follow.
- Be a good person: Develop a reputation as a responsible and ethical human being. Even if the audience does not know much about you before the speech, that good character will still come through.
- Demonstrate concern for the audience: With both your nonverbal behavior and speaking, show the audience that you are happy to be with them and that you care about them. You might consider mentioning your concern for them directly. Express gratitude to the audience to be having the opportunity to speak.

Some ancient teachers of public speaking, such as Gorgias from chapter 1, were said to have argued that they could persuade audiences to trust their political expertise even if they had no political experience.

Is there something wrong with such a claim? Why or why not?

demonstration of practical wisdom, or prudence (*phronesis*); a demonstration of our moral virtues, or being a good person (*arete*); and a demonstration or evidence of goodwill toward the audience (*eunoia*). For a speaker to have a strong, influential presence (or *ethos*), he or she will need to come across as being competent, having common sense, successfully performing his or her roles (e.g., a job), and having the audiences' best interests at heart.

Ethos as Self-Evidence

Ethos is all about using yourself as part of the evidence that supports your speech. What does this mean? It means that the audience is influenced by your demeanor as a speaker as well as by your reputation. If you are attempting to persuade someone, your underlying message should be "trust me, I have your best interests at heart." For this reason, you should always take care to present yourself as someone who is competent, has good sense, knows what you're talking about, and cares about the welfare of your audience. Stories, testimonials, and confessions about your own beliefs, attitudes, values, and behaviors in your personal life contribute to and inform an audience's perception of your character.

What is the difference between a persuasive appeal and a persuasive argument? What are Aristotle's three main forms of persuasive appeal? Define the focus of each.

using aristotle's triangle to analyze
speeches

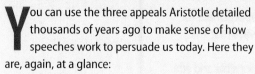

Paul Zimmerman/Getty Images

DIGITAL DIVE

Senator Elizabeth Warren

Y ou can use the three appeals Aristotle detailed thousands of years ago to make sense of how speeches work to persuade us today. Here they are, again, at a glance:

Logos: Persuasive appeals to reasoning and logical processes. Depending on the context of use in the ancient Greek language, the term *logos* can also refer to argument, speech, reason, word, or even sentence. **Example:** "Today for most insurance plans, mental health parity is the law, but it sure doesn't feel that way for people who need help. A 2015 survey conducted by the National Alliance on Mental Illness found that nearly 50 percent of respondents had been denied coverage for mental or behavioral health care, compared with only 14 percent denied for physical health care."[8] — Senator Elizabeth Warren

Pathos: Persuasive appeals to feelings and emotion. Depending on the context of use in the ancient Greek language, the term can also refer to emotion or a feeling in the moment. **Example:** "For me, the pain I share with so many other Americans on the issue of gun violence was made extremely personal to me on Thursday, July 23 [2015] when — I'm not even going to say his name, when this — when he sat down for my movie *Trainwreck.* . . . Two lives were tragically lost and others

injured. . . . When I heard about this news, I was completely devastated. I wanted to go down to Louisiana, and then I was angry."[9] — Comedian-actor Amy Schumer

Ethos: Persuasive appeals to character and reputation. Depending on the context of use in the ancient Greek language, the term can also refer to the moral disposition of the speaker. **Example:** "My first children's program was on WQED fifteen years ago, and its budget was $30. Now, with the help of the Sears-Roebuck Foundation and National Educational Television, . . . each station pays to show our program. It's a unique kind of funding in educational television. . . . I'm very much concerned, as I know you are, about what's being delivered to our children in this country. And I've worked in the field of child development for six years, trying to understand the needs of our children."[10] — Child television personality Fred Rogers

LaunchPad
macmillan learning

Aristotle's three basic appeals can be used to make sense of how a speech works to persuade an audience. To get a sense of how you can apply these concepts to speech, visit LaunchPad at **launchpadworks.com** and link to the speech this chapter opened with by Yeb Saño, which was delivered to the United Nations COP19 Climate Change Conference in 2013.

As you watch and listen, answer the following questions:

- How does Saño attempt to establish his authority and expertise in the speech? How does he demonstrate practical wisdom and goodwill toward the audience?
- In what ways does Saño appeal to the feelings and emotions of his audience? In what ways does he demonstrate his own feelings?
- How does Saño appeal to reason? Does he make reasoned appeals to his audience? Does he make arguments (i.e., are his appeals backed up by evidence)?

Appealing to Needs

When we examine the most popular theories of persuasive appeals in our time, few find serious disagreement with Aristotle's three basic categories—after all, we're still teaching and using them. But what, exactly, persuades people? Aristotle's answer was that people can be motivated to change their beliefs, attitudes, values, and behavior through influential appeals to reason, emotion, and character. Today's theories of motivation answer the same question in similar ways but tend to emphasize two kinds of appeals rather than three:[11]

> People can be motivated to change their beliefs, attitudes, values, and behavior through influential appeals to reason, emotion, and character.

- People are motivated to change because of reasoned or rational choices that are in their best interest.
- People are motivated to change because of inherent human *needs*.

Because need appeals are more aligned with the body and emotion, we will focus on needs, reserving rational or reasoned appeals for chapter 16.

In our discussion of audience psychology (see chapter 3), we examined a number of psychological theories for why people are motivated to change. You'll recall that Freud suggests that what motivates most of us is a desire to be acknowledged by others, a drive for recognition. One famous student of psychology that we can trace to Freud's original theories is Abraham Maslow. After years of study, Maslow eventually came to believe that people are fundamentally driven by *needs*, or essential human requirements for basic survival and, later, social happiness. He argued that only if people's more primary needs were met would they be able to focus on social needs.

Building on the psychological theories of others and his own personal observations, Maslow published a series of journal articles and a book outlining his theory of motivation. His 1954 book *Motivation and Personality* advances a visualized representation of human needs arranged in a hierarchy.[12] Maslow argued that basic needs have to be satisfied before one can appeal to higher-order needs. The most basic needs, of course, concern human survival (the need for food, water, shelter, and so on), or biological needs, while needs higher on the model (such as "self-actualization" or "self-esteem") require that these earlier needs be satisfied. Some scholars have criticized Maslow's hierarchy by suggesting that some people are persuaded to act on higher-order needs even when basic physical and safety needs have not been met.[13] For example, we can probably think of friends or family members who have bought extravagant items of clothing or fancy cars when they are having trouble paying their rent. Alternatively, we can think of a number of examples in which an individual's basic needs were sacrificed for those of others, such as a parent foregoing food so that his or her children can eat. Such critiques suggest that Maslow's hierarchy model may be more rational than it initially would seem and that people *do sometimes* behave irrationally. Nevertheless, despite criticisms, Maslow's model

A speaker can study Maslow's hierarchy of needs to gain insight for persuading and motivating audiences.

has been useful for thinking about an audience's needs, providing some hints for explaining why persuasion succeeds or fails with certain audiences.

Appealing to Emotion

Both Aristotle's and Maslow's theories are general, overarching models for thinking about persuasive appeals. Today, we would describe both of them as delving into audience psychology, aiming to give a general account of what motivates audiences toward persuasion. Both perspectives include a number of more specific types of appeals that draw on the feelings or emotions of audiences in ways that are designed to complement, and sometimes even circumvent, reasoning processes. We might think that we know an emotional appeal when we feel one; however, emotional appeals can often seem quite reasonable, too. Although it is often the case that those who deliberately appeal to your emotions are also attempting to circumvent your critical faculties, emotional appeals are often justified. For example, many public service officials will deliberately use fear appeals to persuade people to leave a city threatened by life-threatening weather. Although these fear-based warnings may inconvenience many who hear them, in light of what *could* happen, public officials often believe an appeal to fear is justified.

How do we distinguish between an emotional appeal and a persuasive argument? The two are often intertwined, so the best way to tell the difference is to focus on the most important goal of a persuasive attempt. Emotional appeals often masquerade as persuasive arguments, but their primary goal is to inspire trust or loyalty in a speaker on the basis of feelings. When you are uncertain if a persuasive attempt is primarily for eliciting an emotion or for inspiring critical thinking, determine whether the speaker supplies reasons. If a speaker evokes feeling without offering a series of reasons, he or she is making an emotional appeal and not a persuasive argument. Perhaps the best way to think about the persuasion of emotional appeals is with advertising. Whether in a magazine, on a web page, on the radio, or on television, advertisements are rarely arguments but rather appeals to your emotions, encouraging you to purchase or believe something without thinking critically about doing so.

Speakers use emotional appeals to inspire strong, identifiable feelings, such as happiness, respect, pride, or a feeling of accomplishment, as well as sadness or feelings of loss, compassion, pity, and even hatred. At a sports rally, for example, speakers often attempt to swell feelings of pride for a team to encourage you to support them. A number of philanthropic charities may show you images of rescued animals or hungry children, hoping to inspire your compassion and encourage you to donate funds. The use of emotional appeals is everywhere in our culture. When we are persuaded by a speaker, we are more likely than not responding emotionally as well as rationally. In the West, we tend to prioritize reason and critical thinking as the better way to persuade. Why is that?

Advertisers are experts at appeals to emotions designed to short-circuit your reasoning capacities, especially your sexual response. This advertisement is clearly designed to arouse the viewer.

A distrust of emotional appeals is high in our culture because of a history of war and inhumane treatment of human beings (in scientific research, in the consumer industry, and so on).[14] Much of the evil that humans do to one another is grounded in powerfully destructive emotional appeals that dehumanize others into objects that can be removed, imprisoned, or killed (scholars have tended to study the harm of emotional appeals in respect to propaganda).[15] Because of our complicated history as human beings on this planet, we have learned to be suspicious of persuasive appeals that attempt to circumvent our critical capacities.

There are less horrific appeals to emotions that people distrust, many of which we can reduce to three: fear appeals or scare tactics, propaganda, and false advertising. As with most things human, these three distrusted emotional appeals are often intertwined.

- **Fear appeals or scare tactics.** These represent the broadest category of suspicious emotional appeals, and concern frightening or coercing an audience to think or do something for fear of harm. Sometimes fear appeals are necessary and even warranted, such as explaining to young people why texting while driving is not a good idea with grisly descriptions or images of car accidents. Many public service announcements and related forms of public safety discourse are abused; one doesn't have to look far to find political advertisements suggesting that electing a certain leader will lead to the freeing of hardened criminals from prison or the melting of the polar ice caps.

- **Propaganda.** Deliberately misleading, biased, or even false information to manipulate an audience to agree with or adopt a particular belief system is known as propaganda. The formal and systematic study of propaganda began in the United States in respect to the First and Second World Wars. Various governments—including the United States—tried to bolster popular support for a political regime, policy, or war effort through posters, public service announcements, films, and radio programs. With propaganda, emotional appeals are hidden behind what appears to be appeals to reason or character. The intent of propaganda is to promote a particular worldview or perspective, a political or religious belief system, or other similar large-scale viewpoints.
- **False advertising or fraud.** Most of us are familiar with false advertising, which concerns the promotion of a product or person for the benefit of the speaker, at the expense of the audience. By definition, false advertising is deliberately deceptive and appeals to an audience's emotions, often in ways that are harmful to the deceived. As a label, fraud can be used in both a weak and a strong sense. In the weak sense, fraud typically concerns a person who misrepresents himself or herself, such as an authority who falsifies his or her qualifications, or a person who uses a picture of someone else on his or her online profile on a social networking or dating website. In the stronger sense, fraud is criminal deception and, if detected by authorities, is subject to legal prosecution. Whereas false advertising can concern things, fraud almost always concerns an individual's identity and is consequently related to *ethos* as well.

Our feelings and emotions are easier to change or influence than are our critical faculties, and they are more prone to manipulation. Many emotional appeals can be positive, and it would be impossible to identify any persuasive message that did not make an emotional appeal. Who would be persuaded to do or think something different without *feeling* justified to do so?

In this introductory chapter on persuasive speaking, we examined how persuasion has been understood for centuries as both an ethical and a psychological process. After distinguishing persuasive appeals from arguments, we examined the most well-known kinds of appeals: Aristotle's understanding of *ethos*, *pathos*, and *logos*; appeals to need; and emotional appeals. In chapter 16, we will more closely examine persuasion in terms of rational processes (reasoning) and the structuring of arguments.

Fallacious Appeals to Emotion

In the study of persuasion and argumentation, scholars have identi-fied a number of emotional appeals that are termed "fallacies," which are defined as errors in reasoning. These include, for example, attacks on someone's character (ad hominem) and appeals to join a group or team ("C'mon, everyone's doing it!"). Because emotional fallacies are attempts to short-circuit reasoning processes, we will discuss them in more depth in chapter 16.

(?) How do contemporary theories of persuasive appeals differ from Aristotle's theory? Explain Maslow's theory of motivation. What is the key concept of this theory?

SAMPLE PERSUASIVE SPEECH

South Carolina State Representative Jenny Anderson Horne:
Statement to South Carolina House of Representatives, July 8, 2015

Background: On the evening of June 17, 2015, a number of members of the Eman-uel African Methodist Episcopal Church met in Charleston, South Carolina, to study the Bible. A young man who was not a member of the church was welcomed to join them; later that night, he shot the senior pastor, Clementa Pinckney, and eight others. In part because the massacre was racially motivated, many people began calling for the removal of the Confederate battle flag that had flown on the grounds of the state capitol for decades. As a symbol of slavery, many argued that the removal of the battle flag would begin to heal the racial wounds deepened by the Charleston massacre and signal to the rest of the country that South Carolinians wished to move beyond a racist past.

State lawmakers crafted a bill on July 8 to remove the flag, but before the House could vote on the bill, the legislative body was allowed to entertain speeches for and against it, as well as amendments. Some lawmakers continued to speak against the bill and propose amendments to deliberately delay the vote. Late in the session, a Repub-lican representative from Charleston stepped forward to urge her colleagues to stop delaying the vote. After her speech, the bill passed in the early morning hours of July 9.

Thank you, Mr. Speaker, for your indulgence tonight, and I know the hour is late, so I will be brief. As a member of the Charleston delegation, I would like to express to you how important it is that we not amend this bill. And the rea-son we need not amend this bill at this time is because if we amend the bill in any form or fashion, it is going to a conference committee. It is not going to end quickly. We are going to be doing this all summer long.

Let me tell you: I attended the funeral of Senator Clementa Pinckney, and the people of Charleston deserve immediate and swift removal of that flag

Annotations (right margin):

Horne bolsters her ethos by noting she is from Charleston, the city in which the massacre of African Americans recently occurred.

Horne's thesis comes quickly: she wants her colleagues to stop amending the bill to remove the Confeder-ate battle flag.

Horne supports her thesis and major claim with reasoning. The assumption (or warrant) here is that few lawmakers would enjoy debating and amending such an im-portant bill for weeks, if not months.

Again, Horne rein-forces her credibility as a representative of Charleston and as someone who attend-ed the funeral of one of those massacred.

Horne again reinforces her credibility. She shifts to a discussion of her friendships. When she moves to arguing that the flag offends people, she is developing pathos.

"Heart" is a term that connotes feelings. Horne is making an emotional appeal to ethical decency; the implication is a form of shaming of those who will not pass the bill.

References to surviving family members are an appeal to emotions.

Horne's reasons are primarily emotional and ethical, and secondarily, pragmatic.

Horne dismisses the dominant argument of her opposition: that the Confederate battle flag honors the memory of the Confederate soldiers who died as well as commemorates history.

Horne establishes ethos among her opponents by noting that she is related to the president of the Confederacy. Despite her familial lineage, however, she does not support keeping the Confederate battle flag on state grounds.

Here Horne ends with both a rational and an emotional appeal: history will show that those who support keeping the Confederate flag are misguided. Unless members of the House wish to be remembered as racists, passing the bill sooner rather than later is necessary.

from this [sic] grounds. We can save for another day where this flag needs to go, where the—which flag needs to fly, or where it needs to fly or what museum it needs to be in, but the immediate—[I'm concerned as a member of the Charleston delegation and speaking on behalf of the people in Charleston, this flag offends my friend Mia McCloud, my friend John King, my friend Reverend Neal. . . .]

I cannot believe that we do not have [the heart in this body] to do something meaningful, such as take a symbol of hate off these grounds on Friday. And if any of you vote to amend, you are ensuring that this flag will fly beyond Friday. [And for the widower of Senator Pinckney and his two young daughters, that would be adding insult to injury, and I will not be a part of it.] [And for all of these reasons,] I will not vote to amend this bill today.

We may visit this another session, another year. But if we amend this bill, we are telling the people of Charleston, "*We don't care about you. We do not care that someone used this symbol of hate to slay eight innocent people who were worshipping their god.*"

[I'm sorry. I have heard enough about "heritage."] I have a heritage. I am a lifelong South Carolinian. [I am a descendant of Jefferson Davis. Okay? But that does not matter.] It's not about Jenny Horne. It's about the people of South Carolina who have demanded that this symbol of hate come off of the Statehouse grounds. And I will tell you I do know, and I have it on good authority, that the world is watching this debate, and there is an economic development prospect in Dorchester County that is in jeopardy because we refuse to act. We need to follow the example of the Senate: Remove this flag and do it today, [because this issue is not getting any better with age.]

Thank you. (applause)

Sample Speech Sources

Cary, Nathaniel. "South Carolina Takes Down Confederate Flag." *USA Today*, July 10, 2015, www.usatoday.com/story/news/nation/2015/07/10/south-carolina-confederate-flag/29952953.

Rogers, Katie. "Jenny Horne's Pleas to Remove the Confederate Flag." *New York Times*, July 9, 2015, www.nytimes.com/2015/07/10/us/south-carolina-representative-jenny-anderson-horne-flag-speech.html?_r=0.

Salzillo, Leslie. "With Gut Honesty—South Carolina Republican Jenny Horne Tears Up Party Members over Rebel Flag. *Daily Kos*, July 8, 2015, www.dailykos.com/story/2015/7/8/1400572/-SC-Republican-Jenny-Horne-Brings-Tears-When-Pleading-For-The-Removal-Of-The-Confederate-Flag.

Understanding Persuasion

Persuasion is the process of influencing others to do, think, or believe something through speaking and writing. Persuasive speaking is composed of both appeals and arguments.

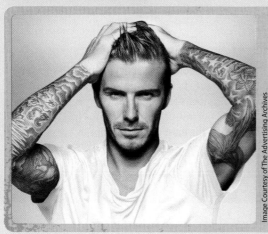

Image Courtesy of The Advertising Archives

The Persuasive Appeal

Persuasive appeals have been traditionally discussed as concerning character (ethos), feelings (pathos), and reason (logos). More recently, however, scholars have focused on appeals in terms of a hierarchy of needs and the power of emotions.

CHAPTER 15

ACTIVITIES

Discerning Kinds of Appeals

Your instructor will put you into a group with classmates. Using a laptop, tablet, or smartphone, together with your group locate a video of an advertisement for a product or service. Then, as a group, find an example in the advertisement of each appeal that Aristotle discusses: ethos, pathos, and logos. Was one kind of appeal stronger than the others? Why or why not?

What's in the Bag?

Your instructor has brought to class a bag that contains a prize. You do not know what the prize is, but you are assured that it is valuable. Your instructor will put you into a group of four or five people and ask you to come up with the most powerful appeal to need and the strongest appeal to emotions you can determine with your group. Create a three- to four-minute persuasive speech with your group, then elect someone to present the speech to the class. Your instructor will award the bag to the group who creates the most persuasive appeals.

KEY TERMS

 Videos in LaunchPad describe many of these terms. Go to launchpadworks.com.

- persuasion 291
- appeal 292
- argument 292

- coercion 294
- rhetoric 296

MAKING ARGUMENTS

CHAPTER 16

Growing up, almost all of us were frustrated by a parent or guardian who would not let us do or have something that we wanted. If we wanted to draw on the wall with crayons or stay out past curfew, we heard the familiar "No!" from a grown-up. Sometimes the frustration we felt over adult denials had less to do with the denial itself and more to do with the reasons *for* the denial: in response to the "No!" you might have pleaded, "But why?" The frequent answer many of us received to that question was "Because I said so!" This stated reason is an *appeal to authority*, which we might paraphrase as, "No, you cannot stay out past curfew because I am the parent and I have power over you." Although "Because I said so!" constitutes an *appeal*, it is not quite an argument. As noted in the previous chapter, an appeal is an attempt to influence another person in general, whereas an argument is a reasoned claim supported by evidence.

Parents often appeal to their authority with children because very young people have yet to develop the capacity for reasoning, which refers to the ability to make an inference or a judgment based on evidence. As we grow older, most of us become better at reasoning; consequently, others are more likely to present us with specific arguments.[1] For example, let's suppose you've gone home to visit your family over spring break, and right before dinner one night you announce that you are going out to meet friends. "I'd rather you didn't," your parent says. "It's supposed to sleet after nine, so I'd worry about your getting home." Instead of appealing to authority, your parent is making an argument that can be paraphrased this way: "You should not go out tonight because the weather will be dangerous for driving." In this argument, the "evidence" offered to you is the possibility that you could have an accident because of icy weather.

In this chapter, we will delve further into the complexities of persuasion by examining the structure of reasoning, which early scholars of public speaking termed *logos* and which we term "logic" today. We will examine the two most important kinds of logical structures in persuasive speaking: (1) arguments and their construction, and (2) the organization of arguments into effective patterns in speeches. At first glance, you might think that the study of arguments and reasoning is complex and philosophical; however, you already rely on the rules of logic in your daily life. This chapter will provide you with names and labels for the reasoning *you already do.*

What's an Argument?

You will learn to

DEFINE "argument," and explain its three basic parts.

DESCRIBE Aristotle's theory of persuasion.

EXPLAIN the three major types of claims and their differences.

DESCRIBE the most common types of fallacies.

What most people refer to as an "argument" in our society is not actually an argument. "Because I said so!" is not an argument; it's a common phrase or appeal that is used to *stop* an argument from happening. The word "argument" often draws to mind an image of two people shouting at each other, but such an image is better labeled as *fighting*. As we noted in the previous chapter, because the image and sound of people fighting is the most popular understanding of "argument," the term unfairly gets a bad rap. In the truest sense, an argument is something you create to *negotiate* with others, not something you (necessarily) strive to *win*.

A true argument includes a claim, some evidence, and reasoning linking the two together. Whether or not you say each part aloud, arguments always have these three parts. For the purposes of public speaking, we can define an **argument** as a claim or series of claims supported by evidence through reasoning.

argument is a claim or series of claims supported by evidence through reasoning.

Distinguishing arguments from fights or simple disagreements can be tricky—often the distinction is only an easy one to make in retrospect. In general, if you are preparing a speech or planning to persuade a person without fighting or engaging in overly passionate exchanges, you are thinking about argumentation. In fact, most speeches are fundamentally arguments. A speech made at a business meeting is easy to understand as an argument ("Vandalay Enterprises should invest in this new vacuum technology"); however, arguments can even be discussions with your children or nieces and nephews about taking turns on the slide at the playground.

reasoning refers to the ability to make an inference or a judgment based on evidence.

As discussed in chapter 15, persuasion is a complex phenomenon that involves both how people *feel* and how people *reason*. Argumentation mostly concerns the **reasoning** side and is an important, if not central, part of persuasion, but it is only a part. In reality, reasoning and feeling are not so easily separated; we only

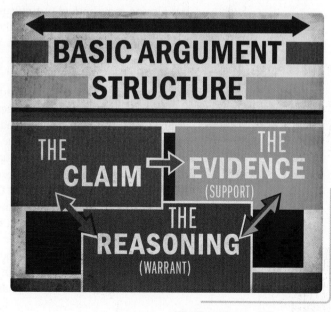

BASIC ARGUMENT STRUCTURE

THE CLAIM → THE EVIDENCE (SUPPORT)

THE REASONING (WARRANT)

do so to make understanding easier and discussion possible.[2] In chapter 15, we explored the feeling dimension of persuasion as the concern of the *appeal*. In this chapter, we will focus on reasoning, or **logic**, which is the concern of the *argument*. Very specific types of appeals that strive to minimize feeling are arguments; these concern *appeals to reason*.

logic refers to the structure of reasoning.

Why Study Argumentation?

The most important reason to study argumentation as a public speaker is cultural: many people tend to follow a number of assumed and often unspoken rules when they argue.[3] We use our inner sense of reasoning when evaluating someone's argument, and that sense often leads us to conclude that an argument is sound or that something seems off. What is this inner sense of reasoning? It's not merely intuition, nor is it simply a feeling of right or wrong. One answer to this and similar questions is that the conviction we feel as people who reason is something that we have picked up as members of our culture. This is to say that the rules of reasoning are learned.[4]

We have already explored a similar inner sense of familiarity with the concept of the genre (see chapter 12): when we listen to a pop song, watch a romantic comedy, or hear a speech at an awards show, we expect to experience a pattern that we have encountered before. As unusual as a new song may sound, as weird as a new movie may be, or as odd as a novel speech may seem, we typically experience a kind of satisfaction when new forms of human expression echo or reflect a pattern we already know. If the song, movie, or speech *never* conforms to a recognizable pattern, we often experience dissatisfaction or discomfort.[5] Reasoning inspires a similar sense of satisfaction or dissatisfaction, because we pick up the rules for reasoning not only formally in our education but also as members of our culture's many conversations. For example, when a friend says something that seems to contradict something she said earlier, we might get a strange sense of discomfort. Such experiences help us sense how feelings and reasoning are actually intertwined.

It is useful to understand that the rules of reasoning are often thought to manage emotions, feelings, and passions. Many people formally study reasoning because they wish to keep strong feelings at bay when discussing difficult, often emotionally charged topics. We use the rules of reasoning to avoid giving too much power to our emotional states so that arguments with others do not become "personal quarrels."[6] For example, relying on the rules of reasoning may help you avoid making a hasty or an expensive purchase (a home, a new vehicle, a large bet at the poker table). It is also useful to understand the rules of reasoning that human beings have developed over the centuries, because knowing them will help you become a better persuader and, perhaps more importantly, a better critical thinker when it comes to the persuasive messages that bombard you every day (e.g., advertisements).

Some thinkers have argued that the rules of reasoning are universal, some have argued that the rules are "hardwired" in our brains, and others have argued that the rules are fundamentally structured by language.[7] Where the rules of reasoning come from is a fascinating topic, no doubt. As a public speaker, however, you need to be familiar with the rules of reasoning in order to moderate feelings, persuade others, and get things done.

Understanding Informal Logic

The persuasive arguments that we hear or witness on an average day usually escape our conscious awareness. In this chapter, our job is to notice how persuasion happens through arguments, and this requires getting familiar with modes of reasoning that we collect under the banner of "informal logic." Formal logic is an analytical study of reasoning processes and is frequently limited to the rigorous examination of propositions and their meanings. Think, for example, of mathematics or analytical philosophy. Informal logic, on the other hand, concerns how people argue with each other in a given culture. Also called logical pragmatics, **informal logic** concerns the study of how people argue on an everyday basis by leaving some things unstated. The key to understanding everyday arguments is noticing what is assumed or *not* said; what is particularly informal about informal logic is that something is missing.[8]

> **informal logic** concerns the study of how people argue on an everyday basis by leaving some things unstated.

The missing or unstated part of everyday reasoning is quickly explained with a joke: "Knock knock!" "Who's there?" "Interrupting Cow." "Interrup—" "MOO!"

This joke does a good job isolating the key insight of informal logic: What makes it humorous is what is unsaid. What is unsaid is the reasoning behind the joke: the knocker interrupts the answerer with a "MOO!" pretending to be Interrupting Cow. What makes the joke funny is this unspoken reasoning of why the joke works, or what we typically isolate in reference to the punch line. If you are ever having trouble remembering what informal logic or the internal mechanics of persuasion are all about, remember: it's the punch line! The unspoken reasoning that makes jokes funny is the same kind of reasoning that very serious arguments require.

Why are we persuaded by informal logic?

One of the reasons that the ancient Greek philosopher Aristotle keeps coming up in this book is that he was among the first thinkers to make a big deal about how persuasion works when speakers leave something unsaid or assumed. In his time as well as ours, we tend to believe that we argue more formally than we actually do. In everyday arguments, we have a habit of making assumptions or relying on unstated premises. To understand how this is the case, let's examine formal arguments first.

A formal argument is one in which all its premises or claims are made explicitly, often deductively, from a general statement about a group of things to a conclusion about one specific thing. The most famous example of deductive reasoning is the **syllogism**, or three-part argument, which Aristotle famously illustrated with a philosophical wise guy, Socrates:

a **syllogism** is an argument that consists of a major premise, a minor premise, and a conclusion drawn from those premises.

1. Major premise: "All men are mortal."
2. Minor premise: "Socrates is a man."
3. Conclusion: "Therefore, Socrates is mortal."

The fate of Socrates is perhaps the most famous syllogism in the history of logic for a reason: reading it, or hearing it said, creates a sense of satisfaction when the conclusion is uttered. Most formal arguments proceed in this way: by explicitly stating all their assertions, or "premises."

Here's the thing: unless you are a philosopher, logician, or mathematician—or Spock of the USS *Enterprise*—you rarely if ever state every one of your premises or assumptions aloud. That is, most everyday arguments

The late, great Leonard Nimoy was most known for his portrayal of Mr. Spock in the *Star Trek* franchise. The character often explicitly stated his premises when making arguments, something that most humans do not do in everyday arguing.

leave something unstated or unsaid because it is commonly understood between the speaker and the listener. Here are two arguments based on Aristotle's famous example that represent everyday argument: (1) Socrates died because he is mortal, and (2) Socrates passed away because he was a man. In both versions of the argument, the premise that humans are mortal is unstated because it is common knowledge.

The kicker for Aristotle—and the fundamental teaching of the study of persuasion for centuries—is this: a speaker is persuasive when he or she invites the audience to fill in the unstated parts. Persuasion cannot be reduced to *what* people actually say or write; persuasion is actually a consequence of the unstated or missing premise supplied by the audience. In other words, the reason people are persuaded by a speaker is because they participate in the creation of arguments with the speaker.

Contemporary Argument: Claims, Evidence, and Warrants

So far we have discussed two important observations about arguments and informal logic that have been taught for centuries: (1) everyday arguments depend on unstated premises, and (2) persuasion relies on audiences to supply unstated premises. How can we use these observations to make and analyze arguments ourselves?

> The reason people are persuaded by a speaker is because they participate in the creation of arguments with the speaker.

In the twentieth century, philosopher Stephen Toulmin developed a useful model of argument in his 1958 study, *The Uses of Argument*.[9] Instead of thinking of arguments as vertical structures (up and down) like a syllogism, Toulmin proposed turning arguments on their sides, making the mental image of argumentation horizontal (see figure on page 311, "Basic Argument Structure"). Instead of thinking about persuasion in terms of premises or other forms of abstraction, Toulmin suggested that we can understand all arguments rather elegantly as having three parts: a claim, evidence, and the warrant (or reasoning) that links the two.[10]

The claim

For Toulmin, the basic element of an argument is a claim. We can think of a claim as an assertion about something. For example, after your flight arrives at your destination, you are often directed to baggage claim to get your luggage. When you check in for a flight and leave a bag, an airline agent gives you a physical piece of paper or a sticker that is proof or a claim to a particular piece of baggage. Similarly, when you make a claim in speech or writing, you are asserting that you have a claim on one or more of three things: (a) that something is a fact, (b) that something is good or bad, or (c) that something should be done. We tend to sort these three kinds of claims as claims of fact, claims of value, and claims of policy.[11]

Toulmin's model of argument consists of a claim, data or evidence, and the reasoning that warrants connecting them.

Types of Claims

In the Western world, arguments typically advance one of three types of claims.

Claim of Fact: A statement that asserts that something has happened, is happening, or will happen, or a statement that asserts that something is true: "X is Y." "I had a waffle for breakfast." A subset of the claim of fact is the *claim of definition*: "A vacuum is a space devoid of matter" or "A vacuum is used to remove dirt from a carpet" are both claims of fact and definition.

Claim of Value: A statement that asserts that something is good or bad. For example, "X is good/bad." What is "good" or "bad" can be of any kind of value (something is or is not useful, something is right or wrong, and so forth). "Jorge is a great dancer" is as much a claim of value as a claim about something morally weighty, like, "Capital punishment is justified." Sometimes claims of value are believed to be claims of fact. The key difference is the role of *judgment*. One is assessing the importance or worth of something in a claim of value.

Claim of Policy: A statement that asserts that something should or should not change, happen, or be done in the future: "We should/ should not do X." "Let's go to the pool today!" is an example, as is "The House of Representatives should reinstate the Glass-Steagall Act." The key to distinguishing a policy claim from other types of claims is the significance or importance of an uncertain future. The claim, "We should not have gone out to such an expensive restaurant last night!" is actually a claim of value, not only because it concerns something that has already happened but also because it makes a judgment about that event. Remember: Policy implies the future!

When making any kind of speech, you'll most likely be making claims of value and fact; we tend to isolate claims of policy as the province and focus of persuasion. To return to our opening example, when a parent argues that you should not drive because the weather is bad, it is a claim of policy. When Aristotle asserts that Socrates will die, he is making a claim of fact. And when a reader of this book says, "Josh's knock-knock joke about the cow is awful!" he or she is making a value claim.

Sometimes it can be difficult to determine whether something is a claim of fact, value, or policy. In everyday arguments, the three are often interwoven in ways that require some thought to untangle them. For example, consider these statements: "I should not have eaten that footlong submarine sandwich, because it made me sick. Stormycloud Subs should not sell sandwiches that large!"

Everyday arguments often merge claims of fact, value, and policy.

All three types of claims are present here in different ways, some implied and some explicit. The claim of fact is that someone ate a foot-long sandwich from Stormycloud Subs and got sick; the claim of value is that eating a huge sandwich is not a good idea; the claim of policy is that the restaurant should not sell huge sandwiches. As a whole, it's tough to decide which claim is *primary* for this argument, and based on these statements alone, there is no way to tell what the argument really concerns. If the statements were from a speech in which the speaker argued against the "super-sizing" of fast food, then the argument is primarily one of policy. If, however, it was a statement made to you by a friend who was trying to be humorous (she really did not think the sub shop was going to stop selling large sandwiches), the argument is basically one of value: "I did a silly thing that caused me to get sick!"

By focusing on the temporal dimension of a claim, you can sometimes determine its type. A claim about whether something did or did not happen is a factual claim. Factual claims concern something that happened in the past or is happening in the present. When something is good or bad—an assertion of value—it can be true of something that happened in the present or the past. Whether one should or should not do something implies the future. This means that claims of policy almost always involve a degree of uncertainty about a time to come. Indeed, policy claims are often the easiest to discern because they concern things that have not yet happened.

Every speech you give will contain a variety of types of claims; you will inevitably make all three kinds to a greater or lesser extent in just

claim vs.  thesis

Bettmann/Contributor/Getty Images

At first glance, it may seem as if a thesis (discussed in chapter 7) is the same thing as a claim. These two things, however, are different. A thesis is an explicit statement about your central claim. The thesis is what you actually write out or say — the words on a page or the words exiting your mouth when you make a speech. More often than not, a thesis is explicitly expressed, and usually in the speech introduction.

A claim may or may not be expressed in a thesis. In general, a claim is an assertion of fact, value, or policy. In fact, just about any spoken or written thesis is some kind of claim. But not all claims are expressly written or spoken; sometimes claims can be implied and go unstated.

This is a tricky distinction, to be sure. If you think about claims as having to do with arguments, and theses as having to do with arguments expressed in language, either spoken or written down, the distinction is easier to make in your head.

You can more easily learn to recognize the difference between a thesis and a claim by visiting LaunchPad at **launchpadworks.com** and linking to the "1961 Kennedy Inaugural Address."

When asked to think about John F. Kennedy's famous 1961 inaugural address, most people remember one of his concluding claims, "Ask not what your country can do for you — ask what you can do for your country." This *policy claim*, however, is not Kennedy's *thesis*.

- Based on your viewing, *what is Kennedy's thesis?*

- Is his thesis his major persuasive claim? Why or why not?

about any type of speech. What matters most when advancing arguments is the *primary*, or most important, claim. The type of argument you advance as primary really depends on your goal: speaking to inform typically centers on claims of fact; speaking to celebrate tends to center on claims of value (about the importance of the community and occasion, for example); and speaking to persuade usually focuses on claims of policy (and secondarily, claims of value), because you want an audience to change their beliefs, attitudes, values, or behaviors.

What are the three major types of claims? ⑦

The evidence

The second basic part of an argument is the evidence one offers to support a claim.[12] In informal or everyday speeches, the kinds of things one can draw on as evidence are limitless. In chapter 15, we examined the types of evidence or support best suited for public speaking (which *are not* limitless), but it doesn't take much imagination to think about all the things one might use as evidence in everyday life. In a persuasive speech calling for tighter regulations on car emissions, you would likely draw on research data, statistics, and health reports for evidence. Yet evidence can also include common knowledge: "Please don't drive tonight because the weather is terrible." For this argument, the evidence is the common knowledge that bad weather can lead to car accidents. For your persuasive speech, you'll be asked to research your evidence from scholarly sources, news reports, and so on. That said, it is useful to remember that evidence refers to *any* material—spoken or unspoken, formal or informal—an arguer uses to support a claim.

The reasoning or warrant

The third and most important part of any argument is the reasoning, which is the connective tissue or link between the claim and the evidence. The warrant is the crux of argumentation; it's the unstated or missing part of an argument that Aristotle isolated as the key component of persuasion. Even if your claim and evidence are clear, bad reasoning can tank an argument. Again, reasoning refers to the thinking and the rules of thinking (logic) that link the claim and evidence together.

Following Toulmin, scholars of argumentation have tended

to describe the link of reasoning as "the warrant." Toulmin picked the term because of its legalistic connotation.[13] Think about the warrant as the answer to the following question: What justifies connecting a given claim to the supplied evidence? In a legal or courtroom setting, for example, reasoning is often based on leads or probable cause. If, for example, police investigators believe someone has committed a crime and wish to search the person's home, they must contact a judge and request a warrant for the home search based on the evidence they have (testimony from an informant, materials found during a routine traffic stop, and so on). In making claims in any speech, whether formal or informal, the speaker is saying to the audience, "Given the context, the relationship between the claims I am making and the evidence I am offering for these claims is warranted."

Let's return to the common scene of toasting a guest of honor as an example. At most retirement parties, there are toasts to the honoree. The claims made during these toasts are almost always fact claims ("She worked for thirty years") or value claims ("He is a great person"). What kinds of evidence do the folks offering these toasts tend to draw on in support of their claims of fact or value? Personal anecdotes about how the speaker knows the retiree, stories recalling a time when he or she observed something the honoree did for another worker, and so on. Notably, the *reasoning* linking personal stories to claims about the honoree is simply one of personal experience and authority: seeing is knowing. The warrant is also an appeal to credibility: "I am a friend and coworker of the honoree, so I am qualified to tell these stories as evidence of her devotion to the company and her work." The "warrant," or the reason the speaker is justified in telling personal stories in support of his or her claims, has everything to do with the widespread cultural belief that we have a right to talk about our friends and coworkers and tell stories about them based on our experiences. The reasoning, in other words, is not necessarily logical in a strict philosophical or analytic sense but rather cultural. At a retirement party in the United States, it is *reasonable* to tell fun and endearing stories about the honoree as a colleague, worker, and manager; at a charity function, it is more reasonable to focus on the honoree's community service, financial donations to good causes, and so on.

Our discussion of reasoning brings us to two very important observations concerning warrants. What is irrational reasoning in one context is perfectly appropriate in another; reasoning is contextually bound. The mistake some public speakers make when thinking about connecting supporting materials to their claims is that the process is simply a matter of logic, not realizing that the rules of logic can change depending on the physical setting of the speech, the kind of speech one is delivering, and the people who are hearing it. For example, when telling a joke, the warrant can often be nonsensical or dependent on punning: "What did the duck say when he bought lipstick? 'Put it on

> What is irrational reasoning in one context is perfectly appropriate in another; reasoning is contextually bound.

my bill!'" Punning logic, however, would not work for a speech about not eating sea bass because it is overfished (the warrant here, of course, is that overfishing is bad and can lead to extinction). The support you use for a speech must be guided by reasons informed by the context of your speech. What appears to be a warrant is often in the eye or ear of the observer or listener. Because warrants are almost always unspoken, and because the audience is supposed to be supplying this part of an argument in most speaking situations, there can be many warrants for an argument, even some not consciously intended by the speaker.[14]

For some arguments, the warrant will be relatively clear, while for others, the reasoning linking a claim to its evidence may be multiple or, worse, muddy. Following are three examples of warrants: one that is straightforward, one that is quirky, and one that very few children (or grown-ups) like:

CLEAR WARRANT

Claim of fact: Having a health-care plan can help you pay for services you could not otherwise afford (evidence). For example, if you paid for an emergency root canal out of pocket, it could run you $1,000 or more. With a good dental plan, the procedure would run you about $500.

> —**Warrant:** A health-care plan saves you money by cutting your health-care expenses.

NOT-SO-CLEAR WARRANT

Claim of value: Having a health-care plan is good for the country because insuring more people reduces general health-care costs (evidence).

> —**Warrant:** A country's overall health is determined by how many people are insured. A good citizen has a health-care plan. A country should support people getting health care. The warrant here is unclear.

TOTALLY UNSATISFYING WARRANT

Claim of policy: You cannot have a cookie because I said so!

> —**Warrant:** I am the boss of you!

You can probably come up with other examples for different claims of fact and value regarding health care, and certainly claims of policy (e.g., You should get health care because it will save you money in the long run, or because preventive medicine leads to a longer, healthier life). In the given examples, the claim of fact has a warrant that is much easier to determine based on the implied links between the evidence (the cost of a root canal with and without health plan support), whereas the claim of value has an uncertain warrant because of the lack of explanation.

A frequent mistake made in analyzing arguments is the assumption that there must be one warrant, or that one warrant is correct while another is incorrect. We should also observe here that the more complex the claim, the more widely variable the reasoning behind it can be. Claims of fact tend to have easily identifiable warrants; claims of value and policy are much more likely to have complex forms of reasoning.

Finally, owing to the unspoken or often assumed character of warrants, when making arguments we may forge links of reason that we do not intend or are relatively unaware of. We are more likely to be unaware of our reasoning when an audience is friendly and familiar to us, and typically more careful about our reasoning when making arguments to unfamiliar audiences. Therefore, we should remind ourselves to think more carefully about our reasoning when making arguments in front of familiar audiences, when we are not prone to do so. No matter who we are presenting to, however, one thing we can and should do is avoid *fallacies*.

? What are the parts of an argument according to Aristotle? What are the parts of an argument according to Stephen Toulmin?

Fallacies: When Reason Slips Up

A **fallacy** is an error in reasoning. Such an error can be deliberate, in which case it is a form of humor or deception, or simply a mistake. Most of us have made and will make fallacious arguments because warrants are often unconscious, especially in more casual settings. We are also prone to fallacious reasoning when we make arguments about

a **fallacy** is an error in reasoning; in argumentation, a fallacy can make an argument invalid.

> ## Tips for Discerning Warrants
>
> A warrant is usually the unspoken or assumed reasoning linking a claim with its evidence. Because this reasoning is usually invisible, warrants rely on an audience to supply them. For this reason, there could be many different warrants discerned by an audience when a speaker is making arguments. Here are some tips to help you more quickly identify reasoning by a speaker:
>
> - Warrants are easier to discern in arguments about facts.
> - Warrants are harder to discern in arguments about values and policies.
> - There may be *more than one* warrant.
> - There may be no "right" or "wrong" warrant; it depends on the argument offered.
> - Warrants *are not always intentional.* A speaker can assume a form of reasoning that he or she is unaware of.
> - There can be "bad" or "unfair" warrants. Bad or unfair warrants are not always unethical — they can simply be mistakes.
>
> **Recall an argument that someone made to you that assumed an unfair or illogical warrant. Do you think the arguer was conscious of this warrant? Why or why not?**

something that we are passionate or emotional about. As speakers, it is generally best to avoid fallacies. Just about the only people in our society who routinely get away with fallacies are comics. A joke is often funny because the reasoning behind it is either fallacious or ridiculous: Why are trees so suspicious on sunny days? Because they're shady!

Just as there are a wide variety of types of warrants, there are a wide variety of types of errors in reasoning. Here are the most common you'll likely encounter in others' speeches—and, alas, sometimes in your own. The first five of these fallacies are based on *appeals* to feelings (discussed in the previous chapter), while the remaining five attempt to short-circuit reasoning or logical thought processes.

Ad Hominem. Literally translated as "to the man" or "to the person," this fallacy reduces an issue to a person's character *unfairly*. Sometimes critiquing a person or something he or she did is not fallacious when the critique is fair. An ad hominem fallacy is *not fair*. Not to be confused with name-calling, which is simply calling someone a bad thing ("You're a dunderhead!"), the ad hominem fallacy is an *argument* that diverts an audience away from an issue to a person, or that *unfairly* suggests some-one's character is to blame for a problem. "Ayn Rand was a cruel and insensitive person; therefore, you should not believe in her philosophy of objectivism" is an ad hominem argument. Why? Because it reduces the philosophy or belief system Rand called "objectivism" to her person, and the two are *not* the same. Of course, most of us are familiar with these sorts of arguments in political campaigns; some politicians are fond of using ad hominem attacks on opponents to win elections.

Ad Baculum ("To the Stick/Club"). The ad baculum is a fear appeal that threatens force or violence if the audience does not accept the will of the speaker: "Either clean the floor with this toothbrush, or you're fired!" As with most emotional appeals, the ad baculum is not necessarily bad. We can think of many public service announcements that are reasonably justified and not fallacious, such as billboards that discourage texting and driving by showing gruesome images of car crashes.

Ad Misericordiam (Appeal to Pity). This is an appeal to the misfortune and plight of another. For example, a familiar appeal to pity is a televi-sion commercial featuring a hungry child; viewers are asked to donate money to alleviate hunger.

Ad Populum ("To the People"). This is an appeal to popular feelings or commonly held emotions about a claim or an assertion that is not sup-ported by good evidence: "Four out of five dentists would recommend chewing Cleenzit gum!"

Bandwagon Fallacy. "Everyone is doing it!" is the motto of the bandwagon fal-lacy, and it's a very common one used in advertising. Celebrity endorsements of products—from cars to sport shoes—rely on the band-wagon fallacy. The term "bandwagon" is actually a reference to the circus. In the past, when circuses came to town, they often had a wagon filled with musicians playing music to attract people to follow them or come to the circus. While we don't have bandwagons today (the closest analogy here would be the ice cream truck that blares music to attract kids), this fallacy is typically exciting and works on the fear that audiences may be missing out.

Either-Or Fallacy.   This fallacy happens when a speaker claims that you have only two choices in making a decision, when there may in fact be many other choices. This fallacy is often common in policy arguments. A related fallacy is the *false dilemma*, which presents an audience with two unhappy choices when there may in fact be different choices to be made: "Either you are with us, or you are against us!"

Non Sequitur Fallacy.   This fallacy typically concerns a conclusion that does not logically follow from one or more premises. "All people are mortal; Socrates is a person; therefore, Socrates cannot dance." The example is ridiculous, but we've gone with this one here because a non sequitur is often harder to notice than other fallacies, as they often appear within otherwise sound arguments. Non sequiturs often follow words like "thus" and "therefore": "Global warming is caused by many factors, including the gas passed by livestock. Therefore, we should all be vegetarians." The argument here about vegetarianism makes *some* sense, but it is logically incoherent.

Red-Herring Fallacy.   Literally, a "red herring" refers to a very stinky fish, also called a "kipper," that turns red when it is smoked. It is so stinky that common lore says that hunters used the stinky fish to distract hunting dogs from finding their actual goal (a rabbit). While this fanciful origin story for the red herring is hard to prove, its imagery is still helpful. In an argument, a red herring is a statement that is *distracting* and actually has no relevance to the issue under discussion; a red herring misdirects the attention of the audience. "If eating deep fried ice cream is wrong, I don't want to be right!" or "I don't need to study public speaking because I never want to go into politics!" are red-herring arguments. Such statements may be funny, but the humor leading to the conclusion introduces something misleading or encourages you to overlook errors in reasoning.

Slippery Slope Fallacy.   This fallacy gets its name from the suggestion that if you walk on a slick surface you will inevitably fall. In other words, when one makes a slippery slope claim, he or she is arguing that something bad or undesirable will *inevitably* happen: "If you eat just one fast-food hamburger, you will get addicted and find yourself eating nothing but fast-food

hamburgers." The fallacy is common because it is very similar to the legitimate reasoning of "precedent" in legal contexts. It is sometimes accepted reasoning when a lawmaker or judge argues that making a change to a law or policy will have undesirable and inevitable legal consequences: "If the state of Oklahoma allows one religious group to erect a monument on state grounds, then all religious groups will erect moments on state grounds." The difference between the fallacy and the legitimate use of slope-style argumentation is usually extreme "all" or "every" language. We typically call a slippery slope argument a fallacy when the undesired consequences of a given action *are not inevitable*.

Straw-Person Fallacy.   When you oversimplify an opponent's argument, or when you claim that your opponent argued something that she or he didn't, you commit the straw-person or straw-man fallacy. This fallacy gets its name from the idea that straw people (e.g., the Scarecrow from *The Wizard of Oz*) are easily taken apart or defeated. Next to the ad hominem fallacy, the straw-person fallacy is the most common reasoning error in political discourse. For example, many "attack ads" for political rivals on television are straw-person arguments *because* they overly simplify policy positions: ads are typically less than thirty seconds!

Where can we locate fallacious reasoning in most arguments? ⑦

Organizing Persuasive Speeches

> *You will learn to*
>
> **EXPLAIN** how persuasive speeches of fact, value, and policy differ.
>
> **LIST** the most common types of policy speech patterns.

When persuading an audience, make sure to craft strong arguments using sound reasoning. The rules of reasoning are not always easy to discern, and making good arguments takes practice. When composing a persuasive speech, keeping an eye out for assumed warrants that may be fallacious is a good way to catch slips in logic. When speaking to inform or celebrate, you are typically not asking an audience to change their minds or behaviors about something, so you don't have to use the same approach to reasoning. When speaking to persuade, however, you're asking for some kind of change in belief, attitude, value, or behavior—that is, you're asking the audience to *take a risk*. Because persuasion entails some degree of risk, you want to make sure your reasons for urging a decision about something hold up under logical scrutiny. This sense of care about your argument is part of your unspoken agreement to an audience whom you implore to trust you.

Although we have already considered how to organize a speech in chapter 7, persuasion requires special attention to organizational formats that are designed specifically for a persuasive purpose. When speaking to persuade, there are times when we are only concerned with reinforcing the values or beliefs of an audience, such as a preacher's sermon among a congregation. "Preaching to the choir," as we say, is an important part of persuading, too.

When speaking to persuade, we often think about ourselves asking an audience to do or think something that they would not ordinarily do or think. This implies that the dominant kind of claim in a persuasive speech is one of policy ("Please vote for Bobby Bobbersons for mayor"). Persuasive speaking in the key of policy tells an audience, in effect, "Y'all should do X." Because persuasive speeches of policy are the most challenging, we will save their discussion for last and begin with a discussion of persuasive speeches of fact and value.

> The condition of persuasion is uncertainty about something in the past, the present, or the future. In the midst of certitude, a speech may inform, celebrate, or coerce, but it does not persuade.

Organizing Persuasive Speeches of Fact

When you attempt to persuade an audience to accept facts or to make a judgment, *a fact or value is open to dispute or disagreement*. Persuasion usually entails some degree of uncertainty about something that has happened, that will happen, or that should happen. For example, documentaries are made to examine historical events in ways previously unconsidered, or sometimes to uncover happenings that may have escaped notice. Here is one stark example of a persuasive argument about facts: For many years historian Harry Elmer Barnes made the argument that the genocide of Jews by the German Nazi government during World War II didn't happen. By the 1950s, Barnes's argument was discredited by counterarguments from other scholars who argued that the facts advocated by "holocaust deniers" are wrong based on historical evidence.[15]

One need not think about persuasive speeches of fact in such grand or grave terms, of course. Most court cases that accuse someone of a crime, even small civil suits on television shows like *Judge Judy* or *The People's Court*, involve a series of arguments of fact designed to persuade a judge or a jury that something did or did not occur. Unlike an informative speech in which the facts shared with an audience are more or less agreed upon by most people, persuasive speeches of fact will orbit some degree of uncertainty (the most direct example, again, are the arguments of lawyers in front of a jury that a crime did or did not occur). Because persuasive speeches of fact almost always concern an event of the past in some way, the most common forms of organization are *temporal* (e.g., chronological) or *topical*, which were discussed in chapter 7.

Organizing Persuasive Speeches of Value

Persuasive speeches of value concern a speaker's attempt to convince an audience to make a judgment about something, to decide whether something is good or bad: "Hamburgers are not bad for you if eaten in moderation," for example, would be the central claim of an argument of value. At issue in such a statement is not what a hamburger is or what moderate eating entails; rather, it is the meaning of "bad"—and, by implication, the meaning of "good." Consequently, speeches that argue for value judgments are typically organized *topically* and usually supply standards of judgment. When you advance standards or rules with which to judge something, you are forwarding a **paradigm**. When you are asking an audience to make a judgment about something, whether it is an event, an object, a person, or even a moral principle, the audience needs to know what the rules of judgment are (or, simply, what is at stake).

> a **paradigm** is generally a pattern or model for something. In the speaking situation, however, a paradigm refers to the standards of judgment you provide to an audience to evaluate something; paradigms reference the coordinates of a judgment of value.

A weighty example that we encounter commonly in the United States news media is the question of gun control and the Second Amendment of the U.S. Constitution, which concludes that the "right of the people to keep and bear arms shall not be infringed." For many decades, those who advocate the right of people to own guns, as well as those who argue for the regulation of guns, have made speeches of value based on how one should interpret this amendment. What does it mean to "bear arms"? Why did the writers of the Constitution think owning weaponry was important? Would they have anticipated automatic weapons? Speakers on both sides of this debate typically organize their speeches topically and almost always in reference to the law and its interpretation as a standard for judgment. Those who advocate for unrestricted gun ownership, for example, typically advance a paradigm based on a limited and literal interpretation of the U.S. Constitution ("strict constructionism" or "textualism") and the values of liberty.[16]

There is, however, a caveat to be made about persuasive arguments of value: they almost always abide by or imply a policy argument. When a speaker advances an argument of value, it is usually in the service of a claim of policy: *Because X is good or bad, you should do Y.* Those who argue for the value of possessing guns typically wish audiences to support legislation that would protect that value, or financially contribute to a political organization that does. Those who argue for the soundness of various nutritional choices probably want us to eat and behave in certain ways. In other words, whenever there is a speech of value, a policy argument is usually close by, even if it is never stated. We could even say the same about speeches of fact, whose organizational structure would seem to suggest that "you should believe X happened" or "you should believe that Z did not commit the crime."

Organizing Speeches of Policy

Because policy arguments hover around issues of uncertainty, they tend to be studied the most when considering persuasive speaking. Speeches of policy ask an audience to believe, judge, or do something, and usually all three to some degree. The structures of policy arguments and speeches have been studied most intently because the ultimate goal of persuasion is to effect change.

Over the past century, scholars of persuasion have identified four basic organizational structures that speakers have found useful and effective: Monroe's motivated sequence, problem-solution, refutation, and comparative advantage. These four forms of persuasive organization do not, of course, exhaust the kinds of organizational structures at your disposal, but they are among the most commonly used and studied.

Persuading with Alan H. Monroe

Known as one of the most talented speech teachers of his time, Purdue University professor Alan H. Monroe developed a persuasive speech organization specifically designed for making policy arguments.[17] Monroe's "motivated sequence" is a way to order a policy speech based on audience psychology (as discussed in chapter 3 on audience analysis), and its primary goal is to elicit action from the audience.

1. *Attention:* Open your speech by making your remarks immediately relevant to the audience.
2. *Need or Problem:* Before you can begin to outline your central policy claim ("Y'all should do X"), you must demonstrate that there is a problem to be solved or that something *needs* to be changed. The stress on "need" here speaks to the way in which motivation is an issue of audience psychology. You can also use Maslow's hierarchy of needs to think about how best to compose your "need" step.
3. *Satisfaction:* In this step of the speech sequence, you introduce your central policy claim. Your claim should be worded such that it directly responds to the need or problem you just described in your opening statement.
4. *Visualization:* For Monroe, this step is where the magic of persuasion happens. After you have exposed a need and suggested a solution, you then help the audience imagine the outcome. Vivid imagery is always good, or perhaps anecdotes and stories of positive outcomes.
5. *Action:* For this final step of your policy speech, you *directly* and *explicitly* ask the audience to do something to actualize change. Speakers use this step to encourage an audience to do something: to vote, to donate money or time, to make a life change, and so on.

An extended sample of a speech that uses the motivated sequence appears in the appendix.

Persuading with Problem-Solution

Monroe's motivated sequence is a persuasive speech structure developed by a speech teacher specifically for policy speeches. The sequence is based, however, on a much more widely used structure, common to everything from toothpaste commercials to doctor-patient discussions about changing one's habits.

1. *Problem*: You tell your audience what the problem is, and perhaps elaborate on its causes.

   Example: "The use of hydraulic fracturing—or fracking—is expanding at a staggering rate in Texas as the demand for natural gas explodes. Although the risks of pollution from fracking—not to mention earthquakes—is increasingly discussed, the gigantic volume of water the practice requires is not. In a state prone to drought, fracking risks the creation of more and more desert towns."

2. *Solution*: You explain your policy for solving the problem and why it will work.

   Example: "Texas legislators are on the right track by passing a law that encourages the recycling of water used in fracking, but it doesn't make it mandatory. Stronger legislation that *requires* the recycling of fracking wastewater should be mandatory, and waterless fracking methods explored."[18]

As members of Western culture, most of us learn this structure without any formal training; most of the more elaborate schemes of organization discussed throughout this book—persuasive and otherwise—are based on it.

Persuading with Refutation.   This organizational pattern often assumes that the audience is at least marginally aware of the speaker or topic. It is a common pattern for debates and similar agonistic speaking situations (e.g., in a courtroom or legislature). For this kind of persuasion, the speaker attempts to move an audience to accept his or her position by responding to or refuting opposing claims. The structure proceeds as follows:

1. Description of the opposing position.
2. Description of consequences or effects of the opposing position.
3. Claims of your position (or your counterposition).
4. Contrast of consequences or effects of your position.

We see the refutation structure used most often in opinion essays and by news commentators on television. Consider political strategist Donna Brazile's remarks defending the Voting Rights Act of 1965:

> The Voting Rights Act put in place sweeping new protections for minority voters in the American South who had been disenfranchised for generations by Jim Crow laws—protections that are in serious jeopardy after

the Supreme Court struck down a key provision that allows the Justice Department to monitor elections and ensure that all those who are eligible to vote can cast their ballots.

Republicans emboldened by the Court's decision have already introduced legislation to limit access to the ballot. In 30 states more than 55 different measures have been introduced and considered over the last several weeks.

Republicans are pushing restrictive voter ID legislation in states around the country that will make it more difficult for people to make their voices heard.

Political analyst Donna Brazile speaks at the 2016 Democratic National Convention.

In North Carolina, Gov. Pat McCrory signed an extreme law that attempts to prohibit parents of college students from claiming them as dependents when they file their taxes if the students register to vote anywhere other than the parents' homes. Under the new law, those same students would be required to provide a government-issued photo identification card at the polls. Student ID cards would not count.

In North Carolina, there are 319,000 voters without a government-issued photo ID. Of those individuals, one-third are black and nearly all are living below the poverty line. Yet they would bear the expense of obtaining an ID.

It isn't right and it isn't fair.

By contrast, the Democratic Party is continuing its fight to expand and defend access to the ballot for all eligible Americans. And make no mistake—nationwide, in red states and blue states, in large states and small ones, we will continue to oppose legislative and political efforts that erode that most precious right.[19]

Although refutation structure is often effective, one must use it with caution. Of all the organizational patterns you can use, refutation is most prone to fallacious reasoning, particularly the straw-person fallacy: because you are recounting an argument you intend to refute, you may be tempted to oversimplify your opposition's points. Care should be taken to explain your points of opposition in a fair manner, and you should reserve your time for refuting only the strongest claims against your position.

Persuading with Comparative Advantage.   When an audience already agrees with you that there is a problem and that something needs to change, you have an advantage as a speaker. For example, most audiences one would encounter today would be inclined to believe that water pollution exists and is a problem. The question is how to respond to the problem. When you are persuading this kind of audience, a "comparative advantage" approach may work well. This form of organization is similar to refutation except that your posture is on the offensive rather than the defensive. It is also based on a problem-solution structure; however, you put your emphasis on the advantages or benefits of your policy in comparison to the alternatives. In other words, you attempt to persuade the audience by amplifying the benefits of your policy in comparison to other policies.

1. Statement of the problem or need for change.
2. Description of your policy or solution.
3. Description of how your policy or solution is better than others.

As with the refutation pattern, the comparative advantage structure is prone to fallacious reasoning during the comparison step. Care should be taken not to oversimplify the alternatives to your policy suggestion.

In this chapter, we investigated the relationship between reasoning and persuasion primarily by focusing on arguments. Taking care to distinguish argumentation from fighting and quarrels, we examined the three-part structure of arguments in terms of Aristotle's syllogism. Then, we updated the basic logic of arguments for our time by examining the Toulmin model: the idea that contemporary arguments have a central claim that is supported by evidence. What links the claim and evidence together is reasoning, often unspoken, that is also termed "the warrant." When linking claims to evidence, however, we can sometimes make mistakes, which are termed "fallacies." Next, we examined the most common organizational patterns for persuasive speeches of fact and value, and the more complex organizational patterns for persuasive speeches of policy: motivated sequence, problem-solution, refutation, and comparative advantage. These different kinds of structures—arguments and speech patterns—do not exhaust the study of informal logic and persuasion, of course, but are offered as places to begin understanding our lifelong attempts to influence others and ourselves.

> **What are the four basic types of organization for a persuasive speech of policy? How and why do these types differ from persuasive speeches of fact and value?** ⍰

end of chapter stuff

Reasoning

Persuasion requires reasoning. We study reasoning in persuasion by more closely examining argument structures and speech organization patterns.

What's an Argument?

Contemporary arguments have three parts: a claim, some evidence, and the warrant or reasoning behind them. Claims can concern facts, values, or policies.

Fallacies: When Reason Slips Up

Fallacies are errors in reasoning. The most common include the ad hominem, the bandwagon, the either-or, the non sequitur, the red herring, the slippery slope, and the straw person.

Organizing Persuasive Speeches

The organization of persuasive speeches differs depending on whether the major claim is one of fact, value, or policy. We tend to think of persuasive speeches as primarily policy oriented. The most common policy speech patterns are the motivated sequence, problem-solution, refutation, and comparative advantage.

Bloomberg/Getty Images

CHAPTER 16

ACTIVITIES

Diagram the Argument

Most arguments we encounter on a daily basis are more complicated than they initially seem. For this reason, diagramming arguments and outlining speeches are powerful tools of analysis that can help you locate the errors and successes of informal logic. Briefly outline one of the persuasive speeches in the appendix of this book, taking care to isolate the thesis statement and the central claim. Then, determine the major points used as evidence for the claim. Finally, determine what the reasoning is that holds the claim and its evidence together (the warrant). Is the warrant justified? Why or why not?

Find the Fallacy in Your Newspaper

Although many people would find the observation fallacious, most of us are guilty of fallacious reasoning. Because we tend to think "enthymematically" — that is, with skips and leaps instead of in some sort of linear progression — most of us will fail at the cultural rules of logic, even on a daily basis. We are most prone to fallacious reasoning when following a pattern or script we have learned on a position we hold (for example, the main "talking points" issued by political parties). With a group assigned by your instructor, locate a school newspaper, either in print or online, and see if you can find examples of the fallacies discussed in this chapter: ad hominem, bandwagon, either-or, non sequitur, red herring, and slippery slope. The most obvious place to look would be on the editorial page or in the letters to the editor, because these are the pages devoted to explicit argument and persuasion. You may find these fallacies in news stories as well. Do the fallacies you find invalidate the arguments in which they are used? Can one make a successful argument using fallacious reasoning? Why or why not?

KEY TERMS

SPEAKING

IN THE WORKPLACE

CHAPTER 17

Whether you currently hold down a job outside school or anticipate getting one in the near future, you probably already realize how what you have learned in your public speaking course applies to workplace speaking: conducting audience analysis, adapting one's message to an expected audience, and stylistically crafting confidence through one's vocal tone and dress are skills that will help you succeed in your chosen vocation.

In this chapter, we will briefly examine common speaking situations and guidelines particular to where one works. Sometimes your profession will involve engaging a public you do not know on a regular basis (such as a tour guide or a job trainer), but a good deal of workplace speaking involves speaking to colleagues in smaller venues and less formal contexts. A common workplace speaking situation we have yet to address is speaking in small groups, either in person or as a virtual team using Internet-based technologies.[1]

Today, team-based presentations are more popular in professional settings than in other speaking contexts. In business and professional contexts, you will more likely be asked to deliver a presentation than a speech, which is typically less formal and relies on visual aids (such as slides created with software, such as Keynote and PowerPoint).

Speaking for Your Vocation

> **You will learn to**
>
> **DEFINE** "vocation," and explain its relation to a job.

Like public speaking in general, the primary purpose of speaking in professional contexts is to establish and maintain relationships with your colleagues. Although workplace speaking often focuses on commercial concerns—increasing profits, business growth, and so on—it also addresses social or political goals and the personal and professional relationships you cultivate to achieve them. For this reason, speaking in professional contexts might be better described as speaking for your vocation. Most people think of a vocation as a profession or a career, but when we consider the origin of the term, it becomes much broader in scope: the term "vocation" comes from the Latin term *vocare*, meaning "to call." In this sense, a vocation refers to one's calling, or whatever it is that beckons an individual toward a meaningful and productive life. A **vocation** refers to a feeling of dedication, if not a sense of duty, to a chosen career.

Much more than a job, our vocations implicate ethical orientations because, as we discussed in chapter 2, all calls are requests to establish relationships built on a sense of trust. If you heed a "calling," you tacitly trust those who practice what you wish to practice as a career. Of course, we cannot formally respond to all the things that call to us, as there are simply too many calls; our time together on the planet is lamentably limited. Yet we will respond to many calls in our lifetimes, if we are lucky, and each of us will figure out which call is truly our own and make it a vocation.

We are certainly called on to find a job or to craft a career, but many calls can stir our passions without the promise of a paycheck. A vocation can also be a hobby, a desire to offer help to others, a need to minister to others, a drive to promote political change, an inspiration to fight for social justice, or even a quest to promote art. Understanding the complex and often *passionate* character of our vocations means that our callings are unique to each individual.

We can identify at least three contexts in which vocational speaking may

> The term "vocation" comes from the Latin term *vocare*, meaning "to call."

vocation refers to a feeling of dedication toward one's occupation.

A vocation is often more than "just a job"—it can be a calling.

be important and applicable to you: in an office space or meeting room, interacting online with groups, and speaking for social change. This and the next two chapters bring *Speech Craft* to a conclusion by addressing each of these contexts in turn.

Speaking at Work

> *You will learn to*
>
> **DEFINE** small group communication.
>
> **LIST** the types of roles for small groups.
>
> **DEFINE** conflict, and explain how to manage it.
>
> **LIST** five types of workplace presentations.

Speaking in the workplace usually takes place before small audiences, or small groups. Many workplace speaking situations involve reporting on work that has been done, communicating results of studies, or making proposals about new ventures, either to one's own organization or as a sales pitch to a potential client. Because many professional speaking contexts are limited to audiences of small groups, the appropriate

Workplace Speaking versus Public Relations

When asked to describe a public speaker, people may talk about someone who is speaking as a professional for his or her job. We might imagine Reshma Saujani, the founder of Girls Who Code, speaking to an audience about women in technology, or the president and CEO of the parent company of Mr. Bubble, Frank Klisanich, holding a press conference to announce a new "bath bomb" product. Although most of the principles of public speaking apply to the professional speaker, workplace speaking involves speaking internally, or inside

Bloomberg/Contributor/Getty Images

Reshma Saujani speaks about the organization she founded, Girls Who Code.

a given organization. Speaking to represent a company is better described as public relations (PR) — a subject that requires its own course and textbook because of the specialized skills it requires. (PR is often taught in more advanced college courses, and you might look to professional programs in advertising or in a business school for more training in this area.)

Can you think of a situation in which speaking inside an organization can simultaneously be PR?

norms to follow will differ widely depending on the culture of the specific organization or business. How to address a group at work is usually best learned by observing how others do it. Some employers may even offer training to familiarize new employees with the speaking norms of the workplace culture. As with any job, a good general rule is to quietly observe at the beginning. By observing before you speak up, you can begin to identify the norms of your organizational culture, including what is appropriate to say and, more importantly, how to say it.

You may be asked to speak at your job before you have had a chance to learn the norms of the culture; this is certainly the case at an interview. In this situation, it's always a good idea to ask your employer what the speaking expectations are and how people typically address one another in the workplace. For example, you might ask your supervisor, "What should I know about expectations for my presentation?" Reviewing the guidelines and tips discussed in chapter 3 on audience analysis will also help you discern what your new workplace audience might expect.

Speaking in Small Groups

Closely related to any speaking you may be asked to do among work groups is small group communication (or small group discussion), which is a genre of speaking in its own right. Unlike every other speech genre discussed so far, small group communication is a speaking situation in which a group comes together to deliberate about a task or to analyze information. In a workplace or professional setting, **small group communication** is commonly understood as an interaction among three or more people (but typically less than twenty) who *self-identify* as a group.[2] Technically, small group discussions are *not* forms of public speaking, although you may at times be asked to kick off a group discussion with a small speech (for which you can plan ahead). Usually, however, communication within small groups is task oriented and impromptu. Discussion within these groups tends to be spontaneous, even if the meeting is scheduled ahead of time.

small group communication concerns the interaction among three or more people who self-identify as a group.

Roles

Although small group discussions may be experienced as spontaneous, researchers who have studied them have discovered a surprising recurrence of communication norms among these groups.[3] Small group discussion is similar to public speaking: just as we know what to expect from many speech genres, we learn the norms of small group discussion from experience and often without formal study. If we think of group discussion as a kind of theater, the most dominant norms that emerge concern *roles*, or the different ways in which people act in groups. You may be a leader, a good listener, a caretaker, or keenly adept at solving problems, but when put into a group, you may find yourself—even unconsciously—playing a role that is unfamiliar to you. For example,

> **?** What are the primary roles of small group discussion?

Everett Collection, Inc.

The 1957 film *12 Angry Men* dramatizes a jury attempting to come to a consensus about a murder verdict; Juror 8 (played by Henry Fonda) is the emergent leader of the group.

you may be accustomed to taking charge of work projects, but in a group you may find yourself working under the leadership of a team manager. Alternatively, you may be accustomed to quietly working on projects on your own, but in a group you may discover others looking to you for leadership. Group dynamics tend to create a constantly changing context that requires adaptation in real time.

When working in groups, a **leader** will typically help guide and influence discussion. If not already assigned to a group, a leader will typically emerge over the course of the discussion. Researchers also identify two types of roles that people can play, either simultaneously or independently. **Task-oriented roles**, or simply "task roles," refer to the actions group members take that directly contribute toward the goal of the discussion, such as taking notes or procuring needed supplies. **Social-oriented roles**, or "interpersonal roles," refer to the forms of discussion group members engage in to help moderate the mood and feelings of participants. Both kinds of roles are important for successful group discussions. When engaged in a group discussion, most participants want to feel valued and heard in addition to believing that the group is being productive and accomplishing something.

a **leader** (in small group communication) is someone who is designated or who emerges to guide and moderate discussion.

task-oriented roles (in small group discussions) are adopted by members to help meet the goals of the group.

social-oriented roles are adopted by members of a group to help moderate the mood and feelings of participants.

groupthink is a common, often unconscious tendency to avoid conflict in a group, usually by failing to challenge ideas or decisions.

Group tendencies

Researchers point out two psychological tendencies that can lead a small group discussion astray: groupthink and conflict. First, small group discussion can often lead to poor or uncritical, even dysfunctional, decisions because of a strong desire for group harmony or unreflective loyalty to the group or a group leader. Although **groupthink** often results in an easy consensus among the group, the consequence is often the silencing of the thoughts or feelings of those who disagree.[4]

Another consequence of groupthink is the stifling of critical thinking and reflection, precisely those things that can help a group avoid bad or hasty decisions. An extreme example of how groupthink can go wrong is a cult, which is a group that has become insular and for which loyalty to the group is prized above critical thought or disagreement. Very rarely will you be part of a group discussion that becomes cultish, of course, but you can use the example as a mental guideline for what you want to avoid.

conflict refers to the inevitable disagreement groups encounter when working on a task together; conflict is positive when it is depersonalized and focused on problem solving.

Because a group is often charged with working together toward a common goal, **conflict** is inevitable.[5] As we discussed in chapter 16 with regard to argumentation, conflict is often incredibly productive if properly understood and embraced.

> Disagreement and tension among group members can actually lead to a deeper understanding of problems, inspiring the kind of critical analyses that make group decisions better. Conflict can be good!

Disagreement and tension among group members can actually lead to a deeper understanding of problems, inspiring the kind of critical analyses that make group decisions better. Conflict can be good!

But conflict can be destructive if it is personalized or if group members make hasty decisions to avoid it. To ensure that conflict is productive, care should be taken to always define and discuss conflict in terms of issues or structures, not people. Arguments discussed and debated in a group should be about ideas, consequences, benefits, and outcomes, not individual personalities. You may perceive that a person's character or behavior is the ultimate cause of conflict, but you're much more likely to discover a productive outcome if you frame disagreement or tension in terms other than person-based issues and challenges. For example, let's suppose your group is tasked with developing a solution to a problem regarding employee training. Instead of saying, "Supervisor Sampson simply does not want to pay us what we need to get this training off the ground," you can reframe the conflict: "The budget the company has developed simply does not

Tips for Avoiding Groupthink

- **Establish the fact that conflict is normal:** When starting to work as a group on a project, explicitly discuss how conflict is both expected and healthy.
- **Oppose ideas, not persons:** Work hard to detach disagreeable ideas from the speakers who offer them. We have a tendency to identify individual people as the cause of problems or difficulties that are actually rooted in or caused by structures or institutions.
- **You are not your ideas:** Remember not to equate your contributions and ideas to your notion of self; groups work on tasks precisely because many minds and bodies often make projects better.
- **Advocate for the devil:** Playing "devil's advocate" refers to adopting a role that offers a critique or counterposition to dominant or consensus suggestions. Such a role is deliberately playful and not intended as mean; rather, opposing or alternative views are offered as a check on groupthink.

When might groupthink be a good thing?

provide us with the resources we need to revise the training program." You'll often be amazed at how productive the discussion of conflicts can be when you depersonalize issues.

There is simply no way to avoid conflict, understood at its most basic as an inability to share the same feelings, experiences, and thoughts of others. Unless you live alone on a desert island, there *is no way to avoid conflict; there are only better and worse ways to manage it.*

Conflict is often a problem, whether in work groups or in life in general, because very few of us are actually taught to understand and manage it. By the time you get to college, you have been taught how to express your individual interests and achieve them on your own, often in ways that avoid conflict. But then you get your first job and are asked to work in groups, with little practice or knowledge about how conflict can be productive. One exception would be if you had participated on a team—sports or academic (e.g., debate)—where you may have learned how to deal with group conflict productively. Even so, the general lack of experience of working in groups or teams in school means that *most people*, at least when starting a career, don't know how to collaborate with a group at work. Practicing active listening (discussed in chapter 2) and avoiding groupthink are two fundamental things you can do to ensure that the inevitable conflicts of group discussion result in more positive outcomes.

What is the best way to manage conflict? ⓘ

When is conflict productive? ⓘ

Making Presentations in the Workplace

Because working in small groups is common in professional and workplace contexts, a team may be asked to give a presentation. If you are asked to create and deliver a presentation as a team, care should be taken among your group to establish roles for the speaking parts as well as assign different tasks (e.g., creating slides). Practice with your team to determine transitions between different speakers, and make sure you reference and handle your presentation aids with ease.

Whether a workplace presentation is delivered by a team or a single speaker, much of what you have learned about speaking to inform and persuade in previous chapters is easily applied to your professional presentations. You may be asked to deliver a sales pitch that explains to buyers or potential partners why they should work with your business, which is a combination of informational and persuasive speaking. Or you may need to speak to coworkers and then write a report about productivity, compile the results of studies or market research, or write a description of the progress that you or a group are making on an assigned task. In most cases, the principles of public speaking can be applied to work presentations, especially the tips described in the chapter on visual aids and using slide presentation software. As with presentations at school, PowerPoint, Keynote, Prezi, and other software programs are popular in workplace presentations (see chapter 11).

Finally, we should note that workplace presentations are different from public speaking presentations because they are constrained by the norms of a workplace culture. More often than not, the presentations you make in front of your colleagues or your superiors will be less formal and more conversational in tone because your audience will be familiar to you. Unlike in a public speaking setting, where many of your audience members will be strangers, your workplace audience may be small, and many of them may know you personally. In addition, there may be times you may even conduct a workplace meeting or presentation over the Internet through a **virtual group**. Whether your work group or work audience consists of people you know well or only slightly, whether online or in "real space," you must be careful to moderate your degree of formality in respect to workplace expectations. You may be tempted, for example, to use inside jokes or adopt a sarcastic tone because those with whom you are meeting are very familiar to you; however, care should be taken to remember that *you are at work*. Unless you work for the Ringling Bros. and Barnum & Bailey Clown College, save most of your jokes and playful innuendoes for after-work meetings.

The team working on this textbook at Bedford/St. Martin's meets to discuss marketing strategies via Google Hangouts.

a **virtual group** is a collection of people brought together to work on a common task through long-distance technologies (teleconferencing, Skype, and so on); today, such groups are as common in the workplace as they are in video gaming.

Types of workplace and professional presentations

There are as many types of workplace speeches and presentations as there are businesses and organizations. Each type of presentation will entail different audience expectations. Many businesses and professional organizations harbor a number of expectations and norms particular to themselves. For example, each kind of workplace has its own kind of specialized language or jargon, and whether or not you use specialized terms depends on your audience. Will the CEO of a communication technology company be interested in the minute technical details of your engineering assignment, or will you be expected to provide simplified details? Will you be speaking to an audience who will be familiar with specialized terms, or will you be giving a more general pitch to a client? Before you participate in a presentation, ask others who have had experience with the particular audience what the expectations are and if they have any advice for you. If you have the opportunity, watch a colleague at your workplace give the kind of presentation you will be giving to help you better discern expectations.

Despite the wide variety of formats, the most common types of speaking for business and professional settings include the following:

Keynote Speeches. Many businesses and professional organizations hold meetings, annual or semiannual, for various reasons: to debut new services or products, to provide a self-assessment of how the company is doing, and so on. Keynote speeches at these events are often given by workplace leaders or invited guests. Like celebratory speaking, the emphasis in keynote presentations is inspirational in tone. For example, the president of a company might deliver the keynote address at an annual meeting. While she may report profits or address concerns internal to the company, her ultimate goal is to celebrate the employees and the company. Because these kinds of addresses are typically for all employees or volunteers in an organization, the language is typically less specialized and the message more general and celebratory in tone. (The norms for keynote speeches are discussed extensively in chapter 13.)

Training Sessions.   As a speaker representing an organization, you may be asked to train a number of colleagues to assume new roles and responsibilities, or to facilitate discussion among them. In this capacity, you are primarily speaking to inform. In the context of a training session, your colleagues are probably going to be less familiar with the language culture of the organization; therefore, each specialized term or concept will need to be clearly defined. Training sessions tend to be less formal because of their "how-to" character.

Proposals.   A proposal is a plan for change that is presented to others for discussion and deliberation. Proposals are usually written first, then introduced to others in the form of an oral presentation. All types of organizations—from political think tanks to restaurant chains—must make decisions about possible changes. Whether that change is a different strategy for reaching voters or a new theme for a restaurant menu, speakers must either inform their colleagues of options or persuade them to take a course of action. By definition, a proposal presentation is delivered to an audience that has not yet deliberated or discussed the proposal; as a result, these types of presentations tend to veer from informative to persuasive.

Sales Pitches.   Sales presentations are fundamentally persuasive speeches designed to convince an audience to purchase a product or service, or perhaps adopt an approach, address a problem, or embrace an opportunity that your organization is recommending. A problem-solution or motivated sequence style of organization is typical in sales pitches. Because persuasion is central to any sales presentation, pitches should always build on values that are commonly shared with the audience (review chapters 15 and 16 for a refresher).

Reports.   Whether delivered to customers or colleagues, a report is a researched presentation that informs clients or colleagues as to the status of specific aspects of the business or organization. A speaker or team might deliver a report on profits, for example, or update staff on progress or potential challenges and changes to the workplace.

Interviewing for a Job

> **You will learn to**
>
> **EXPLAIN** the equality ideal of interviewing.
>
> **LIST** and **DEFINE** two types of workplace interviews.

Strictly speaking, a job or position interview is not public speaking. We are addressing this topic, however, because the techniques and skills of public speaking have a direct application to interview contexts: you should research your audience, and you should strive to establish goodwill and common values. The guidelines for style and delivery (language use, vocalics) discussed in chapters 9 and 10 also apply.

In chapter 3, we discussed interviewing as a research tool that you can use to gather information about a topic. In a workplace context, you and your interviewer are the topic! A workplace interview typically refers to a series of questions and answers between an employer and a potential employee. In popular culture, interviews are sometimes portrayed as one-sided plays of power in which an employer interrogates a desperate job seeker. Although such inequities do occur, interviews are best and most ideally understood as an equal opportunity for employers and potential employees to learn more information about each other. In a workplace setting, the two most common kinds of interviews are the *screening interview* and the *selection interview*.

Screening Interviews

A screening interview is one in which an employer attempts to reduce a large number of job applicants to a smaller and more manageable number. Typically, an employer conducts these short interviews over the phone, via the Internet (with Google Hangouts, Skype, or WebEx), or in person. Screening interviews typically involve questions about basic qualifications and fit. In these contexts, applicants have the least amount of power and, consequently, should be very well prepared. Here are some tips for screening interviews:

- Dress professionally if the interview is in person or through a virtual meeting or videoconference.
- Before your interview, research the organization's history and mission and, if possible, the professional background of your interviewer(s). Employers are impressed by applicants who demonstrate a familiarity with the organization or company and its mission.
- Interviews at restaurants are more manageable if the restaurant is quiet, although you will likely have little choice in this regard.

Still, if meeting in public, request a quiet space away from others if you are able. If on the phone or Internet, conduct your interview in a quiet space away from pets or people who might interrupt your conversation.

- If using the phone or Internet, secure a stable connection (such as a landline or a reliable Wi-Fi connection). Dropped calls or spotty connections are frustrating for both parties, and you want to create the best possible impression.
- After the interview, send a thank-you e-mail to the potential employer. Thank your interviewer for his or her time, mention two or three things that you took away from the meeting, and reiterate your interest in the company and the position. Follow up with a handwritten thank-you note—it will help you stand out from the crowd.

Selection Interviews

Most people will encounter the selection interview during their career, and often more than once. A selection interview is one in which an employer seeks personal contact, either through videoconferencing or in person, with a potential employee. Employers design their questions to further assess a workers' qualifications and predict his or her work-related behavior. The potential employee's questions help discern if he or she would be a good fit for the position and satisfy the employer's needs. In essence, the selection interview is a conversation between the employer and the potential employee about whether they would work well together.[6]

the **behavioral interview** is a popular form of interviewing that asks candidates questions about past behavior to predict future work-related outcomes.

In the past, standard selection interview questions from an employer were designed to assess the applicant's values, qualifications, and future behavior through hypothetical situations (e.g., "Where do you see yourself in our company in three years?"). Owing to research that suggested that traditional interviews that relied on open-ended questions about imaginary scenarios were ineffective,[7] the **behavioral interview** was created and has subsequently become the most dominant type of interview.[8] Rather than focus on the future, the behavioral interview asks candidates about past behavior in work-related situations in an attempt to predict future behavior based on the answers. Common behavioral questions or prompts include, "Describe a time in your past position in which you had to work in a team," or "Tell us about a recent conflict with a coworker and how you resolved or managed it." These kinds of invitations for discussion benefit both the employer and the interviewee because

H. Armstrong Roberts/ClassicStock/Getty Images

Although selection interviews are sometimes conducted virtually, they usually occur in person.

no one has to guess about a hypothetical situation with the interviewee drawing on the memories of past events.

To help prepare for a behavioral interview, John R. Cunningham developed what he terms the STAR method of responding, which he collaborated on with his colleague Blair W. Browning.[9] When you are asked behavioral questions, these job interview experts recommend the following:

1. Explain the **S**ituation and **T**ask thoroughly: What is the context of the situation you have been asked about? When and where did it occur? Were other colleagues involved? What led you to take action?
2. Describe what **A**ction you took in response to the situation: What did you do, and how did you do it? What steps did you take to prepare your response?
3. Describe the **R**esult in detail: What were the outcomes of your behavior? Were you successful? If you were not successful, what did you learn from the experience, and how would you respond differently?

? How do you prepare for a screening interview? A selection interview? What is the STAR method of interviewing?

Although most selection interviews are held in person, companies may choose to conduct selection interviews online, using videoconferencing software. If this is the case, review the detailed guidelines for speaking online in chapter 18.

Although your chosen vocation may not necessarily be what earns you a living, almost everyone is destined to labor in some kind of workplace. In this chapter, we have rehearsed the kinds of speaking that occur most frequently in workplace contexts, from small group communication and team speaking, to the delivery of keynotes, proposals, and reports. We also examined the forms of speaking most people encounter when pursuing a job: screening and selection interviews. Finally, we touched on the importance of thinking about how your workplace speaking may influence and affect others. In the next chapters, we examine two forms of vocational speaking in more depth: online speaking, which has become a common mode of communication in our time, particularly in an era when our friends, families, and work colleagues are located across the globe (chapter 18); and speaking that seeks social change, a brand of vocational speaking that transcends the interests of wages and profit (chapter 19).

ethical considerations
for speaking in the workplace

Magic Car Pics/REX/Shutterstock

Ford marketed and sold its Pinto from 1971 to 1980.

We have already examined listening and the ethical dynamics for public speaking in a way that stressed the significance of building relationships, responding to others, generating goodwill, and helping to constitute a sense of community (see chapter 2). In the workplace context, speeches, presentations, and other forms of verbal communication entail an added degree of complexity; you are representing not only yourself when you speak but often your organization, clients, or colleagues. In other words, in a workplace context, your speaking may have consequences that affect the livelihood of others, and this may require extra attention to mindfulness (e.g., when speaking informally on social media, like Facebook or Twitter). Because there are so many different types of workplaces, it is challenging to address every ethical consideration, but there is at least one guideline that is useful across most organizational contexts: honesty. Communicating honest and true information in the workplace environment is almost always the best policy, even if you have to deliver bad news. In general, deception — even to save someone's feelings — can do more harm than good over time.

If you work for a for-profit company, sometimes a morally appropriate decision compromises the profit. In the United States, there are a number of businesses whose employees have spoken publicly in defense of their companies, which were engaged in unethical activities.

For example, in 1971 the Ford Motor Company rushed into production a compact car called the Pinto, which was designed to compete with more inexpensive cars from Asia. Despite the fact that the company's own crash tests revealed a design flaw with the gas tank — which could explode upon rear impact — Ford made the decision to produce and market the vehicle because it was more cost effective to settle injury lawsuits than halt production. For its part, Ford has never admitted that the Pinto was an unsafe vehicle; however, its employees and associates in the industry did successfully lobby for delaying the adoption of crash-safety standards by the National Highway Traffic Safety Administration.[10]

LaunchPad
macmillan learning

To see video footage of crash tests, visit LaunchPad at **launchpadworks.com** and link to the video for Ford Pinto crash test. Although the case of the Ford Pinto is extreme, it highlights how workplace speaking can challenge you ethically as a speaker.

Consider the following critical questions:

- Would you have lobbied for Ford with the knowledge that the Pinto was an inferior product that could potentially cause drivers or passengers harm?
- Would you market a product that you knew did not work the way it was supposed to?
- Could you speak on behalf of a company about a product that you did not believe in?

Speaking for Your Vocation

Workplace speaking tends to be less formal than more traditional or "public" forms of speaking. Presentations and discussions are more common than speeches, as are small group discussions and team presentations.

Speaking at Work

Workplace speaking often poses ethical challenges that are different from those of more traditional forms of public speaking. This is because the welfare of customers, fellow employees, and the professional organization is often implicated in workplace contexts.

BloombergContributor/Getty Images

Interviewing for a Job

Most people will be interviewed for a job or some sort of position in their lifetime. Screening interviews are designed to reduce the applicant pool for an employer. Selection interviews — predominantly behavioral — are designed to assess a fit between an employer and a potential employee.

H. Armstrong Roberts/ClassicStock/Getty Images

CHAPTER 17

ACTIVITY

Small Group Discussion in the Workplace

In a group assigned by your instructor, consult an editorial from the school newspaper (online or in print) about a challenge that your school is facing. Now imagine you are a think tank assigned by your employer to develop a policy for your school that will help address the problem. Remember, as we discussed in the chapter on argumentation (chapter 16), a policy claim is one that states, "We should do _____ to solve this problem." In the time allowed by your instructor, discuss with your group the problem and possible solutions. Draft a brief statement that explains your policy proposal, then select a spokesperson for your group. When the class reconvenes, instead of sharing your policy proposal, answer the following questions as a class:

1. When you were discussing your policy ideas, did any particular roles among your group members emerge? Was there a clear leader in your group? How could you tell? Did some members engage more in task-oriented roles and others in social-oriented roles? Can you share examples of each?
2. Did you encounter conflict? How do you know? Did you manage the conflict, and if so, how? If not, why not?
3. Did you experience groupthink? If so, how do you know? If not, how can you be sure?

Of course, after you discuss the answers to these questions, your instructor may ask you to share your group's proposal!

KEY TERMS

 Videos in LaunchPad describe many of these terms. Go to launchpadworks.com.

vocation 337
 small group
   communication 339
leader 340
task-oriented roles 340

social-oriented roles 340
groupthink 340
conflict 340
virtual group 343
behavioral interview 346

·SPEAKING·ONLINE·

CHAPTER 18

How often do you keep in touch with friends and loved ones through Apple's FaceTime, Google Hangouts, or Skype? Although many of your online encounters are likely with friends and loved ones, many schools, workplaces, and professional organizations have been using online media for decades to connect people across distances in speaking situations. In college, for example, online education is very common and increasingly an option for students.[1] Many businesses and professional organizations rely heavily on videoconferencing, too, because company employees may reside in other states or countries — or, in the case of science fiction films, other solar systems! We increasingly interact through speakers and screens instead of face to face (F2F) with friends, classmates, and coworkers.

Aside from overcoming the limitations of geography, there are many convenient advantages to online speaking. Before we address these, however, we need to acknowledge that realizing these benefits requires hard work to compensate for the disadvantages of speaking online. Even the newest communication technologies can't engage the human eye or ear as directly as F2F speaking can. In F2F encounters, we are able to pick up more physical information and feelings from both speakers and listeners.[2]

However we seize the advantage of an online speaking presence today, new challenges to online speaking will arise that we cannot anticipate as technologies continue to develop and transform. For this reason, when learning about speaking and listening in online environments, it is prudent to focus on basic principles instead of particular forms of technology, software, or media. In this chapter, we will identify and study four basic dimensions of addressing others over a screen or speaker that are not likely to change for some time: the purpose and types of online presentations, adapting to the amorphous audience, reckoning with technology, and navigating the increasingly blurry line between public and private.

Understanding Online Presentations: Purpose and Type

> **You will learn to**
>
> **EXPLAIN** the key differences between face-to-face and online speaking.
>
> **LIST** the two types of online presentations, and give examples of each.

Originally, the term "on-line" simply meant something or someone who is connected to a computer. Today, the term has lost its hyphen and typically connotes a connection to the Internet through a modem, Wi-Fi, or cellular service on a variety of computing devices, from desktop computers to smartphones to tablets.[3] Consequently, an **online presentation** refers to a prepared speech, podcast, or video that is broadcast on a computing device.

an **online presentation** is a prepared speech, podcast, or video that is broadcast on a computing device.

The primary reason speakers create and deliver online presentations concerns the limitations of space, however, concerns about time and saving money can play a role as well. Some readers may be taking online courses that have no physical classroom and, as a result, presentations can only occur in an online environment.

> When preparing for an online presentation, most of the principles of traditional F2F public speaking apply.

Online versus F2F

When preparing for an online presentation, most of the principles of traditional F2F public speaking apply. The techniques and guidelines we have already studied for celebrating, informing, and persuading in a speech are just as useful for online environments as they are for F2F environments. Online presentations have a number of distinct advantages. Not only can it save you and others time and money, but it can also provide a wider degree of flexibility for you and your audience. Unlike presenting in a physical space, which limits your audience size, your online audience can range in size from one person to thousands of people. If you record your presentation to upload and broadcast at a later time, you have the luxury of editing your presentation or simply redoing it. Recorded presentations also allow your audience members to watch or listen to your presentation at a time and place that is convenient for them.

Speaking F2F is different from speaking through a computer.

Whether recorded or live, however, online presentations pose a number of challenges to speakers and listeners alike. The most obvious problem is technology failure, which happens to just about anyone who regularly delivers online presentations. You can lose your online connection, your software can develop a glitch, your camera or sound recording device can fail, and so on. The best way to prepare for technology or equipment failure is to check your equipment ahead of time and, if you are presenting live, prepare for an alternative presentation method just in case (e.g., if you lose your Skype connection, plan to conduct a conference call on a telephone line instead).

A less obvious yet significant challenge of online presentations concerns the sensory limitations of online recording and broadcasting technologies. When you speak in an F2F environment, you adapt to your audience through the feedback you receive from them using all of your senses. The immediacy of speaking face to face provides you, as a speaker, with the kind of information—some of which is even unconscious—that enables you to appear more genuine and to more easily connect with your audience. By necessity, online presentation technologies rely on cameras, microphones, and speakers, which reduce sensory information. For example, have you ever tried to take a photograph with your smartphone that didn't come out because there was not enough light? The human eye is capable of perceiving much more information in low light than is a camera; thus, to shoot yourself or objects with a camera, you must have—or have to create—"good light."[4] Whenever you create and broadcast an online presentation, you have to take extra steps in order to be seen and heard. We will discuss techniques for working with the limitations of communication technologies later in the chapter.

Because you are receiving less verbal and nonverbal information and feedback from your audience than you would in F2F contexts, another challenge online speakers have is a tendency to seem wooden or stiff. When creating and delivering an online presentation, you have to work harder to appear animated, perhaps using more hand gestures than you would in a F2F speech. Because you will be using a microphone

A Skyping We Will Go! Two colleagues discuss a group project over Skype.

and broadcasting your voice online, your voice will be stripped of higher and lower frequencies, which simply means that you'll have to work harder to maintain vocal variety. In order to engage your audience, your vocal tone will need to be more conversational, and you will need to attend carefully to varying your vocal qualities. Alternations in pitch, tone, volume, speech rhythms, and so on, will need to be more pronounced, so that you appear lively on the audience's screens and speakers.

Matching Eyes, Camera, and Screen. When speaking using a computer or a smartphone, you have to remember to *look at the camera*, not your screen, to create a sense of eye contact with viewers.

Eye Contact Online. In traditional face-to-face public speaking contexts, it is expected that speakers will attempt to scan the audience and make eye contact with as many individuals as they can. When speaking online, this task is difficult because of where the camera is located. It is common for computer manufacturers to place the webcam at the top of the computer screen, and when interacting or presenting online, we have a tendency to stare at our screen, not at the camera. To audiences watching a speaker online, the speaker will appear to be looking down rather than directly at them. You can create the sense of eye contact in online presentations by looking directly into the camera instead of at your computer screen.

Types of Online Presentations

Online presentations exist in a variety of formats and styles. The biggest dividing line among types concerns whether your presentation is live or prerecorded. Among scholars who research and teach about online environments, live (or real-time) speaking is referred to as **synchronous communication**, and recorded presentations are termed **asynchronous communication**.[5]

Each type can be subdivided into a number of formats, the most common of which are detailed here.

Synchronous Presentations. The most common formats for speaking in real time include streaming video (such as with Skype and videoconferencing) and webinars. Both formats have the advantage of audience

synchronous communication takes place in real time.

asynchronous communication is either written or prerecorded before it reaches an audience.

? **What are the advantages and disadvantages of online speaking?**

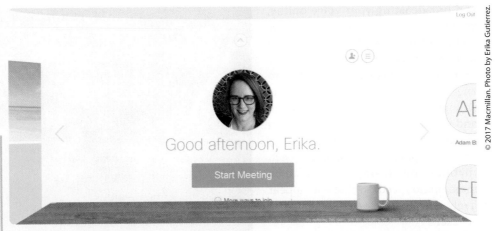

Share Your Desktop Live! Some webinar software allows you to share a live shot of your desktop with others online.

interaction and provide the speaker with more opportunities to adapt to the audience in real time. When using *streaming video*, the speaker typically faces a camera on a computer or a smartphone and addresses an audience elsewhere, either collectively viewing a projection on a screen (such as in a classroom or a boardroom) or individually on other computers or smartphones. With Skype or FaceTime, for example, speakers are usually presented with an image of the audience, as well as a smaller square or box that allows them to see themselves.

Webinars sometimes employ streaming video, but they are more specialized in character: they are real-time meetings that bring together speakers and audiences in deliberately interactive ways. Webinar software, such as Cisco's WebEx, combines multiple ways for speakers and audiences to engage each other, including "chat" or dialogue boxes, the ability to share files, videocasting, and screencasting. **Screencasting** refers to sharing whatever appears on your desktop with others online. For example, when making a presentation online in WebEx, you can screencast a video or even a slide presentation you have created to your audience. Webinars differ from videocasting because they do not have to feature video. During a webinar, for example, an audience might hear your voice while watching a slide presentation.

Asynchronous Presentations. If you've ever watched a YouTube video, you are already familiar with the advantages and limitations of recorded presentations. On the one hand, you will not be able to interact with your audience and thus cannot adjust or adapt to their needs at the moment of playback. On the other hand, you will have the time to carefully prepare your recording, perhaps even redo or edit it to improve its quality.

a **webinar** is a seminar with three or more people conducted over the Internet using software created for this purpose.

a **screencast** refers to a live or recorded broadcast of a speaker's computer desktop to others online.

Using Visual Aids Online

In some online presentations, especially when screencasting, a speaker may use visual aids like graphics or even a slide show. During some screencasts, for example, the speaker is heard but not seen. Instead of seeing the speaker, the audience sees a series of images or slides. In webinars, for example, speakers sometimes deliver a speech while showing the audience a PowerPoint, Keynote, or Prezi slide show. When using images or slide software in an online presentation, use the same principles of composition and content discussed in chapter 11. Before using visual aids online, be sure to research audience expectations and make sure you provide ample screen time for yourself *and* your visual aids.

During what kind of online speaking situations are visual aids helpful? Why? Can you think of any online speaking situations for which visual aids would be a hindrance?

(?) What are the two basic types of online presentations? Which of the two do you think would be most effective?

The most common formats, of course, are *videos*, *podcasts*, and *vodcasts*. A podcast is simply an audio recording that you share with others on the Internet, whereas a vodcast is a podcast that includes images or video clips (not necessarily of the speaker).

On Mediascapes

Owing to quickly evolving communication technologies, various online contexts have emerged that enable us to speak on various pages and screens to small groups or large faceless audiences who share our interests. Anthropologist Arjun Appadurai defines the term *mediascape* to refer to a general context of communication enabled or created by media technologies (akin to a "landscape"). The Internet is a mediascape, but more narrowly, so is the world of podcasts and social networking.[6] A key feature of any mediascape is that its boundaries are blurry and hard to easily distinguish. How you craft an online presentation really depends on the specific mediascape you are working in and its attendant audience.

Mediascapes are dynamic and change with media technology. How has the mediascape of the Internet changed during your lifetime? What are the reasons for this change?

Adapting to the Amorphous Audience

> **You will learn to**
>
> **DEFINE** an amorphous audience.
>
> **EXPLAIN** the relationship between publicity, circulation, and promotion.

Most of the public speaking situations discussed in your public speaking course presume a concrete audience, or at least an audience that you can research ahead of time, analyze, and then compose a speech for based on their predicted identities and characteristics. In many online presentation contexts, especially those for a class at school or for a meeting with workplace colleagues, you may know who your audience is. When developing online presentations for known audiences, most of the principles of audience analysis discussed in chapter 3 are applicable and helpful.

The online environment is a bit different from the traditional F2F speech situation, however. When you upload or post a presentation for your public speaking class, it is likely that only you, your classmates, and your instructor will see it (your instructor should let you know if this is not the case). When you upload a presentation for *anyone* to see, hear, and download, however, you may not know who constitutes your audience. For example, when you upload a video to YouTube or a social networking site, you may not know much about who might be listening or watching. So what do you do? As is the case with known audiences, the tips and principles discussed in the chapter on audience analysis — avoiding stereotyping, making yourself aware of differences, and so on — still apply. When speaking publicly over a broadcast or digital stream to anyone, your audience is **amorphous**, or without discernible shape, size, or form.

an **amorphous** audience is one that you know exists but whose size and demographic information are unknown.

Because of the massive volume of information available to those with access to the Internet, individuals tend to seek out the messages they want to see and hear, forming audiences for those messages. To put it another way, audiences are created by messages because they do not necessarily exist before the messages.[7] Think about it this way: historically, mass communication audiences were thought of as relatively stable because there was a limited number of channels on radio and television and therefore a limited number of messages. Before cable and satellite television and streaming services such as Hulu and Netflix, television audiences were concentrated and could be easily studied, and programming could be developed to address their needs and desires. Today, however, there are so many messages and channels that it makes more sense to think about online audiences as something that a program or message helps to create. When addressing an amorphous audience, the questions you need to ask yourself first include the following: What kind of audience do I want for my message? What audience would I like to create for what I have to say? The answers you develop in response to these and related questions will guide you in crafting your speech or media content.

Because many forms of online presentations are crafted for an amorphous audience, your goals as a speaker (to celebrate, to inform, or to persuade) may also have the *additional* goal of publicity. Generally speaking, **publicity** is the mediated sharing and circulation of a message to promote something—information, ideas, a persuasive message, even yourself. Two concepts are central to publicity: circulation and promotion.

publicity refers to the distribution and circulation of information or a message for promotional purposes.

By "circulation," we refer to the way in which a message is taken up by audiences through repeat listening or viewing: how many views your video receives on YouTube, how many times one of your tweets was retweeted, and so on. Publicity often involves figuring out ways to promote your message that encourage continual circulation, so that your message can be heard by more and more people. A video that has gone "viral," for example, has achieved high circulation, whereas a video that is shared and viewed among only a small group of family and friends has low circulation.

The Possibilities and Perils of Pride

Over the last decade, some scholars have reported a marked rise in feelings of entitlement and an inflated sense of self among different publics, usually dubbed narcissism.[8] The argument is that narcissism is on the rise, not necessarily because of moral shortcomings but because our hypermediated environment is changing how we present ourselves to others.

So named after the Greek myth of Narcissus, a beautiful hunter who fell in love with his reflection and died staring at it, "narcissism" is a psychological concept that references our own perceptions of self-importance. *Strictly speaking, narcissism is necessary: we all need to have some regard for our self-importance.* Even so, while everyone needs narcissism, too much self-regard can blind

Narcissus today.

one to the needs and requests of others, disabling one's sense of response-ability. Narcissism can become a problem for online speakers who seek fame or notoriety at the expense of others or by deliberately doing something embarrassing. Generally speaking, fame seeking and self-promotion should be *secondary* to an audience-centered goal of celebrating, informing, or persuading. The reason fame seeking should take a back seat to other goals is an ethical one: when seeking publicity or trying to promote your ideas, speaking responsibly entails a consideration of, or response to, others, *even your future self.* Failing to consider the welfare of even an imagined amorphous audience will not establish the goodwill necessary for effective communication. And perhaps even more importantly, failing to consider others may lead you to publicize a message that you may later regret, a topic addressed in the discussion of the public/private distinction at the end of the chapter.

Narcissism is a trait all people share. Explain why *some* narcissism is necessary for speaking publicly, online and otherwise.

What is an amorphous audience? How does an online speaker address this kind of audience?

By "promotion," we do not necessarily mean that a speaker pursues publicity for a profit; rather, promotion is primarily about creating an audience for the goals of entertaining, informing, and persuading. Promotion fundamentally concerns bringing an audience into being on the basis of securing their attention; what the audience does after that really depends on your goals and the content of your message.

Because the specific purposes of online presentations vary quite dramatically, how you craft and circulate your message is dependent on what you wish to show, say, or do. Do you want to entertain? Do you want to inform people about an important issue or cause? Do you want to persuade others to your political viewpoint or sell a product? For an online message to be productive—that is, to have an impact on the beliefs, attitudes, values, or behaviors of an audience—the primary goal of publicity needs to be coupled with the speaker's goals.

Conducting Online Presentations

You will learn to

LIST the compositional elements of video presentations.

LIST the three kinds of lighting needed for online videos.

EXPLAIN how a speaker can avoid technological problems.

Setting Up an Online Presentation

Neither this book nor your instructor can provide detailed tips on how to bring an audience into being for networked or online contexts, if only because doing so is dependent on your message and goals. We can, nevertheless, offer some tips to make the content of your message better for speaking online. The first step is to make sure that you and your message can be seen and heard clearly.

Equipment is necessary for an online speech.

One of the most intriguing developments of popular culture in our time is the explosion of digital technologies—computers, smartphones, webcams, and so on—that have made it possible for more and more people to broadcast themselves to audiences big and small. As with any technology, however, when something electronic or digital works, it is also prone to not working. Therefore, you should always have a backup plan for equipment failure, especially if your online presentation will be live.

Making Videos and Podcasts for Amorphous Audiences

- **Remember That You Create the Audience.** Remember that the content of your message brings an audience into being. Always ask yourself, "What audience would I like to see my message?" Your answer to this question can help you in the process of brainstorming.
- **Remember the Importance of Publicity.** Select media channels that are most likely to distribute your message to the audience you wish to call into being. If your speaking context is not online and your audience is known in some way, your goal will be the message itself.
- **Disseminate and Circulate.** Think about the ways in which you can promote viewing or listening to your message: Can you e-mail family and friends a link to your message? Can you post about it on social networking websites? Can you promote your message in chat rooms or on message boards and blogs?

Let us use the video-sharing network YouTube as an example. When speakers post videos of themselves sharing an opinion, reviewing an album or a film, or performing a funny prank, the video quality may be crisp and easy to see, or grainy and out of focus. The better the quality of the video, the more likely a viewer is going to want to watch it. To be an effective online speaker, think about messages that you have enjoyed watching and that were memorable, and aim toward crafting your message with similar qualities. Whatever content you create, it is important to make sure that your message is clear, easy to see and hear, and promoted in a way that engages the audience that you wish to address or cultivate.

The Digital Divide

Although cellular, Internet, and satellite technologies have made it possible for many ordinary people to get themselves seen and heard by large audiences, not everyone has this access. If you're reading this book, you probably have access to the Internet or a smartphone, but it is important to remember that not everyone has access to technology. The "digital divide" is a term that refers to the social or economic inequality of access to information technologies like the Internet. Contrary to common opinion among those who have access to the latest communication technologies, the gap between those who do and those who do not is growing.[9] Individuals who live in poverty or less industrialized societies may not have access to digital resources. When speaking online, one should be mindful and consider all the individuals who are excluded from your message; even if there is little you can do about the divide now, you may be in a position in the future to help close it. How to resolve this divide among the world's populations, based on social and economic inequality, is one of the major challenges of the twenty-first century.

We tend to think of the digital divide in global terms; however, the problem is also local. Where would you locate the divide in the town you live in? What are the reasons for access and lack of access to digital technologies?

Although it is important to know how to use communication technologies (cameras, microphones, and computers), it is just as important to understand the general aesthetic principles of any form of online presentation that depends on video or images. Depending on your message, you may emphasize one of the following principles more than the others.

Compositional elements of online presentations using video

Taking the creation of a video or a live online speech as our default forms of messaging (think, again, of YouTube videos or videoconferencing), make sure to address—or at least think about—the following aesthetic principles when starting out:

- **Lighting:** Whether videoconferencing or making a video to share with friends and family on the Internet, your audience should be able to see you. Most cameras cannot register, or "see," the variations of light and dark that can be seen with the human eye; thus, when filming, you must make sure to be in brighter light than you are normally accustomed to in "real" space. See the feature on page 364 on lighting for more tips.
- **Color:** How elements are colored communicates information, and care should be taken to coordinate your background and wardrobe in a way that is consistent with your message. Think about what certain colors may symbolize to your audience. In addition, some colors are too muted or vivid to capture on camera, so be sure to experiment to determine what colors can be used (white can wash out the screen, for example, and yellow does not tend to show up correctly on computer screens).
- **Composition, movement, and background:** The way in which you present yourself—or your subject, such as a pet or a sculpture—in

Composition and Background. Which of these shots of an online speaker is more pleasing?

the frame of a screen references your video's composition. How you compose the visual field of your message communicates information to your audience. Traditionally, online speakers tend to orient themselves in the center of the screen, which communicates to the audience that they are to pay attention to what the speaker does and says. Closely related to composition is the movement of the camera. When making videos for either live broadcast or for replaying later, you want to make sure the camera is stable and not drifting. If you are using a smartphone, care should be taken to position the camera at eye level, so that your audience is not forced to watch your speech hunched over (or worse, to look up your nostrils!). Finally, consider the background of your video: make sure you are positioned in front of a plain background, or one that is appropriate for the speaking situation (e.g., if academic, a bookshelf). Few audiences are interested in seeing a messy closet or a sink full of dirty dishes behind you!

- **Sound:** In some presentation situations—for example, if your emphasis is on imagery, video, or sign language—you may not want your video to have sound. Most online presentations use audio, however, and require good sound quality. Audiences should be able to *hear* what you are saying if you are speaking, and should be able to discern any soundtrack (music, sound effects, and so on) you intend to be heard. Make sure your microphone or playback device is working correctly, adjusting for volume. Finally, care should be taken to eliminate background noise—from dogs barking and the sloshing of a washing machine, to the clanging of your bracelets and earrings—as microphones are prone to amplify everything. If available, a headset with a microphone may be a good solution for you, because it better enables you to hear your audience—and they you!

Obviously, if your online speech involves sound only, as with a podcast, you would not need to attend to lighting, color, and the composition of the screen. Even so, because the sound of someone's voice does not communicate as much information as it does when combined with facial expressions and body language, how you structure and choose words for your message becomes even more important. Structure and word choice in sound-only messages substitute for things like color and composition, so think about your sound presentations as "word videos" of sorts. A sound-based message will be more memorable to audiences if you choose words that are vivid or evocative of vibrant imagery. In addition, the structure or outline of your message should be emphasized with enumerations and very clear transitions to give listeners a sense of its order in their heads.

tips for do-it-yourself
home video lighting

Y ou do not have to be a professional or be in a studio to achieve good lighting for your own video productions. When using a webcam, tablet, or smartphone, you can manually adjust the brightness setting to control for glare on your eyeglasses or what appears to be strange colors. Aside from adjusting the brightness settings on your devices, however, the trick to good lighting is controlling for shadows. A shadowy video can communicate mystery, and a brightly lit video can communicate vibrancy and excitement. A poorly lit video (too bright or too dark) can communicate incompetence or, worse, that you do not care about the audience enough to help them see you.

Professional photographers and videographers have learned sophisticated ways to communicate mood and information with lighting. The study of lighting begins with "three-point lighting."[10]

Key light: The key light is the main light directed on the subject of a camera. It could be the light in the room or sunlight, but in general, the key light refers to a light aimed directly at a subject.

Back light: The back light refers to the light behind the subject of the camera. The back light helps an audience distinguish between the subject and his or her background.

Fill light: A fill light is typically the light that is between the back and key light, usually beside the

Good lighting is crucial to online video presentations.

subject. We use fill lighting to control the way in which light and shadow are contrasted.

When lighting yourself, another person, or an object for a video project, you might be able to achieve the lighting you want without doing anything (an overcast day often provides perfect lighting for filming outside). You can assemble various lights from your home to create a professional look even without expensive lighting equipment. For example, you could use a desk lamp on the floor for a backlight, a table lamp for the fill, and a friend holding a flashlight for the key light.

Since the invention of photography, lighting techniques have been developed to help capture subjects clearly. Go online to find a video tutorial or how-to guide using the search term "three-point lighting."

After reviewing the video, visit LaunchPad at launchpadworks.com and consider the following questions:

- What is three-point lighting? What are the three points?
- Using lights and lamps you already own, how might you achieve three-point lighting in your living room or bedroom?

Online aesthetics: A checklist

_____ Lighting: Can the audience see me or my subject clearly? Do I have enough lighting for audiences to see me or my subject?

_____ Color: What do the colors on the screen possibly symbolize for my audience? Does the color contribute to or detract from my message? Is it intentional?

_____ Composition: Am I or is my subject in the center of the screen? If not, is there a purpose for being off-center? Is my background pleasing to the eye?

_____ Sound: Can my audience hear my soundtrack or me? Is the volume adjusted appropriately?

Prepare for technology failures

In F2F speaking situations, the worst kind of equipment failure is the loss of your voice. In online contexts, however, you often depend on files (videos, slide shows, audio clips, and so on), software, and various kinds of computing hardware, which increase the possibility of technological failure. When presenting live, or in real time, you have much less control when you lose your Wi-Fi connection or encounter a technological problem. Here are some tips to keep in mind to avoid or minimize technology mishaps:

- **If possible, test your equipment ahead of time:** Before recording or broadcasting yourself live, test and retest your camera, microphone, and any software you intend to use. This can help you troubleshoot before beginning your presentation.
- **Make backups:** Before recording or broadcasting your presentation, duplicate and back up all the files you intend to use, such as videos, slide shows, and audio clips. If you are making a video, podcast, or vodcast recording, back up the file on a zip drive or portable hard drive.
- **Select a reliable Internet connection:** At the time of this writing, a cabled (or "wired") connection (e.g., Ethernet) to the Internet is the most reliable connection for online speaking. If you cannot have a wired connection to the Internet for your online presentation, find the strongest and most reliable Wi-Fi that you can before broadcasting or uploading a presentation.
- **Avoid relying on hyperlinked media:** If using video or audio clips in your online presentation, download them to your device; avoid using hyperlinks to them or relying on someone else's web server or web page. Especially when presenting in real time, dropped signals or Wi-Fi outages can make it impossible for you to rely on presentation elements that are not already on your computer. If you must rely on a hyperlink dependent on an Internet connection, test and retest the link before your presentation, and have the link open and ready to click by the time you begin.

- **Practice your presentation using your technology:** Whether your online presentation will be recorded or live, practice your presentation by running through it at least a couple of times. This will help you identify problems and instances where possible technological failures could happen.

What is the purpose of three-point lighting? Do you typically prepare for equipment failure? If so, how? If not, why not?

Practice, Practice, Practice!

Because online presentations mute some of the information we get from our senses and limit the opportunities to interact with audiences as we speak, they require more practice. Even if your presentation is to be live, record yourself practicing it first to help you identify possible areas of improvement and to anticipate potential technology issues. Remember that online speaking requires more vocal variety and gesturing to compensate for the information that is lost in online environments. Practice leads to polished presentations, and polished presentations are more effective to audiences, whether you know who they are or not.

Tips for Effective Online Presentations

Because online presentations are mediated by cameras, microphones, speakers, and screens, you have to amplify your face-to-face behaviors to engage audiences elsewhere. Keep these tips in mind:

- **Be Energetic!** Remember to vary your pitch, volume, rhythm, and related vocalic elements to bring your presentation to life. Look at the camera from time to time to create the feeling of eye contact. Many online presentations are done from a sitting position, requiring powerful gestures to compensate for the lack of movement.
- **Maintain Your Focus!** Because you're likely at a computer in a familiar setting, it can be easy to become distracted when creating or broadcasting an online presentation. Remove baubles, knickknacks, and pets, and silence your phone — unless of course you are using it to do your online presentation. In that case, be sure to turn off the ringer and enable "do not disturb" mode. Is your fire alarm "chirping"? Replace the battery! Minimize any forms of distraction that you can anticipate to help you maintain your focus.
- **Keep the Audience Engaged!** Online audiences like visual aids, so use them if you can. If the format of your presentation allows, engage the audience by encouraging them to ask questions. If you are using a "chat" feature to interact with your audience, be sure to pause to allow them an opportunity to respond (and to accommodate the inevitable broadcast time delay).

Public or Private? It's Hard to Say

> **You will learn to**
>
> **DESCRIBE** what public means in an online context.

Thus far we have discussed mostly practical considerations for creating, uploading, and broadcasting online presentations. What we have not addressed is a more ethical and philosophical concern that is only going to become more pressing in the future: What is, or what should be, public? One of the most recent, befuddling developments in our time concerns the way in which increasing access to digital technology allows for the mass circulation of messages by everyday people. An uploaded video that you created of your dog begging for his toy, "Mr. Squeaky," might end up being viewed by hundreds, perhaps millions, of strangers. If your video post or tweet starts to trend or "goes viral," it might be read, shared, or retweeted by thousands. The point here is that in our mediated world, you never know who is listening or watching. Online presentations intended for a small group in a closed online platform (e.g., WebEx) could be recorded and distributed to others without your knowledge. When sharing presentations on social networks or video sites, not only is the amorphous audience hard to discern, but there's a good chance that some of the folks included within it are watching you. In other words, we have to modify the old adage to be careful what you wish for: Be careful what you broadcast!

Traditional, face-to-face public speaking often relies on a distinction between what is public, or what is accessible to everyone or members of a particular community, and what is private, or what is assumed to be personal and not subject to widespread circulation. Public speaking assumes that what a speaker shares is open and subject to the scrutiny and consideration of others. The Internet and other digital or cellular contexts, however, constitute a special situation because of the way in which many of us assume a degree of privacy when there may actually be none. Think about it this way: When a person posts a photograph of you that

When broadcasting to an amorphous audience, you never quite know who might be watching!

is unflattering, you may refuse to be "tagged" in the image because you don't like it; however, this image will remain for others to see unless the original poster takes it down. Similarly, if you post a video on YouTube or Vimeo, it is released into the world of the amorphous audience. Even if you elect to remove the video, it may continue to circulate because someone has downloaded it or captured it with video capturing software.

The older or more traditional distinction between public and private is seriously challenged by the contemporary demands to promote and circulate one's ideas in online environments for education, work, politics, and socialization. The consequence of this and similar challenges is that you must be mindful and careful when sharing information and crafting messages for online environments. The age-old adage to "say only what you wish to be repeated" holds triple-fold for online and networked environments. A failure to think about what you share online can result in unintended consequences. Stories abound about people who have lost a job, spouse, or friendship because of something he or she shared online. One day after work a young person expressed reasonable frustration with her job—"I hate my job!"—on her social media page. Weeks later she was fired because the post was circulated outside her friend network, and her employer came to believe she set a bad example for other employees.[11]

Are most online presentations public or private? How do online presentations differ from face-to-face presentations in regard to publics?

Because it is very hard to determine what is public and private in our digital world, it is always best to use caution when creating messages for the Internet or similar contexts. Like a tattoo, *Facebook is forever!* Tattoos can be removed, of course, but not without a lot of pain and perhaps unsightly remainders. Similarly, with a lot of effort, one may be able to erase or remove an online video or message from the Internet, but traces will undoubtedly remain. Even videos made for class projects can circulate among Internet views years after you created them, so think carefully about what you release into the digital world.

In this chapter, we have examined two types of online presentations—synchronous (live) and asynchronous (recorded)—and detailed a number of formats. Because they are filtered through communication technologies, each with its own limitations, online presentations provide you and the audience with less sensory information. Consequently, online speakers must compensate with a vivid delivery style and increased attention to sound and image reproduction. It is also a good idea for online presenters to test their equipment and prepare for possible technology issues before their presentation. Finally, special care must be taken with online presentations because of the potential for them to reach wider audiences than originally intended.

Understanding Online Presentations: Purpose and Type

As online communication becomes increasingly popular, online presentations are increasingly prevalent forms of public speaking.

Adapting to the Amorphous Audience

Most principles of public speaking apply in an online context. For an online speech, speakers must carefully prepare what they are going to say and how they will present the material and themselves.

Conducting Online Presentations

Setting up an online presentation requires gathering the appropriate equipment, planning, and practice.

Public or Private? It's Hard to Say

Care should be taken when uploading or broadcasting an online presentation, as you may have audience members that you have never considered.

 **LaunchPad**
macmillan learning

LaunchPad for *Speech Craft* includes a curated collection of speech videos and encourages self-assessment through adaptive quizzing. Go to **launchpadworks.com** to get access to:

 LearningCurve adaptive quizzes

 Video clips to help you improve your speeches

ACTIVITIES

Quick Video and Review

Your instructor will put you into groups. Together with your group, plan, prepare, and write a short speech of introduction or a toast to a beloved pet or popular woodland creature on campus. Select a speaker from your group, and then, using a smartphone or a laptop, record the speech you prepared. Review the recording with your group, and identify the strengths and weaknesses of the presentation: Is the recording good enough to share online? Why or why not?

Get Your Publicity On!

Whether you are seeking to entertain, inform, or persuade, public speaking in the context of new media often requires an ability to use technology effectively, as well as experience promoting your message in new media environments. In a group assigned by your instructor, use a camera or a smartphone to create a short video on any topic (e.g., advertising a new invention or product, explaining how to do something, or promoting a social or political cause — it does not matter *what* the video is about). Upload the video to a video sharing service like Vimeo or YouTube. Over a period of time set by your instructor, try to publicize and promote your video on the Internet, following any guidelines set by your instructor. The point of this activity is to learn about what works and does not work for garnering publicity and encouraging circulation. After the set period, examine how many "hits" or "views" your video received, then consider the following questions:

- What promotional techniques worked to increase your viewership? What techniques failed?
- Did the content of your video effect how many hits or views your video received? Why or why not?
- Did you use deceptive techniques to promote your video? Why or why not?
- What kind of reaction or comments did your video receive? Did any of these surprise you?

KEY TERMS

 Videos in LaunchPad describe many of these terms. Go to launchpadworks.com.

online presentation 353

synchronous communication 355

asynchronous communication 355

webinar 356

screencast 356

amorphous 358

publicity 359

SPEAKING
FOR SOCIAL CHANGE

CHAPTER 19

I f you asked most people what they thought about public speaking, their answer would typically register in the realm of things that cause them anxiety (snakes, public nudity, a sharp stick in the eye). And if you asked most people about their imagined vision of public speaking as an art, they might respond with a description of a power- ful woman or man, such as a world leader or a CEO, speaking to a large audience. But if you asked most people to identify a speech that they believe is among the most *influential* and important speeches in history, they would likely reference a speech delivered by a civil rights leader, such as Susan B. Anthony's "On Women's Right to Vote" from 1873; Martin Luther King Jr.'s "I Have a Dream Speech" from 1963; or, perhaps more recently, a speech delivered by a politician or activist in support of the Black Lives Matter movement.[1]

In North America, at least, the loftier ideals we harbor about public speaking tend to center on speeches of political advocacy or social protest in the popular imagination. Perhaps this is the reason why speeches of political advocacy and social protest are among the most common we see and hear in the national news media. I have chosen to bring *Speech Craft* to a close by addressing our loftiest ideals as they register in political advocacy and social protest, but not because we must all aspire to such speechmaking — that would be a rather high bar to set. Instead, I close with an examination of this genre of public speaking because the community-centered values that underlie it *underwrite all kinds of public speaking*, bringing the reasons why we study this craft as a whole into their starkest relief. To this end, we will examine three dimensions of political advocacy and social pro- test: (1) it is usually a *group* effort, rather than an individual one; (2) it is not lim- ited to "the street" but takes place over (sound) speakers and screens (including "new media"); and (3) it often *violates* cultural norms and conventions.

Public Speaking and Social Movements

For many people, the most memorable speeches about our country or a particular community are those that evoke deep emotions or buck the status quo in favor of massive social, legal, or political change. For these reasons, we should not be surprised that public speaking teachers in the United States have identified Martin Luther King Jr.'s "I Have a Dream" speech as the most important, eloquent, and influential speech of the twentieth century.[2] King delivered his speech arguing for racial equality

Rosa Parks's refusal to give up her seat to a white passenger on a bus in 1955 is one of many events that inspired the civil rights movement, which led to dramatic cultural and legal changes in the United States.

and spiritual unity on August 28, 1963, on the steps of the Lincoln Memorial during the Great March on Washington, which was one of the largest rallies for human rights in the history of the United States (estimates range from 200,000 to 300,000 people). Unquestionably, "I Have a Dream" is one of the most moving, genre-busting speeches *of all time*—celebratory, informative, and persuasive all at once. King's landmark speech sets just about the highest bar for advocacy speaking that one can imagine.

As much a product of the speech itself and the charisma of the speaker as it is the context of its delivery, King's speech is hard to use as a measure for our own speechmaking. We reference King's monumental speech as the embodiment of the loftiest ideals we have for speaking: a value and concern for the community, a celebration of the community, and an attempt to urge social change for the betterment of the community.

Whether a speech of political advocacy or social protest is delivered by King on the National Mall or by a local activist on the steps of your state capitol, it is often described as participating in the rhetoric or discourse of social movements. Although there is no scholarly consensus about how to define a **social movement**, many communication scholars characterize a social movement as a group (or collective) of like-minded individuals who promote a particular cause, politics, or ideology.[3] The civil rights movement in the United States is a familiar example, which is often said to have begun with the refusal of a number of activists, most famously Rosa Parks, to sit in the back of buses during the era of racial segregation.[4]

Other famous examples of social movements include the women's rights movement; the widespread, counterculture protests against the wars in Vietnam, Iraq, and more recently Afghanistan; and contemporary movements, such as that of the Tea Party and Occupy Wall Street. As social movement scholar Herbert W. Simons points out, social movements are often characterized as "outside the mainstream" or "*uninstitutionalized*."[5] Finally, a social movement is characterized by the promotion of social and political change over a long period, meaning that the speeches given as part of a social movement are not localized to one person but often to many speakers. Political advocacy and social protest speeches are not dependent on a single speaker and do not obey

a **social movement** refers to a group (or collective) of like-minded individuals who promote a particular cause, politics, or ideology.

Characteristics of Social Movements

- Group (or collective) driven; community oriented
- Promote a nonmainstream cause, politics, or ideology
- Not institutionalized
- Consist of many activists, speakers, and leaders
- Push for social or political change

commonly recognized rules, norms, or laws. Indeed, social protest and political advocacy often concerns a push to change law, policy, or convention by a group of like-minded, like-feeling people who are not considered part of an established or well-recognized institution.

On Genre Hybridity and Personal Commitment

Over the course of writing *Speech Craft*, I have tried to stress that the most personally meaningful speeches are those delivered to and among friends and family. As a result, I have argued that celebratory or special-occasion speaking is the foundation of the other speech genres. When we think about our communities or country, the speeches most lauded and remembered are those that commemorate a moment, celebrate a community, and inspire social change, which are in some sense also celebratory in character.

Speaking for political advocacy and social change is different, however, because it tends to be less intimate and more formal, and speakers often pursue persuasive goals in addition to celebrating a community. *Speaking for political advocacy and social protest, in other words, is a hybrid genre, combining the goals of celebratory speaking with the functions of persuasive speaking.* One reason for this hybridity is the deeply personal investments people make in social movements that are ultimately about a collective or even society as a whole. For this reason, speeches of advocacy should be understood in a much different way than more traditional celebratory or persuasive speeches. Almost all speeches of political advocacy and social protest are given in a moment of

Social Activism with a Bullhorn! Communication scholar Dana Cloud leads a protest in downtown Austin, Texas.

contingency, when change could go any number of unpredictable ways, or at least when things could truly be otherwise. In this respect, political advocacy and social protest speaking combines the celebratory focus on the present moment with the future-oriented aims of persuasion: the speaker celebrates communal bonds in pursuit of change in the face of an uncertain future.

> The speaker celebrates communal bonds in pursuit of change in the face of an uncertain future.

What is social protest and political advocacy? What forms can it take? How is it related to social movements?

New Media and the Publicness of Social Movements

One reason to study social protest and political advocacy as the last form of public speaking is that it doesn't necessarily have to be public, nor is advocacy limited to speeches. For example, beginning in late 2010, a series of social and political revolutions began in the Arab world that has come to be known as the Arab Spring. Collectively composed of a series of demonstrations, protests, riots, and wars, the Arab Spring resulted in the ousting of a number of political leaders in Egypt, Libya, and Yemen, among others, by 2013.

Because it was multinational in scope, analysis of the Arab Spring is exceedingly complex; but at the time of this writing, many scholars were puzzling over how *social media*—namely, Twitter and Facebook—helped generate social change for numerous advocacy groups, allowing them

Peter Macdiarmid/Getty Images

In 2011, protesters gathered in Tahrir Square in Cairo, hastening a democratic revolution that led to the resignation of Egyptian president Hosni Mubarak.

to organize and mobilize thousands upon thousands of people and distribute messages advocating change.

Scholars of social movements have noticed relationships between the Arab Spring and the Occupy Wall Street and Tea Party movements, as all of them appear to have relied heavily on media spectacles and social networking for making their causes visible to larger publics and political leaders. News media coverage of these very different movements even led *Time* magazine to declare "the Protester" as its annual Person of the Year in 2011.[6] Clearly we are living in a time when social protest and political advocacy are no longer limited to demonstrations in public streets or squares, as advocacy has globalized—however paradoxically—on our computers and television screens as well.[7] Unlike social movements of the past, the social movements of our time often entwine what happens on the street with what happens on the screen. Regardless, public speaking is implicated on every level and on every medium.

Closely related to the new media dimension of social protest and political advocacy is widespread observation that social movements rely as much on private contexts as they do on public ones. In her study of the women's liberation movement, Karlyn Kohrs Campbell argues that

The Feminists of Color Collective Group meets weekly in New York City.

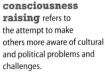

> Karlyn Kohrs Campbell argues that feminist advocacy cannot be understood in relation to an emergent leader, as cultural and political advocacy often depend on "meetings of small, leaderless groups in which each person is encouraged to express her personal feelings and experience."

feminist advocacy cannot be understood in relation to an emergent leader, as cultural and political advocacy often depend on "meetings of small, leaderless groups in which each person is encouraged to express her personal feelings and experience." Such small meetings raise awareness, termed "**consciousness raising**," which in turn makes public advocacy possible.[8]

Assessing speaking in non- or quasi-public contexts—from living rooms to chat rooms—is difficult, because what is said in private groups to cultivate understanding and the feelings of common cause are not open to the public record. A larger public may be made aware of a given social or political cause because of an influential leader or speaker, but a very large part of advocacy is the organization and mobilization that takes place in private. In these more intimate contexts, the guidelines for small group discussion in the workplace (chapter 17) often apply.

To add to the complexity of social movement advocacy, it is sometimes the case that very different groups of people can come together to advocate for a common social or political cause despite apparent differences. Historically, for example, many of those fighting for an end to slavery were also fighting for women's rights, and vice versa. As social movement scholar Karma R. Chávez has argued, many successful forms of social and political advocacy involve coalitions forged "behind the scenes" or in protected "enclaves," where advocates feel safe to share and express their views and experiences.[9]

A **coalition** is an alliance or a temporary grouping of people for the purpose of collective social or political advocacy. As Chávez has shown, in many contexts groups desiring or advocating related but different causes will temporarily come together—such as labor unions and political parties, or queer activists and groups struggling for migrant rights—to fight for the same policy change. In short, when we examine speaking for advocacy or social movements—public, private, and everything in between—we see that social change is as much a product of behind-the-scenes coalition building and consciousness raising as it is a result of public speeches made on a screen or in the streets. How to apply the principles of public speaking to private (living rooms, meeting rooms), public (television, the Internet), and in-between (social networks,

consciousness raising refers to the attempt to make others more aware of cultural and political problems and challenges.

a **coalition** is a temporary grouping of people for the purpose of collective social or political advocacy.

text messaging, even a classroom) spaces and places really depends on your group, what you are advocating, and what you wish to achieve.

Civic Engagement: To Obey or Not to Obey

A third reason we are addressing speaking for political and social advocacy in the last chapter of *Speech Craft* is the complex concept of civic engagement at its center. **Civic engagement** can be both law abiding and law challenging, even law breaking. In general, speeches of social and political advocacy engage a citizenry or a people who identify with one another as members of an organized social and political system of some sort, such as a community, a neighborhood, a city, a state, a nation—even the globe! In democratic societies, civic engagement is often thought about in terms of voting, participating in the "political process," deliberating on important policy issues and laws, rallying, protesting, or otherwise vocally supporting or listening to a diversity of perspectives and views. These forms of engagement, often discussed in social studies and civics classes in high school, are only one part of civic engagement. Another part concerns **social agitation**, a deliberate violation of the sanctioned norms of social or political culture.[10]

In recent decades, a number of political commentators and civics scholars have bemoaned a decline in civic engagement in terms of decreasing numbers of voters.[11] Other scholars have linked a decline in voting behavior or a general willingness to participate in official political processes to a larger cultural erosion of civility. **Civility** has many meanings, but the most common understanding of civility refers to speech or behavior that is seen as polite, courteous, or appropriate to a given social or public situation: raising one's hand to speak; taking turns when speaking; affording other speakers, especially those with whom you disagree, a degree of respect; and so on. Other scholars, such as Thomas Benson, have argued that some "public behavior . . . is not necessarily . . . courteous and considerate, and consequently it is difficult to maintain that civic engagement is or *should be* 'polite.'"[12] It's hard to argue that when Rosa Parks protested inhumane segregation laws by refusing to give up her bus seat to a white passenger on December 1, 1955, in Montgomery, Alabama, she was not performing civility. Similarly, we would be hard-pressed to maintain that the confrontational signs and speeches used at political rallies are "uncivil." Similar to what they say about beauty and obscenity, what appears to be civil and uncivil speech depends on which side of an issue you are on.

When we think about political or social advocacy as a form of civic engagement, then, we have to think outside of a box that is sometimes too simplistically reduced to a voting box. Engaging through advocacy can mean following the rules, but it can also mean breaking them. This is yet another reason why we have to be careful when discussing public speaking in a context of advocacy.

civic engagement is the manner in which citizens participate in the political or social processes and governance of a given community.

social agitation refers to the deliberate violation of widely accepted or sanctioned norms of a social or political culture.

civility refers to speech or behavior that is seen as polite, courteous, or appropriate to a given social or public situation.

To Be Civil or Uncivil? That Is the Question!

After reviewing textbooks and research on public speaking and composition, communication studies scholar Craig Rood has suggested that civic engagement researchers tend to argue for two competing approaches to civility: an *invitational* approach and a *confrontational* approach. The *invitationalists* argue that because we "do not always know what is best for others," it is better to be polite and courteous and observe the norms of a given culture and context of discussion because it reduces the potential for suffering and possible violence. The *confrontationalists* counter by arguing that the civil norms of politeness and courtesy assume equality — social, political, and economic — and that "people might need to be uncivil if they hope to attract the attention of those in power."[13]

Against taking either side, Rood suggests that those seeking civil engagement with others adopt a radically contextualized stance, deciding when to be invitational or confrontational depending on the moment. He terms this stance *situational civility*: "While the baseline version of rhetorical civility [courtesy, politeness] can function as a norm, the precise meaning, degree, and fittingness of civility must be considered within the messier contexts of unique rhetorical situations. The medium, topic, context, and [speakers] — including their histories and goals — all affect the type of communication that is desirable, possible, and ethical."[14]

In what kind of speaking situation is an invitational speech best suited? In what kind of speaking situation is a confrontational speech appropriate?

Civil Obedience and Civil Disobedience

You will learn to

DEFINE "civil disobedience" and explain its purpose.

EXPLAIN the difference between a rally and a protest.

Rather than focus on what is and is not civil, perhaps a more helpful way to take up the complexities of civil engagement is in reference to obedience, or the degree to which an advocate or activist of a political or social cause complies with existing norms or laws. There are myriad forms obedient speech can take, from platform speaking or speaking at rallies (political, but also music venues — think about Woodstock or Coachella), to speaking for or against an issue in front of a small group or a large crowd, to participating in large-scale protests and marches.

In most democratic societies, civilly obedient forms of speech are permitted, even encouraged. The most visible types of social and political advocacy are rallies and protests, which often get featured in mainstream news programs—both online and on television. A rally is simply a meeting of people to support a social or political cause, whether it's the success (or future success) of a sports team or the campaign of a political party or candidate. A protest can also be a rally; however, a protest is typified by its opposition or objection to something, be it a cause, a person, a policy, or even an idea.

Whether a rally or a protest (or both), there are two basic goals of each: (1) to publicize one's cause, gathering, and message; and (2) to motivate and find common cause among the like minded and like feeling. The goal of a rally or a protest is to bring a community together and, if one is seeking wider publicity for an issue, to draw media attention (e.g., newspaper or television coverage). Because protests and rallies are held for and among those who have common interests and investments, they are more properly considered special occasion or celebratory events, and only secondarily persuasive events. Consequently, the techniques and tips discussed in chapter 13 on celebratory speaking apply more directly to social and political advocacy than do the techniques of persuasion. As St. Augustine noted of preaching over a thousand years ago, rallies and protests are for preaching to the converted. What Augustine could not have predicted, of course, is that rallies and protests are also about getting outside media attention.

Most forms of advocacy are nonviolent, peaceful, and law abiding; however, there are also rallies, protests, and other forms of advocacy that are consciously designed to violate norms and laws. Often associated with forms of nonviolent resistance, **civil disobedience** refers to a refusal to comply with the norms, demands, or laws of a given group or government. American writer and critic Henry David Thoreau famously advocated civil disobedience in his 1849 lecture *Resistance to Civil Government*, in which he argues that it was the responsibility of citizens to oppose morally abhorrent injustices (such as slavery) through nonviolent means, such as refusing to pay taxes that went to support immoral causes. Because he believed that democratic governments are created by human beings, Thoreau argued that there is always some possibility that governments can be reasoned with, but—and this is a big but—it may entail seeking attention though civil disobedience. Mahatma Gandhi—a leader of the movement to end the British rule and control of India in the 1930s and 1940s, as well as numerous attempts to challenge the rigid caste system in India—cited Thoreau as an inspiration for his nonviolent disobedience, which involved leading massive marches, sit-ins, and boycotts. Rosa Parks's refusal to give up her bus seat in protest of local laws was an act of civil disobedience that drew national attention to the larger social and political movement to end segregation.

In a community, state, or country in which people are permitted to speak their minds and express their views, civil obedience is usually an effective way to garner support and work toward change, whether social,

civil disobedience is a refusal to comply with the norms, demands, or laws of a group or government for the purpose of social change.

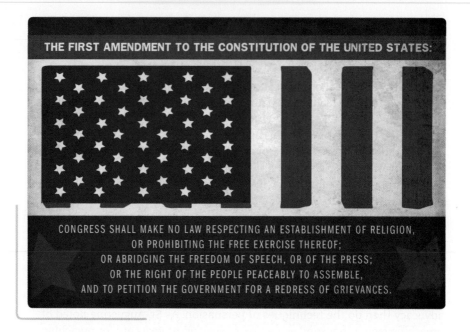

THE FIRST AMENDMENT TO THE CONSTITUTION OF THE UNITED STATES:

CONGRESS SHALL MAKE NO LAW RESPECTING AN ESTABLISHMENT OF RELIGION,
OR PROHIBITING THE FREE EXERCISE THEREOF;
OR ABRIDGING THE FREEDOM OF SPEECH, OR OF THE PRESS;
OR THE RIGHT OF THE PEOPLE PEACEABLY TO ASSEMBLE,
AND TO PETITION THE GOVERNMENT FOR A REDRESS OF GRIEVANCES.

political, or otherwise. Parades and rallies, speeches, even groups of people marching down a public street, are usually compliant with local, state, and national laws, especially in the United States, in which *the First Amendment* to the Constitution—the very first one!—affords citizens the right to freedom of speech and assembly. For larger gatherings, a group or a group's leaders may need to apply for a permit or license to speak or gather on public grounds; the usual stated reason for why such permits or licenses exist is to protect the rights of the freedom of speech and assembly "for everyone." Martin Luther King Jr.'s "I Have a Dream" speech was delivered during a massive rally in Washington, D.C., for which its leaders worked with government officials—actually, directly with U.S. president John F. Kennedy—to secure permission and government support and prepare the city for an influx of hundreds of thousands of activists.

Although civil disobedience has been successful, there is no question that civil disobedience has also been a profoundly important rhetorical strategy used by social and political leaders in the histories of many countries, especially the United States. A group may assemble spontaneously, or one might even participate in a rally or march that is in violation of local or state laws. If you are engaged in a political or social movement for change, you may be part of a community that chooses disobedience as a way to draw attention to an issue that you consider problematic. To this end, there are many forms civil disobedience might take:

- **Using Forbidden Speech:** Saying or doing things that are not allowed or illegal, such as using profanity on regulated broadcasting networks or interrupting a speaker during a lecture.

Civil rights leaders meet with President John F. Kennedy and Vice President Lyndon Johnson about the March on Washington in 1963.

- **Boycotts and Tax Refusals:** Actively refusing to participate or engage in a compulsory practice; refusing to buy or pay for a product or service; or avoiding fees, fines, or taxes levied against one's person or group. Draft dodging was a historically important form of civil disobedience during the U.S. war in Vietnam.
- **Hacking and Data Leaks:** Releasing classified or private information to the public, disclosing proprietary documents or computer data, exposing government or trade secrets, and so on. For example, the American computer administrator Edward Snowden famously leaked documents from the National Security Agency, which revealed a number of controversial U.S.-sponsored surveillance programs.
- **Sit-Ins:** A group of individuals plant their bodies (sitting, of course, but also standing, lying, or even camping) in a physical location until removed, forcibly or otherwise. Sit-ins were a common nonviolent strategy used during the civil rights movement and remain one of the most visible and widely used forms of civil disobedience today.

Unlike norm- or law-sanctioned forms of activism, choosing civil disobedience as a strategy of political or social advocacy can be risky, even dangerous. When engaging in any form of public advocacy, it is important to think about possible consequences and to prepare for them.

Whether legal or illegal, obedient or disobedient, activism almost always entails a risk. Advocating social or political change is risky *because no one can predict the future*; consequently, when you advocate for change, you are typically asking for or demanding a reality that has never existed before. Advocacy in whatever form also entails a risk because, inevitably, you are pushing for a social or political change that someone else does not want. Thus, you are engaging in a confrontation or exposing a conflict, and as we noted in the chapter on workplace speaking (chapter 17), very few of us are trained to embrace, understand, or manage conflict in a productive way.[15]

Public Activism as Civic Engagement

Cultural and political activism often takes the form of public demonstrations and protests, and such events almost always entail a variety of forms of public speaking, from collective chants and rally cries to more formal speeches of motivation and consciousness raising. Dr. Bryan McCann is an organizer and activist for a number of social justice causes, including prison reform, abolishing the death penalty, and labor issues. He is also a communication studies professor at the Louisiana State University in Baton Rouge. McCann's academic research informs and is informed by his community organizing and activism. He reports that working for social and political change is not only difficult and time consuming: surprisingly and perhaps unexpectedly to many, he is careful to observe that activism, especially forms of civil disobedience, can be boring! Too many of those who are moved to join a social movement or organization romanticize involvement in ways that reflect television news reporting and Hollywood films. In reality, he says, working for social or political change involves "pushing paper" and requires tedious, often grueling, work behind the scenes — and the patience to wait for something to happen.

McCann's bits of advice for activism in general, and civil disobedience in particular, are as follows:

1. **Most of the work is behind the scenes.** Much of what you will do as an activist is uneventful and relies on small group communication in quasi-public settings. McCann says that working with a social movement often "involves meetings, literature tables, recruiting, fundraising, making posters, and so on. The public only sees the big rallies or public education panels you help to orchestrate." The public will not see most

Bryan J. McCann

Activist-scholar Bryan McCann at an anti–death penalty demonstration in Houston, Texas.

of the work you will do as an activist or advocate, he says; what they *will* remember are the speeches activists give at rallies.

2. **Activism is primarily for the insider.** Understand that the audience for your social or political advocacy is rarely and certainly not primarily the average citizen. Social movements exist because the ideas they advance and promote are not mainstream. For this reason, in the early stages of social advocacy, your job is to find or recruit folks who are already on your side; rarely do activists try to engage or convince those opposed to their side of an issue, at least at the beginning or early stages of social and political advocacy. "Preaching to the choir is [especially] essential if the singers never show up to the practice," quips McCann. In other words, most of the speaking you do as an activist is aimed primarily at like-minded group members and secondarily at the mass media (in the hopes of coverage).

3. **Stay motivated.** Staying motivated and keeping in touch with the joy and passion that originally attracted you to your cause is essential. This is where public speaking—either internal to the group or at public events—is crucial, in order to continue to motivate the group and reinforce its commitment.

4. **Vary your strategies of public engagement.** Before the arrival of digital media and social networking, activists had to rely on word of mouth, canvassing, posters, and, if they were lucky, coverage in a broadcast news story. Today, however, social media allows for the massive and speedy distribution of information; use those channels! While the resources of the Internet are tremendously useful, however, they should not lead one to forget how important and influential face-to-face communication can be. Organizing and activism still require pressing the flesh, the default condition of public speaking.

5. **Learn how to talk to news media.** Practice how you should speak to reporters, journalists, and others who may distribute your message. Study the principles of public speaking and use them! A very short message with succinct language is more likely to be featured in a broadcast on television or an Internet media report.

6. **Violate norms sparingly.** Use the techniques of civil disobedience carefully and sparingly: breaking rules, norms, and laws to get attention from the mass media or those who have the power to effect change is a form of speech, but it is effective only if it achieves the goals of the group. Breaking the law simply for excitement or romantic fantasy is self-centered and loses sight of the purpose of advocating for social or political change.

arresting developments
protesting and the police

Forms of social and political activism that involve protests and demonstrations may invite the attention of legal authorities, such as the police. Depending on the size of the protest, the issue of concern, and the place in which it occurs, police may and certainly can intervene. It is even more likely that police will intervene if the protest involves expressions of civil disobedience, such as sit-ins or human blockades. Activists and protesters can be arrested and taken into custody when laws are violated, but arrests do occur even when there is only the perception of a legal violation or a perceived threat of possible harm. Advocacy that involves lively demonstrations and protests often invites police involvement and arrests. If you participate in a social protest that may invite arrest, you should be aware of the complexities of the law and your rights.

LaunchPad
macmillan learning

Learn more about your rights as a social activist and protester in the United States, as well as tips for avoiding arrest and what to do if you are arrested, by visiting LaunchPad at **launchpadworks.com** to read "Arresting Speech."

Consider the following questions:

- What are the reasons to avoid a request to be searched at a protest?

- What is the Miranda rule, and why should you know it?

- Why should you avoid speaking to law enforcement at a rally? If you do speak to the police, what can you say?

- What things can you do to protect yourself if you anticipate an arrest at a protest?

When speaking out in favor of or against a given social or political issue, you should always try to anticipate possible consequences. Ideally, the consequences that most social movement groups desire is a renewed sense of cohesion and **solidarity**—a sense of united agreement and mutual feeling among the group—and perhaps some attention from the mass media and those who are in power to effect social or political change, including authorities, politicians, policy makers, and voters. Even so, any review of the history of social or political activism in the West quickly reveals that speaking out for or against a political or social issue, however obedient or disobedient you are, can result in aggression from those who disagree, legal conscription or arrest, and even violence.

solidarity is a feeling of agreement or unity in a community about a belief, a cause, an event, or a proposed action.

Speech, Not Swords: The Humane Alternative of Public Speaking

> **You will learn to**
>
> **EXPLAIN** the relationship between the study of public speaking and violence.

It is at the closing juncture of this book, and deliberately in the context of political advocacy and social protest, that we can finally embrace why public speaking was developed as a craft thousands of years ago: our ancestors dreamed of an end to aggression—to an end to war—by substituting words for weapons. As an art form that has been developed and studied for thousands of years, oratory has been seen as a way to negotiate differences among people, substituting violence with arguments. The author of this textbook shares this dream, even though history teaches us it is not always realized; the reasoning behind the First Amendment of the U.S. Constitution, however, expresses this dream nevertheless. We study public speaking because we have a commitment to keeping this dream alive, whether it is realized by bringing your family and friends together, by negotiating a disagreement in the workplace, or by fighting for social change as part of a social movement.

violence is the use of physical or psychological force to injure, harm, or alter something or someone in order to cause or stop change.

As we noted in chapter 1, the art of public speaking emerged with the advent of democracy, a form of government that seeks to replace physical violence with the contest and collaboration of voices, seeking deliberation instead of war. Broadly speaking, **violence** is the use of physical or psychological force to injure, harm, or alter something or someone in order to cause or stop change. In general, most of us want *to avoid violence* because it can

During an anti-Vietnam protest march to the Pentagon, photographer Bernie Boston captured the image of George Edgerly Harris III putting a carnation into the barrel of a gun held by a National Guardsman.

Everett Collection Inc./Alamy Stock Photo

cause harm to others and ourselves. As a general moral principle, most cultures across the globe teach us that violence is to be avoided. Avoiding violence, especially in the context of complex social or political issues about which people on all sides feel passionately, is often more easily said than done. Although many of those involved in civil rights movements in the twentieth century practiced nonviolent forms of protest and activism, there are countless stories of people who were severely injured or killed for marching, protesting, and staging sit-ins and boycotts. If anything, the history of civil rights movements is a history of brutality, for which the assassinations of Indira Gandhi, Bobby Kennedy, Martin Luther King Jr., Abraham Lincoln, and too many others are well-known examples of the murderous rage against those fighting for social, political, and legal equality. From the 1969 Stonewall riots that galvanized the LGBTQ community into a civil rights movement, to the violent, state-sponsored oppression of Syrian citizens during the Arab Spring uprisings, the most serious social and political struggles in history are frequently, and sadly, marked by violence.

Although there is a valid sense in which we can speak of violence "metaphorically" through speech—for example, a verbal argument can be violent because it dismantles an opposing viewpoint—the craft of public speaking as it has been practiced and taught for centuries has been promoted as a substitute for violence; a sense of "care" or "caring" is connoted by the term "craft." Again, it bears repeating that the study of oratory and public speaking has rarely flourished outside of a democracy, if only because those who would celebrate, inform, and persuade others are simply not allowed to do so. Speech changes hearts and minds; thus, as the ancient Greeks observed, it can be perceived as a powerful threat to those in power.

Rhetorician and theorist Kenneth Burke dedicated one of his books on speech and persuasion with a Latin phrase, *ad bellum purificandum*, which translates as "toward the purification of war." What Burke seems to suggest with this phrase, which carries the contradictory nouns "purification" and "war," is that the study and use of speech can reduce or help to avoid violence, and perhaps that the use of argument can replace weapons. Certainly you would not be taking a course in public speaking if centuries of speaking had not met this goal with some success. Ultimately, we study public speaking and the art of building community, informing others, and persuading others because we seek to avoid hurting other people. We study public speaking because we have achieved a society and culture in which speech is prized above the use of force. We study public speaking because we are free to do so, which is indeed something to celebrate. Or to say the same thing in a different way, and as we have encountered over and over again through the course of this book, *we study public speaking for love.*

Chuck Fishman/Getty Images

Speaking for Social Change

Although it is the least likely kind of public speaking most of us will do, speaking for social protest and political advocacy are often thought of as embodying the loftiest ideas of democracy.

Bryan J. McCann

Public Speaking and Social Movements

Speeches of social protest and political advocacy are usually associated with social movements, or collectives of like-minded individuals who promote a cause, politics, or ideology that is not "mainstream." Today, social movements include both on-the-ground as well as mediated (online) advocacy and organizing.

Civil Obedience and Civil Disobedience

Political advocacy and social protest speaking are forms of civil engagement. Such engagement can be "obedient" or "disobedient," both of which have been historically effective.

Everett Collection Inc./Alamy Stock Photo

Speech, Not Swords: The Humane Alternative of Public Speaking

We study and practice public speaking for love.

 **LaunchPad**
macmillan learning

LaunchPad for *Speech Craft* includes a curated collection of speech videos and encourages self-assessment through adaptive quizzing. Go to **launchpadworks.com** to get access to:

✓ LearningCurve adaptive quizzes

 Video clips to help you improve your speeches

ACTIVITY

Movement Speech and Social Change

Think of a social movement that you find interesting, whether or not you believe with the political or social changes it advocates. Research speeches related to the movement and make a list of the speakers and the context for their speeches. Then answer the following questions:

1. Do the speeches stress the movement or the speaker? How do you know?
2. Did the movement result in social change? If so, in what ways? If not, how do you account for the failure to catalyze change?
3. Is the social movement still thriving, or has it passed? How do you know?

KEY TERMS

 Videos in LaunchPad describe many of these terms. Go to launchpadworks.com.

 social movement 374
consciousness raising 378
coalition 378
civic engagement 379
social agitation 379

civility 379
civil disobedience 381
solidarity 387
violence 387

SAMPLE ANNOTATED SPEECHES

STATEMENT OF SENATOR JETON ANJAIN
OF RONGELAP ATOLL BEFORE
THE FOURTH COMMITTEE OF THE UNITED NATIONS

OCTOBER 30, 1985
PAGE 392

COMMENCEMENT SPEECH
AT WELLESLEY HIGH SCHOOL
BY DAVID MCCULLOUGH, JR.

JUNE 1, 2012
PAGE 398

APPENDIX

SAMPLE ANNOTATED PERSUASIVE SPEECH

Senator Jeton Anjain of Rongelap Atoll

Right Livelihood Award Foundation

Rongelap Atoll is a collection of sixty-one islands, roughly eight square miles, that is part of the Marshall Islands in the Pacific Ocean. It is close to the neighboring Bikini Atoll, where the U.S. government tested numerous atomic weapons in the 1940s and 1950s (for example, the "Operation Crossroads" and the "Castle Bravo" tests). The tests caused widespread radioactive contamination in the Marshall Islands. Although in 1957 the United States claimed the area was "clean and safe," the resettled residents of the Rongelap Atoll developed cancer; children died. The magistrate Jeton ("John") Anjain appealed for help from the United States and the United Nations, but did not receive it. Below is a copy of a speech Anjain delivered to the United Nations in 1985 in which he appealed for help. Anjain's persistence eventually led to the evacuation of the island with the assistance of Greenpeace. The U.S. government later agreed to conduct a health and radiation survey. The speech is a masterful use of appeals to reason and to emotion, and is demonstrative of the motivated sequence.

The author thanks Karlyn Kohrs Campbell of the Department of Communication Studies at the University of Minnesota for this example.

> This is a formal opening of gratitude, which befits the dignity of the event of speaking before the United Nations.

> In this short paragraph, Anjain establishes his credibility by explaining who he is and why he is speaking. This is a straightforward appeal to ethos. Notably, the last sentence also helps to establish goodwill: he devotes all of his "time and energy" to helping his people.

Statement of Senator Jeton Anjain of Rongelap Atoll before the Fourth Committee of the United Nations, October 30, 1985

Mr. Chairman and distinguished delegates,

I greatly appreciate this opportunity to address the Fourth Committee of the United Nations, and I wish to congratulate the new chairman on his recent election.

My name is Jeton Anjain and I am the senator from Rongelap Atoll in the Marshall Islands in Micronesia. Having been trained as a dentist, I practiced dentistry for twenty-five years in the Marshall Islands, and in 1982 I was appointed as the Minister of Health for the Marshall Islands. I now serve as senator for my people on Rongelap and devote all of my time and energy to that task.

At the end of World War II, the United States took control of the more than two thousand islands that make up the island group called Micronesia in the central Pacific Ocean. In 1947, Micronesia became a territory of the United States under the United Nations trusteeship system, and of the eleven trust territories created after the Second World War, it was the only one designated as a "strategic trust." Under Article VI of the trusteeship agreement, the United States made a promise to the international community that it would "protect the inhabitants against the loss of their lands and resources," and that it would "protect the health of the inhabitants" of the trust territory.

In July of 1946, the United States selected Bikini Atoll as the site to explode two atomic bombs in an experiment known as "Operation Cross-roads." It should be pointed out that the "Able" and "Baker" atomic bombs of "Operation Crossroads" were detonated the year before the signing of the 1947 trust agreement, and we now view that fact of history as evidence of how the United States would administer its "trust" in the Pacific. Under a United Nations trust agreement, the United States exploded sixty-six atomic and hydrogen bombs in our islands, and even as I speak to you today, my people are continuing to suffer from the radioactive legacy of these barbaric nuclear weapons tests. In my traditional language there is no word for "enemy," but yet, we now consider it an act of war that the United States came to our islands for only one purpose: to explode nuclear weapons in the name of United States national security.

In the early hours of a still day on March 1, 1954, a bright flash of light streaked across the morning sky. Several of my people on Rongelap were confused, as they thought they saw the light coming from the west instead of a normal sunrise in the east. Minutes later, several loud sounds, like claps of thunder, pierced the morning air. A little while later, the bright morning sky turned grey, and a gritty ash fell out of the sky and covered our island. Little did we know then that our lives would be forever changed by that gritty ash that fell out of the sky thirty-one years ago. And little did my people know that we were the world's first victims of radioactive fallout from a hydrogen bomb.

After several days, my people—and the people of Utirik several hundred miles away—were evacuated to Kwajalein Atoll to the south of Rongelap. The people began to feel very sick and weak, and many began to have burns on their bodies. Hair began falling out of their heads, and the United States doctors told us that their blood counts went below fifty percent the normal level. Many people thought that they were going to die from this new sickness, and in fact, we have been slowly dying ever since that tragic day in 1954.

Here the first element of the motivated sequence begins: Ajain gains the attention of his audience by explaining the relevance of the U.S. government's promises to the international community, represented by the United Nations. This paragraph also doubles as a preview of the problem that needs to be addressed: a broken promise to the people of Micronesia.

Anjain introduces the problem step of the motivated sequence in plain language.

This is a bold statement sure to get the attention of Anjain's international audience.

The imagery of "two suns" here is vivid. The description of the ash also creates a powerful mental image.

Anjain repeatedly mentions the ignorance of his people, underscoring their innocence.

Anjain starkly describes the problem that needs to be addressed: his people are dying because of nuclear contamination.

Mysteriously, most of the pregnant women at the time either had miscarriages, or else gave birth to creatures that did not resemble human beings. After thirty-one years, the women of Rongelap continue to have these problems with reproduction, and we believe that lingering radiation is the cause of this. Because our home islands were so contaminated, we were forced to abandon our home of Rongelap. For three years we became refugees, and lived on Ejit Island in Majuro Atoll. Then, in 1957, the Atomic Energy Commission told us that we could return home. Packing up our belongings, we made the happy journey back to our ancestral home of Rongelap. After several years back home on Rongelap, we thought that things were slowly getting better, and that perhaps our lives would return to a normal state. How wrong we were.

> Anjain repeatedly returns to the ignorance of himself and his people. This reinforces the impression of an innocent people caught unawares by the negligence, if not aggression, of the U.S. government.

In 1963, the United States doctors discovered a thyroid tumor in the neck of a Rongelap woman. The next year a few more thyroid tumors were discovered. We began to see that with every passing year, more and more of our people were being stricken with thyroid disease, and one by one my people were taken to the United States, where major surgery was performed to remove their thyroid glands. Beginning in 1969, the people of Utirik—who were three hundred miles downwind of the hydrogen bomb at Bikini—began to experience the same problem with thyroid tumors. The thyroid disease among my people has reached epidemic levels, and several children suffered from stunted growth because of their injured thyroid glands.

> Anjain devotes a paragraph to thyroid disease. This gives his audience something specific and detailed to think about as an example.

In 1972, a nephew of mine named Lekoj Anjain died of leukemia when he was nineteen years old: Lekoj was one year old during the "Bravo" hydrogen bomb test of 1954 when he played in the snowlike fallout on the ground. Not long afterward, my brother John—the father of Lekoj—and his wife Mijjua both developed thyroid tumors. And I have had a cancerous tumor removed from my body. The radiation from the 1954 "Bravo" fallout has not only killed and maimed the people of my island, but it has taken a personal toll on the lives of my family members. Mr. Chairman and distinguished delegates, I do not think this radioactive legacy is what the international community had in mind when it turned our islands over to the United States under a sacred trust agreement in 1947!

> Anjain now describes the personal effects of U.S. bomb tests on his family. This testimony comprises a powerful appeal to pathos.

> Anjain reinforces the idea of a broken promise.

As health problems continued to proliferate many years after our original exposure to high-level radioactive fallout, we found it odd when the United States doctors and scientists kept telling us that things were getting better, and that the radiation in our islands was going away. We also began to wonder who was really benefiting from the annual medical surveys conducted by the United States government. It is funny that although many U.S. agencies have come

> Note that Anjain always describes his people's thoughts and feelings in innocent terms: his people found it "odd," but stopped short of distrust or accusations.

out to our islands with supposedly the "best" doctors in the world, we still have never been taught even the most basic facts about our unique exposure to radioactive fallout. First the Atomic Energy Commission came to our islands, then came the Energy Research and Development Administration, and now we have the Department of Energy. They keep changing the names of these agencies, but they never change the people in the agencies.

In 1978, the Department of Energy conducted a radiological survey of the northern Marshall Islands. At the conclusion of their survey, it was revealed that in addition to Rongelap and Utirik, twelve other atolls and islands were contaminated with dangerous levels of fallout from the hydrogen bomb test program. In other words, our worst fears were realized when the U.S. government admitted for the first time in 1978 that literally thousands more Marshallese had been exposed to fallout and were continuing to live in a radioactive environment. Yet, despite this very important admission, only Rongelap and Utirik are receiving U.S. medical surveys. This fact makes a simple mockery of Article VI of the trust agreement whereby the United States pledged to "protect the health of the inhabitants."

Following the 1978 D.O.E. survey, the people of Rongelap were told to abandon the northern half of their atoll because of dangerous radiation levels. You can imagine the great fears and anxieties this caused my people when they realized that since their return after "Bravo" in 1957 they had been eating foods and living on islands in an area now under quarantine! And it is likewise easy to imagine why my people began accusing the United States government of using them as "guinea pigs" in an ongoing human experiment to study the long-term effects of how radiation enters the human food chain. I have often thought that those Americans who allowed my people to be exposed to radioactive fallout, and subsequently used us as human guinea pigs, should face a Nuremburg-like tribunal for the callous disregard for human life.

Following the 1978 Department of Energy survey, the D.O.E. produced a bilingual booklet about radiation in the northern Marshall Islands. When we compared the radiation levels of Bikini—where twenty-three atomic and hydrogen bomb tests occurred—and Rongelap, we found very little difference. And yet, as this committee knows, Bikini is off-limits for at least the next hundred years while the people of Rongelap have been allowed to remain in a very dangerous situation since our return in 1957 after the fallout came to our islands.

It was after we were told that one-half of our atoll was under quarantine, and after we saw in the Department of Energy's own words that many islands

Here Anjain further develops the need to address a problem: despite a parade of medical experts, the people of Rongelap remain uninformed about their conditions.

The problem-solution pattern is set up neatly in this paragraph: the United States has admitted there is a problem, but thousands of Marshallese residents are not getting tested. The solution is to conduct medical surveys for everyone affected by the bomb tests.

Again, Anjain stresses the broken promise of the U.S. government, implicating the oversight of the United Nations.

Here the speaker communicates that the problem is perhaps worse than neglect; Anjain says that some of his constituents believe they are part of a human experiment, and that the Americans who conducted or allowed this to happen should be tried in international court for crimes against humanity (as were a number of Nazis after the Second World War).

Notably, this statement is the first policy claim made in the speech: if the people of Rongelap were experimented on, then those who permitted it should be tried in court. In part, this argument helps the audience to visualize a possible action step.

The mention of "action" cues both the visualization and action components of the motivated sequence pattern.

on Rongelap were as contaminated as islands at Bikini, that we decided to take some action. In 1983, President Amata Kabua and I introduced a resolution into our parliament calling for the evacuation of the Rongelap people. That resolution passed unanimously.

In May of this year, the people of Rongelap finally decided to take appropriate action. With the help of the environmental group Greenpeace, the people of Rongelap took the drastic step of moving away from the dangerous situation on Rongelap. With the kind assistance of Greenpeace's flagship, the *Rainbow Warrior*—which the French saw fit to blow up in Auckland Harbor—we moved our entire community to Mejato Island at Kwajalein Atoll. I am currently helping to organize an international independent radiological and health survey of Rongelap in the next year so that we may—at long last—make an intelligent and informed decision about whether to return to Rongelap, or whether to abandon our home islands.

Here another policy claim is implicated: a radiological health survey is needed to make informed health decisions, and to determine if Rongelap should be permanently abandoned.

In this paragraph, Anjain describes the specific U.S. policy changes he is against.

At present, the United States Congress is about to terminate the strategic trust agreement with the United Nations. Under a questionable legal document known as the Compact of Free Association, we will enter into an ambiguous relationship with the United States that is neither independence nor complete annexation. However, the one certain fact under the compact is that the U.S. will maintain a military grip on Kwajalein for at least the next thirty years. Perhaps the most troubling part of the compact concerns the radiation victims in the Marshall Islands. At the moment, more than four thousand Marshallese have filed lawsuits in United States courts for radiation-induced damages to property and health. Under the so-called "espousal" clause of Section 177 of the compact, all of these lawsuits will become null and void, and all future lawsuits for latent radiation disease will be canceled. Because we have never had the benefit of a truly independent and non-governmental health study of our contaminated islands, we still do not know just how extensive the radiation damage really is. Furthermore, we have no idea about the future outlook for our unborn generations who will be exposed to radioactivity on many islands in the Marshalls.

Anjain reiterates his policy claim, that an independent radiological study of his people is needed.

Therefore, we find it rather peculiar that the U.S. is so eager to prevent us from all judicial proceedings stemming from the nuclear tests, and we honestly fear that the U.S. may know something about our future health that they do not want us to know about. Certainly, this violates both the letter and the spirit of the 1947 trust agreement.

Anajain returns, once again, to the broken promise. This repetition is helpful and appeals to the audience's sense of justice.

Recently a research arm of the U.S. Congress known as the Congressional Research Service did an analysis of the espousal clause in the compact.

According to this analysis by C.R.S., it has been determined that espousal is unconstitutional and violates U.S. law. The reason given by C.R.S. is that because the government of the Marshall Islands does not have sufficient sovereignty either under the trust agreement or under the compact, it could not legally enact the espousal provision of the compact. I have attached a copy of this five-page C.R.S. analysis to my statement.

In conclusion, I must confess my deep-felt disappointment with the nearly forty-year history of United States administration of our once-peaceful and unpolluted islands. My people continue to ask me why the United Nations has never really helped us. In fact, under the watchful eyes of the Trusteeship Council, the United States exploded nuclear bombs in our islands, caused irreversible destruction to our health and environment, and tampered with our culture in a way that has divided us into opposing camps. In the aftermath of U.S. administration, suicide—unknown among the Micronesian people before the period of American rule—has one of the highest rates in the world in our once-peaceful land.

In closing, I formally request that the Decolonization Committee send a special visiting mission to our islands to see firsthand what forty years of U.S. rule has done to my people and to our islands. Surely, on this fortieth anniversary of the United Nations, it would seem most appropriate for the Decolonization Committee to directly observe the last remaining trust territory before the termination of the trust agreement.

Last August, the members of the South Pacific Forum signed a treaty calling on the French government to stop its nuclear testing in the Pacific. The reason the forum nations are demanding an end to nuclear testing in their backyard is that they fear the possible adverse health effects associated with exposure to radiation. When you think about it, these nations are trying to prevent what has already happened to my people. If nothing else, my people serve as a warning to all of humanity about what nuclear weapons do to human beings. Please, for the sake of our children and our children's children, let us heed the warning by replacing an unchecked nuclear arms race with international cooperation and a sane world order.

Thank you.

> Here the speaker argues that the policy change proposed by the United States is unconstitutional. In addition to the broken promise of the U.S. government, disease, and death, the proposed policy change is illegal.

> Previously Anjain reserved his criticism to the United States government. In this paragraph, he now implicates the United Nations as having a responsibility as well. By waiting until the end of his speech to make this move, Anjain is much more likely to persuade his audience. There are now emotional, moral, and legal reasons to help the people of Rongelap.

> Here Anjain introduces his first action step: send representatives to see the problems on the island firsthand. The reasoning here is that if members of the United Nations are personally moved, they will be more likely to help the evacuees.

> In a powerful closing, Anjain argues that the plight of his people is a warning to all human beings about the horrors of nuclear weaponry.

SAMPLE ANNOTATED CELEBRATORY SPEECH

Visit LaunchPad to answer discussion questions about this speech.

David McCullough Jr.
David McCullough

On a spring day in 2012, English teacher David McCullough Jr. delivered the commencement address to the graduating class of Wellesley High School. Located in an affluent neighborhood outside of Boston, the seniors of Wellesley High probably expected a celebration of their accomplishments because a commencement speech generally: (1) acknowledges the experiences of graduates; (2) celebrates their hard work; and (3) challenges them to seize the future. In this way, the commencement speech constitutes the community and celebrates them in the present, the two key purposes of celebratory speaking in general.

Interestingly, Mr. McCullough achieves the ends of celebratory speaking by warping the commencement genre, brilliantly demonstrating the discussion at the conclusion of chapter 12 on genres: once a speaker has a firm grasp of a given genre, she or he can playfully violate conventions — *as long as the general purpose is met in the end.* Because the speech was so well done, the teacher found himself at the center of media interest as a video of his address went viral on the Internet. McCullough's commencement speech demonstrates how a firm grasp of commencement speech commonplaces can permit deviation and yet still achieve the twin purpose of constituting the community and celebrating it in the present.

This is a conventional opening: the speaker thanks dignitaries and the audience, and expresses that speaking is an honor.

Commencement Speech at Wellesley High School, June 1, 2012

Dr. Wong, Dr. Keough, Mrs. Novogroski, Ms. Curran, members of the board of education, family and friends of the graduates, ladies and gentlemen of the Wellesley High School class of 2012, for the privilege of speaking to you this afternoon, I am honored and grateful. Thank you.

So here we are . . . commencement . . . life's great forward-looking ceremony. (And don't say, "What about weddings?" Weddings are one-sided and insufficiently effective. Weddings are bride-centric pageantry. Other than conceding to a list of unreasonable demands, the groom just stands there. No stately, hey-everybody-look-at-me procession. No being given away. No identity-changing pronouncement. And can you imagine a television show dedicated to watching guys try on tuxedos? Their fathers sitting there misty-eyed with joy and disbelief, their brothers lurking in the corner muttering with envy. Left to men, weddings would be, after limits-testing procrastination, spontaneous, almost inadvertent . . . during halftime . . . on the way to the refrigerator. And then there's the frequency of failure: statistics tell us half of you will get divorced. A winning percentage like that'll get you last place in the American League East. The Baltimore Orioles do better than weddings.)

But this ceremony . . . commencement . . . a commencement works every time. From this day forward . . . truly . . . in sickness and in health, through financial fiascos, through midlife crises and passably attractive sales reps at trade shows in Cincinnati, through diminishing tolerance for annoyingness, through every difference, irreconcilable and otherwise, you will stay forever graduated from high school, you and your diploma as one, 'til death do you part.

No, commencement is life's great ceremonial beginning, with its own attendant and highly appropriate symbolism. Fitting, for example, for this auspicious rite of passage, is where we find ourselves this afternoon, the venue. Normally, I avoid clichés like the plague, wouldn't touch them with a ten-foot pole, but here we are on a literal level playing field. That matters. That says something. And your ceremonial costume . . . shapeless, uniform, one-size-fits-all. Whether male or female, tall or short, scholar or slacker, spray-tanned prom queen or intergalactic X-Box assassin, each of you is dressed, you'll notice, exactly the same. And your diploma . . . but for your name, exactly the same.

All of this is as it should be, because none of you is special.

You are not special. You are not exceptional.

Contrary to what your soccer trophy suggests, your glowing seventh-grade report card, despite every assurance of a certain corpulent purple dinosaur, that nice Mister Rogers and your batty Aunt Sylvia, no

Here the speaker signals the genre of commencement speaking itself. This cues the audience to think about the norms of such a speaking genre (because, of course, he intends to violate them).

The speaker foreshadows a coming critique by playfully making fun of wedding ceremonies. Such a comparison indirectly implicates celebratory speaking as a whole as well.

The speaker conflates commencement and wedding ceremonies for humorous effect, as if commencement ceremonies were a corrective: you cannot divorce a graduation. This signals the coming violation of commencement norms.

The speaker pokes fun at commencement speaking conventions, building audience anticipation for a coming violation.

While humorous, the speaker here is actually constituting the community by pointing out commonalities (in this case, graduation garb).

This is the thesis statement. Appears to be a direct violation of the norms of commencement speaking.

The speaker uses repetition of the same idea and same sounds to create a rhythm.

Repetition, yet again: the speaker has created a kind of chorus that he will return to repeatedly. While the statement is not immediately clear, the audience knows he means to be humorous because the preceding introduction was humorous.

In each stage the speaker describes — infancy, adolescence, young adulthood — note that he is actually stressing the support of parents along each stage. In this way, the speaker acknowledges both the graduates and their supporters in the audience; he constitutes two communities as one.

Note the speaker *does not* define what he means by "special." Usually speakers define their terms. Something is afoot: perhaps by "special" the speaker does not mean what we think he means by the term?

McCullough's discussion of the relative insignificance of the individual in relation to all of humanity and the cosmos begins to hint that what he means by "special" may not be a common sense of the term. Here, the comparison recalls descriptions of humanity by astrophysicists and philosophers.

matter how often your maternal caped crusader has swooped in to save you . . . you're nothing special.

Yes, you've been pampered, cosseted, doted upon, helmeted, bubble-wrapped. Yes, capable adults with other things to do have held you, kissed you, fed you, wiped your mouth, wiped your bottom, trained you, taught you, tutored you, coached you, listened to you, counseled you, encouraged you, consoled you, and encouraged you again. You've been nudged, cajoled, whee-dled, and implored. You've been feted and fawned over and called sweetie pie. Yes, you have. And, certainly, we've been to your games, your plays, your recitals, your science fairs. Absolutely, smiles ignite when you walk into a room, and hundreds gasp with delight at your every tweet. Why, maybe you've even had your picture in the *Townsman!* And now you've conquered high school . . . and, indisputably, here we all have gathered for you, the pride and joy of this fine community, the first to emerge from that magnificent new building. . . .

But do not get the idea you're anything special. Because you're not.

The empirical evidence is everywhere, numbers even an English teacher can't ignore. Newton, Natick, Nee . . . I am allowed to say Needham, yes? . . . that has to be two thousand high school graduates right there, give or take, and that's just the neighborhood Ns. Across the country no fewer than 3.2 million seniors are graduating about now from more than 37,000 high schools. That's 37,000 valedictorians . . . 37,000 class presidents . . . 92,000 harmonizing altos . . . 340,000 swaggering jocks . . . 2,185,967 pairs of Uggs. But why limit ourselves to high school? After all, you're leaving it. So think about this: even if you're one in a million, on a planet of 6.8 billion that means there are nearly 7,000 people just like you. Imagine standing somewhere over there on Washington Street on Marathon Monday and watching sixty-eight hundred yous go running by. And consider for a moment the bigger picture: your planet, I'll remind you, is not the center of its solar system, your solar system is not the center of its galaxy, your galaxy is not the center of the universe. In fact, astrophysicists assure us the universe has no center; therefore, you cannot be it. Neither can Donald Trump . . . which someone should tell him . . . although that hair is quite a phenomenon.

"But, Dave," you cry, "Walt Whitman tells me I'm my own version of perfection! Epictetus tells me I have the spark of Zeus!" And I don't disagree. So that makes 6.8 billion examples of perfection, 6.8 billion sparks of Zeus.

You see, if everyone is special, then no one is. If everyone gets a trophy, trophies become meaningless. In our unspoken but not so subtle Darwinian competition with one another—which springs, I think, from our fear of our own insignificance, a subset of our dread of mortality —we have of late, we Americans, to our detriment, come to love accolades more than genuine achievement. We have come to see them as the point—and we're happy to compromise standards, or ignore reality, if we suspect that's the quickest way, or only way, to have something to put on the mantelpiece, something to pose with, crow about, something with which to leverage ourselves into a better spot on the social totem pole. No longer is it how you play the game, no longer is it even whether you win or lose, or learn or grow, or enjoy yourself doing it. . . . Now it's "So what does this get me?" As a consequence, we cheapen worthy endeavors, and building a Guatemalan medical clinic becomes more about the application to Bowdoin than the well-being of Guatemalans. It's an epidemic—and in its way, not even dear old Wellesley High is immune . . . one of the best of the 37,000 nationwide, Wellesley High School . . . where good is no longer good enough, where a B is the new C, and the midlevel curriculum is called Advanced College Placement. And I hope you caught me when I said "one of the best." I said "one of the best" so we can feel better about ourselves, so we can bask in a little easy distinction, however vague and unverifiable, and count ourselves among the elite, whoever they might be, and enjoy a perceived leg up on the perceived competition. But the phrase defies logic. By definition there can be only one best. You're it or you're not.

If you've learned anything in your years here I hope it's that education should be for, rather than material advantage, the exhilaration of learning. You've learned, too, I hope, as Sophocles assured us, that wisdom is the chief element of happiness. (Second is ice cream . . . just an FYI.) I also hope you've learned enough to recognize how little you know . . . how little you know now . . . at the moment . . . for today is just the beginning. It's where you go from here that matters.

As you commence, then, and before you scatter to the winds, I urge you to do whatever you do for no reason other than you love it and believe in its importance. Don't bother with work you don't believe in any more than you would a spouse you're not crazy about, lest you too find yourself on the wrong side of a Baltimore Orioles comparison. Resist the easy comforts of complacency, the specious glitter of materialism, the narcotic paralysis of

The speaker finally explains his understanding of "special." Until this point, the speaker deliberately deployed an equivocation fallacy (or a slip between two or more meanings of a word) to create a sense of humorous anticipation. In a sense, the speaker calls himself out for his own equivocation, which creates an "ah-ha!" for his audience.

The speaker is arguing that the values of any group or communal practice — sport, for example — have been eclipsed by individual gain. In this way the speaker introduces a persuasive argument into his celebratory speech. It should be stressed, however, that this argument of value is already shared by his audience; he is pointing out a tension between what the audience values. In this way a persuasive argument is offered in the service of constituting and celebrating the community.

The speaker foreshadows his conclusion: education is a good in itself, and wisdom is the pursuit of the community. Humility is the lesson of learning.

self-satisfaction. Be worthy of your advantages. And read . . . read all the time . . . read as a matter of principle, as a matter of self-respect. Read as a nourishing staple of life. Develop and protect a moral sensibility and demonstrate the character to apply it. Dream big. Work hard. Think for yourself. Love everything you love, everyone you love, with all your might. And do so, please, with a sense of urgency, for every tick of the clock subtracts from fewer and fewer; and as surely as there are commencements there are cessations, and you'll be in no condition to enjoy the ceremony attendant to that eventuality no matter how delightful the afternoon.

The fulfilling life, the distinctive life, the relevant life, is an achievement, not something that will fall into your lap because you're a nice person or mommy ordered it from the caterer. You'll note the founding fathers took pains to secure your inalienable right to life, liberty, and the pursuit of happiness—quite an active verb, "pursuit"—which leaves, I should think, little time for lying around watching parrots roller-skate on YouTube. The first President Roosevelt, the old rough rider, advocated the strenuous life. Mr. Thoreau wanted to drive life into a corner, to live deep and suck out all the marrow. The poet Mary Oliver tells us to row, row into the swirl and roil. Locally, someone . . . I forget who . . . from time to time encourages young scholars to carpe the heck out of the diem. The point is the same: get busy, have at it. Don't wait for inspiration or passion to find you. Get up, get out, explore, find it yourself, and grab hold with both hands. (Now, before you dash off and get your YOLO tattoo, let me point out the illogic of that trendy little expression—because you can and should live not merely once, but every day of your life. Rather than You Only Live Once, it should be You Live Only Once . . . but because YLOO doesn't have the same ring, we shrug and decide it doesn't matter.)

None of this day-seizing, though, this YLOOing, should be interpreted as license for self-indulgence. Like accolades ought to be, the fulfilled life is a consequence, a gratifying by-product. It's what happens when you're thinking about more important things. Climb the mountain not to plant your flag, but to embrace the challenge, enjoy the air and behold the view. Climb it so you can see the world, not so the world can see you. Go to Paris to be in Paris, not to cross it off your list and congratulate yourself for being worldly. Exercise free will and creative, independent thought not for the satisfactions they will bring you, but for the good they will do others, the rest of the 6.8 billion—and those

> The speaker finally indicates the "real" community he would like students (and their families) to be: all of humanity.

who will follow them. And then you too will discover the great and curious truth of the human experience is that selflessness is the best thing you can do for yourself. The sweetest joys of life, then, come only with the recognition that you're not special.

Because everyone is.

Congratulations. Good luck. Make for yourselves, please, for your sake and for ours, extraordinary lives.

This three word sentence, because of its point and brevity, is powerful.

This completion of the speech indicates the speaker has goodwill for the audience, and undoes the equivocation with which he began.

glossary

accent: the way in which a person's speech pronunciation can indicate class allegiance or where she or he is from.

active listening: a technique of observing and responding to a speaker's spoken and nonverbal messages with the goal of mutual understanding.

alliteration: the recurrence of the same sound in a series of words.

amorphous audience: an audience that you know exists but whose size and demographic information are unknown.

appeal: a request made to another person with the intent of influencing him or her.

argument: a reasoned claim, or series of claims, supported by evidence.

asynchronous communication: communication that is either written or prerecorded before it reaches an audience.

attitude: a set of beliefs that cluster around a common object and that predispose behavior.

audience analysis: the process of studying an audience before, during, and after a speech.

audience disposition: how the audience feels about you, your topic, and the occasion for your speaking, and what you do with this information while speaking.

behavioral interview: a popular form of interviewing that asks candidates questions about past behavior to predict future work-related outcomes.

belief: an idea about reality.

bias: a preference for something or even for beliefs, ideas, and values that benefit you or others unequally.

brainstorming: the creative process of developing ideas and solutions to problems.

civic engagement: the manner in which citizens participate in the political or social processes and governance of a given community.

civil disobedience: a refusal to comply with the norms, demands, or laws of a group or government for the purpose of social change.

civility: speech or behavior that is seen as polite, courteous, or appropriate to a given social or public situation.

coalition: a temporary grouping of people for the purpose of collective social or political advocacy.

coercion: influencing someone to do or think something by threats, unwarranted emotion, and/or force that includes distorting, hiding, or preventing conscious choices.

color vision deficiency (CVD): an inability to see certain colors or to distinguish particular colors, most frequently the colors red and green.

commencement speech: an inspirational speech delivered to graduating students at an educational institution, such as a university.

common knowledge: events, ideas, things, or even beliefs that are widely known and understood in a given community.

communication: the coordination of behavior using symbols.

communication apprehension: the anxiety or fear experienced by communicators.

concept map: a visual representation of the relationships between different concepts, usually depicted with arrows and lines.

conflict: the inevitable disagreement groups encounter when working on a task together. Conflict is positive when it is depersonalized and focused on problem solving.

connotation: refers to the feelings one associates with a sign.

consciousness raising: the attempt to make others more aware of cultural and political problems and challenges.

contextual reasoning: thinking about the kinds of support you can use for a speech given its contextual demands and constraints.

definition: an explanation or description of the meaning of a term or concept.

demography: the study of the statistical characteristics of a given population.

denotation: refers to the literal and primary meaning of a sign, what you would expect to find in a dictionary.

description: evoking sights, sounds, and smells to give an audience a mental sense of an event, process, or object.

dialect: forms of language—including pronunciation, idioms, slang, and so forth—that are particular to a geographic region.

direct quotation: a word-for-word reference to what someone else has said.

enumeration: explicitly numbering an order of things. In public speaking, enumeration refers to the composition of transitions in oral delivery, or mental signposts. Many terms and phrases are handy for this purpose, for example: "first," "second," "third," "one," "two," "next," and "finally."

ethics: the study of how we should and should not respond to others.

ethnic identification: understanding oneself to share and/or participate in the language, culture, style, and history of a given group of people.

examples: descriptive representations used to illustrate claims.

expertise: refers to having knowledge or skills particular to a given field. In the context of public speaking, expertise is closely associated with credibility.

extemporaneous delivery: a speech that is delivered with few notes or that *seems* to be delivered with little or no preparation.

extemporaneous speaking: a form of public speaking that appears to require little or no preparation.

facts: verifiable truths or information; often contrasted with opinions and beliefs.

feedback: the unpleasant sound created when an audio input is too close to an output (e.g., a loudspeaker); in public speaking, feedback refers to verbal or nonverbal responses to a speaker that indicate an understanding or misunderstanding of a message.

form: the activation and satisfaction of expectations in audiences.

formal audience analysis: employing various tools and methods for gathering information about people, such as focus groups, interviews, or surveys.

gender: the socio-cultural identification of "male," "female," or something different than these. As a general rule, when referencing identity you will be more inclusive thinking about gender than you will be thinking about biological sex, if only because the relationship between sex and gender is culturally variable.

general speech purpose: answers the question "why?" with regard to the topic, audience, and occasion, and is framed around informing, persuading, or celebrating.

genre: a label for a widely recognized form or pattern of discourse in a given culture.

gesture: the movement of the head, hands, and arms to communicate an idea or feeling.

groupthink: a common, often unconscious, tendency to avoid conflict in a group, usually by failing to challenge ideas or decisions.

historical arrangement: how a given object or event occurred in documented, historical fact.

identification: the shared sense of identity between or among two or more people, usually in reference to a common thing, experience, or event.

identity crisis: a concept developed by Erik Erikson that refers to the realization that one's ideal self and actual self are very different.

impression management: refers to the way in which a person navigates his or her self-presentation in body and language.

informal audience analysis: the way in which a speaker gathers information about his or her audience in an unsystematic way.

informal logic: concerns the study of how people argue on an everyday basis by leaving some things unstated.

informative speaking: speech that attempts to introduce or impart new knowledge and information to audiences.

internal previews and summaries: more detailed forms of transitions that review major points to come, or that summarize points that have been said, respectively.

invention: the process of discovering materials and arguments for a speech.

irony: the trope for saying one thing but meaning another.

jargon: the specialized or peculiar language of a particular community or group.

jeremiad: a prophetic speech of woe and moral or spiritual shortcoming. Jeremiads typically admonish communities to repent or change their ways to avert doom.

keynote address: a featured speech at a convention, meeting, or political gathering that is designed to highlight the tone and purpose of gathering; sometimes keynote speeches advance a collective goal or agenda.

leader: someone who is designated or who emerges to guide and moderate discussion.

lecture: in the context of celebratory speaking, a speech of blame or admonishment. In the context of informative speaking, however, a lecture is simply an educational speech.

listening: the process of actively making meaning of messages.

logic: refers to the structure of reasoning.

malapropism: the accidental confusion of ideas or similar-sounding words, sometimes referred to as a "Freudian slip."

metaphors: tropes or figures of speech that compare two seemingly dissimilar things.

misinformation: sometimes termed "disinformation," misinformation is false, inaccurate, or misleading information.

misunderstanding: the inability of one or more communicators to apprehend meanings, feelings, or identities, and to coordinate their behaviors.

motivational speaking: speeches that are primarily intended to inspire an audience to feel or think something about themselves or their community.

narration: the telling of a story, or a verbal account of an event or series of events.

narrative arrangement: sequences a speech like a story moving from the beginning to the end.

noise: anything that distracts from a message in the context of communication. Noise can be internal or external to the listener.

nudity dream: a common dream in which the dreamer realizes he or she is naked in front of a group of people.

online presentation: a prepared speech, podcast, or video that is broadcast on a computing device.

opinions: judgments that may or may not depend on facts or knowledge.

paradigm: generally, a pattern or model for something. In the speaking situation, however, a paradigm refers to the standards of judgment you provide to an audience to evaluate something; paradigms reference the coordinates of a judgment of value.

paraphrase: to summarize the ideas or remarks of others without directly quoting them.

persuasion: the process of influencing others to do, think, or believe something through speaking and writing.

plagiarism: the representation of someone else's ideas or words as your own; plagiarism is intellectual theft.

presentation software: programs that allow speakers to present visuals.

prop: any physical object that helps you illustrate a point in your speech.

protest: a type of rally in which people are objecting to something, be it a cause, a person, a policy, or even an idea.

psychological audience analysis: the anticipation of audience feelings and an attempt to marshal those feelings in order to change beliefs, attitudes, values, or behavior.

publicity: the distribution and circulation of information or a message for promotional purposes.

race: a group of people identified as having the same or similar physical characteristics based on genetic heritage. Many scholars argue that race is a vexed social construction and has no basis in genetics or biology.

rally: a meeting of people to support a social or political cause, from the success (or future success) of a sport team to the campaign of a political party or candidate.

rally speech: an enthusiastic oration, designed to inspire and motivate a community, delivered at an event for a social or political cause.

reasoning: refers to the ability to make an inference or a judgment based on evidence.

response-ability: the ability to respond to others, which is the foundation of listening and speaking.

rhetoric: the study of the ways in which speaking and writing influence people to do or think what they otherwise would not ordinarily do or think.

screencast: a live or recorded broadcast of a speaker's computer desktop to others online.

selective exposure: a psychological theory suggesting that people prefer information that supports their views and avoid information that does not.

selective listening: the ways in which a person attends to some auditory information (speech or sound), ignoring other information.

selective perception: the ways in which people attend to the things they like, ignoring things that they do not.

sermon: a speech by a religious leader or spiritual person. Sermons often include references to religious or spiritual texts, such as the Hebrew or Christian bibles or the Koran.

sexual orientation: the gender identity of those with whom you choose to be intimate.

simile: metaphors that use or imply the word "like."

small group communication: the interaction among three or more people who self-identify as a group.

social agitation: the deliberate violation of widely accepted or sanctioned norms of a social or political culture.

social movement: a group or collective of like-minded individuals who promote a particular cause, politics, or ideology.

social norms: rules that govern what is normal in a given culture.

social-oriented roles: roles adopted by members of a group to help moderate the mood and feelings of participants.

solidarity: a feeling of agreement or unity in a community about a belief, a cause, an event, or a proposed action.

sound reinforcement: the use of microphones, sound processors, and amplifiers to enhance the quality or volume of sounds.

specific purpose statement: a single sentence, often beginning with the word "to," that explains the specific topic and goal of your presentation.

speech: the meeting place of the body and language, typically understood as meaningful, vocal expression.

speech anxiety: the communication apprehension specific to speech making.

speech situation: both the exigency or reason for giving a speech as well as those things that constrain what can be said. The primary characteristic of the speech situation is the reason and purpose of a speech. Secondary elements include the space and place of a speech, as well as the characteristics of the audience.

statistics: numerical facts or measurements about a large group or collection.

stereotype: an overgeneralization about a person or group based on their assumed characteristics.

stories: accounts of real or imagined events or people for the purpose of illustration and/or entertainment.

style: refers to the way in which a person presents himself or herself to others. In the context of public speaking, style refers to the relationship between what one says and how he or she says it.

supporting material: the facts, statistics, testimony, examples, and stories that bolster your claims.

synchronous communication: real-time communication.

task-oriented roles: roles adopted by members of a group to help meet the goals of the group.

techne: a habit of mind and body that is cultivated to make something; a craft.

testimony: the sharing of an individual's viewpoints, perspectives, or opinions.

thesis statement (central idea): a single sentence that expresses the topic and purpose of a speech.

tone: the emotional quality or character of human expression; in public speaking, tone references the feelings of the speaker as they are expressed in delivery.

tonework: the labor of the speaker to craft, control, or change the expression of feeling in public speaking.

tropes: figures of speech. Popular tropes include metaphor, simile, and irony.

truth: a fact or belief that is widely accepted by a given community or group of people.

unknown audience: a group of individuals who are brought together by a given message who may or may not share common characteristics.

value: a deeply held core belief.

verbal fillers: "vocalized pauses" in your speaking that distract from your speech and which should be avoided.

violence: the use of physical or psychological force to injure, harm, or alter something or someone to cause or stop change.

virtual group: a collection of people brought together to work on a common task through long-distance technologies (teleconferencing, Skype, etc.); today, such groups are as common in the workplace as they are in video gaming.

visualization: imagining the outcome of a possible course of action or behavior.

vivid language: concerns words that are sensuous and evocative.

vocalics: the study of the nonverbal character and expressiveness of the human voice.

vocation: a feeling of dedication toward one's occupation.

voice projection: the way in which speakers use the strength of their voice to control volume and express confidence in a speaking situation.

webinar: a seminar with three or more people conducted over the Internet using software created for this purpose.

references

Chapter 1

1. Gorgias, "Encomium of Helen," trans. George A. Kennedy, in *The Rhetorical Tradition: Readings from Classical Times to the Present*, ed. Patricia Bizzell and Bruce Herzberg (Boston: Bedford/St. Martin's Press, 2001), 44–46.

2. Isocrates, "Against the Sophists," trans. George Norlin, in *The Rhetorical Tradition: Readings from Classical Times to the Present*, ed. Patricia Bizzell and Bruce Herzberg (Boston: Bedford/St. Martin's Press, 2001), 74.

3. Gorgias, "Encomium of Helen."

4. Jerry Seinfeld, "No. 1 Fear," *I'm Telling You for the Last Time* (UMVD, 1998), CD.

5. Karen Kangas Dwyer and Marline M. Davidson, "Is Public Speaking Really More Feared than Death?" *Communication Research Reports* 29 (2012): 99–107.

6. J. C. McCroskey, "Oral Communication Apprehension: A Summary of Recent Theory and Research," *Human Communication Research* 4 (1977): 78–96.

7. Ian Robertson, *The Stress Test: How Pressure Can Make You Stronger and Sharper* (New York: Bloomsbury, 2016).

8. James M. Honeycutt, Charles W. Choi, and John R. DeBerry, "Communication Apprehension and Imagined Interactions," *Communication Research Reports* 26 (2009): 228–36.

9. Merrill Fabry, "This Is How the Town Hall Meeting Became a Campaign-Season Staple," *Time*, January 22, 2016, time.com/4190233/town-hall-meeting-history.

10. William Keith and Christian Lundberg, "Creating a History for Public Speaking Instruction," *Rhetoric and Public Affairs* 17 (2014): 139–46.

11. Magda Walczak, "Public Speaking (In & Out of China)," *Magda's Blog*, November 19, 2009, www.magdawalczak.com/posts/public-speaking-in-out-of-china.

12. Plato, *Phaedrus*, trans. H. N. Fowler, in *The Rhetorical Tradition: Readings from Classical Times to the Present*, ed. Patricia Bizzell and Bruce Herzberg (Boston: Bedford/St. Martin's Press, 2001), 138–68.

13. Aristotle, *On Rhetoric: A Theory of Civic Discourse*, trans. George A. Kennedy (New York: Oxford University Press, 2007).

14. William Fleeson, Adriane B. Malanos, and Noelle M. Achille, "An Intraindividual Process Approach to the Relationship between Extraversion and Positive Affect: Is Acting Extraverted as 'Good' as Being Extraverted?" *Journal of Personality and Social Psychology* 83 (2002): 1409–22.

15. Sarah E. Williams and Jennifer Cumming, "Sport Imagery Ability Predicts Trait Confidence, and Challenge and Threat Appraisal Tendencies," *European Journal of Sport Science* 12 (2012): 499–508.

16. Joe Ayres and Brian L. Heuett, "An Examination of the Impact of Performance Visualization," *Communication Research Reports* 16 (1999): 29–39.

17. Amy Cuddy, *Presence: Bringing Your Boldest Self to Your Biggest Challenges* (Boston: Little, Brown, 2015).

18. Robert K. Merton, "The Self-Fulfilling Prophecy," *Antioch Review* 8 (1948): 193–210.

19. Public speaking classes are specifically designed to give you that experience. See Karla M. Hunter, Joshua N. Westwick, and Laurie L. Haleta, "Assessing Success: The Impacts of a Fundamentals of Speech Course on Decreasing Public Speaking Anxiety," *Communication Education* 63 (2014): 124–35.

Chapter 2

1. The approach to listening and ethics adopted in this chapter is heavily indebted to two French intellectuals—philosopher Jacques Derrida and psychoanalyst Jacques Lacan—and the author's friend and colleague Diane Davis. See references 14, 15, and 16 in this chapter.

2. For a related formulation drawing on the work of Emmanuel Levinas, see Lisbeth Lipari, "Listening Otherwise: The Voice of Ethics," *International Journal of Listening* 23 (2009): 44–59.

3. International Listening Association, "An ILA Definition of Listening," *Listening Post* 53 (April 1995): 4–5.

4. I. A. Richards, *The Philosophy of Rhetoric* (New York: Oxford University Press, 1936): 1–10.

5. For an overview of the scientific literature of individual-based listening research, see Graham D. Bodie, Debra Worthington, Margarete Imhof, and Lynn O. Cooper, "What Would a Unified Field of Listening Look Like? A Proposal Linking Past Perspectives and Future Endeavors," *International Journal of Listening* 22 (2008): 103–22.

6. For an overview, see for example Leda M. Cooks and Mark P. Orbe, "Beyond the Satire: Selective Exposure and Selective Perception in 'In Living

Color,'" *Howard Journal of Communications* 4 (1993): 217–33.

7. Graham D. Bodie, "Listening as Positive Communication," in *The Positive Side of Communication*, ed. T. Socha and M. Pitts (New York: Peter Lang, 2012): 109–25.

8. Steven McCornack, *Reflect & Relate: An Introduction to Interpersonal Communication* (Boston: Bedford/St. Martin's, 2007): 188–98.

9. Margarete Imhof, "What Makes a Good Listener? Listening Behavior in Instructional Settings," *International Journal of Listening* 12 (1998): 81–105.

10. Diane Davis, *Inessential Solidarity: Rhetoric and Foreigner Relations* (Pittsburgh: University of Pittsburgh Press, 2010).

11. For a robust discussion of communication ethics, see Rita Manning and Scott R. Stroud, *A Practical Guide to Ethics: Living and Leading with Integrity* (Boulder, CO: Westview Press, 2007): 131–68.

12. For a fascinating review of research about how our imagined interactions with others influences how we communicate, see James M. Honeycutt, *Imagined Interactions: Daydreaming about Communication* (New York: Hampton Press, 2002).

13. Matt Apuzzo, Michael S. Schmidt, William K. Rashbaum, and Sam Borden, "FIFA Officials Arrested on Corruption Charges; Sepp Blatter Isn't among Them," *New York Times*, May 27, 2015, www.msn.com/en-us/sports/soccer/fifa-officials-arrested-on-corruption-charges-sepp-blatter-isn%E2%80%99t-among-them/ar-BBkhpSl?li=BBgzzfc&ocid=UP97DHP.

14. Graham D. Bodie and David E. Beard, "Listening Research in the Communication Discipline." *The Unfinished Conversation: 100 Years of Communication Studies*, Pat Gherkin and William M. Keith, eds. (New York: Routledge, 2014): forthcoming.

15. Diane Davis, *Inessential Solidarity: Rhetoric and Foreigner Relations* (Pittsburgh: University of Pittsburgh Press, 2010).

16. Jacques Derrida, "A Number of Yes," trans. Gabriel Motzkin. *The Journal of Philosophy* 85 (1988): 632–644.

Chapter 3

1. Aristotle, *On Rhetoric: A Theory of Civic Discourse*, 2nd ed., trans. George A. Kennedy (New York: Oxford University Press, 2007), 149.

2. Robert James Branham and W. Barnett Pearce, "The Conversational Frame in Public Address," *Communication Quarterly* 44 (1996): 423–39.

3. Sigmund Freud, *Group Psychology and the Analysis of the Ego*, trans. James Strachey (New York: W.W. Norton, 1959).

4. Joshua Gunn, "For the Love of Rhetoric, with Continual Reference to Kenny and Dolly," *Quarterly Journal of Speech* 94 (2008): 131–55.

5. Kenneth Burke, *A Rhetoric of Motives* (Berkeley: University of California Press, 1969).

6. Milton Rokeach, *Beliefs, Attitudes, and Values: A Theory of Organization and Change* (San Francisco: Jossey-Bass, 1968).

7. Antonio Damasio, *Descartes' Error: Emotion, Reason, and the Human Brain* (New York: Avon, 1994).

Chapter 4

1. *Oxford English Dictionary Online*, s.v. "Invention," def. 1, accessed June 10, 2015, www.oed.com/view/Entry/98969?redirectedFrom=invention#eid.

2. James Ward, "The Enduring Genius of the Ballpoint Pen," *Wall Street Journal*, June 5, 2015, www.wsj.com/articles/the-enduring-genius-of-the-ballpoint-pen-1433512313.

3. Lloyd Bitzer, "The Rhetorical Situation," *Philosophy and Rhetoric* 1 (1968): 1–14; Richard E. Vatz, "The Myth of the Rhetorical Situation," *Philosophy and Rhetoric* 6 (1973): 154–61; Scott Consigny, "Rhetoric and Its Situations," *Philosophy and Rhetoric* 3 (1974): 175–86.

4. Teresa Brennan, *The Transmission of Affect* (Ithaca: Cornell University Press, 2004).

5. Ibid.

6. Keith Dresser, "Making the Most of Salt," *Cooks Illustrated* (November–December 2010): 16–17.

Chapter 5

1. Rick Caulfield, "'Trust Yourself': Revisiting Benjamin Spock," *Early Childhood Education Journal* 26 (1999): 263–65; Benjamin Spock and Robert Needlman, *Dr. Spock's Baby and Child Care*, 9th ed. (New York: Pocket Books, 2011); Elizabeth Suoboda, "Parental Guidance," *Science and Spirit* 15 (March/April 2004): 66; John B. Watson, *Psychological Care of Infant and Child* (New York: Amo Press, 1972).

2. "Study Finds Every Style of Parenting Produces Disturbed, Miserable Adults," *Onion*, October 26, 2011, www.theonion.com/article/study-finds-every-style-of-parenting-produces-dist-26452.

3. Terri Pous, "Parents Believe *Onion* Article, Freak Out Accordingly," *Time*, November 2011, newsfeed.time.com/2011/11/01/parents-believe-onion-article-freak-out-accordingly.

4. Thomas Reid, *An Inquiry into the Human Mind: On the Principles of Common Sense*, ed. Derek R. Brookes

(University Park: Pennsylvania State University Press, 1997).

5. Frederic Flament et al., "Effect of the Sun on Visible Clinical Signs of Aging in Caucasian Skin," *Clinical, Cosmetic and Investigational Dermatology* 6 (2013): 221–32.

6. Elizabeth Khaykin Cahoon et al., "Individual, Environmental, and Meteorological Predictors of Daily Personal Ultraviolet Radiation Exposure Measurements in a United States Cohort Study," *PLoS ONE* 8 (2013): 1–9.

7. Gabrielle Jonas, "A Textbook Case of Anti-science," *Newsweek Global* 162 (2014): 83–87.

8. Min Jiang, "The Business and Politics of Search Engines: A Comparative Study of Baidu and Google's Search Results of Internet Events in China," *New Media and Society* 16 (2014): 212–33; Andrew Langford, "gMonopoly: Does Search Bias Warrant Antitrust or Regulatory Intervention?" *Indiana Law Journal* 88 (2013): 1559–92.

9. Brian K. Pinaire, "Internet Conspiracies: Where the Absence of Evidence Is Confirmation of the Claim," *Skeptic* 12 (2005): 26.

10. "Our Mission," FactCheck.org, accessed July 5, 2015, www.factcheck.org/about /our-mission.

11. Dave Levitan, "Fiorina Shortchanges Marijuana Research," FactCheck.org, July 2, 2015, www.factcheck.org/2015/07/fiorina -shortchanges-marijuana-research.

12. For more in-depth tips on Internet research, see Karen Hartman and Ernest Ackermann, *Searching and Researching on the Internet and World Wide Web*, 5th ed. (Portland, OR: Franklin, Beedle, 2010).

13. Leo Cendrowicz, "The Smurfs Are Off to Conquer the World—Again," *Time*, January 14, 2008, content.time.com/time/world /article/0,8599,1703303,00.html.

14. "Global Climate Change: Vital Signs of the Planet," National Aeronautics and Space Administration, accessed July 11, 2014, climate.nasa.gov.

15. Annette Lamb and Larry Johnson, "Wicked or Wonderful: Revisiting Wikipedia," *Teacher Librarian* 40 (2013): 68–73.

16. Andrea A. Lunsford and Marcia F. Muth, *The St. Martin's Pocket Guide to Research and Documentation*, 5th ed. (Boston: Bedford/St. Martin's, 2011).

Chapter 6

1. "Perspectives: Casey Gerald, MBA 2014," Harvard Business School, Spring 2013, www.hbs.edu/mba /student-life/people/Pages/perspectives .aspx?profile=cgerald.

2. John A. Byrne, "Most Stirring Speech Ever by an MBA," Poets and Quants, June 22, 2014), poetsandquants.com/2014/06/22/the-most -stirring-speech-ever-given-by-an-mba.

3. Robert Saifan, "'We Need a New Field Manual for Business': Casey Gerald," *Fast Company*, October 14, 2015, www.fastcompany.com/3036583 /generation-flux/we-need-a-new-field-manual -for-business-casey-gerald.

4. For more on the complexity of beliefs, see Robert Jervis, "Understanding Beliefs," *Political Psychology* 27 (2006): 641–63.

5. D'Vera Cohn, "Love and Marriage," Pew Research Center, February 13, 2013, www.pewsocialtrends .org/2013/02/13/love-and-marriage.

6. Theodore M. Porter, *Trust in Numbers: The Pursuit of Objectivity in Science and Public Life* (Princeton, NJ: Princeton University Press, 1995).

7. Arnold Barnett, "How Numbers Can Trick You," *MIT Technology Review* 97 (October 1994), www.rci .rutgers.edu/~hallman/PDF/Numbers.pdf.

8. Ibid.

9. For more examples of misused, misinterpreted, and misleading statistics, see Tyler Vigen's website, Spurious Correlations, at www .tylervigen.com/spurious-correlations.

10. D'Vera Cohn et al., "Barely Half of U.S. Adults Are Married—a Record Low," Pew Research Center, December 14, 2011, www.pewsocialtrends .org/2011/12/14/barely-half-of-u-s-adults-are -married-a-record-low.

11. Lori Robertson and Jess Henig, "A False Appeal to Women's Fears," September 4, 2009, www.factcheck.org /2009/09/a-false-appeal-to-womens-fears.

12. Carol Tavris and Elliot Aronson, *Mistakes Were Made (but Not by Me): Why We Justify Foolish Beliefs, Bad Decisions, and Hurtful Acts* (Boston: Houghton Mifflin Harcourt, 2007).

13. David Rose, "Forget Global Warming—It's Cycle 23 We Need to Worry About (and if NASA Scientists Are Right the Thames Will Be Freezing Over Again)," *Daily Mail*, January 29, 2012, www .dailymail.co.uk/sciencetech/article-2093264 /Forget-global-warming--Cycle-25-need-worry -NASA-scientists-right-Thames-freezing-again. html#ixzz1ktghEAPl.

14. Peter Gleick, "'Global Warming Has Stopped'? How to Fool People Using 'Cherry-Picked' Climate Data," *Forbes*, February 5, 2012, www.forbes.com/sites/petergleick/2012/02/05 /global-warming-has-stopped-how-to-fool -people-using-cherry-picked-climate-data.

15. "Changing Attitudes on Gay Marriage," Pew Research Center, May 12, 2016, www.pewforum.org/2016/05/12 /changing-attitudes-on-gay-marriage.

16. Sasha Frere-Jones, "Show Runners," *New Yorker*, June 27, 2011, www.newyorker.com /magazine/2011/06/27/show-runners.

17. See Gerard A. Hauser, "Aristotle's Example Revisited," *Philosophy and Rhetoric* 18 (1985): 171–80.

18. Aristotle, *On Rhetoric: A Theory of Civic Discourse*, trans. George A. Kennedy (New York: Oxford University Press).

19. Alasdair MacIntyre, *After Virtue*, 2nd ed. (Notre Dame: University of Notre Dame Press, 1984), 216.

20. William F. Lewis, "Telling America's Story: Narrative Form and the Reagan Presidency," *Quarterly Journal of Speech* 73 (1987): 280–302.

21. Chimamanda Ngozi Adichie, "The Danger of a Single Story," filmed July 2009, TED video, 18:49, posted October 2009, www.ted.com/talks/chimamanda _adichie_the_danger_of_a_single_story /transcript?language=en.

22. Douglas N. Walton, *Informal Logic: A Handbook for Critical Argumentation* (New York: Cambridge, 1989).

23. Readers familiar with the Greek rhetorical tradition may recognize that what I am describing as contextual reasoning harks back to the centuries-old concept of *to prepon* (the appropriate). See John Poulakos, "Toward a Sophistic Definition of Rhetoric," *Philosophy and Rhetoric* 16 (1983): 35–48.

Chapter 7

1. Nelson Cowan, "What Are the Differences between Long-Term, Short-Term, and Working Memory?" *Progress in Brain Research* 169 (2008): 323–38.

2. George A. Miller, "The Magical Number Seven, Plus or Minus Two: Some Limits on Our Capacity for Processing Information," *Psychological Review* 63 (1956): 81–95.

3. Jean-Luc Doumont, "Magical Numbers: The Seven-Plus-or-Minus-Two Myth." *IEEE Transactions on Professional Communication* 45 (2002): 123–27.

4. Angelica Moé and Rossana De Beni, "Stressing the Efficacy of the Loci Method: Oral Presentation and the Subject-Generation of Loci Pathway with Expository Passages," *Applied Cognitive Psychology* 19 (2005): 95–106.

5. This method of organizing and memorizing a speech is called the "method of loci," and much research has supported its efficacy. See Jennifer A. McCabe, "Location, Location, Location! Demonstrating the Mnemonic Benefit of the Method of Loci," *Teaching of Psychology* 42 (2015): 169–73.

6. Mandell, Andrea. "Justin Timberlake's Voting Selfie May Have Broken the Law." *USA Today*, 26 Oct. 2016, www.usatoday.com/story/life /people/2016/10/25/justin-timberlakes-voting -selfie-may-have-broken-law/92728472/.

7. Steven A. Beebe, "Eye Contact: A Nonverbal Determinant of Speaker Credibility." *Speech Teacher* 23 (1974): 21–25.

Chapter 8

1. Jonathan M. Cheek and Lisa A. Melchior, "Shyness, Self-Esteem, and Self-Consciousness," in *Handbook of Social and Evaluation Anxiety*, ed. Harold Leitenberg (New York: Springer, 1990), 47–82.

2. For strategies for reducing social anxiety, see David Shinji Kondo and Yang Ying-Ling, "Strategies for Reducing Social Anxiety," *Communication Research Reports* 11 (1994): 153–59.

3. Aristotle, *On Rhetoric: A Theory of Civic Discourse*, trans. George A. Kennedy (New York: Oxford University Press, 1991).

4. Solomon E. Asch, "Forming Impressions of Personality," *Journal of Abnormal and Social Psychology* 41 (1946): 258–90.

5. Gender and attractiveness play an important role, as does vocal clarity, rate of speech, and perceived preparedness. See Mark Hickson III, Sidney R. Hill, and Larry Powell, "The Foundations of Perceived Similarity," *Communicator* 9 (1979): 43–51; and John Batten et al., "An Exploratory Investigation Examining Male and Female Students' Initial Impressions and Expectancies of Lecturers," *Teaching in Higher Education* 19 (2014): 113–25.

6. Stephen Colbert, "University of Virginia 2013 Commencement Speech," May 18, 2013, genius .com/Stephen-colbert-university-of-virginia-2013 -commencement-speech-annotated.

7. Jamie Oliver, "Teach Every Child about Food," filmed February 2010, TED video, 21:53, posted February 2010, www.ted.com/talks/jamie_oliver /transcript?language=en.

8. Jon Huntsman, "Energy Speech," November 1, 2011, www.p2012.org/issues/huntsman110111en.html.

9. Ibid.

10. Research on the effect of primacy and recency on public speaking audiences is dated; most research in this area, known as "serial position effects," is centered on consumer behavior and memory studies. For a review, see Rik G. M. Pieters and Tammo H. A. Bijmolt, "Consumer Memory for Television Advertising: A Field Study of Duration, Serial Position, and Competition Effects," *Journal of Consumer Research* 23 (1997): 362–72.

11. William D. Crano, "Primacy versus Recency in Retention of Information and Opinion Change,"

Journal of Social Psychology 101 (1977): 87–97; also see Ray Ehrensberger, "An Experimental Study of the Relative Effectiveness of Certain Forms of Emphasis in Public Speaking," Speech Monographs 45 (1945): 94–112.

12. For a review of the emerging research on attention and "mind-wandering," see Jason G. Randall, Frederick L. Oswald, and Margaret E. Beir, "Mind-Wandering, Cognition, and Performance: A Theory-Driven Meta-Analysis of Attention Regulation," Psychological Bulletin 140 (2014): 1411–31; and Jonathan Smallwood and Jonathan W. Schooler, "The Science of Mind Wandering: Empirically Navigating the Stream of Consciousness, Annual Review of Psychology 66 (2015): 487–518.

13. Huntsman, "Energy Speech."

14. Jeanne Theoharis, "'The Northern Promised Land That Wasn't': Rosa Parks and the Black Freedom Struggle in New York," OAH Magazine of History 26 (2012): 23–27.

15. Oprah Winfrey, "Eulogy for Rosa Parks," AmericanRhetoric.com, October 31, 2005, www.americanrhetoric.com/speeches/oprahwinfreyonrosaparks.htm.

Chapter 9

1. Project Runway. "Finale, Part I." Season 10, Episode 13. Directed by Craig Spirko. Lifetime, October 11, 2002.

2. Aristotle, On Rhetoric, trans. George A. Kenney, 2nd ed. (New York: Oxford University Press, 2007).

3. Edwin G. Flemming, "A Comparison of Cicero and Aristotle on Style," Quarterly Journal of Speech Education 4 (1918): 61–72; also see Ralph Pomeroy, "Aristotle and Cicero: Rhetorical Style," Western Speech 25 (1961): 25–32.

4. Barry Brummett. A Rhetoric of Style (Carbondale: Southern Illinois University Press, 2008).

5. In addition to Brummett, see Robert Hariman, Political Style: The Artistry of Power (Chicago: University of Chicago Press, 1995).

6. In the field of communication studies, the teachers and scholars of performance studies and oral interpretation have programmatically examined the relation between the body and communication in many contexts. For an introductory overview of this research, see Tracy Stephenson Shaffer, John M. Allison Jr., and Ronald J. Pelias, "A Critical History of the 'Live' Body in Performance within the National Communication Association," in A Century of Communication Studies: The Unfinished Conversation, eds. Pat J. Gehrke and William M. Keith (New York: Routledge, 2015), 187–206.

7. For in-depth investigations of style and expertise, see E. Johanna Hartelius, The Rhetoric of Expertise (Lanham, MD: Lexington Books, 2011); and

Anna M. Young, Prophets, Gurus, and Pundits: Rhetorical Styles and Public Engagement (Carbondale: Southern Illinois University Press, 2014).

8. Gorgias, "Encomium of Helen," trans. D. M. MacDowell, in Reading Rhetorical Theory, ed. Barry Brummett (Fort Worth, TX: Harcourt College, 2000), 31–33.

9. Barack Obama, "Remarks by the President in Eulogy for the Honorable Reverend Clementa Pinckney," WhiteHouse.gov, June 26, 2015, www.whitehouse.gov/the-press-office/2015/06/26/remarks-president-eulogy-honorable-reverend-clementa-pinckney.

10. Stephen Colbert, "2006 White House Correspondents Dinner," C-SPAN, April 29, 2006, www.c-span.org/video/?192243-1/2006-white-house-correspondents-dinner.

11. Kenneth Burke, Language as Symbolic Action: Essays on Life, Literature, and Method (Berkeley: University of California Press, 1968).

12. Roderick P. Hart, Sharon E. Jarvis, William P. Jennings, and Deborah Smith-Howell, Political Keywords: Using Language That Uses Us (New York: Oxford University Press, 2004).

13. For a discussion of teaching political correctness in schools, see Richard Rorty, Achieving Our Country: Leftist Thought in Twentieth-Century America (Cambridge, MA: Harvard University Press, 1998).

Chapter 10

1. Jeff Chang, Can't Stop Won't Stop: A History of the Hip-Hop Generation (New York: Picador, 2005).

2. Jim Fricke and Charlie Ahearn, Yes Yes Y'all: The Experience Music Project Oral History of Hip-Hop's First Decade (Cambridge, MA: De Capo Press, 2002).

3. Jonah Weiner, "Funny Things Rappers Do with Their Hands," Slate.com, November 11, 2009, www.slate.com/blogs/browbeat/2009/11/11/funny_things_rappers_do_with_their_hands.html.

4. Herman Cohen, The History of Speech Communication: The Emergence of a Discipline, 1914–1945 (Annandale, VA: Speech Communication Association, 1994), 1–12.

5. Leslie Ramos Salazar, "Reducing Vocalized Pauses in Public Speaking Situations Using the VP Card," Communication Teacher 28 (2014): 213–17.

6. John Bourhis and Mike Allen, "The Role of Videotaped Feedback in the Instruction of Public Speaking: A Qualitative Synthesis of Published Empirical Research, Communication Research Reports 15 (1998): 256–61.

7. Joe Ayres et al., "Two Empirical Tests of Videotape Designed to Reduce Public Speaking Anxiety," Journal of Applied Communication Research 21 (1993): 132–47.

8. Edward T. Hall, *Silent Language* (New York: Doubleday, 1959).

9. Kris Rugsaken, "Body Speaks: Body Language around the World," NACADA *Clearinghouse of Academic Advising Resources*, 2006, www.nacada.ksu.edu/Resources/Clearinghouse/View-Articles/body-speaks.aspx.

10. Jürgen Streeck, *Gesturecraft: The Manu-Facture of Meaning* (Philadelphia: John Benjamins, 2009).

11. Ibid.

12. Peter J. Marshall and Andrew N. Meltzoff, "Neural Mirroring Mechanisms and Imitation in Human Infants," *Philosophical Transactions of the Royal Society B: Biological Sciences* 369 (2014): 1–11.

13. Melinda Wenner, "Smile! It Could Make You Happier," *Scientific American*, September 1, 2009, www.scientificamerican.com/article/smile-it-could-make-you-happier.

14. Ronald Schmidt-Fajlik, "Introducing Non-Verbal Communication to Japanese University Students: Determining Content," *Journal of Intercultural Communication* 15 (2007): 2.

15. Steven A. Beebe, "Eye Contact: A Nonverbal Determinant of Speaker Credibility," *Speech Teacher* 23 (1974): 21–25.

16. Nick Morgan, "What Should a Speaker Wear?" *Forbes*, July 18, 2011, www.forbes.com/sites/nickmorgan/2011/07/18/what-should-a-speaker-wear.

17. Omri Gillath et al., "Shoes as a Source of First Impressions," *Journal of Research in Personality* 46 (2012): 423–30.

Chapter 11

1. For a cultural history of recorded laughter, see Jacob Smith, "The Frenzy of the Audible: Pleasure, Authenticity, and Recorded Laughter," *Television and New Media* 6 (2005): 23–47.

2. Timothy J. Lawson, Brian Downing, and Hank Cetola, "An Attributional Explanation for the Effect of Audience Laughter on Perceived Funniness," *Basic and Applied Social Psychology* 20 (1998): 243–49; Michael J. Platow et al., "'It's Not Funny If They're Laughing': Self-Categorization, Social Influence, and Responses to Canned Laughter," *Journal of Experimental Social Psychology* 41 (2005): 542–50.

3. Michael P. Verdi et al., "Organized Spatial Displays and Texts," *Journal of Experimental Education* 65 (1997): 303–17; Livingston Alexander, Ronald G. Frankiewicz, and Robert E. Williams, "Facilitation of Learning and Retention of Oral Instruction Using Advance and Post Organizers," *Journal of Educational Psychology* 71 (1979): 701–7.

4. N. Katherine Hayles, "Hyper and Deep Attention: The Generational Divide in Cognitive Modes," *Profession*, 2007, 187–99.

5. Dale Cyphert, "Presentation Technology in the Age of Electronic Eloquence: From Visual Aid to Visual Rhetoric," *Communication Education* 56 (2007): 168–92.

6. Mark Zachry and Charlotte Thralls, "An Interview with Edward R. Tufte," *Technical Communication Quarterly* 13 (2004): 447–62.

7. William S. Cleveland and Robert McGill, "Graphical Perception and Graphical Methods for Analyzing Scientific Data," *Science* 229 (1985): 828–33; Rocio Garcia-Retamero and Ulrich Hoffrage, "Visual Representation of Statistical Information Improves Diagnostic Inferences in Doctors and Their Patients," *Social Science and Medicine* 83 (2013): 27–33.

8. Michael Tortorello, "Hard to Kill: Houseplants for the Inept," *New York Times*, November 10, 2010, www.nytimes.com/2010/11/11/garden/11houseplants.html?pagewanted=all.

9. Cyphert, "Presentation Technology," 168.

10. Kristi Hedges, "Six Ways to Avoid Death by PowerPoint," *Forbes*, November 14, 2014, www.forbes.com/sites/work-in-progress/2014/11/14/six-ways-to-avoid-death-by-powerpoint/#2715e4857a0b73a9fefd34cb.

11. Edward R. Tufte, *The Cognitive Style of PowerPoint: Pitching Out Corrupts Within*, 2nd ed. (Cheshire, CT: Graphics Press, 2006).

12. Edward R. Tufte, "PowerPoint Does Rocket Science—and Better Techniques for Technical Reports," September 6, 2005, www.edwardtufte.com/bboard/q-and-a-fetch-msg?msg_id=0001yB.

13. Elisabeth Bumiller, "We Have Met the Enemy and He Is Powerpoint," *New York Times* April 26, 2010, www.nytimes.com/2010/04/27/world/27powerpoint.html.

14. Ibid., paras. 7 and 10. Others, however, have responded thoughtfully to these critiques and defended the use of presentation software. Simon Marks, one-time product manager at Microsoft, has responded that like any tool or technology, PowerPoint can be abused, and that fans of "information density" like Tufte will not generally like the program (Clive Thompson, "PowerPoint Makes You Dumb," December 14, 2003, *New York Times Magazine*, 88). In other words, using slide software may be inappropriate for detailed academic or technical analyses.

15. Jean-Luc Doumont, "The Cognitive Style of PowerPoint: Slides Are Not All Evil," *Technical Communication* 52, no. 1 (2005): 64. In his defense of the medium, Doumont states that "slides are not all evil" and that slide software is used most effectively in oral presentations: we should not treat slides as written documents to be "read" but as something to be viewed "while the presenter is speaking."

16. Cyphert, "Presentation Technology," 169.

Chapter 12

1. Kenneth Burke, *Counter-Statement* (Berkeley: University of California Press, 1968), 22–29; Debra Hawhee, *Moving Bodies: Kenneth Burke at the Edges of Language* (Columbia: University of South Carolina Press, 2009).

2. Burke, *Counter-Statement*, 31.

3. For an insightful discussion of how Burke theorized the relationship between body and form—including Burke on music and other intoxicants—see Debra Hawhee, *Moving Bodies: Kenneth Burke at the Edges of Language* (Columbia: University of South Carolina Press, 2009).

4. For more on the complex relationship between form and genre, see Karlyn Kohrs Campbell and Kathleen Hall Jamieson, eds., *Form and Genre: Shaping Rhetorical Action* (Falls Church, VA: Speech Communication Association, 1978); and Joshua Gunn, "The Rhetoric of Exorcism: George W. Bush and the Return of Political Demonology," *Western Journal of Communication* 68 (2004): 1–23. For notable, in-depth studies of genre, see Karlyn Kohrs Campbell and Kathleen Hall Jamieson, *Presidents Creating the Presidency: Deeds Done in Words*, 2nd ed. (Chicago: Chicago University Press, 2008); and Carolyn R. Miller, "Genre as Social Action," *Quarterly Journal of Speech* 70 (1984): 151–67.

5. Aristotle, *On Rhetoric*, trans. George A. Kennedy (New York: Oxford University Press, 2007), 83–100.

Chapter 13

1. Aristotle, *On Rhetoric: A Theory of Civic Discourse*, 2nd ed., trans. George A. Kennedy (New York: Oxford University Press, 2007), 47–50; Eugene Garver, "Aristotle on the Kinds of Rhetoric," *Rhetorica* 27 (2009): 1–18. For a nuanced discussion of the "present" temporality in Aristotle's understanding of epideictic, see Megan Foley, "Time for Epideictic," *Quarterly Journal of Speech* 101 (2015): 209–12.

2. "State Law Officiants Requirements," Marriage Laws, accessed March 19, 2016, www.usmarriagelaws.com/marriage-license/officiants-requirements.shtml.

3. "Become Ordained," Universal Life Church, accessed March 17, 2016, www.ulc.org.

4. Véronique Nahoun-Grappe, "France," *International Handbook on Alcohol and Culture*, ed. Dwight B. Heath (Westport, CT: Greenwood Press, 1995), 75–87.

5. For further discussion of this unique genre, see Katherine Henry, "'Slaves to a Debt': Race, Shame, and the Anti-Obama Jeremiad," *Quarterly Journal of Speech* 100 (2014): 303–22; Nancy E. Mitchell and Kim S. Phipps, "The Jeremiad in Contemporary Fundamentalism: Jerry Falwell's Listen America," *Religious Communication Today* 8 (1985): 54–62.

6. "The Table Lodge: A History," PhoenixMasonry.org, accessed March 17, 2016, www.phoenixmasonry.org/table_lodge_history_ritual.htm; Heather Morrison, "'Making Degenerates into Men' by Doing Shots, Breaking Plates, and Embracing Brothers in Eighteenth-Century Freemasonry," *Journal of Social History* 46 (2012): 48–65.

7. Kathleen Hall Jamieson and Karlyn Kohrs Campbell, "Rhetorical Hybrids: Fusions of Generic Elements," *Quarterly Journal of Speech* 68 (1982): 146–57.

Chapter 14

1. Temple Grandin, *Thinking in Pictures, and Other Reports from My Life with Autism* (New York: Random House, 1995), 17.

2. Lois Parshley, "Temple Grandin on How to Raise Resilient Animals," *Popular Science* 287 (July 2015): 30.

3. Temple Grandin, "My Mind Is a Web Browser: How People with Autism Think," *Cerebrum*, January 1, 2000, dana.org/Cerebrum/2000/My_Mind_Is_a_Web_Browser__How_People_With_Autism_Think.

4. For more on this, see Grandin, *Thinking in Pictures*.

5. For a remarkable example of Grandin's public speaking, see Temple Grandin, "Helping Different Kinds of Minds Solve Problems," SXSWedu, Austin Convention Center, Austin, TX, March 6, 2016, youtu.be/Ycd1kxoySWk.

6. Milton J. Wiksell, "On Being Objective in Speaking," *Today's Speech* 4 (1956): 25–27.

7. For an example persuasive speech on this topic, see Temple Grandin, "Animals Are Not Things: A View on Animal Welfare Based on Neurological Complexity," Grandin.com, 2002, www.grandin.com/welfare/animals.are.not.things.html.

8. Technically speaking, the ancients used topoi to denote the relationships among different objects in order to invent arguments. These included cause/effect, whole/part, and so forth. The topics discussed here deviate substantially from the ancient topics and are updated for our time. For more information, see Sara Rubinelli, *Ars Topica: The Classical Technique of Constructing Arguments from Aristotle to Cicero* (New York: Springer, 2009).

9. Rickie Lee Jones, sampled in "Little Fluffy Clouds," by the Orb, on *The Orb's Adventures beyond the Ultraworld*, Mercury, 1991, compact disc.

10. *Oxford English Dictionary Online*, s.v. "social security," def. 1, accessed May 8, 2016, www.oed.com/view/Entry/183757?redirectedFrom=social+security#eid.

11. *Merriam-Webster's Collegiate Dictionary*, 11th ed., s.v. "courage."

12. *Online Etymology Dictionary*, s.v. "courage," accessed April 26, 2016, www.etymonline.com /index.php?term=courage&allowed_in_frame=0.

13. Linda Coffey, Margo Hale, and Ann Wells, "Goats: Sustainable Production Overview," ATTRA: Sustainable Agriculture, August 2004, attra.ncat .org/attra-pub/summaries/summary.php?pub=212; Melinda A. Zeder and Brian Hesse, "The Initial Domestication of Goats (*Capra hircus*) in the Zagros Mountains 10,000 Years Ago," *Science* 287 (2000): 2254–57.

14. Walter Fisher, "Narration as a Human Communication Paradigm: The Case of Public Moral Argument," *Communication Monographs* 51 (1984): 2.

15. Chris Maynard and Bill Scheller, *Manifold Destiny: The One! The Only! Guide to Cooking on Your Car Engine!* rev. ed. (New York: Simon & Schuster, 2008), 6.

16. Ibid., 7.

17. David Newhardt and Robert Genat, *American Cars of the 1950s* (St. Paul, MN: Motorbooks, 2008), 6–7.

18. Lawrence Ulrich, "The Internal Combustion Engine Is Not Dead," *Popular Science*, May 6, 2010, www.popsci.com/cars/article/2010-04 /most-advanced-engines.

19. Maynard and Scheller, *Manifold Destiny*, 14.

20. Maynard and Scheller list five no-nos; see *Manifold Destiny*, 19–20.

Chapter 15

1. Imelda V. Abano, "Philippine Climate Envoy Steps Down to Lead 'Pilgrimage,'" Reuters, April 22, 2015, www.reuters.com/article/2015/04/22/us -climatechange-philippines-politics-idUSKBN0ND 1G320150422#9PCKA1Lf21IjdOjW.97.

2. John Vidal, "Will Philippines Negotiator's Tears Change Our Course on Climate Change? *Guardian*, December 6, 2012, www.theguardian.com/global -development/poverty-matters/2012/dec/06 /philippines-delegator-tears-climate-change.

3. "'It's Time to Stop This Madness'—Philippines Plea at UN Climate Talks," Climate Home, November 13, 2013, www.climatechangenews .com/2013/11/11/its-time-to-stop-this-madness -philippines-plea-at-un-climate-talks.

4. See the National Association of Colleges and Employers website for detailed guidelines; for a university-specific example, see "HireUTexas and Campus-Wide Recruiting Policies." RecruitUT, accessed May 2, 2016, recruit.utexas.edu /employers/policies.

5. Charles U. Larson, *Persuasion: Reception and Responsibility*, 12th ed. (Boston: Wadsworth, 2010), 29–31.

6. Some scholars have argued, however, that coercion is a form of persuasion. See James R. Andrews, "The Rhetoric of Coercion and Persuasion: The Reform Bill of 1832," *Quarterly Journal of Speech* 56 (1970): 187–95; Parke G. Burgess, "Crisis Rhetoric: Coercion vs. Force," *Quarterly Journal of Speech* 59 (1973): 61–74; Cal M. Logue, "Transcending Coercion: The Communicative Strategies of Black Slaves on Antebellum Plantations," *Quarterly Journal of Speech* 67 (1981): 31–46.

7. Aristotle, *On Rhetoric: A Theory of Civic Discourse*, 2nd. ed., trans. George A. Kennedy (New York: Oxford University Press, 2007); Amélie Oksenberg Rorty, ed., *Essays on Aristotle's Rhetoric* (Berkeley: University of California Press, 1996).

8. Elizabeth Warren, "HELP Committee Hearing on Mental Health," Dirksen Senate Office Building, Washington, DC, January 20, 2016, www.warren .senate.gov/?p=video&id=1046.

9. Amy Schumer, "Read the Transcript of Amy Schumer's Emotional Speech on Gun Control," *Time*, August 3, 2015, time.com/3982553/amy -schumer-gun-control-transcript.

10. Fred Rogers, "Senate Statement on PBS Funding," May 1, 1969, American Rhetoric, www.americanrhetoric.com/speeches /fredrogerssenatetestimonypbs.htm.

11. For foundational overviews, see J. Anthony Blair, "Argumentation as Rational Persuasion," *Argumentation* 26 (2012): 71–81; R. Barry Fulton, "Motivation: Foundation of Persuasion," *Quarterly Journal of Speech* 49 (1965): 295–308; Donald K. Smith and Robert L. Scott, "Motivation Theory in Teaching Persuasion: Statement and Schema," *Quarterly Journal of Speech* 47 (1961): 378–83.

12. Abraham H. Maslow, *Motivation and Personality* (New York: Harper & Row, 1954).

13. This is the position of a number of Marxist and post-Marxist scholars who define the study of ideology as "an inquiry into the ways in which people may come to invest in their own unhappiness"; Terry Eagleton, *Ideology: An Introduction* (New York: Verso, 1991), xiii. For other critiques of Maslow's theory, see Mahmoud A. Wahba and Lawrence G. Bridwell, "Maslow Reconsidered: A Review of Research on the Need Hierarchy Theory," *Organizational Behavior and Human Performance* 15 (1976): 212–40; Patrick A. Gambrel and Rebecca Cianci, "Maslow's Hierarchy of Needs: Does It Apply in a Collectivist Culture," *Journal of Applied Management and Entrepreneurship* 8 (2003): 143–61.

14. For an account of how the study of feelings, emotions, and the body were gradually downplayed in communication studies, see Joshua Gunn, "Speech's Sanatorium," *Quarterly Journal of Speech* 101 (2015): 18–33.

15. Everett Hunt, "Ancient Rhetoric and Modern Propaganda," *Quarterly Journal of Speech* 37 (1951): 157–61; J. Michael Sproule, "Authorship and Origins of the Seven Propaganda Devices: A Research Note," *Rhetoric and Public Affairs* 4 (2001): 135–43; J. Michael Sproule, *Propaganda and Democracy: The American Experience of Media and Mass Persuasion* (New York: Cambridge University Press, 2005).

Chapter 16

1. Although common wisdom holds that one should not argue with children, such wisdom is based on a misunderstanding of what an argument and arguing are (e.g., as fighting). Janet Lehman, "Why You Can't Really 'Win' an Argument with Your Child," Empowering Parents, April 2013, www.empoweringparents.com /article/why-you-cant-really-win-an-argument -with-your-child. Research supports the idea that children benefit from learning reasoning through argumentation in multiple contexts. See, for example, Clotilde Pontecorvo and Francesco Arcidiacono, "Development of Reasoning through Arguing in Young Children," *Cultural-Historical Psychology* 4 (2010): 19–29; Tilmann Habermas, "Autobiographical Reasoning: Arguing and Narrating from a Biographical Perspective," *New Directions for Child and Adolescent Development* 2011 (Spring 2010): 1–17.

2. Antonio R. Damasio, *Descartes' Error: Emotion, Reason, and the Human Brain* (New York: Avon Books, 1994); Antonio R. Damasio, *The Feeling of What Happens: Body and Emotion in the Making of Consciousness* (New York: Harcourt Brace, 1999).

3. There are a number of theories about how we come to learn the norms of argument. The author tends to believe those who suggest we pick up argument norms pragmatically and conversationally, and then only formally through secondary and higher education. For this approach, see Frans H. van Eemeren and Rob Grootendorst, *A Systematic Theory of Argumentation: A Pragma-Dialectical Approach* (Cambridge: Cambridge University Press, 2004).

4. Many scholars assume that norms of reasoning differ from one culture to another, especially in respect to moral reasoning. For an example, see Hannah Soong, Richard Lee, and George John, "Cultural Differences in Justificatory Reasoning," *Educational Review* 64 (2012): 57–76. Some scholars argue that norms of reasoning may be universal; see, for example, Hugo Mercier, "On the Universality of Argumentative Reasoning," *Journal of Cognition and Culture* 11 (2011): 85–113. The author tends to agree with those researchers who believe norms of reasoning are culturally relative; see Joseph Henrich, Steven J. Heine, and Ara Norenzayan, "The Weirdest People in the World," *Behavioral and Brian Sciences* 33 (2010): 61–135.

5. Kenneth Burke, *Counter-Statement* (Berkeley: University of California Press, 1968), 29–44.

6. Douglas N. Walton, *Informal Logic: A Handbook for Critical Argumentation* (New York: Cambridge University Press, 1989), 3–4.

7. See Mercier, "On the Universality"; Henrich, Heine, and Norenzayan, "Weirdest People."

8. Frans H. van Eemeren, "The Study of Argumentation," in *The SAGE Handbook of Rhetorical Studies*, ed. Andrea A. Lunsford, Kirt H. Wilson, and Rosa A. Eberly (Thousand Oaks, CA: Sage, 2009), 109–24.

9. Stephen Edelston Toulmin, *The Uses of Argument*, updated ed. (New York: Cambridge University Press, 2003): 87–134.

10. Diagram adapted from ibid., 87–134.

11. These three basic types of argument claims are sometimes said to derive from "stasis theory," a classical method of developing arguments based on the context or situation: Does the situation concern facts? A definition? An evaluation? A proposal to do something? For an overview, see Andrea A. Lunsford, John J. Ruszkiewicz, and Keith Walters, *Everything's an Argument with Readings*, 6th ed. (Boston: Bedford/ St. Martin's, 2013); Jeanne Fahnestock and Marie Secor, "The Stases in Scientific and Literary Argument," *Written Communication* 5 (1988): 427–43.

12. Toulmin prefers the term "data" over that of "evidence." See Toulmin, *Uses of Argument*, 90.

13. Ibid., 88–91. Toulmin's notion of the warrant is much more technical and complex than is treated here; for a deeper account, see David Hitchcock, "Toulmin's Warrants," in *Anyone Who Has a View: Theoretical Contributions to the Study of Argumentation*, ed. Frans H. Van Eemeren, J. Anthony Blair, Charles A. Willard, and A. Francisca Snoeck Henkemans (Dordrecht, Netherlands: Springer Netherlands, 2003), 69–82.

14. For more information on warrants, see David Hitchcock, "Toulmin's Warrants," 69–82.

15. See, for example, Deborah Lipstadt, *Denying the Holocaust: The Growing Assault on Truth and Memory* (New York: Plume [Penguin], 1994).

16. Laura J. Collins, "The Second Amendment as Demanding Subject: Figuring the Marginalized Subject in Demands for an Unbridled Second Amendment," *Rhetoric and Public Affairs* 17 (2014): 737–56.

17. Alan H. Monroe, *Principles and Types of Speeches* (Chicago: Scott, Foresman, 1953).

18. Based on arguments advanced in "Texas Water Crisis," editorial, *Houston Chronicle*, August 16, 2013, www.chron.com/opinion /editorials/article/Texas-water-crisis-4739205 .php. Also see Anna Driver and Terry Wade, "Fracking without Freshwater at a West Texas Oilfield." *Scientific American*, November 21,

2013, www.scientificamerican.com/article/fracking-without-freshwater-at-a-texas-oilfield/#.

19. Donna Brazile, "Voting Rights Act Needs Help," *USA Today*, August 6, 2013, www.usatoday.com/story/opinion/2013/08/06/voting-rights-act-scotus-column/2623797.

Chapter 17

1. Gregory R. Berry, "Enhancing Effectiveness on Virtual Teams," *Journal of Business Communication* 28 (2011): 186–206.

2. For a more in-depth discussion of communicating in groups, see Dan O'Hair and Mary Wiemann, *The Essential Guide to Group Communication* (Boston: Bedford/St. Martin's, 2009).

3. Ibid.

4. Rebecca J. Welch Cline, "Detecting Groupthink: Methods for Observing the Illusion of Unanimity," *Communication Quarterly* 38 (1990): 112–26.

5. Linda L. Putnam and M. Scott Poole, "Conflict and Negotiation," in *Handbook of Organizational Communication*, ed. Fredric M. Jablin, Linda L. Putnam, Karlene H. Roberts, and Lyman W. Porter (Newbury Park, CA: Sage, 1987), 549–99.

6. For more information on the selection interview, see Lawrence S. Kleiman and Joan Benbek-Rivera, "A Four-Step Model for Teaching Selection Interviewing Skills," *Business Communication Quarterly* 73 (2010): 291–305.

7. Deborah Bowers and Brian H. Kleiner, "Behavioral Interviewing," *Management Research News* 28 (2005): 107–14.

8. J. R. Cunningham, *Get a Job! Interview Survival Skills for College Students* (New York: McGraw-Hill, 2009).

9. Blair W. Browning and John R. Cunningham, "Students Better Be on Their Best Behavior: How to Prepare for the Most Common Job Interviewing Technique," *Communication Teacher* 26 (2012): 152–57.

10. William H. Shaw and Vincent Barry, *Moral Issues in Business*, 8th ed. (Belmont, CA: Wadsworth, 1980), 83–86.

Chapter 18

1. Tamyra Pierce, "Social Anxiety and Technology: Face-to-Face Communication versus Technological Communication among Teens," *Computers in Human Behavior* 25 (2009): 1367–72.

2. Such feelings are not simply conveyed in speech but are also chemical. See Teresa Brennan, *The Transmission of Affect* (Ithaca: Cornell University Press, 2004).

3. *Oxford English Dictionary*, 2nd ed., s.v. "online."

4. Michael Mauser, "Eye vs. Camera," TedEd, accessed March 31, 2016, ed.ted.com/lessons/eye-vs-camera-michael-mauser.

5. For more information about the differences, as well as an increasing tendency to prefer asynchronous modes, see Morton Ann Gernsbacher, "Internet-Based Communication," *Discourse Processes* 51 (2014): 359–73.

6. Arjun Appadurai, "Disjuncture and Difference in the Global Cultural Economy," *Public Culture* 2 (1990): 1–24.

7. For more on the "fiction" of audiences, see John Hartley, "Invisible Fictions: Television Audiences, Paedocracy, Pleasure," *Textual Practice* 1 (1987): 121–38.

8. Jean M. Twenge and W. Keith Campbell, *The Narcissism Epidemic: Living in the Age of Entitlement* (New York: Atria Books/Simon & Schuster, 2010).

9. Cecilia Kang, "Bridging a Digital Divide That Leaves Schoolchildren Behind," *New York Times*, February 22, 2016, www.nytimes.com/2016/02/23/technology/fcc-internet-access-school.html?_r=2.

10. Adam Leipzig, Barry S. Weiss, and Michael Goldman, *Filmmaking in Action* (Boston: Bedford/St. Martin's, 2016).

11. John Sloop and Joshua Gunn, "Status Control: An Admonition Concerning the Publicized Privacy of Social Networking," *Communication Review* 13 (2010): 289–308.

Chapter 19

1. Jamelle Bouie, "Elizabeth Warren Just Gave the Best Response to Black Lives Matter," *Slate.com*, September 20, 2015, www.slate.com/articles/news_and_politics/politics/2015/09/elizabeth_warren_s_black_lives_matter_speech_was_the_best_one_yet_it_s_still.html; Annie Karni, "Black Lives Matter Protesters Disrupt Clinton Speech," *Politico.com*, October 30, 2015, www.politico.com/story/2015/10/hillary-clinton-black-lives-matter-protest-215396.

2. Stephen L. Lucas and Martin J. Medhurst, *Words of a Century: The Top 100 American Speeches, 1900–1999* (New York: Oxford University Press, 2008).

3. Herbert W. Simons, "Social Movements," in *Encyclopedia of Rhetoric*, ed. Thomas O. Sloane (New York: Oxford University Press, 2001), 724–32.

4. Barry Schwartz, "Collective Forgetting and the Symbolic Power of Oneness: The Strange Apotheosis of Rosa Parks," *Social Psychology Quarterly* 72 (2009): 123–42. Also see Paul Hendrickson, "The Ladies before Rosa: Let Us Now Praise Unfamous Women," *Rhetoric and Public Affairs* 8 (2005): 287–98.

5. Simons, "Social Movements," 724. For a fine collection of speech examples from social movements, see Charles E. Morris III and Stephen Howard Browne, eds., *Readings on the Rhetoric of Social Protests*, 3rd ed. (State College, PA: Strata, 2013).

6. Rob Bishop, "The Professional Protester: Emergence of a New Media Protest Coverage Paradigm in *Time* Magazine's 2011 Person of the Year Issue," *Journal of Magazine and New Media Research* 14 (2013): 1–19.

7. See Michael P. Boyle and Mike Schmierbach, "Media Use and Protest: The Role of Mainstream Media and Alternative Media Use in Predicting Traditional and Protest Participation," *Communication Quarterly* 57 (2009): 1–17; and Joel Penney and Caroline Dadas, "(Re)Tweeting in the Service of Protest: Digital Composition and Circulation in the Occupy Wall Street Movement," *New Media and Society* 16 (2014): 74–90.

8. Karlyn Kohrs Campbell, "The Rhetoric of Women's Liberation: An Oxymoron," *Quarterly Journal of Speech* 59 (1973): 74–86.

9. Karma R. Chávez, "Counter-Public Enclaves and Understanding the Function of Rhetoric in Social Movement Coalition Building," *Communication Quarterly* 59 (2011): 1–18.

10. See John W. Bowers, Donovan J. Ochs, Richard J. Jensen, and David P. Schulz, *The Rhetoric of Agitation and Control* (Long Grove, IL: Waveland Press, 2009).

11. Robert D. Putnam, *Bowling Alone: The Collapse and Revival of American Community* (New York: Simon & Shuster, 2001).

12. Thomas W. Benson, "The Rhetoric of Civility: Power, Authenticity, and Democracy," *Journal of Contemporary Rhetoric* 1 (2011): 22–30. See also Shelley D. Lane and Helen McCourt, "Uncivil Communication in Everyday Life: A Response to Benson's 'The Rhetoric of Civility,'" *Journal of Contemporary Rhetoric* 3 (2013): 17–29; Craig Rood, "Rhetoric of Civility: Theory, Pedagogy, and Practice in Speaking and Writing Textbooks," *Rhetoric Review* 32 (2013): 331–38; and Nina M. Lozano-Reich and Dana L. Cloud, "The Uncivil Tongue: Invitational Rhetoric and the Problem of Inequality," *Western Journal of Communication* 73 (2009): 220–26.

13. Rood, "Rhetoric of Civility," 332.

14. Ibid., 334.

15. For more on this perspective, see Dean Pruitt, Jeffrey Rubin, and Sung Hee Kim, *Social Conflict: Escalation, Stalemate, and Settlement*, 3rd ed. (New York: McGraw-Hill, 2003).

acknowledgments

Page 76. Definition of "invention." By permission. From *Merriam-Webster's Collegiate® Dictionary*, 11th Edition © 2017 by Merriam-Webster, Inc. (www.Merriam-Webster.com).

Page 78. Bob Dylan lyrics. © 1962 by Warner Bros. Inc.; renewed 1990 by Special Rider Music. All rights reserved. International copyright secured. Reprinted by permission.

Page 120. "Changing Attitudes on Gay Marriage." Pew Research Center, Washington, D.C. (May 2016) www.pewforum.org/2016/05/12/changing-attitudes-on-gay-marriage/.

Page 149. "The Science of Dreams." Reprinted by permission of Victoria Filoso.

Page 222. "U.S. Market Share of the Major Labels in the Recording Industry, 2013." *Media and Culture* 2016 Update edition, by Richard Campbell, Christopher R. Martin, and Bettina Fabos, reprinted by permission of Bedford/St. Martin's.

Page 277. Definition of "social security." By permission. From *Merriam-Webster's Collegiate® Dictionary*, 11th Edition © 2017 by Merriam-Webster, Inc. (www.Merriam-Webster.com).

Page 278. Definition of "courage." By permission. From *Merriam-Webster's Collegiate® Dictionary*, 11th Edition © 2016 by Merriam-Webster, Inc. (www.Merriam-Webster.com).

Page 290. Excerpt from speech. Reprinted by permission of Naderev "Yeb" Sano.

Pages 330–31. Excerpt from speech. Reprinted by permission of Donna Brazile, copyright © 2013.

Pages 315–16. Toulmin's model. *The Uses of Argument*, updated edition. New York: Cambridge University Press, 2003.

Pages 398–403. Sample celebration speech. Reprinted by permission of David McCullough Jr.

index

accents, 207
acceptance speeches, 253–254
accountability, 35–36
accuracy, in language, 187
Achille, Noelle, 13
action, call to, 173, 329
active listening, 23, 31–33, 41
ad baculum appeal, 324
Adele, 114, 116, 121–122
ad hominem fallacy, 324
Adichie, Chimamanda Ngozi, 125
ad misericordiam appeal, 324
ad populum appeal, 324
after-dinner speeches, 257–258
age, of audience members, 54–57
alliteration, 189
Amanpour, Christiane, 40
AMA style, 106
American Legacy, 123
American Sign Language (ASL), 209
amorphous audiences, 50–51,
    358–360, 361, 367–368
ancient Greeks, 3, 9, 12–13, 37, 81,
    242–243
anecdotes, 125
Anthony, Susan B., 372
anxiety
    about public speaking, 7–9, 13,
        16, 162
    introductions and, 162
APA style, 106
aphantasia, 124
Appadurai, Arjun, 357
appeals, 292–293, 295–305
    analyzing, 300
    to authority, 310
    to character (ethos), 298–299, 300
    to feelings and emotions
        (pathos), 297–298, 300,
        302–305, 324
    to needs, 301–302
    to pity, 324
    to reason (logos), 296–297, 300
    rhetorical triangle and, 295–299
appearance, 212–214
Apple Keynote, 49, 50, 119, 223,
    229, 232
Arab Spring, 376–377
argumentation, reason to study,
    312–313
arguments, 292–293, 295, 302–303,
    309–334
    claims, 316–320, 322, 327–329
    contemporary, 315–323
    defined, 311–312
    enthymeme, 316
    evidence, 320

of fact, 317, 318, 322, 327
fallacies in, 323–326
vs. fights, 311
informal logic and, 313–315
organization of, 326–332
reasoning or warrant, 320–323
Aristotle
    on celebratory speeches, 252
    on examples, 124
    on expertise, 186
    on goodwill, 65, 162
    on knowing age of audience,
        56–57
    rhetorical triangle of, 295–299
    on speaker's responsibility, 37
    on speech genres, 242–243
    study of public speaking by, 9,
        12, 13
    on style, 179
    on syllogisms, 314–315
articulation, 204
Asch, Solomon, 163
assassinations, 388
asynchronous communication, 355
asynchronous presentations,
    356–357
attending, in active listening, 31–32
attention, 24, 171–172
attention getters, 164–166
attire
    of audience members, 186–187
    of speaker, 212–214
attitudes, 67–68, 69, 294–295
audience
    age of, 54–57
    amorphous, 50–51, 358–360, 361,
        367–368
    attention of the, 171–172
    attire of, 186–187
    for celebratory speech, 252
    characteristics of, 51–62
    expectations of the, 239,
        240–241, 245
    eye contact with, 158, 210–211
    familiar vs. unfamiliar, 185
    identification with, 65–67
    impression formation by,
        163–164
    outsiders vs. insiders, 185–186
    psychology, 64–70, 301
    respect for, 41
    scanning, 211
    size, 50–51
    speech preparation and, 16
    speech support and, 112
    stereotypes, 51, 53, 59–60
    support from, 7–8

television, 51
topic choice and, 79
unknown, 50–51
word choice and, 184–186
audience analysis, 16, 45–74
    audience disposition, 70–72
    beliefs, attitudes, and values,
        67–70
    defined, 47
    demographic analysis, 51–62
    formal, 63–64
    informal, 62–63
    love and identification and,
        64–67
    psychological, 71
    speech location and, 47–51
audience disposition, 70–72
audio aids, 218–220, 223
    See also presentation aids
Austin, Gilbert, 202
authority, appeals to, 310
authorship, 102

background, in online
        presentations, 362–363
back light, 364
bandwagon fallacy, 324–325
Barnes, Harry Elmer, 327
Barnett, Arnold, 115
behavior, 70
behavioral interviews, 346–347
beliefs, 68, 69
beliefs, attitudes, and values
    (BAVs), 67–69, 294–295
Benson, Thomas, 379
bias, 118
biased language, 193–194
bibliographies, 105–106, 154
bin Laden, Osama, 4
Bíró, László, 76
blank slides, 233
Bodie, Graham D., 31
body, 182
body language, 203–211
    eye contact, 210–211
    facial expression, 210
    gestures, 206, 208–210
    vocalics, 203–206
boycotts, 383
brainstorming, 79–85
Branham, Robert James,
    60–61
Brazile, Donna, 330–331
Brummett, Barry, 181
Burke, Kenneth, 66–67, 192,
    240, 388
business casual dress, 213

of persuasion, 293–294
as self-evidence, 299
of speaking as a listener, 33–42
study of, 4
tips for developing, 299
workplace speaking and, 348
ethnic identification, 59–61
ethos, 37, 38, 40, 298–299, 300
etymological definitions, 278
eulogies, 138–139, 202, 239, 242, 259–265
eunoia, 162
evidence, 320
examples, 112, 122, 124–125, 278
expertise, 37–38, 40–41, 186–187
expert testimony, 121–122
explanations, 278
extemporaneous delivery, 158
extemporaneous speaking, 17, 158
external noise, 26, 27, 30
eye contact, 158, 210–211, 354, 355

FaceTime, 356
facial expression, 210
FactCheck.org, 99–100, 117
facts, 112, 113
factual claims, 317, 318, 322, 327
faith, 123
fallacies, 297, 305, 323–326
false advertising, 304
false dilemma, 325
Faulkner, William, 111
fear
    appeals to, 303–304
    of public speaking, 6, 7–9, 46
feedback, 32, 41–42, 206
feelings, 70–72
femininity, 58
fifties, 54, 56
fighting, 311
fill light, 364
Filoso, Victoria, 148, 155
final note, 173
First Amendment, 6, 382, 387
first impressions, 163–164
Fisher, Walter, 279
flattery, 67
Fleeson, William, 13
flowcharts, 222
focus groups, 63
fonts, 226
footwear, 213–214
forbidden speech, 382
Ford Motor Company, 348
forensic speeches, 242–243
form, 240–242
formal audience analysis, 63–64
formal language, 186–187
formal logic, 313
forties, 54, 56
fraternal orders, 257–258
fraud, 304

Freemasons, 258
free speech, 4, 6
Frere-Jones, Sasha, 122
Freud, Sigmund, 64, 65, 140
Freudian slip, 193
functional/operational definitions, 278

Gale Academic OneFile, 99
Gandhi, Mahatma, 381
gay marriage, 120
gender, 53, 57–59, 194
general speech purpose, 85–86
generational differences, 54–57
genre
    defined, 241
    familiarity with, 312
    hybridity, 375–376
    movie, 238, 239, 241
    music, 241
    speech. *See* speech genres
    violation of, 245–246
Gerald, Casey, 110
gestures, 206, 208–210
Girls, 59
Gleick, Peter, 119
Golden Rule, 34, 194
Goldilocks Rule, 231
goodwill, 38, 40, 65, 162, 163, 164, 210
Google, 98
Gore, Al, 257
Gorgias of Leontini, 3, 5, 12, 189
Grandin, Temple, 270, 279
graphs, 221–223
grooming, 212–214
group affiliations, 53, 61–62
groups
    conflict in, 340–342
    small. *See* small groups
    virtual, 343
groupthink, 340, 341
Guddy, Amy, 14
Gunn, Tim, 178, 183

hacking, 383
Hall, Edward T., 208
handouts, 228, 234
Harris, Robert, 101
headsets, 363
hearing, 24, 25
Helen of Troy, 5
heterosexuality, 59
hierarchy of needs, 301–302
high context cultures, 208
hip-hop, 200, 202–203, 241
historical arrangement, 141
Hitler, Adolf, 4
hoaxes, debunking, 94
honesty, 348
Houston, Whitney, 138–139

humor
    in introductions, 166
    ironic, 191
    misunderstanding and, 192
Huntsman, Jon, 168–169, 172, 173
hyperlinks, 232, 365
hypothetical examples, 124

identification, 65–67
identity
    gender, 57
    racial and ethnic, 59–61
    self, 27–28
    sexual, 59
identity crisis, 54, 55, 57
"I Have a Dream" (King), 123, 124, 198, 373–374, 382
imagery, concrete, 188
impression formation, 163–164
impression management, 182–183
inclusive language, 186
Independent Women's Forum (IWF), 117
inductive approach, 143
inductive reasoning, 314
inform, as speech purpose, 85, 86, 88
informal audience analysis, 62–63
informal language, 186–187
informal logic, 124, 128, 313–315
information design, 219
informative speaking, 129, 240, 244, 269–288
    defined, 271
    definitions, 277–278
    demonstrations, 278–279
    description, 276–277
    example, 282–285
    explanations, 278
    goal of, 271
    K.I.S.S. rule for, 279–280
    narrations, 279
    objectivity and, 272, 274
    personal relevance and, 281
    vs. persuading, 271–274
    strategies for, 275–279
    tips for, 279–281
    topic choice, 274–275, 276
    types of, 275
    uniqueness and, 280–281
inspiration, 80
inspirational speeches, 256–259
instrumental values, 68–69
interests, topic choice and, 78–79
interference, 25–27
internal noise, 26, 27–28
internal previews, 169
internal summaries, 169
Internet audiences, 50–51
Internet connection, 365
Internet links
    in online presentations, 365
    in slides, 232